THE INVENTION OF
DECOLONIZATION

The Algerian War and the Remaking of France

TODD SHEPARD

CORNELL UNIVERSITY PRESS
ITHACA AND LONDON

First published 2006 by Cornell University Press
First printing, Cornell Paperbacks, 2008

Printed in the United States of America

Design by Scott Levine

Library of Congress Cataloging-in-Publication Data
Shepard, Todd, 1969–
  The invention of decolonization : the Algerian War and the remaking of France / Todd Shepard.
    p. cm.
Includes bibliographical references and index.

  ISBN 978-0-8014-7454-5 (pbk. : alk. paper)

  1. Algeria—History—Revolution, 1954–1962—Influence. 2. Decolonization—France—History—20th century. 3. Decolonization—Algeria—History—20th century. 4. France—Ethnic relations—Political aspects—History—20th century. 5. Algeria—Ethnic relations—Political aspects—History—20th century. 6. Repatriation—France—History—20th century. 7. National characteristics, French. 8. France—Civilization—1945– I. Title.
  DT295.S477 2006
  325.650944'09046—dc22   2005028791

Paperback printing   10 9 8 7 6 5 4

To my parents, David and Catherine Shepard,
and my brother, Bradley Shepard,
for making so much possible

CONTENTS

ACKNOWLEDGMENTS

I gratefully acknowledge the friends and colleagues who made this book possible. They are in no way responsible for any lapses of judgment or knowledge. I am grateful to my parents, David and Catherine Shepard, and my brother, Bradley Shepard, for their love and encouragement. My late French "father," Roger Langlade, introduced me to French history, John Steinbeck, and his emphatic belief in justice and constant debate. I thank John Ackerman at Cornell University Press for his encouragement, patience, and attention. I also am grateful to the anonymous referees who read the manuscript, to Katy Meigs, for her copyediting, and to Susan Barnett and Ange Romeo-Hall at Cornell University Press for their fine work.

I came to graduate school already inspired by the teaching of Henry Abelove, Claire Bond Potter, and Ann-Louise Shapiro. The Rutgers History Department was exceedingly generous in their support. Among my teachers at Rutgers, Omer Bartov, Belinda Davis, and Michael Adas gave form to my understanding of history. Donald R. Kelley's teaching and scholarship helped me conceptualize a project that focuses on just a couple of years in a context several centuries longer.

Françoise Gaspard, who welcomed me into her gay studies seminar in Paris, has been particularly generous with her knowledge and her humor, and even traveled from Paris to Norman, Oklahoma, to talk to my students about the "veil question" in France. I thank her and Claude Servan-Schreiber for their friendship and their support.

As an undergraduate, reading Joan W. Scott led me to pursue a career in history, and I had the good fortune of being one of her graduate students. Joan led me to archives, pushed me to ask new questions, and made overarching connections. She has read more drafts of this project than anyone else and continues to inspire me with her rigor and commitment.

I was fortunate to work under the direction of Bonnie G. Smith. She taught me how to be a historian and how important writing well is to doing history. Her confidence in my work and her support have been critical. Bonnie saw the potential of my topic before anyone else, including me. As a person and a scholar, she remains my model.

Scott Sandage, Suzanne Kaufman, Carol Helstosky, and Martin Summers made my first years in graduate school much more pleasant than they are supposed to be. I am thankful that Noah Elkin, Rick Jobs, Roxanne Panchasi, and Patrick McDevitt were in my cohort. I continue to miss the late Becca Gershenson.

In France, Daniel Borrillo and Didier Eribon, especially, as well as Pierre Tévanian, Sidi Mohammed Barkat, Eric Fassin, Sylvie Thénault, Raphaëlle Branche, Emmanuelle Saada, and Gérard Noiriel asked many questions and helped me clarify my ideas. The archivists at the CARAN, the CAC, the SHAT, the Quai d'Orsay, the Bureau of the Prime Minister, Catherine Aubel at the Ministry of the Interior, Chantal Alexis at the Ministry of Justice, Edward Arkwright at the Archives of the Senate, Chantal Blondeau at *L'Express,* Sylvian Girandon at *Paris-Match,* Ruth Valentini at *Le Nouvel Observateur,* and others have left me in their debt and far more aware of what I still need to study. I thank Siné for permission to reprint one of his cartoons.

In Paris, I thank my friends Frédéric Biamonti, Stuart Michaels, Olivier Trimon, Zina Iouravskaia, Antoine Guitton, Noëlle Dupuy, Marc Siegel, Sandrine Sanos, David Halperin, Larry Norman, Daniel Hendrickson, Chuck Walton, Hee Ko, and the late Michael Camille. Frederick Cooper, Joshua Cole, and Patricia Lorcin helped me to think about decolonization in new ways. Serguei Emeline helped me so much and made my life richer. Juliette Cadiot, Judith Surkis, Oliver Samour, Sylvie Tissot, Sandrine Bertaux, and Nicolas Jabko each contributed to my intellectual life and my world.

The University of Oklahoma offered a supportive environment in which to work, especially the chair of the History Department, Robert Griswold, and my colleagues, Jamie Hart, Norman Stillman, and Judith Lewis. The department, the School for International and Area Studies, and the Oklahoma Humanities Council supported my research and allowed me time to write. Michael Alexander, Cathy Kelly, Elizabeth Miller, and Matthew Stratton offered their friendship and their intellectual support. Richard Immerman, Beth Bailey, and David Farber welcomed me to Temple University.

Nicolas Jabko, Michael Alexander, and Sandrine Sanos read the entire manuscript, and others read large portions of it, including Juliette Cadiot, Judith Surkis, Jennifer Milligan, Dagmar Herzog, Amelia Lyons, and Laure Blévis. My special thanks to the editing pens, probing questions, and thick skins of Richard Kaye and Daniel Sherman.

I owe more than I can say to my friends Jennifer Milligan, Barbara Balliet, Cheryl Clarke, and Rich Hamerla.

Finally, I thank Saïd Gahia. He already knew what I have been trying to think about for years, and a lot more. Everything is clearer now.

ABBREVIATIONS

AIU   International Israelite Alliance
ALN   National Liberation Army
AN   National Archives, Paris
CAC   Center for Contemporary Archives of the National Archives, Fontainebleau
FLN   National Liberation Front
FMA   Muslim French citizen from Algeria
FNSA   French of North African Origin
FSE   French of European Origin
GPRA   Provisional Government of the Algerian Republic
GPRF   Provisional Government of the French Republic
MAE   Archives of the French Ministry of Foreign Affairs, Paris
MJ/FA   Archives of the Nationalities Office of the French Ministry of Justice, Paris
MTLD   Movement for the Triumph of Democratic Liberties
OAS   Secret Army Organization
PCA   Algerian Communist Party
PCF   French Communist Party
PSU   Unified Socialist Party
RG   French Bureau of Investigations
RPF   Rally of the French People
RNUR   National Rally for the Unity of the Republic
SAM   Service for Muslim Affairs
SFIO   Socialist Party
SHAA   Archives of the French Air Force, Vincennes
SHAT   Archives of the French Army, Vincennes

CHRONOLOGY OF FRENCH OCCUPATION
OF ALGERIA

July 1830: French troops invade and occupy Algiers and surrounding territories.

Military Directive of *22 October 1830* recognizes the jurisdiction of "local"—"Muslim" and "Israelite" (their term for Jewish)—courts and law over their respective communities.

Ordinance of *22 July 1834* annexes French-occupied land ("Algeria") to France.

Ordinances of *22 July 1834* and of *28 February 1841* limit purview of local law to "civil" or personal status: marriage, divorce, paternity, and inheritance.

1848: The Second Republic extends department status to France's Algerian territory.

Senatus-Consulte of *14 July 1865* asserts that every "indigenous Muslim is French," establishes possibility for qualified "indigenous" men to obtain French citizenship.

Crémieux Decree of *24 October 1870:* "The native Israelites of the Algerian departments are declared French citizens."

Law of *26 June 1889* affirms that any individual born in France (including Algeria) of a parent (French or foreign) born in France is automatically French.

Law of *4 February 1919* proposes a simpler and more widely accessible means for men from Algeria with Koranic local civil status to acquire citizenship.

Ordinance of *2 August 1945* guarantees adult French women the vote, a right first promulgated under the French Committee for National Liberation in Algiers on *21 April 1944.*

Statute for Algeria of *20 September 1947,* which established the Algerian Assembly and affirmed that all Algerians have French citizenship.

1 November 1954: A series of armed attacks and a communiqué announce the existence of the National Liberation Front (FLN), which demands the "reestablishment of the sovereignty of the Algerian nation."

May 1958: Protests in Algiers on *13 May* in defense of "French Algeria" lead the French government of Pierre Pflimlin to resign; Charles de Gaulle goes to Algiers, then agrees to lead a government that will propose a new constitution.

4 October 1958: The Constitution of the Fifth Republic, adopted by a referendum on *28 September 1958,* takes effect.

16 September 1959: De Gaulle calls for "a peace of the brave" with the FLN and embraces the previously taboo idea of Algerian self-determination.

January 1960: The "Week of the Barricades" in Algiers: a failed coup d'état in defense of French Algeria.

21 April 1961: Failed coup d'état in Algiers, led by Generals Challe, Jouhaud, Salan, and Zeller.

The Boulin Law of *26 December 1961* establishes repatriate status.

18 March 1962: Signing of the "Evian Accords" between representatives of the French Republic and the Provisional Government of the Algerian Republic (GPRA).

19 March 1962: Official announcement of the Evian Accords.

Referendum of *8 April 1962,* in which inhabitants of the Algerian departments do not participate, approves the Evian Accords.

Law of *13 April 1962* incorporates the decisions approved by referendum into French law.

14 April 1962: Appointment of Georges Pompidou as prime minister after Michel Debré resigns.

20 April 1962: Arrest of ex-General Raoul Salan, head of Secret Army Organization.

Referendum of *1 July 1962* in the departments of Algeria supports independence in cooperation with France.

3 July 1962: The French Republic recognizes results of the 1 July referendum; all deputies and senators from Algeria are excluded from the French Parliament.

5 July 1962: Declaration of the Algerian Republic in Algiers.

Ordinance of *21 July 1962:* Requires French citizens from Algeria with local civil status to apply for French nationality before *1 January 1963.*

Referendum of *28 October 1962* approves the election by direct universal suffrage of all subsequent presidents of the Republic.

18 and 25 November 1962: Legislative elections in France produce a pro-Gaullist majority and see the reemergence of a "Popular front"–style alliance on the Left.

Introduction

The Algerian Revolution (1954–1962) won independence for Algeria. For many people, it also became the very archetype of the mid-twentieth-century struggle to end Western colonialism. The "Mecca of the revolutionaries" stirred militants such as the young African National Congress leader Nelson Mandela, who trained at a nationalist military camp in Morocco; the Palestinian nationalist Yassir Arafat, who witnessed the entry of liberation forces into Algiers on 3 July 1962; and the American radical Angela Davis, who in 1961 discussed what the triumph over imperialism meant with Algerian students in Paris. Those who fought them also studied its lessons: the police of apartheid-era South Africa relied on French military theories about "revolutionary war"; FBI agents in the 1960s watched Gillo Pontecorvo's magnificent film *The Battle of Algiers* (1965) to help them crush groups like the Black Panthers; and Israeli prime minister Ariel Sharon kept a copy of Alistair Horne's magisterial recounting of the conflict, *A Savage War of Peace* (1977), on his nightstand. In 2003, after the United States occupied Iraq, the Algerian War once again drew the attention of commentators and policymakers.[1]

The Algerian Revolution was at the same time a French revolution. As a

---

[1] The most important general history of the Algerian Revolution is Sylvie Thénault's *Histoire de la guerre d'indépendance algérienne* (Paris, 2005), which takes into account all of the scholarly work published in French since the opening in 1992 of most French government archives concerning the war. The most well-known English-language history is Alistair Horne, *A Savage War of Peace: Algeria, 1954–1962* (New York, 1977). Other synthetic overviews of the war include Benjamin Stora, *Histoire de la guerre d'Algérie, 1954–1962* (Paris, 1992); Pierre Miquel, *La guerre d'Algérie* (Paris, 1993); and John Talbott, *The War without a Name: France in Algeria, 1954–1962* (New York, 1980). Among archivally based studies, see esp. Gilbert Meynier, *Histoire intérieure du FLN, 1954–1962* (Paris, 2002), and Matthew Connelly, *A Diplomatic Revolution: Algeria's Fight for Independence and the Origins of the Post–Cold War Era* (Oxford, 2002). On Algeria as Mecca, see John P. Entelis, *Algeria: The Revolution Institutionalized* (London, 1986), 189; on Mandela, Arafat, and the South African police, see Connelly (2002), 279. On Sharon, see Amos Elon, "No Exit," *New York Review of Books* 49, no. 9 (23 May 2002): 15–20.

French revolution, the Algerian War posed fundamental questions about who was French and how the country must be governed. It was only at the close of armed conflict between the Algerian nationalists united around the National Liberation Front (FLN) and French forces, a short period of several months in 1962, that unexpected and still largely unknown decisions and events forged lasting answers. What I will term "the invention of decolonization" made these messy episodes disappear. As we'll see, French responses to the Algerian Revolution gave birth to the certainty that "decolonization" was a stage in the forward march of history, of the Hegelian "linear History with a capital H."[2] This allowed the French to forget that Algeria had been an integral part of France since the 1830s and to escape many of the larger implications of that shared past. Through this forgetting, there emerged novel definitions of French identity and new institutions of the French state. The French political system was radically transformed. In most ways, what resulted in France resembles a counterrevolution, one that curtailed both the protection of liberties and the possibilities for securing equality and fraternity that earlier generations of revolutionaries had struggled to expand.[3]

Two blind spots determined this restructuring of French state structures and national identity. In their tardy but urgent maneuvering to exclude Algeria and Algerians from France, French officials sought to avoid the appearance that they had accepted the arguments of their anticolonialist opponents. Such obfuscation continued even after a cease-fire with Algerian nationalists had been signed at the town of Evian in the French Alps on 18 March 1962; President Charles de Gaulle personally blocked projects to prepare the transfer of power that in any way seemed to admit FLN claims to sovereignty in Algeria. Throughout the same period, in their determination to exorcize Algeria, officials ignored French laws and French history. This willful denial of nationalist claims and French codes had unrecognized and lasting effects on France.

Most people from Algeria who had French citizenship in March 1962 (some nine million) had it taken away by 1963: those who were "Muslims" became Algerians (official documents refer to "Algerians of Muslim origin"); the minority—called "Europeans" (roughly one million)—continued to be French. Race and ethnicity appeared as meaningful markers to explain who could be considered French at a moment when definitions premised on legal

---

[2] On Hegel's vision of history in the context of Europe's relations with non-Europeans, see Herman L. Bennett, "The Subject in the Plot: National Boundaries and the 'History' of the Black Atlantic," in "Rethinking the African Diaspora," ed. Judith Byfield, special issue, *African Studies Review* 43, no. 1 (April 2000): 101–24.

[3] On the centrality of Algeria to modern French history, see Etienne Balibar, "Algeria, France: One Nation or Two?" in *Giving Ground: The Politics of Propinquity,* ed. Joan Copjec and Michael Sorkin (London, 1999), 162–72. For a critique of uses of historical inevitability to describe decolonization, see Anne McClintock, "The Angel of Progress: Pitfalls of the Term 'Post-Colonialism,'" *Social Text* 31–32 (1990): 84–98.

codes or tradition proved weak. Further, the means and procedures that the
government set up to exclude Algeria (definitively) and "Algerians" (provi-
sionally, yet emphatically) from both the French Republic and the French nation also—and not coincidentally—allowed President Charles de Gaulle and
his associates to reshape, radically so, republican legitimacy, civil liberties,
and the state.[4]

What Is "Decolonization"?

The history of how Algerian independence transformed France provides crucial insights into a broader concern: How did "decolonization" reshape the
West?[5] The so-called end of empires—events that the Senegalese essayist and
historian Abdoulaye Ly imagined in 1956 as "a ring of fire burning all along
the Tropics"—was characterized in the same year by the French anthropologist Georges Balandier as "the insurrection of poor and dominated peoples." Balandier argued that "this is the event that defines the twentieth
century." The expectations that Ly and Balandier's statements reveal were
not to be realized. Decolonization did not become the alternate pole to the
black hole of the Holocaust, nor did the period mark the end of the pursuit
by some states of empires. Yet decolonization was certainly one of the century's foundational "events," like the world wars, the Bolshevik Revolution,
and the cold war. Historians of the West have not given it due attention.[6]

What decolonization means has preoccupied many scholars of African
and Asian states and peoples who gained independence. The historians W. R.
Ochieng' and Atieno Odhiambo, writing about Kenya, argue that "decolonization as a theme is a much wider concept than the mere 'winning of independence' or 'transfer of power.' . . . It entails the exploration of dreams,

[4] On the relationship between "techniques of government" and the definition of "population," see Michel Foucault, "Governmentality," in *The Foucault Effect: Studies in Governmentality*, ed. Graham Burchell, Colin Gordon, and Peter Miller (Chicago, 1991), 99–101.

[5] On the importance of colonial developments and references in the elaboration of metropolitan thinking, see Ann Laura Stoler, *Race and the Education of Desire: Foucault's History
of Sexuality and the Colonial Order of Things* (Durham, N.C., 1995). For the United Kingdom,
see Paul Gilroy, '*There Ain't No Black in the Union Jack': The Cultural Politics of Race and Nation* (Chicago, 1991); Antoinette Burton, *At the Heart of the Empire: Indians and the Colonial
Encounter in Late-Victorian Britain* (Berkeley, 1998). For France, Herman Lebovics, *True
France: The Wars over Cultural Identity, 1900–1945* (Ithaca, 1992); Alice Conklin, *A "Mission
to Civilize": The Republican Idea of Empire in France and West Africa, 1895–1930* (Stanford,
1997); Paul Rabinow, *French Modern: Norms and Forms of the Social Environment* (Cambridge, Mass., 1989); and Gwendolyn Wright, *The Politics of Design in French Colonial Ur-
banism* (Chicago, 1991).

[6] Abdoulaye Ly, *Les masses africaines et l'actuelle condition humaine* (1956), 12; Georges
Balandier, introduction to *Le "tiers monde": Sous-développement et développement*, ed. George
Balandier (1956), 13. Note: all translations from the French, unless otherwise indicated, are my
own. On the Holocaust and twentieth-century history, see Omer Bartov, "The Holocaust as
Leitmotif of the Twentieth Century," in *Lessons and Legacies VII: The Holocaust in Interna-
tional Perspective*, ed. Dagmar Herzog (Evanston, Ill., forthcoming).

the analysis of struggles, compromises, pledges and achievements, and the rethinking of fundamentals."[7] As such claims suggest, there has been much debate about what happened and how, as well as to what effect, in the period after World War II when dozens of lands that had been under foreign control gained independence. One point of disagreement appears in the contrast that Ochieng' and Odhiambo highlight between the concepts "winning of independence" and "transfer of power." The former focuses on anticolonialist struggle, whereas the latter (a term popularized by certain historians of the British Empire) foregrounds negotiations and planning among colonial officials and with colonized elites. Histories of Europe and the West, meanwhile, still describe "decolonization" primarily as the break point between "empire" and "after," with some analyses of overseas or foreign policy focusing on a shift from "new imperialism" to "neocolonialism." Within Europe itself, debates concentrate on decolonization as the moment when the "question of colonialism" ends and the "immigrant question" begins.[8]

My analysis of the decolonization of Algeria shows how French bureaucrats, politicians, and journalists rewrote the history of imperialism and antiimperialism so that decolonization was the predetermined end point. This book's main aim, then, is not to settle questions that dominated public debates during the period. Instead it calls into question the apparent inevitability of the divisions this moment produced in and between peoples. Its genealogical approach attends to the often unexpected ways that Algeria's independence, like that of other European colonies after World War II, crystallized previous changes and durably reshaped the people and states that were involved. It details as well how there emerged a congeries of understandings that have continued to frame political debates about immigration to Europe.[9]

This instance of decolonization had exceptional consequences internationally as well as in France. The Algerian War was the most traumatic case of decolonization in the French Empire. The historian of colonialism Raymond Betts evokes the institutional effects of "events in Algeria" on France as "turbulence . . . the onrush of opposing forces into a political vacuum . . . the near paralysis of the national government." A number of scholars have identified the French experience of the Algerian Revolution as the starting point for the avalanche of events around "May 1968," and the ac-

---

[7] W. R. Ochieng' and E. S. Atieno Odhiambo, "On Decolonization," in *Decolonization and Independence in Kenya, 1940–1993,* ed. B. A. Ogot and W. R. Ochieng' (London, 1995), ix–xviii; xii.

[8] On "transfer of power," see Prosser Gifford and William Roger Louis, eds., *The Transfer of Power in Africa: Decolonization, 1940–1960* (New Haven, 1982) and *Decolonization and African Independence: The Transfers of Power, 1960–1980* (New Haven, 1988).

[9] On the need to understand France's colonial history in order to analyze contemporary debates on race, immigration, and national identity, see Laurent Dubois, "*La République métisée:* Citizenship, Colonialism, and the Borders of French History," *Cultural Studies* 14, no. 1 (2000): 15–34.

companying intellectual rethinking of post-Enlightenment conceptions of politics, values—such as the Rights of Man, rationality, and universalism—and possibilities for progress. In 1971, for example, the French philosopher Jacques Derrida argued that modern Western metaphysics was a "white mythology which reassembles and reflects the culture of the West," a mythology (about how to determine the fundamental nature of all reality) that "the white man takes . . . for the universal form of . . . Reason." Derrida, whose family fled their Algerian homeland in 1962, later identified the Algerian Revolution as one of the historical contexts that most immediately informed his thinking.[10]

What has gone unremarked is that French efforts to end the Algerian Revolution gave birth to the notion that the historical category "decolonization" was a causal force with an all but irresistible momentum. Oddly enough, the word itself first appeared in an 1836 tract "Decolonization of Algiers." Journalist Henri Fonfrède called on France to end the six-year-old occupation of territory in North Africa, lands that in 1838 the French government would name "Algeria." In the late 1920s, a few social scientists and Communists began to employ the term "decolonization" in their works.[11] By the 1950s, European and American scholars and politicians hesitantly applied it to describe specific shifts of sovereignty in particular territories. Like the French ethnologist Henri Labouret, who in 1953 published the first book with "decolonization" in its title, most Western scholars argued that such develop-

---

[10] Raymond Betts, *France and Decolonization, 1900–1960* (New York, 1991), 3. Jacques Derrida, "White Mythology: Metaphor in the Text of Philosophy," in Jacques Derrida, *Margins of Philosophy,* trans. Alan Bass (Chicago, 1982), 213. On the sense of upheaval and possibilities in the increasingly self-conscious "Third World," see Robert Malley, *The Call from Algeria: Third Worldism, Revolution, and the Turn to Islam* (Berkeley, 1996), 79–82; Eric Hobsbawm, *The Age of Extremes: A History of the World, 1914–1991* (New York, 1994), 436. On the genealogical connections between the Algerian Revolution and "'68," see Robert Young, *White Mythologies: Writing History and the West* (New York, 1990); Kristen Ross, *Fast Cars, Clean Bodies: Decolonization and the Reordering of French Culture* (Cambridge, Mass., 1995), and *May '68 and Its Afterlives* (Chicago, 2002). On Derrida and Algeria, see Jacques Derrida and Geoffrey Bennington, *Jacques Derrida,* trans. Geoffrey Bennington (Chicago, 1991), and Lee Morrissey, "Derrida, Algeria, and 'Structure, Sign, and Play'," *Postmodern Culture* 9, no. 2 (January 1999).

[11] Charles-Robert Ageron, "Décolonisation," in *Encyclopedia Universalis,* Corpus 7 (2004), 11–16, and *La décolonisation française* (1994), 5. See the book by Indian Communist leader Manabendra Nath Roy, *The Future of Indian Politics* (London, 1926). For the first English-language use of the term "decolonization" in a scholarly journal, see Benjamin Semenov-Tian-Shansky's "Russia: Territory and Population: A Perspective on the 1926 Census," *Geographical Review* 18, no. 4 (October 1928): 616–40. It provides no elaboration of the term. More important, the next such articles were German economist Moritz Bonn's "Imperialism," in *The Encyclopedia of the Social Sciences,* VII, ed. E. P. A. Seligman (New York, 1932), 613, and "The Age of Counter-Colonisation," *International Affairs* 13, no. 6 (November–December 1934): 845–47, precursors to his widely read *The Crumbling of Empire* (London, 1938). A number of historians, following Bonn himself, have identified Bonn as the inventor of the term; this was not the case, but his reintroduction of the term into English was that which took hold (in English and in French). On Bonn, see Ageron, "Décolonisation"; and David E. Gardinier, "Decolonization," in *Handbook of World History,* ed. Joseph Dunner (New York, 1967).

ments were wrongheaded, at least in the short term, and could be avoided through wise political choices made in Europe's imperial capitals.[12]

In the last years of the Algerian War, French discussions transformed this descriptive term into a historical category, an all but inevitable stage in the tide of History. In Algeria, as elsewhere, decolonization now appeared as wholly consistent with a narrative of progress—the ongoing extension of national self-determination and its corollary values: liberty, equality, fraternity, and the Rights of Man—that had begun with the French Revolution. A comparable story (under the guise of "the civilizing mission" or the "white man's burden") had been used to explain the building of European empires up until World War II. Similarly, during the French fight against the FLN, officials had reframed their civilizing mission as a "modernizing mission." And now, faced with the collapse of efforts to keep Algeria French, many claimed that this development, too, reinforced, rather than challenged, understandings that modern France, its form of government, and its values offered a universal template for progress.[13]

On 18 March 1962, government representatives signed a series of agreements with envoys of the FLN. With the so-called Evian Accords, the government met Algerian nationalists' demand for liberation. The French recognized that Algerians were so different, as a group, from other French citizens that they could not be accommodated within the French Republic. This was what the FLN had always proposed, arguing that Algerians formed a nation, defined by Arab culture, Berber roots, and Islamic tradition, that needed an independent state. Yet until the final years of the Algerian War, French leaders energetically rejected this contention.[14]

Virtually every French politician had waved off any consideration of the possibility of Algerian independence, a dismissal they backed up with force. When Prime Minister Pierre Mendès-France, straight-talking hero of the modernizing Left, responded in November 1954 to the FLN's first armed actions and political demands with a statement before the National Assembly that "Algeria is France, not a foreign country," and when François Mitter-

[12] Henri Labouret, *Colonisation, colonialisme, décolonisation* (Paris, 1952).

[13] On arguments about the civilizing mission, see Aimé Césaire, *Discourse on Colonialism,* trans. Joan Pinkham (New York, 2000); Michael Adas, *Machines as the Measure of Men: Science, Technology, and Ideologies of Western Dominance* (Ithaca, 1989); and "Contested Hegemony: The Great War and the Afro-Asian Assault on the Civilizing Mission Ideology," *Journal of World History* 15, no. 1 (2004): 31–63; Thomas August, *The Selling of Empire: British and French Imperialist Propaganda, 1890–1940* (Westport, Conn., 1985); Raoul Girardet, *L'idée coloniale en France, 1871–1962* (Paris, 1972). On French efforts to define their fight against the FLN as a "modernizing mission," see Connelly, *Diplomatic Revolution* , 17–38; on the intersection of decolonization and the rise of modernization theory and developmentalism, see Malley, *Call from Algeria,* 69–70.

[14] Authors such as Paul Clay Sorum and Raoul Girardet have analyzed the remarkable shift in attitudes among intellectual and political circles as well as the populace during the war. See Paul Clay Sorum, *Intellectuals and Decolonization in France* (Chapel Hill, N.C., 1977), and Girardet, *L'idée coloniale en France,* 282.

rand, his minister of the interior (and future Socialist president, 1981–1995), argued that they are French departments, they were representative of most French leaders and people. The conviction that Algeria was part of France remained dominant throughout the 1950s. Legally, as is sometimes forgotten, all Algerians were French citizens and all of Algeria was part of the French Republic. Even to consider negotiating these facts was alien to French political tradition and ideology and violated fundamental French laws. Rather, over the course of the "events in Algeria," French officials worked to make these ties stronger: they exponentially expanded citizenship rights for Algerian "Muslims" (a term I place in quotes because official references to those Algerians legally categorized as "Muslim" did not necessarily refer to people who practiced Islam) and established extensive, aggressive affirmative action–style policies to benefit Algerian "Muslims," both in mainland France (the metropole) and Algeria.[15]

With the advent of the notion that decolonization was a tide of History, however, French elites came to see Algerian independence as necessitated by the logic of history itself. No longer the exception among European overseas possessions, Algeria now became the emblematic example. In April 1963, one year after announcing the Evian Accords, de Gaulle referred to French Algeria as part of a colonial project that had "passed its expiration date." Several months earlier, a classified report on groups organized by and for the repatriates from North Africa stated that such people were "the victims of that unavoidable and planetary evolution that has been called decolonization." The lessons these French officials drew were not limited to France. Just months after Algerian independence, de Gaulle pointed to the United Kingdom's failure to decolonize fully as a sign of its lack of commitment to building Europe—one key reason, the French president explained, why Britain should be kept out of the European Community. Embarrassed, the British, with what R. F. Holland terms "unseemly bustle," pushed most of their remaining colonies toward independence.[16]

Squarely focused on questions of statehood and sovereignty, this structural understanding of decolonization has allowed politicians, historians, political scientists, and others to follow the dominant French approach to Algerian independence in 1962: to avoid grappling with questions of "ra-

---

[15] Mendès-France, quoted in Jean Lacouture, *Pierre Mendès-France*, trans. George Holoch (New York, 1984), 306; Mitterrand quoted in Frantz-Olivier Giesbert, *François Mitterrand, ou la tentation de l'histoire* (Paris, 1977), 131. On reforms during the war, see chapter 1.

[16] See "Allocution radio-télévisée du Général de Gaulle" (19 April 1963), 2, in Service historique de l'Armée de Terre (hereafter, SHAT) SHAT 1H/2467 bis/5; "Les Associations de rapatriés en France [1ère partie]" in *Bulletin de documentation de la direction des Renseignements Généraux* (hereafter, RG) 78 (September 1962), 5, in Centre d'accueil et de récherches des Archives nationals, Paris (hereafter, AN) F/7/15581. (The reports I consulted are the summaries of reports submitted by undercover agents within France, classified "Confidential".) R. F. Holland, "The Imperial Factor in British Strategies from Attlee to Macmillan, 1945–63," in *Perspectives on Imperialism and Decolonization: Essays in Honour of A. F. Madden,* ed. R. F. Holland and G. Rizvi (London, 1984), 184.

cial" or "ethnic" difference, or with racism. After 1962, there was no longer any need to try to explain the seemingly commonsensical belief that "Algerians" were, somehow, not the same as "the French." Yet the difficulty of explaining or making policy based on this difference, now admitted as obvious, was precisely what had made it so hard for the French to admit even the possibility of Algerian independence. For almost eight years, the blood-soaked conflict had forced the French to confront how they defined the boundaries of the nation: Could French people still imagine that Algerians were French? By conceiving of decolonization as a tide of History Western observers could avoid coming to terms with what Malcolm X saw in the worldwide flowering of struggles against colonialism: a "tidal wave of color." Grants of independence would suffice; the deeper issues could be ignored.[17]

After 1962, the 130-year French insistence that Algeria was French was simply abandoned—with numerous consequences. Algeria and, to a lesser extent, "Algerians," had been foundational elements of modern French history, a fact epitomized by the now tainted—but in the 1950s often cited—formula "l'Algérie, c'est la France" (Algeria is France).[18] Accepting Algerian independence entailed the disappearance of the legal, institutional, and economic mechanisms the French had used to make Algeria French. These mechanisms had begun to emerge almost immediately after the conquest of Algiers in 1830 and included tactics and procedures later applied in other colonized territories, both of France and other colonizers: armed violence, "native codes," racist thinking and discrimination, and the malignant neglect of disease, starvation, and ignorance. The French governance of Algeria was unique, however, in that France defined Algeria as an extension of itself. Efforts to make Algeria part of France and, more important, part of the French Republic after 1871, led to the emergence of several of the features that struc-

---

[17] On Malcolm X, see Robin D. G. Kelley, "A Poetics of Anticolonialism," *Monthly Review* 51, no. 6 (November 1999): 1–21. On the emergence of the nation-state as the most important "imagined community" among anticolonial activists in Africa, see Frederick Cooper, "Conflict and Connection: Rethinking Colonial African History," *History after the Three Worlds: Post-Eurocentric Historiographies*, ed. Arif Dirlik, Vinay Bahl, and Peter Gran (Lanham, Md., 2000), 157–90; Benedict Anderson, *Imagined Communities: Reflections on the Origins and Spread of Nationalism*, rev. ed. (London, 1991); and Partha Chatterjee, *The Nation and Its Fragments: Colonial and Postcolonial Histories* (Princeton, 1993). On ways that Western commentators place anticolonial and postcolonial developments within Western understandings of the nation-state, see Dipesh Chakrabarty, "Postcoloniality and the Artifice of History: Who Speaks for 'Indian' Pasts?" *Representations* 37 (1992): 1–26; Edouard Glissant, *Caribbean Discourse: Selected Essays* (Charlottesville, Va., 1989); Bennett, "The Subject in the Plot", 101–6. On how to think outside of such approaches, see Antoinette Burton, "Introduction: On the Inadequacy and the Indispensability of the Nation," in *After the Imperial Turn: Thinking with and through the Nation*, ed. Antoinette Burton (Durham, N.C., 2003), 1–23.

[18] Familiar to anyone who has studied the war, this was one of the slogans that rallied those in the French metropole and in Algeria who denied Algerian nationalists' demands for independence.

tured the government of all French people. Definitions of citizenship and nationality were among them.[19]

With independence, Algeria became the first dramatic failure of French state institutions on French territory to convince people to identify themselves as French. Since the French Revolution, of course, many groups and individuals in continental France had rejected official efforts to call them French or had resisted thinking of themselves in the ways that Paris-based legislators and mandarins ordained. Into the last decades of the nineteenth century, many of the inhabitants of the metropolitan departments preferred other languages to French, while provincial, local, and religious specificities sparked episodes of often spectacular intransigence against nationalizing and homogenizing measures. Whether it confronted the Vendée of the 1790s and its *chouans*, the village of Hautefaye in 1870 and its "cannibals," or the Bretons who joined the fight against forced secularization of the schools in the early 1900s, however, the French state always had maintained its claims to be in the right and, if necessary, enforced these claims with violence. The French historians Sylvie Thénault and Raphaëlle Branche separately show how colonialist racism determined the forms that French attempts to crush the Algerian Revolution took—in particular the systematic use of physical torture, summary executions, and massive population dislocations, which together led to the deaths of at least 250,000 Algerians. But to understand the vigor and duration of these efforts, we also need to see them as a continuation of approaches that governments previously had pursued in the metropole, in the name of liberalism and universalism.[20] This, of course, also raises questions about what it meant when France gave up trying to force Algerians to be French.[21]

[19] On French governance in Algeria, see Kamel Kateb, *Européens, "indigenes," et Juifs en Algérie, 1830–1962: Représentations et réalités des populations* (Paris, 2001). In English, see David Prochaska, *Making Algeria French: Colonialism in Bône, 1870–1920* (London, 1990), chap. 2. For an excellent cultural history of the paradoxes, possibilities, and limitations of claims in Algeria before the Revolution that Algeria was at once a part of France and had a colonial population, see Jonathan Gosnell, *The Politics of Frenchness in Colonial Algeria, 1930–1954* (Rochester, N.Y., 2002).

[20] The history of France in Algeria, that is, offers a *mise en abîme* of metropolitan history, as well as of the French Republic's relationship to its colonial empire.

[21] The classic text on French "nationalizing" efforts within the metropole is Eugen Weber, *Peasants into Frenchmen: The Modernization of Rural France, 1870–1914* (Stanford, 1976), while the seminal challenge to such a Paris-centric view is Peter Sahlins, *Boundaries: The Making of France and Spain in the Pyrenees* (Berkeley, 1989), which shows the centrality of negotiations and resistance on the boundaries to nation making. On language use among fin-de-siècle peasants in France, see Weber, *Peasants into Frenchmen*, 67–94, and Jean-Francois Chanet, *L'ecole républicaine et les petites patries* (Paris, 1996); on the Vendée, see Charles Tilly, *The Vendée: A Sociological Analysis of the Counter-Revolution of 1793* (Cambridge, Mass., 1994); on Hautefaye, see Alain Corbin, *The Village of Cannibals: Rage and Murder in France, 1870* (Cambridge, Mass., 1993); on Brittany and secularization, see Caroline Ford, *Creating the Nation in Provincial France: Religion and Political Identity in Brittany* (Princeton, 1993). On torture and "exceptional" justice, see Raphaëlle Branche, *La torture et l'armée pendant la guerre*

The Algerian Revolution, as writers such as Frantz Fanon and Jean-Paul Sartre who supported it explained, summoned France and the world to see the paradoxes, limits, and incoherencies of Western universalism, as well as the violence it required and thus produced. Along with writers from colonized Africa such as Albert Memmi (Tunisia), Sembène Ousmane (Senegal), and Mongo Beti (Cameroon), the Caribbean-born Fanon demanded answers to the biting question posed by French-Martinican poet and theorist of Negritude Aimé Césaire: "Colonization and civilization?" They expected more in response than the transfer of power. These critics did not reject all the values associated with Western universalism; they fought for the emergence of what Césaire's *Discourse on Colonialism* (1950) termed a "new humanism," one that would open up unimagined possibilities, a "new plenitude," to the decolonized. In turn, Sartre emphasized that this hoped-for Third World revolution had universal pretensions. His preface to Fanon's *Wretched of the Earth* (1961) stated that "we, too, the people of Europe, we are being decolonized . . . let us look at ourselves, if we dare, and see what it makes of us."[22] Yet, when France ceased contesting Algeria's independence, the government and most French actors did so while avoiding any engagement with the problems these radical thinkers identified. Instead, the ways France came to terms with Algerian independence only exacerbated them.[23]

Premises

In 1962 the French government abandoned its twinned efforts in Algeria—to make French a territory that had been French for decades and to turn the inhabitants of this territory, despite their being French nationals, into Frenchmen. This was unprecedented. Yet the specific ways France chose to effect the division between the metropole and Algeria erased the rupture and made its dramatic effects on France appear natural. French actors, within the

---

d'Algérie (Paris, 2001), and Sylvie Thénault, *Une drôle de justice: Les magistrats dans la guerre d'Algérie* (Paris, 2001). For a summary of efforts to count the number of dead and wounded, see Guy Pervillé, *Pour une histoire de la guerre d'Algérie* (2002), 237–47. The demographer Kamel Kateb has criticized the demographic method that French historians have used to establish estimates that between 250,000 and 350,000 Algerians died during the conflict. He argues that a more rigorous analysis of the same numbers leads to estimates of roughly 430,000 deaths and upwards of 578,000. See Kamel Kateb, *Européens, "indigènes" et juifs en Algérie (1830–1962). Representations et réalités des populations* (2001), 313.

[22] Preface to Frantz Fanon, *Les damnés de la terre* (Paris, 1991), 54.

[23] See Paul A. Silverstein, *Algeria in France: Transpolitics, Race, and Nation* (Bloomington, 2004); Françoise Gaspard, *A Small City in France: A Socialist Mayor Confronts Neofascism*, trans. Arthur Goldhammer (Cambridge, Mass., 1995); Maxim Silverman, *Deconstructing the Nation: Immigration, Racism, and Citizenship in Modern France* (London, 1992); and Peter Fysh and Jim Wolfreys, *The Politics of Racism in France* (New York, 1998).

government and without, made decisions at the war's close that effaced what was going on and expunged the importance of Algeria from French history.[24]

Rather than pursue recent approaches to memory in terms of commemoration, or in relation to trauma, this book explores how a rewriting of the Algerian history of France took place at the moment of independence.[25] Critical thinking about the formative role played by Algeria and the "new imperialism" in the construction of the French nation-state disappeared. In its place there emerged the fiction that the "Algerian experience" had been an unfortunate colonial detour, from which the French Republic had now escaped. This fiction set the stage for what the political scientist Adrian Favell identifies in French debates since the 1980s as a "mysterious reinvention of the republican tradition . . . trumpeting the grand moments of modern French self-definition . . . and forgetting the rest."[26] Many French people came to imagine their acceptance of decolonization as a victory, celebrating the daring of "de Gaulle the decolonizer," or the signatories of the 1961 "Manifesto of the 121" in support of conscientious objection and against the Algerian War. Efforts in 1962 and since to exclude the minority of French people who continued to argue that Algeria was French from the realms of French and republican memory or history helped make such a story seem feasible. Only "fascists"—symbolized by the terrorist OAS (Secret Army Organization), a group led by deserters from the French military, which had enjoyed wide support among Algeria's roughly one million so-called Europeans—had opposed independence, or so many have been led to believe.

---

[24] On the effects and durability of this forgetting, see Benjamin Stora, *La gangrène et l'oubli: La mémoire de la guerre d'Algérie* (Paris, 1991).

[25] On memory as memorialization, see, in particular, Daniel J. Sherman, *The Construction of Memory in Interwar France* (Chicago, 1999), esp. the introduction; John R. Gillis, ed., *Commemorations: The Politics of National Identity* (Princeton, 1994); and Pierre Nora, ed., *Les lieux de mémoire*, vols. 1–3 (Paris, 1984–1992). On memory in terms of trauma, see, in particular, Dominick LaCapra, *Representing the Holocaust: History, Theory, Trauma* (Ithaca, 1994); Saul Friedlander, "Trauma, Transference and 'Working Through' in Writing the History of the *Shoah*," *History and Memory* 4, no. 1 (Spring–Summer 1992); and Stoler, *Race and the Education of Desire*, 62.

[26] Adrian Favell, *Philosophies of Integration: Immigration and the Idea of Citizenship in France and Britain* (New York, 2001), 59. "New imperialism" refers to the renewal, in the last decades of the nineteenth century, of European enthusiasm for conquering and governing foreign countries. This renewal led to a European "scramble" for parts of the globe, which the United State and Japan eventually joined. On the cultural effects of "new imperialism," see John M. MacKenzie, *Propaganda and Empire: The Manipulation of British Popular Opinion, 1880–1960* (Manchester, 1984), 10. For an analysis of how MacKenzie's approach can be applied to France see the editors' introduction to *Promoting the Colonial Idea: Propaganda and Visions of Empire in France*, ed. Tony Chafer and Amanda Sackur (New York, 2002); and Owen White, *Children of the French Empire: Miscegenation and Colonial Society in French West Africa, 1895–1960* (Oxford, 2000), 117. On the rise of scientific racism, see Adas (1989); Michael A. Osborne, *Nature, the Exotic, and the Science of French Colonialism* (Bloomington, Ind., 1994); on colonialism and racism, see William B. Cohen, *The French Encounter with African: White Response to Blacks, 1530–1880* (Bloomington, Ind., 1980); August (1985); Julia Clancy-Smith and Frances Gouda, eds., *Domesticating the Empire: Languages of Gender, Race, and Family Life in French and Dutch Colonialism* (Charlottesville, Va., 1998).

Such amnesia encourages us to view divisions fabricated by recent historical events (France and the French, different from Algeria and the Algerians) as obvious.[27]

Understandings premised in newly clear racial and ethnic differences proved the most secure harbor for French universalism in its stormy exit from the reassuring certainties that overseas empire had seemed to offer. For French officials from the 1830s until independence in 1962, Algerian "Muslim" was above all a legal, rather than a religious category. In 1962, invocations of "Muslim origin" gave way to descriptions of "North Africans" or "Algerians" who could not be "European" or "French." With no public debate, the French government made common-sense understandings of racial or ethnic difference the basis of laws that denied most people from Algeria the right to remain French.[28]

In this revolutionary moment, political institutions and the law joined with, reinforced, and sometimes redefined other crucial definitions (scientific, medical, bureaucratic, and cultural, for example) of who was French and how France should be governed, definitions in which race and ethnicity were already explicit. This is why, in studying the disappearance of a France that included Algeria, my focus on political institutions and the law is particularly telling. I understand the law and formal politics, first, as specific modes of representation, which act to define the people each claims to regulate, represent, and govern. As modes of representation, law and formal politics also inform how such people relate to other people and to institutions. Second, in this book I examine law and formal politics for the ways they discipline debates and people: I pay particular attention to how both rely on institutions to produce subjects who can be categorized through specific characteristics (e.g., gender, sexuality, nationality, religion, and ethnicity), and to shape these subjects' possibilities for acting.[29] Attending to formal politics and the law also allows us to use investigations of imperialism to assess the real importance of "sameness" and universality in post-1789 French politics and thinking.[30] It was in these twinned domains that

---

[27] On what he terms the "heroic narrative" of decolonization in post-independence histories of Africa, see Cooper, "Conflict and Connection", 163.

[28] For an overview of how cultural historians analyze these discourses of French colonialism and "difference," see Daniel J. Sherman, "The Arts and Sciences of Colonialism," *French Historical Studies* 23 (2000): 700–29.

[29] On integrating the law and political institutions into the critical schemas that Michel Foucault elaborated, see Michel Foucault, *Il faut défendre la société* (Paris, 1997) and *The History of Sexuality, vol. 1, The Will to Knowledge,* trans. Robert Hurley (New York, 1978); see also Nicos Poulantzas, *State, Power, Socialism* (London, 1978); Alan Hunt, "Foucault's Expulsion of Law: Towards a Retrieval," *Law & Social Inquiry* 17, no. 1 (Winter 1992): 1–38; and Pierre Bourdieu, "The Force of Law: Toward a Sociology of the Juridical Field," trans. Richard Terdiman, *Hastings Law Journal* 38, no. 5 (July 1987).

[30] On the need to take seriously claims to "sameness," see Alice L. Conklin, "Colonialism and Human Rights, A Contradiction in Terms? The Case of France and West Africa, 1895–1914," *American Historical Review* 103, no. 2 (April 1998): 419–42.

modern France had maintained some semblance of color blindness. In discussions of Algerian "Muslims" in Algeria from the conquest on, or alongside other workers and soldiers from the colonies in the metropole during and after World War I, scholars have shown how racial thinking framed official as well as other (scientific, popular, and so forth) understandings.[31] Yet, as a number of these authors rightly note, despite the sometimes frequent appearance of racist affirmations, and even the use of explicitly ethnic or racial categories in state documents, France never made these categories official, never gave them legal or codified definition.[32]

The French had remained most reticent toward "scientific" understandings of race-based distinctions, and most attached to universalist principles, in precisely those areas where the law was implicated. French legislators after 1789 avoided placing racial classifications into law. Inspired by the goals and achievements of the French Revolution (as democrats, socialists, writers, and politicians of the nineteenth century defined them and as the Third Republic institutionalized them[33]), French law and republican ideology resisted the embrace of racial categories. Such attempts at embodying French revolutionary ideas, of course, were only partly successful. Studies of French anti-Semitism offer the most insight into this phenomenon and its paradoxes.[34] Yet, as the formulation of post-Vichy immigration policy illustrates, republican commitment to keeping French law "color blind" had real effects. The most influential French proponents of recognizing ethnic and racial categories, demographic experts such as Georges Mauco and Albert Sauvy, wrote the official recommendations. They invoked science to affirm that group membership should determine suitability for immigration. The policy

---

[31] Emmanuelle Saada offers the best description of the way that understandings of race, ethnicity, or place of origin shaped how the French dealt with and thought about their colonial subjects in Algeria and other colonies. See "Une nationalité par degré. Civilité et citoyenneteé en situation coloniale," in *L'esclavage, la colonisation, et après*, ed. Parick Weil and Stéphane Dufoix (2005), 193–227. On such practices in metropolitan France, see, e. g., Tyler Stovall, "The Color Line behind the Lines: Racial Violence in France during the Great War," *American Historical Review* 103, no. 3 (June 1998), 737–69; Laurent Dornel, "Les usages du racialisme: Le cas de la main-d'oeuvre coloniale en France pendant la Première Guerre mondiale," *Genèses* 20 (September 1995); Laura Levine Frader, "Gender, 'Race,' and the Body at Work in France, 1919–1939," *International Review of Social History* 44, supplement 7 (1999): 123–47; Elisa Camiscioli, "Producing Citizens, Reproducing the 'French Race': Immigration, Demography, and Pronatalism in Early Twentieth-Century France," *Gender & History* 13, no. 3 (November 2001): 593–621; and Sandrine Bertaux, "Entre ordre social et ordre racial: Constitution et développement de la démographie en France et en Italie, de la fin du XIXe siècle à la fin des années cinquante," PhD diss., European University Institute, 2002.

[32] See Erik Bleich, "The French Model: Color-Blind Integration," in *Color Lines: Affirmative Action, Immigration, and Civil Rights Options for America*, ed. John David Skrentny (Chicago, 2001), 270–96.

[33] See William Sewell, *Work and Revolution in France: The Language of Labor from the Old Regime to 1848* (Cambridge, 1980); and Philip Nord, *The Republican Moment: Struggles for Democracy in Nineteenth-Century France* (Cambridge, Mass., 1995).

[34] See, e. g., Pierre Birnbaum, *Jewish Destinies: Citizenship, State, and Community in Modern France*, trans. Arthur Goldhammer (New York, 2000); and Paula E. Hyman, *The Jews of Modern France* (Berkeley, 1998).

that French politicians codified, however, rejected such advice, and contained no reference to place of origin, race, or ethnicity.[35]

In ways that surpassed rhetoric, France's hegemonic political tradition and its laws—unlike those of other Western countries such as the United States, the United Kingdom, and Germany—hewed to principles that explicitly avoided references to race and ethnicity. The French Republic remained confident in its capacity to turn even men perceived as belonging to different (and less "civilized") races into French individuals. In areas such as higher education, popular entertainment, sports, and the arts, assimilation—or at least color blindness—existed to the degree that at least token individuals could succeed. In all of these areas, the limited possibilities for access and success offered to people of color were well in advance of any other predominantly white Western nation.[36]

It was in the area of representative politics that France was most successful in offering a semblance of racial equality to all of its citizens. From the late 1920s through the first Vichy government, men of color regularly held cabinet-level posts. From 1944, when women were given the right to vote, until 1962, every government included at least one man or woman of color. Between 1949 and 1969, Gaston Monnerville, a black man from French Guiana, was the president of the Senate, the second highest state office. Between October 1958 and July 1962, Algerian "Muslims" made up some 9.5 percent of the French Parliament—roughly "representative" of their numbers.[37] Although the details of this history remain largely unstudied, these facts give some support to the description by certain scholars of a "color blind" French model, which differs from what they identify as "color-conscious" U.S., British, and German models. Yet, with the events of 1962, this history of relatively successful (formal) representation came to an end.[38]

[35] See Patrick Weil, *La France et ses étrangers: L'aventure d'une politique de l'immigration 1938–1991* (Paris, 1991), 53–61. On Mauco's racism, see Camiscioli, "Producing Citizens" ; Bertaux, "Entre ordre social et ordre racial"; and Karen Adler, *Jews and Gender in Liberation France* (Cambridge, 2003), 106–43; for Sauvy, see Bertaux, "Entre ordre social et ordre racial". On the attention many republican French politicians paid to racist theories in the interwar period, see Clifford Rosenberg, "Albert Sarraut and Republican Racial Thought," in *French Politics, Culture & Society* 20, no. 2 (Fall 2002): 97–114.

[36] On the possibilities for nonwhite French men to participate in sports, see Pierre Lanfranchi and Alfred Wahl, "The Immigrant as Hero: Kopa, Mekloufi, and French Football," in *European Heroes: Myth, Identity, Sport,* ed. Richard Holt, J. A. Mangin, and Pierre Lanfranchi (London, 1996), 114–27.

[37] On the question of representation in France, see, e.g., Pierre Rosanvallon, *Le peuple introuvable: Histoire de la représentation démocratique en France* (Paris, 1998). Since at least Rousseau, and on beyond Karl Marx, theorists have analyzed the problematic concept of representation. See *The Social Contract,* trans. Maurice Cranston (London, 1968); *Eighteenth Brumaire of Louis Bonaparte* (New York, 1963); for an interesting reflection on Marx's analysis of "representation," see Gayatri Chakravorty Spivak, "Can the Subaltern Speak?" in *Marxism and the Interpretation of Culture,* ed. Cary Nelson and Lawrence Grossberg (Urbana, Ill., 1988).

[38] Among the members of government in the 1930s were Blaise Diagne, Henry Lemery, Alcide Delmont, Gratien Candace, and Gaston Monnerville. See chapter 10.

This book explores the disappearance of an imperial state that attempted until its last months, although fitfully, to make real the principles of race-blind equality and republican universality that were rooted in the history of France after the 1789 Revolution. France did this in order both to maintain control over Algeria's land and people and to reaffirm French self-under-standings. After it had achieved military dominance over the armed rebellion, yet proved incapable of stymieing growing support for the Algerian Revolution, the Fifth Republic still ignored the ideological arguments of those who did not want to be French or to be ruled by France. These efforts to avoid engaging with the challenges of Algerian nationalism continued until after Algerian independence. This silence allowed the foundation, as this book charts, of the now wholly "European" republic that emerged in the process of excluding Algeria and Algerians from France and French history.

An Overview

The book's chapters are organized into three sections. Chronologically, the first section covers the period from 1830 to 1962, the second returns to 1961–62, while the third focuses on the nine months that followed the 19 March 1962 cease-fire. The four chapters of part 1, "The Making and Forgetting of French Algeria," trace French claims that Algeria was part of France from the conquest of Algiers, in 1830, through the Algerian Revolution (1954–1962). The three chapters of part 2, "Between France and Algeria," consider how, from 1961 until the Evian Accords, French officials and metropolitan opinion discussed and worked to define the "French of Algeria" in anticipation of Algerian independence. The three chapters of part 3, "The Exodus and After," detail the effects of the unexpected flight, in the months that followed the Evian Accords, of over eight hundred thousand people from Algeria to continental France, and map how the crisis of the "exodus" crystallized the structures of a "post-Algerian" France.

PART I

THE MAKING AND FORGETTING
OF FRENCH ALGERIA

From that moment the whole world moved into a phase of social
development to which the French have recently given
a name, the useful word *décolonisation*.
C. E. CARRINGTON

In a sense, every modern nation is a product of colonization.
ETIENNE BALIBAR

Chapter 1

Muslim French Citizens from Algeria

A Short History

French leaders, and most particularly those of the French Republic, struggled for over twelve decades to manage the paradoxes and incoherencies of ruling Algeria—the land and its people—as if it was a part of France. During these years (1830s–early 1960s), France asserted that Algeria was an extension of French national territory and that its native-born inhabitants were national subjects; for most of that period, when and whether most Algerians would be citizens remained an unresolved question. In 1958, all Algerians became full citizens of the French Republic, and from 1956 until 1962 France put in place an impressive array of novel policies to concretize long-deferred pretensions that all Algerians, including "Muslims," were part of the nation.[1]

In this chapter I outline the history of French Algeria until just before it became clear to almost all French people that this history would end. I primarily reference the law, how France established and used legal codes and institutions to manage its territory and subjects across the Mediterranean. France with Algeria became a republic within an empire (1870–1940; 1944–1962), which placed Algeria at the heart of the conflicts and concerns entailed by the twinned flourishing of liberal modernity and modern colonialism—what some scholars compellingly term "colonial modernity." This meant that French decisions concerning Algeria often directly formed modern French self-understandings and government institutions, citizenship and

---

[1] On citizenship in France since the Revolution, see Joan Wallach Scott, *"Only Paradoxes to Offer": French Feminists and the Rights of Man* (Cambridge, Mass., 1996); Pierre Rosanvallon, *Sacre du citoyen: Histoire du suffrage universel en France* (Paris, 1992); on before the Revolution, see Peter Sahlins, *Unnaturally French: Foreign Citizens in the Old Regime and After* (Ithaca, 2004).

nationality among them. France in Algeria was, like other modern polities, a "taxonomic state," to use the anthropologist Ann Laura Stoler's terms, in which categorizing and defining people and their possibilities authorized state action. The identities that French laws and codes assigned people in Algeria also shaped—in often stark and brutal ways—their situations, their options, and their history.[2]

Between Assimilation and Coexistence, 1830–1944

The French conquest of the lands that now make up Algeria began with the invasion of the city of Algiers in 1830, the last whimper of the Bourbon Restoration (1815–1830) and the dawn of the July Monarchy (1830–1848). The successful invasion of the Ottoman-ruled Barbary Coast, which the French court infamously explained as a response to the Dey of Algiers's offensive use of a flywhisk on a Bourbon envoy, failed, however, to prop up King Charles X at home. The Orléanist (liberal) regime of King Louis-Philippe that replaced him aggressively pursued military repression of widespread local resistance across the Mediterranean and annexed French-occupied land to the national territory (Ordinance of 22 July 1834). The Crown speech of 23 December 1839, read before the parliament, declared Algeria "a land forever French."[3]

From the 1830s on, French officials maintained that Algerian territory was part of France and that Algeria's inhabitants were all French subjects.[4] After the Revolution of 1848, as a sign of its commitment to the values of 1789, the Second Republic declared, along with the abolition of slavery, that French territory in North Africa was an extension of the republic. It became three departments (Algiers, Oran, and Constantine).[5] However, full mem-

---

[2] Ann Laura Stoler, *Carnal Knowledge and Imperial Power: Race and the Intimate in Colonial Rule* (Berkeley, 2002), 206–8.

[3] Quoted in Kamel Kateb, "Histoire statistique des populations algériennes pendant la colonisation française, 1830–1962," PhD diss., Ecole des hautes études en sciences sociales, 1998, 188.

[4] One of the urtexts in recent discussions of citizenship, the sociologist Rogers Brubaker's *Citizenship and Nationhood in France and Germany* (Cambridge, Mass., 1992), considers what he terms a "French model" of the relationship between membership in the nation, national territory, and the law. In his influential formulation these three terms have anchored modern conceptions of national identity. Brubaker counterposes postrevolutionary France, where citizenship was "to be defined expansively, as a territorial community," or in terms of *jus soli* (also called *droit du sol* or citizenship by birth in the territory), and a German history of citizenship and nationhood, where an ethnic definition of membership in the nation, in terms of *jus sanguinis* (also called *droit du sang* or citizenship by bloodline), took shape that was not tightly linked to a bounded national territory.

[5] The lands that the French later conquered south of what had been Ottoman territory, in the Sahara, remained distinct from Algeria and from France until the 1950s. The Law of 24 December 1902 established this distinction, defined them as an extension of French territory, and named them the Southern Territories.

bership in the nation (in the form of citizenship) for the inhabitants, nearly all of them so-called indigenous people, was repeatedly postponed. Until 1944, in Algeria as elsewhere in France, the law maintained that full citizenship was a possibility only for men.

The history of the exclusion from citizenship of most people in or from French Algeria in some, but not all, ways resembles that of women's relationship to French citizenship. From the time of the 1789 French Revolution, the state relied on the legal category of citizenship to recognize some of its subjects as individuals with the capacity for rational decision making. Citizenship identified those individuals who had the right to participate in governing the nation. When the government was a republic (1792–1799; 1848–1851; 1870–1940; 1945 to the present), all full citizens had equal formal rights, both before the law and to vote for and serve in government. From the Revolution until 1944, most republican politicians argued that the exclusion of the category "women" from full citizenship was necessary for republican democracy. Republican opponents of women's suffrage used arguments about the "complementarity" of men and women and/or claims of female irrationality to insist that the law should neither efface nor ignore distinctions between "men" and "women."[6]

Most commentators, however, considered the exclusion of the majority of Algerian men from the polis as temporary. The characteristics that distinguished them from other French nationals were considered to be regrettable and surmountable, not complementary, natural, or necessary. This problem should be resolvable without substantially altering either the meanings or the mechanisms of citizenship or republicanism.[7] In discussing Algerians, some politicians and polemicists did make routine sallies that such men could never become French citizens because they were too different, by which they meant inherently inferior. But far more often there were generous and egalitarian republican arguments about why "Muslim" men would eventually have citizenship.[8]

---

[6] For the most compelling elaboration of these historical arguments, see Carole Pateman, *The Sexual Contract* (Stanford, 1988); Joan W. Scott, *"Only Paradoxes to Offer"* and *Gender and the Politics of History*, rev. ed. (New York, 1999); and Geneviève Fraisse, *Reason's Muse: Sexual Difference and the Birth of Democracy* (Chicago, 1994); see also Steven C. Hause and Anne Kenney Hause, *Women's Suffrage and Social Politics in the French Third Republic* (Princeton, 1984).

[7] The situation of Algerian "Muslim" men is thus also different from France's male West African colonial subjects. For an analysis of the structural similarity in French explanations of noncitizenship for French women and its colonial subjects, see Alice Conklin, "Colonialism and Human Rights, A Contradiction in Terms? The Case of France and West Africa, 1895–1914," *American Historical Review* 103, no. 2 (April 1998): 434.

[8] See Laure Blévis, "Les avatars de la citoyenneté en Algérie coloniale ou les paradoxes d'une categorization," *Droit et Société* 48 (2001): 557–80. Wendy Brown's comparative analysis of the emergence of the "Woman Question" and the "Jewish Question" in eighteenth- and nineteenth-century Europe offers suggestive insights into a similar distinction. See "Tolerance and/or Equality? The 'Jewish Question' and the 'Woman Question'," *differences: A Journal of Feminist Cultural Studies* 15, no. 2 (2004): 1–31.

Until World War II and the Vichy regime, French officials, whether republicans or not, relied on two models for their perspectives on and policies concerning the relationship of the vast majority of Algeria's inhabitants to the nation. The first was the assimilation model. In this view, officials expected all male inhabitants of Algeria to become French citizens eventually. Guided by assimilationism, the state and its local agents would break down what they described as local traditions and structures that promoted superstition and ignorance, conditions that prevented men from acting as individuals and joining the corps of citizens. French institutions would offer them access to a legal system, training, and education premised in universal principles and rationality. Irrationality and religious fanaticism, Muslim in particular, would crumble. Such mechanisms would create individual French men out of all adult male Algerians and would open access to full membership in the nation.[9]

The second model, following the terminology of French jurists in the 1950s, was coexistence. The policies of coexistence recognized that different groups existed in Algeria and that their relationship to the state and to the nation necessarily would be different. This principle was very similar to the late nineteenth-century French policy of associationism. Connecting "coexistence" to associationism highlights the central role of imperialist domination in both. The form and effects imposed on local people by the coexistence model and the associationist policy were not notably distinct.[10]

It is analytically important to distinguish "coexistence" from "association," however. Associationism explicitly recognized that distinct "cultures" existed and had to pursue distinct paths toward "civilization." The French referred to the principles of assimilationism when they first sought to administer the vast territories they colonized during the post-1884 "scramble for Africa," as well as the lands they conquered in North Africa (Tunisia, 1881, and Morocco, 1912) and Indochina (from 1859). Faced with the enormous resources assimilationist policies demanded—and with the realization that in many situations such policies worked to undermine French control—the Third Republic soon embraced a new theory that promoted parallel development. Like the theory of assimilation, the concept of association offered a rationale—"the mission to civilize"—for why the French Republic, sup-

---

[9] It was during Year III of the Revolution that the French legislator Boissy d'Anglas coined the term "assimilation" in reference to the West Indian colonies. See Rosanvallon, *Sacre du citoyen,* 424 n. 1. In 1960 a group of French jurists in Algiers defined assimilation as "the pursuit of a unitary conception of the state that excluded, in principle, all particularities for ethnic, religious, or social groups. If such a particularism exists, this approach can afford an exceptional status, presumed transitory, en route to the equality of all subjects before the law." By dint of political and institutional measures, "progressive assimilation would bring to a close such temporary juridical exceptions." See Commission rélations entre les communautés, La Cour d'Appel d'Alger, "Le régime juridique des statuts privés et des juridictions civiles en Algérie" (Algiers, 9 December 1960), 1, in Centre des Archives contémporaines des Archives nationales, Fontainebleau (hereafter, CAC/AN) 950395/76.

[10] Ibid.

posedly committed to "liberty, equality, fraternity" and the Rights of Man, had embarked on the conquest and domination of millions of people across the globe. Associationism recognized "peoples" who, as colonial subjects under French guidance (and through their exposure to French civilization, laws, science and knowledge, and ideals), would eventually become civilized nations.[11]

The practice of coexistence in Algeria began well before the idea of associationism, and it never became an official policy. During the Third Republic numerous writers, scientists, legislators, and officials argued for the application of association to Algeria. The idea was widely popular among Algeria's "Europeans," yet their representatives and allies were unable to convince French legislators or ministers to adopt associationism as policy in Algeria. Indeed, officials avoided using the word "association" in discussing French policy in Algeria until the 1950s. They did not officially admit the existence of "peoples" or "cultures" in Algeria (except during the Second Empire), recognizing only legal systems that governed groups of designated individuals. All male French "subjects" in Algeria, unlike those in the new colonies of the late nineteenth century, were destined, their rulers said, to become French citizens.[12]

The tension between approaches based on assimilation and coexistence, which shaped the history of French Algeria, emerged in the first months that followed the French conquest of Algiers. A military directive of 9 September 1830 declared French-occupied lands legally a tabula rasa on which to inscribe French law. One month later, the directive of 22 October 1830 reversed that decision. Threatened with the revival of armed resistance, the French army reestablished "Muslim" and "Israelite" (a French term for "Jewish") jurisdictions over their respective communities. This embrace of pragmatism over principle was, of course, emblematic of European overseas

---

[11] Numerous scholars have analyzed associationism as it emerged in French theoretical considerations of their imperial project and, more recently, as an approach that had significant ramifications on lands and people under colonial control. On the development of the concepts of assimilation and associationism, see Raymond F. Betts, *Assimilation and Association in French Colonial Theory, 1890–1914* (New York, 1970), and Martin Demming Lewis, "One Hundred Million Frenchmen: The 'Assimilation' Theory in French Colonial Policy," *Comparative Studies in Society and History* 4, no. 2 (January 1962): 129–53. On associationism as "paternal authoritarianism," see William B. Cohen, *Rulers of Empire: The French Colonial Service in Africa* (Stanford, 1971). The most important reevaluation of the importance of these theories is Alice Conklin, *A "Mission to Civilize": The Republican Idea of Empire in France and West Africa, 1895–1930* (Stanford, 1997). See also Eric T. Jennings, "Monuments to Frenchness? The Memory of the Great War and the Politics of Guadeloupe's Identity, 1914–1945," *French Historical Studies* 21, no 4 (Fall 1998). On the concept of "civilization" as used in postrevolutionary French colonization, see Conklin, *A Mission to "Civilize"*, 1–15.

[12] Patricia M. E. Lorcin, *Imperial Identities: Stereotyping, Prejudice and Race in Colonial Algeria* (London, 1995), 165–225. As detailed below, after 1865 all Algerian autochthones became French nationals and thus were no longer termed "subjects" in the sense that France's "colonial subjects" were. I thank Laure Blévis for discussing with me official reticence to employ the term "association."

imperialism. Yet from then on this "forced" decision proved crucial to how France defined the inhabitants of the territory that officials soon began to call "Algeria." Until the end of World War II, while forms of administration and domination grounded in coexistence predominated, most officials in Algeria and politicians in the metropole insisted that their goal was assimilation.[13]

It was through their recognition of stark differences between legal systems that the French laid the groundwork for policies of coexistence. From October 1830 until Algerian independence in July 1962, France admitted the legitimacy of what came to be called "local law," that is, the distinct ensemble of legal codes, courts, and jurists that predated the French arrival. In 1830, this meant Koranic (Islamic) and Mosaic (Jewish) laws and institutions; eventually, the French also recognized Berber and Mozabite customary laws. Local laws governed only those people living under it at the moment of French conquest, and their descendants. In French Algeria, there was no way for groups or individuals to "adopt" a local law, neither through conversion nor marriage. (Nor did abjuring religious belief offer a way out.) Only through *jus sanguinis* (also called *droit du sang*, or "by descent") did an individual come under the rule of local law.[14] However, by the end of the 1830s, the French had limited the questions that fell under the control of Koranic and Mosaic courts and jurisprudence.[15] The Ordinance of 28 Febru-

---

[13] On these developments, see Commission relations entre les communautés, "Le régime juridique des statuts privés et des juridictions civiles en Algérie," 9; Kateb, "Histoire statistique des populations algériennes". First used in 1831, according to Charles-Robert Ageron in *Histoire de l'Algérie contemporaine, 1830–1999*, 11th ed. (Paris, 1999), 3, the name "Algérie" was adopted officially in 1838 to designate the French possessions in the north of Africa. See Guy Pervillé, "Comment appeler les habitants de l'Algérie avant la définition légale d'une nationalité algérienne," *Cahiers de la Méditerranée* 54 (June 1997): 55–60. I employ the term "Israelite" advisedly and contextually; as a name used in French to identify Jews, its valence—from respect to disdain—has varied over time. See Dominique Schnapper, *Juif et israélite* (Paris, 1980).

[14] See Allan Christelow, *Muslim Law Courts and the French Colonial State in Algeria* (Princeton, 1985), and Louis-Augustin Barrière, *Le statut personnel des musulmans d'Algérie de 1834 à 1962* (Dijon, 1993). On the multiplicity of law systems in comparative imperial contexts, see M. B. Hooker, *Legal Pluralism: An Introduction to Colonial and Neo-colonial Laws* (Oxford, 1975). On the impossibility of using religious conversion to leave "Muslim" status, see André Bonnichon, "La conversion au christianisme de l'indigène musulman algérien et ses effets juridiques (Un cas de conflit colonial)," JD diss., Paris, 1931.

[15] Local law applied only to questions of what was termed "civil status"—marriage, divorce, paternity, and inheritance—while the government established "French" law (also, in this context, referred to as "common" law) and French courts to regulate criminal and public affairs. First autochthones governed by Mosaic law (Ordinance of 22 July 1834), then people governed by Koranic and Berber customary law (Ordinance of 28 February 1841) were subjected to the French penal code, while the Ordinance of 26 September 1842 established that judgments rendered under the *droits locals* that still governed civil or personal status—at that time Koranic, Mosaic, and Berber customary—could be appealed before the French Court of Algiers. See Kateb, "Histoire statistique des populations algériennes", 7. From then until local jurisdictions disappeared in 1962, the judgment on appeal was supposed to be based on that of the original jurisdiction. For a study of this rule that covers the 1930s and 1940s, see Laurent Bellon, "Logiques judiciaires et couples mixtes," *Genre humain*, special issue "Juger en Algérie" (September 1997): 63–74.

ary–27 April 1841 (Article 50) put an end to the role of Mosaic courts, and officials soon restricted the authority of Berber customary law courts as well.[16]

Government acceptance of the coexistence of different legal systems in French Algeria did not stop successive French governments from pursuing assimilation. They did so by extending the reach of French law and institutions. French legal institutions served what the government planned would be a large and growing community of settlers from mainland or "metropolitan" France; they drew indigenous Algerians into contact with French ways of governing as well. Civilian officials justified their increasing encroachment on the daily lives of people under the jurisdiction of Koranic or Mosaic law as an attempt to encourage all of Algeria's inhabitants to assimilate. This was most explicit in the case of Jewish "natives," whose assimilation was a constant concern for metropolitan Jewish organizations and their allies in government up through 1962. (Such a support system did not exist for "Muslims" until the 1950s.) In 1842 the government-commissioned "Altaras Report" laid out "a blueprint for a long-term civilizing project of a wide scope" for what it presented as a backward Jewish community. The report declared that the Jewish community's existing civil and judiciary system was "contrary to progress and encompasses principles that cannot be harmonized with our civilization." French planners assumed that male Algerian "Muslims" and "Israelites" would quickly grow to prefer French law and want to become fully French, to become citizens.[17]

References to the law anchored official discussions of "differences" or distinctions between groups. Although the state admitted the existence of multiple legal systems, each of which governed a specific group of people, French officials largely avoided describing these groups in organic terms, such as race, nationality, ethnicity, or even religion. The historian Jean-Robert Henry notes that it was during the conquest of Algeria, in a 9 June 1831 military command decision concerning private contracts, that the category "European" appeared for the first time in French legal language.[18] French governance in Algeria also gave legal definition to the categories "Muslim," "Arab," "Indigenous," and "Jew." The appearance of what Henry qualifies

---

[16] Isaac Uhry, *Receuil des lois décrets, ordonnances, avis du Conseil d'Etat, arêtés, règlements et circulaires concernant les israélites 1850–1903, précédé de l'ordonnance du 25 mai 1844,* 3rd ed. (Bordeaux, 1903), 214. On the limits on Berber customary law courts, see Hooker, *Legal Pluralism,* 211.

[17] Rochdi Younsi, "Caught in a Colonial Triangle: Competing Loyalties within the Jewish Community of Algeria, 1842–1943," PhD diss., University of Chicago, 2003, 47; Jacques Altaras and Joseph Cohen, "Rapport sur l'état moral et politique des israélites de l'Algérie et des moyens de l'améliorer," reproduced in *Les Juifs d'Algérie et la France, 1830–1855,* ed. Simon Schwarzfuchs (Jerusalem, 1981). On the effects of French efforts, see Elizabeth Friedman, *Colonialism and After: An Algerian Jewish Community* (South Hadley, Mass., 1988).

[18] Jean-Robert Henry, "L'identité imaginée par le droit: De l'Algérie coloniale à la construction européenne," in *Cartes d'identité: Comment dit-on "nous" en politique?* ed. Denis-Constant Martin (Paris, 1994), 44.

as "primary categories" in French law, however, was "rapidly associated with measures" that were meant to lead to "their transformation and their disappearance." The term "Arab," for example, which was employed to refer to people in military-controlled areas, disappeared from official use after the 1870s.[19]

During the rule of Napoleon III (the Second Empire, 1851–1870), the ongoing tension at the heart of French rule of Algeria revealed itself most fully. Military command replaced civilian control, official colonization slowed (after 1860), and the army pursued southern conquests, elements of a policy termed le Royaume Arabe (Arab Kingdom). In a 6 February 1863 letter, Napoleon III wrote that "Algeria is not strictly speaking a colony, but an Arab Kingdom." This imperial fantasy, in which French rationalizing and modernizing oversight and instruction would contain and shape "Arab" control and character, encompassed the existing Algerian departments. The historian Patricia M. E. Lorcin summarizes the policy as one in which "the practices and religion of the Arabs were respected," yet one that, to quote the emperor of France, "sought to mold them to our laws, accustom them to our domination and convince them of our superiority." To these ends, decrees in 1854 and 1866, the first since October 1830, gave official expression to the principle of the coexistence of communities.[20]

In affirming the centrality of policies based in coexistence, the emperor also introduced a new variant of assimilation, which was at once more aggressive in its effects and more limited in its reach. Through the affirmation of French nationality for all, the extension of full citizenship to a limited few, and the establishment of a process of so-called naturalization, the Second Empire gave institutional form to the promise of assimilation in Algeria. The Senatus-Consulte of 14 July 1865 asserted that every "indigenous Muslim is French" (thus recognizing their French nationality) and extended French citizenship to a small number of "indigenous" men and their descendants. In exchange for full citizenship, these men abandoned their "local civil status": the right, in personal or civil matters, to be governed by local laws, what the text termed "Muslim law" for "Muslim natives" and "personal status" for "Israelite natives." By the end of the 1860s, French officials began to call indigenous Algerians not simply "natives" but also people "with local civil sta-

---

[19] Jean-Robert Henry, "Algeria and Germany: The Paradoxical Benchmarks of French Identity," *International Scope Review* 3, no. 6 (Winter 2001): 49; Henry, "L'identité imaginée par le droit," 45. On the establishment of civilian control, see Charles-Robert Ageron, *Histoire de l'Algérie contemporaine*, vol. 2, *1871–1954* (Paris, 1979), 19–21, 31.

[20] Lorcin, *Imperial Identities*, 76. On this period see Annie Rey-Goldzeiguer, *Le Royaume Arabe: La politique algérienne de Napoléon III, 1861–70* (Algiers, 1977). The Senatus-Consultes of 1854 and 1866 established government by executive decree over Algeria, which remained in place through the 1880s. See Lewis, "One Hundred Million Frenchmen,", 136. On the Decree of 8 August 1854, which established official registration (*état civil*) with the "Muslim" authorities of all "Muslims" (abolished through the Imperial Decree of 18 August 1868), see Kamel Kateb, *Européens, "indigènes," et juifs en Algérie, 1830–1962: Représentations et réalités des populations* (Paris, 2001), 22–24.

tus" or "Koranic civil status," "Mosaic civil status," and the like. This signaled that, in civil law matters, Koranic or Mosaic laws (and Koranic courts
in the first instance) could regulate these French nationals.[21] Officials termed
a minority of Algerian inhabitants "Algerians with French civil status" or
"with common civil status." This category comprised immigrants from Europe along with a very small number of people who had abandoned their
"local civil status" to obtain full citizenship. (Note that for many decades
the term "Algerian" referred exclusively to people of French or other European origin; the term *pieds noirs* first appeared in the late nineteenth century
in reference to "Muslims," though it later—first in a pejorative sense, then
embraced with pride—denominated "European" Algerians.)[22]

The 1865 directive also established the principle that Algerian men with
"local civil status" who fulfilled certain criteria could obtain full citizenship;
to do so they were required to abandon their right to be judged under local
civil law or by local law courts. The vast majority of the small number of
men who met the criteria for French citizenship did not obtain it. Many rejected this option because of their attachment to their religion or their desire
not to be seen as apostates or collaborators. Only 1,309 men completed citizenship applications between 1865 and 1899 (out of a total "Muslim" population of some four million by 1901). Concurrently, local administrators
used delay and red tape, as the political scientist Patrick Weil demonstrates,
to prevent significant numbers of Algerian men with Koranic civil status
from obtaining the citizenship they requested.[23] The procedure, which the
French termed "naturalization," prefigured French practice in the colonies
they conquered in the late nineteenth century. Although French governance
of the Four Communes of Senegal (St. Louis, Gorée, Dakar, and Rufisque),
French since before 1789, particularly shaped subsequent colonial rule in
West Africa, the quite different approach to local populations France pursued in Algeria offered the primary template.[24] The historian Alice Conklin
describes the emergence in the early twentieth century of an official policy to
"naturalize" as French citizens "deserving" members of the local elite in

---

[21] In another sign of assimilationism, Algerians with local civil status had the option of seeking redress in matters governed by "local law" before a French court in the first instance. See
Martine Fabre, "Le recours en cassation en Algérie: De la colonisation à la décolonisation," paper presented 22–23 October 2002, Droit et justice en Algérie (19–20ème siècles), Paris.

[22] On use of the terms *pieds noirs* and *Algerians*, see Pervillé, "Comment appeler les habitants de l'Algérie".

[23] "Sénatus-Consulte du 14 juillet 1865 sur l'état des personnes et la naturalisation en Algérie," *11 bulletin* 1315 n. 13-504. On "Muslim" resistance to accepting French citizenship as
proposed and on local administrators' efforts to prevent the naturalization of "Muslim" men,
see Patrick Weil, *Qu'est-ce qu'un Français? Histoire de la nationalité française depuis la Révolution* (2002), 236–37. For statistics between 1865 and 1900, see Charles-Robert Ageron, *Les
Algériens musulmans et la France (1871-1919)*, vol. 2 (Paris, 1968), 1118.

[24] For a comparison between the Four Communes (Senegal) and Algeria, see Ruth Dickens,
"Defining French Citizenship Policy in West Africa, 1895–1956," PhD diss., Emory University,
2001, 42–53.

French West Africa. In West Africa, according to Conklin, the policy worked to reassure French claims that policies premised on ideas of association did advance the goal of equality, despite the obvious inequalities they left in place (in the colonized societies) and created (between the French colonizers and the colonized). The French offered a limited number of local elite men the kind of rights and responsibilities that their policies were designed to eventually allow to local peoples, under French guidance. Naturalization in the Algerian context (which gave men who already had French nationality the exercise of French citizenship) provided the model for subsequent policy in the empire (which gave citizenship including nationality to colonial subjects), yet it had a different meaning. Qualified individuals obtained French citizenship as a precursor to what all Algerians, as French people, eventually would obtain. By the twentieth century, when naturalizations began in certain other colonies, French officials usually presented the "evolved" (evolués) as exemplary models for the progression, through French rule, of colonized peoples into associated nations, which eventually would establish the types of "universal" rights for all of their citizens that citizens of the Republic (including the newly naturalized) already had.[25]

The most important and consistent use of the model of assimilation that the French elaborated in Algeria was in the metropole, in the process that Eugen Weber outlines in *Peasants into Frenchmen*.[26] Indeed, if developments in Second Empire Algeria offer key insights into later decisions and practices in the new French overseas empire, subsequent Algerian developments had much more to do with the evolving governance of France itself. The collapse of the Second Empire and the establishment in 1870–71 of what would become the Third French Republic marked the high point of assimilationist practice specifically targeted at Algeria. The famed Crémieux Decree of 24 October 1870 announced that "the native Israelites of the Algerian departments are declared French citizens; consequently, their real status and their personal status will be, as of the promulgation of this decree, regulated by French law."[27] This decree announced a renewed French willingness to ad-

---

[25] Conklin, "Colonialism and Human Rights, a Contradiction in Terms?": 434–36.

[26] Henry, "Algeria and Germany," 48, and Eugen Weber, *Peasants into Frenchmen: The Modernization of Rural France, 1870–1914* (Stanford, 1976), esp. the concluding chapter, 485–96. On the colonial inspiration for "assimilating" the French provinces, see also: Edmund Burke III, "The Terror and Religion: Brittany and Algeria," in *Colonialism and the Modern World: Selected Studies,* ed. Gregory Blue, Martin Bunton, and Ralph Crozier (Armonk, N.Y., 2002), 40–51. For a philosophical comparison between French efforts to incorporate peripheral regions of metropolitan France and to assimilate the colonies, see Simone Weil, *Simone Weil on Colonialism: An Ethic of the Other,* ed. and trans. J. P. Little (Lanham, Md., 2003), 19, 123.

[27] See "Décret du 24 octobre 1870 qui déclare citoyens français les Israélites indigènes d'Algérie," in *Bulletin n. 8–XII* (1870–71). This decree was tightened and completed by the "Décret du 7 octobre 1871 rélatif aux Israélites indigènes d'Algérie," in *Journal Officiel* (hereafter, *J.O.*) of 9 October 1871. This second, so-called Lambrecht Decree was enacted following a virulently anti-Semitic campaign in the metropole. It sought more closely to regulate which Jews in Algeria were eligible for citizenship. The more restrictive decree demanded proof of birth or descent

dress general populations and not just exceptional individuals, as had been the policy under the Second Empire. It recognized that policies based on the voluntary abandonment of civil status had failed: since 1865, only 144 Algerians with Mosaic civil status had sought to become French citizens. In addition, while Crémieux built on the new institutional measures Napoleon III's government had established with the Senatus-Consulte of 1865, it also sidelined the imperial attachment to local "peoples." The Third Republic, however, implemented no such proposal for Algerians who were governed by Muslim or Berber customary law.[28] Instead, the continued recognition of their local civil status flagged the implicit pursuit of a policy of coexistence.

French governments, from the 1880s until independence, dealt with the relationship between people in Algeria and the nation mainly through laws that affected all of France. These laws redefined French nationality and citizenship and also codified the marginalization of Algerians with local civil status. In 1889, the Third Republic affirmed the principle of *jus soli* ("*droit du sol*"), that is, by birth in the territory for the attribution of French nationality. Nationality was itself a prerequisite for citizenship, but not concomitant with it. *Jus soli* emerged via two measures, both contained in the Law of 26 June 1889. The first established the rule of "double *jus soli*," which gave French nationality to any individual born in France (including Algeria) of a parent born (French or foreign) in France. The individual had no say in the matter. The second gave French nationality at his or her majority to any individual who, born on French territory of two foreign-born parents, still lived in France (including Algeria). The individual had one year in which to decline French nationality. Legislators and jurists from Algeria played key roles in writing and voting in this new law. They argued that the large numbers of noncitizens in Algeria made reform imperative. The census of 1886 revealed that there were 219,627 "French" inhabitants of Algeria and 202,212 inhabitants with another European nationality, mostly Italian or Spanish. The massive foreign "colonies" of people from Spain, the Italian peninsula, Malta, and elsewhere resulted from French policies, but they now threatened French rule in Algeria.[29] Beginning with the July Monarchy

---

from inhabitants born in Algeria before 1830. Thus Jews from other parts of the Maghreb, in particular, could be excluded. See Kateb, "Histoire statistique des populations algériennes," 196. (Given the great difficulty in obtaining preconquest documentary proof, this requirement, of course, could be and was maliciously applied to harass Algerian Jews.) Laure Blévis shows that this second decree became the legal basis by which entry into any local law civil status in Algeria was available only via *jus sanguinis*. See Blévis, "Droit colonial algérien de la citoyenneté," 561 n. 15.

[28] On Jewish reticence to "naturalize," see Charles-André Julien, *Histoire de l'Algérie contemporaine*, vol. 1, *1827–1871* (1964), 476; and Friedman, *Colonialism and After*, 10. On ultimately successful efforts to prevent the National Assembly from naturalizing Algerian "Muslims," see Christelow, *Muslim Law Courts and the French Colonial State*, chap. 8.

[29] On the importance of the Law of 1889, see Gérard Noiriel, *La tyrannie du national: Le droit d'asile en Europe, 1793–1993* (Paris, 1993), 88. Weil, *Qu'est-ce qu'un Français?* 56–57.

(1830–1848), the French government and local administrators had first allowed and then established and pursued policies to encourage the immigration of Europeans, French or foreign. The Second Empire discouraged all immigration between 1860–70, as part of the planned Royaume Arabe.[30] These incitements to immigration included and were accompanied by measures—primarily military, but also administrative and medical—that, as the Algerian historian of demography Kamel Kateb argues, sought to eliminate local "Muslim" populations, or did so de facto. Kateb demonstrates that large-scale "Muslim" emigration from Algeria and a precipitous increase in "Muslim" mortality rates during most of the nineteenth century reflected what he terms "the existence of demographic policies, the first aim of which was to substitute an imported population (European and Christian) for the indigenous population (Arabo-Berber and Muslim)."[31] Most important were the military campaigns France conducted to suppress armed resistance to French rule. Large-scale actions continued until 1871, when Gen. Patrice MacMahon crushed the last significant armed rebellion against French rule in Kabylie.[32]

In the late 1880s, numerous Algerian officials and French legislators insistently argued that the republic had to guarantee that the many people with foreign origins living on the boundaries of the republic—in the metropole's northern departments as well as Algeria—would remain loyal to France.[33] They supported a law that would naturalize the children of foreign-born residents of France and establish a clear hierarchy within France between nationals and foreigners. The Law of 26 June 1889 recognized that living in France made people French; a modern "republican" version of *jus soli* now was conjoined with *jus sanguinis* (the principle of descent) in determining nationality. What makes "republican *jus soli*" different from the feudal kind is its premise, which Weil identifies as "socialization" or a "sociological approach to nationality." The state recognized residence in France of an individual born in France as a sign that the individual has been or will be educated in France, because of which he or she will necessarily become at-

---

On concerns about foreign "European" settlers, see Andrea L. Smith, "The Colonial in Postcolonial Europe: The Social Memory of Maltese-Origin Pieds-Noirs," PhD diss., University of Arizona, 1998, 147–49. Weil notes that in 1891 "the Cour de Cassation ruled that [double *jus soli*] applied to children born in France to a foreign woman who, herself, was born in France. Up until then, administrators had decided that the term '*étranger*' referred only to the father" (*Qu'est-ce qu'un Français?* 215 and 327 nn. 16 and 17).

[30] A small group of legitimists, various individuals loyal to Charles X, were the colony's first settlers. A number of groups of families came to Algeria, encouraged by the military, which distributed plots of land in an effort to establish a human wall of defense. France began a policy of official colonization in 1841. See Ageron, *Histoire de l'Algérie contemporaine,* and Kateb, "Histoire statistique des populations algériennes,", 112–13.

[31] Kateb, "Histoire statistique des populations algériennes," 15.

[32] A smaller rebellion was fought between 1881 and 1884 around Sidi-Cheikh, while local uprisings occurred in Marguerite in 1902 and the Aurès in 1916. See ibid., 131.

[33] Peter Sahlins, *Boundaries: The Making of France and Spain in the Pyrenees* (Berkeley, 1989), shows the centrality of such negotiations at the boundary to nation making.

tached to the nation. Weil goes so far as to suggest that "socialization" may not just have supplemented family ties but replaced them as the principle underlying attribution of nationality. In his interpretation, by the late nineteenth century blood ties (one or both parents having French nationality), like birthplace (born and raised on French territory,) were signs indicating that socialization as French would take place. Besides naturalizing individuals born in France, the Law of 26 June 1889 aimed at encouraging foreign-born inhabitants of France (including Algeria) to obtain French nationality. It did so by eliminating numerous privileges French law previously offered to foreigners residing in France as well as by clearly codifying the process of naturalization.[34]

At the same time as these laws were taking hold (part of a series of measures meant to "assimilate" the territory and people of Algeria to the metropole) inequality between Algerian colonized and European colonizers was, as the U.S. historian of colonial Algeria David Prochaska remarks, "widening rather than narrowing in virtually every sphere of colonial life."[35] The end of large-scale French military activity, which accompanied the emergence of the Third Republic, saw a renewed emphasis on juridical measures to manage the Algerian departments. In 1881, French repression was codified in the so-called native code, which, on top of the penal code, instituted exorbitant penalties for thirty-three infractions limited to "natives." (In 1890 the number was reduced to twenty-one, and some remained in place until 1944.)[36] In the same context as the Law of 26 June, the Decree of 17 April 1889 codified the submission of the personal or civil status of most Algerians to local law, whether Koranic or Berber customary This inscription of local civil status in French law, symbolically and practically, signaled the close of an active French policy of legal assimilation. Although limited possibilities for "naturalization" remained in place for "qualified" individuals, nothing was done to try to induce the mass of Algerians with local status to conform to French civil law or to make them into French "individuals." The requirements for an Algerian "Muslim" to become a citizen remained governed by the tight restrictions of the 1865 Senatus-Consulte until after World War I.

After the Senatus Consulte of 1865, Algerian "Muslims" had French nationality, a status that a number of court decisions in subsequent decades reaffirmed. Their nationality, however, gave them no political rights until 1919, and then only restricted political rights until 1958. There were also

---

[34] See Weil, *Qu'est-ce qu'un Français?* 58–61 and 225.

[35] On the use of the term "assimilate" in relation to Algeria in the early Third Republic, see Blévis, "Droit colonial algérien de la citoyenneté," 101–2; David Prochaska, *Making Algeria French: Colonialism in Bône, 1870–1920* (Cambridge, 1990), 155.

[36] See Charles-Robert Ageron, *Les Algériens musulmans et la France, 1871–1919,* vol. 1 (Paris, 1968), 168–76; Weil, *Qu'est-ce qu'un Français?* 223; Isabelle Merle, "Retour sur le régime de l'indigénat: genèse et contradictions des principes répressifs dans l'Empire français," *French Politics, Culture and Society* 20, no. 2 (Summer 2002): 77–97.

punitive limitations on their exercise of other nonpolitical rights, most notably as a result of the native code. This situation—combined with the existence of Koranic and other local law civil statuses—has led other scholars to downplay the claim that "Muslims" had French nationality. Weil argues in *Qu'est-ce qu'un français?* (What Makes a Frenchman?) that "Muslims" had a *nationalité denaturé* (denatured—or meaningless—nationality). The historian Emmanuelle Saada has made a more compelling case for dismissing the French nationality of Algerian "Muslims" by connecting it to the French nationality of other French colonial "subjects." International law—as it emerged in the nineteenth century—considered all people from French colonies who did not possess another nationality to be in possession of French nationality. I find her argument instructive for understanding the mechanisms of colonial domination. Nonetheless, the distinction between the legal situations of Algerian "Muslims" in French law and colonial subjects in international law remains significant. Both Weil and Saada disregard the most important indication of the legal reality of "Muslims'" nationality: adult "Muslim" men did have other nonpolitical rights after 1865 (eligibility for civil service jobs and a recognized status as a witness and plaintiff in French courts) and limited political rights after 1919, rights which were not available to French subjects in the colonies. They were also not available to women who had French citizenship and nationality.[37]

Beyond its legal existence, two developments provide strong evidence for the real importance of the nationality, however "denatured," that Algerian "Muslims" received. The French nationality of Algerian Jews, like "Muslims," had been affirmed by the 1865 decrees. When in 1870 the government of national defense "naturalized" Algerians with Mosaic civil status as citizens with French civil status, the approach used was consistent with previous republican histories of French nationals receiving citizenship rights (like male workers in 1848, for example)—and differed starkly from the naturalization of foreigners. The similarity between "Muslims" and other groups of nationals with restricted rights, further, allows us to make sense of the fact that all "Muslims" received French citizenship in 1944, while French colonial subjects received French Union citizenship only.

Such quibbles among scholars over how to assess the nationality of Algerian "Muslims" signal the differences between our analyses of their his-

[37] On the nationality of "Muslims," see Laure Blévis, "Droit colonial algérien de la citoyenneté: conciliation entre des principes républicains et une logique d'occupation coloniale (1865–1947)," in *La guerre d'Algérie au miroir des décolonisations françaises* (2000), 561 n. 15; Louis Rolland and Pierre Lampué, *Précis de droit des pays d'outre-mer, territoires, departments, Etats associés*, 2nd ed. (1952), 97; Weil, *Qu'est-ce qu'un Français?*; Emmanuelle Saada, "Une nationalité par degré. Civilité et citoyenneté en situation coloniale," in *L'esclavage, la colonisation, et après,* ed. Patrick Weil and Stéphane Dufoix (2005), 193–227. On French West African colonial subjects, see Owen White, *Children of the French Empire: Miscegenation and Colonial Society in French West Africa, 1895–1960* (Oxford, 2000); and Conklin, "Colonialism and Human Rights, a Contradiction in Terms?": 419–42.

torical relationship to definitions of French nationality—and republican institutions. For Weil, the exclusion of Algerian "Muslims" from French nationality consolidates his larger argument about the coherence of the model of republican nationality that emerged through the history he details and still, he argues, persists. In other words, by denying their nationality or conceiving of it as "denatured," he effectively leaves in place a normative and coherent conception of French nationality as race-blind and egalitarian (which came to fruition when women got the vote after World War II), while defining the case of Algerian "Muslims" as an aberration. For Saada, on the contrary, the continuity between Algerian "Muslims" and other colonial subjects emphasizes the central role in modern French history she attributes to the racialized exclusion of the colonized from membership in the nation. This division, her work suggests, authorized the republican embrace of egalitarian citizenship by delimiting who could be included. For Saada, the French Republic, like the United States, depended on race to institutionalize its understanding of the individual, universal rights, and democracy.

Against Weil's presumption, I emphasize the crucial role that building an overseas empire had in structuring republican institutions in France. At the same time, my research suggests that, against Saada's claim, race did not play the fundamental role in post-1789 understandings of who could be a French citizen as it did in American history, or as gender did in France. The Algerian War, as the following pages demonstrate, changed this. For Algerian "Muslim" men, in my view, exclusion from citizenship until after World War II was not "paradoxical," as was the case in the exclusion of woman from citizenship until 1944 described by Joan Wallach Scott, or French explanations for why their colonial subjects in West Africa were not destined for citizenship, as explained by Conklin. By this I mean that there was never a widely embraced principle—on the model of sexual difference or respect for local cultures—to explain the situation of dramatic inequality in Algeria. Theoretical or principled explanations were far less important than the acknowledged success of resistance to the assimilation of Algeria's "Muslims." Effective resistance came from both Algerian "Muslims" themselves and from racists north and south of the Mediterranean.[38]

Neither racial, ethnic, nor religious criteria entered into official definitions of Algerians with local civil status, as they did in other colonies. Nonetheless, by the late nineteenth century assumptions about the inferiority of Algerian "Muslims" joined continued assertions that France needed to respect the attachment of "Muslims" to their Koranic or customary law status as explanations for the continued exclusion of most from full citizenship. Racial thinking and racist theorizing were very important in late-nineteenth-

---

[38] Scott "Only Paradoxes to Offer," Conklin, "Colonialism and Human Rights, a Contradiction in Terms?": 434–6. Alexis Spire, "Semblables et pourtant différents. La citoyenneté paradoxales des 'Français musulmans d'Algérie' en metropole," *Genèses* 53 (December 2003): 48–68, 49, uses "paradoxical" as a synonym for "inequality."

century Western debates. A number of the most widely discussed participants were French. Joseph-Arthur de Gobineau, Ernest Renan, and Gustave Le Bon were the most visible figures among a swarm of French writers, scientists, officials, and legislators who proposed and espoused the "recognition" of hierarchies among racially distinguished "populations," hierarchies supposedly anchored in nature and demonstrable by science.[39] Prominent proponents of such views pushed to redefine French colonial policies to take account of racial theory. Léopold de Saussure relied on racist categorization explicitly to attack assimilationism in the colonies in his widely cited *Psychology of French Colonization in its Relationships with Native Societies* (1899).[40] Speaking at the opening session of the International Colonial Congress of Paris, in 1889, Le Bon bemoaned "the fatal results of the system known as assimilation." Yet, despite these attacks, French law continued to avoid codifying racially—or ethnically—based categories. There were a variety of reasons, which were distinct from imperial concerns; both Weil and Henry point to the importance Germany played as a counter model, while Hannah Arendt highlights how the embrace of race-thinking by English nationalists and French anti-republicans also contributed. The heated response to Le Bon's statement was fairly typical: speaker after speaker, including prominent politicians (one of them, a deputy from the French Antilles, made reference to his own African descent), stood up to reject his views, and did so in the name of republican values. Because Algeria was legally an extension of the metropole, neither racial, ethnic, nor even religious criteria entered into official definitions of Algerians with local civil status, as they did in other colonies.[41] In Algeria as in all of France, the law sustained the pretense that "ethnicity" and "race" did not matter, a state of affairs that continued until the Algerian Revolution.[42] The fact that local civil status was assigned on the basis of descent, which the Lambrecht Decree of September 1871 confirmed, suggests how tenuous such race-blind claims were.[43]

Racism had an enormous and direct effect on the daily experience of Algerians with local civil status as well as on popular, intellectual, and official thinking about "Muslim" Algerians. Local officials in Algeria encountered few sanctions when they ignored "race-blind" French laws and regulations. The refusal by numerous bureaucrats to "naturalize" qualified Algerian men with local civil status exemplifies this impunity, as does the failure of elected

---

[39] Joseph-Arthur de Gobineau, *Essai sur l'inégalité des races humaines* (Paris, 1853–55).

[40] *La Psychologie de la colonisation française dans ses rapports avec les sociétés indigènes* (Paris, 1899).

[41] Lewis, "One Hundred Million Frenchmen," 140.

[42] Lorcin, *Imperial Identities*, 225; Henry, *Algeria and Germany*; Weil, *Qu'est-ce qu'un Français?* . As Emmanuelle Saada shows, the French did codify laws based on race in the colonies. See "La 'question des métis' dans les colonies françaises: Socio-histoire d'une catégorie juridique (Indochine et autres territoires de l'Empire français; années 1890–années 1950)" PhD diss., Ecole des hautes etudes en sciences sociales, Paris, 2001.

[43] See n. 27.

officials in Algeria to fund schools for children with local civil status despite the "Ferry" Laws (1879–1886) on universal education.[44] The National Assembly's repeated reauthorization of the supposedly temporary native code offered constant reaffirmation of the presumed inferiority of "Muslims." The French criminal justice system as a whole, particularly in its growing reliance on expert medical and scientific testimony, embraced racist assumptions not codified in the law. Other institutions and practices that the French Republic established or encouraged in Algeria relied on racialized or "ethnic" categories and assumptions, for example the official census and psychiatric medicine. Kateb cites Instruction 295 of the governor general of Algeria concerning the census; while it noted that the law required classifying "naturalized indigenous Israelites with the French Europeans," it asked for a way to count Jewish citizens separately from non-Jewish citizens. From 1872 until 1931 the censuses asked for and tallied responses to such questions. Only mass protest by Jewish Algerians put an end to this practice. By the 1880s, as Kateb shows, census takers asked "Muslims": "What is your origin: Arab, Kabyle, Mozabite, Moroccan, Tunisian, Other (specify)?" Such questions were (and remain) explicitly excluded from census questionnaires in the metropole. Likewise, Lorcin's examination of the Kabyle myth shows how "racial" definitions of Algeria's people shaped ideas about how to extend and maintain French domination. Racism's most direct effect was economic, what the French ethnologist Germaine Tillion, writing in the 1950s, termed the "pauperization" of the majority of Algeria's population.[45]

Yet the goal of assimilation still remained government ideology, if never the grounds for an effective policy, until the end of the Third Republic, despite the government's reticence to pursue the assimilation of Algeria's "Muslims" and repeated calls to abandon it. In conjunction with the Paris World's Fair of 1900 (Exposition Universelle Internationale), for example, three international scientific congresses concerning colonial issues published statements in favor of indirect rule, or associationism. Polemicists in the French press and legislators in the National Assembly joined many local administrators in Algeria in calling for France to adopt a "British" or even "Dutch" model of rule and abandon efforts to assimilate Algerian "Muslims." Saada shows to what extent racial and ethnic understandings informed how jurists, judges, and bureaucrats relied on these alternate models in their interpretations of French law. Yet when the National Assembly discussed the possibil-

---

[44] Charles-Robert Ageron, *Modern Algeria: A History from 1830 to the Present* (London, 1992), 75. For analyses of evolving French scientific racism toward "Algerian Muslims," see Kateb, "Histoire statistique des populations algériennes,", 258–65, and Lorcin, *Imperial Identities.*

[45] Kateb, *Européens, "indigènes," et juifs en Algérie,* 192 and 197; Lorcin, *Imperial Identities.* On racial categorization and racist practice in psychiatry, see Richard Keller, "Action Psychologique: French Psychiatry in Colonial North Africa, 1900–1962 (Algeria, Tunisia, Morocco)," PhD diss., Rutgers University, 2001. On pauperization, see Germaine Tillion, *L'Algérie en 1957* (Paris, 1957).

ity around 1900, the legislators voted overwhelmingly to maintain the policy of assimilation for Algeria.[46] Given the availability of alternatives and the increasing disregard in Algeria for the actual pursuit of assimilation, it is noteworthy that such attempts to define "Muslims" out of the nation did not affect laws of citizenship and nationality, and that reformers continued to advance and, in limited ways, legislate plans to overcome distinctions between Algerians with local civil status and other French nationals.[47]

In 1911 *La Revue indigène*, which its French founders envisioned as a forum to debate ways to improve life among the colonized, proposed an idea that French legislators had already discussed in the 1880s: "naturalization with local status." In a series of articles, the journal asked law professors from various metropolitan law schools to comment on the compatibility of such a process with republican law. All but one expressed favorable opinions. This study went much further than previous efforts to impose "naturalization with local status," such as the proposed laws of 15 June 1887, of 27 July 1890, or of 16 January 1897. Legislators took up the study's proposals at various times between 1913 and 1916, but without success. The failure was due to politics—the successful opposition of deputies and senators from Algeria and their allies—rather than legal constraints or matters of principle.[48] French colonial subjects in their Indian possessions and in the Four Communes of Senegal (the so-called *originaires*) already had a combination of citizenship rights (the exercise of which was limited to the territory in which they were born) alongside the right to be governed in their "civil status" by Koranic or Hindu caste laws and courts.[49] The propositions concerning Algeria went further, calling for full citizenship and the maintenance of local civil status for all Algerian men with local civil status. During World War I, the National Assembly also debated extending other rights to Algeri-

---

[46] On the congresses, see Nancy Lee Turpin, "The Blue Ticket: Paradoxes and Revolt at the 1900 Paris World's Fair," PhD diss., University of Illinois–Chicago, (2004), 201–4.

[47] Betts, *Assimilation and Association in French Colonial Theory* , 45 and 116. For an analysis of the debate between French and British scholars on whether, in practice, French colonialism in West Africa was different than British "indirect rule," see Véronique Dimier, "Le discours idéologique de la méthode coloniale chez les Français et les Britanniques de l'entre-deux guerres à la décolonisation (1920–1960)," *Travaux et documents du Centre d'étude de l'Afrique noire* 58–59 (1998). On references to the Dutch, see H. L. Wesseling, "The Netherlands as a Colonial Model," in *Imperialism and Colonialism: Essays on the History of European Expansion* (Westport, Conn., 1997), 38–58, esp. 45–58.

[48] See "La naturalization des musulmans dans leur statut," *Revue indigène* 63–64 (July–August 1901): 397–456; "Notre première enquête sur la naturalization," in no. 66 (October 1901): 525–36, and "Sur la naturalisation," in no. 67 (November 1901): 589–93. For an analysis of these discussions, see Kateb, *Européens, "indigènes," et juifs en Algérie*, 199.

[49] See Damien Deschamps, "Une citoyenneté différée: Cens civique et assimilation des indigènes dans les établissements français de l'Inde," *Revue française de science politique* 47, no. 1 (February 1997): 49–69; Mamadou Diouf, "The French Colonial Policy of Assimilation and the Civility of the *Originaires* of the Four Communes (Senegal): A Nineteenth Century Globalization Project," *Development and Change* 29 (1998): 671–96; and Catherine Coquery-Vidrovitch, "Nationalité et citoyenneté en Afrique occidentale française: Originaires et citoyens dans le Sénégal colonial," *Journal of African History* 42 (2001): 285–305.

ans with local civil status, in order to facilitate their assimilation. Finally, in response to the sacrifice and the loyalty of thousands of Algerians on the battlefields (as well as in the factories) of wartime France, the Law of 4 February 1919 offered a simpler and more widely accessible means for such men to acquire citizenship, though it still required the renunciation of local civil status, making it far more restrictive than other reforms that had been discussed. The Law of 4 February 1919, by opening more civil service posts to Algerian men with local civil status and by establishing a "double college" for local, municipal, and cantonal elections, further entrenched these restrictive and theoretically "transitory" legal regimes.[50] The Law of 18 August 1929 allowed Algerian women with local civil status to apply for citizenship (with all the limits French law imposed on female citizens) under either the 1919 or 1865 procedures.[51]

Until after 1944, France accommodated neither the desire of "Muslims" for greater control of their lives nor the arguments of many French citizens in Algeria and racists in the metropole to exclude definitively Algeria's indigenous populations from potential citizenship. Yet both positions grew in importance. Among immigrants from Europe, and their descendents, anti-indigenous politics helped consolidate a new "Algerian" identity. (While there were some calls to establish a state separate from France, most "European" Algerians embraced their relationship to the metropole.) Anti-Semitic campaigns during the belle epoque (1890s–1914) to repeal the Crémieux Decree, which failed to achieve their goal, articulated the argument that assimilation of indigenous Algerians threatened the very foundations of republican government. Racist campaigns deployed such theses in successful efforts to limit the extension of rights to Algerians with local civil status, as with the Law of 4 February 1919, or to prevent any extension whatsoever, as with the defeat of the Blum-Viollette bill in 1937.[52]

---

[50] Eligibility for most posts in the *fonction publique* and the addition of local officials elected by *indigènes* were extended in Title II, Articles 12–16 of "Loi du 4 février 1919 sur l'accession des indigènes d'Algérie aux droits politiques," *J.O.* of 6 February 1919. The "double college" system allowed certain Algerian men with local civil status to elect certain local officials. These local officials formed a separate "college," inferior in number and in authority, from their fellows elected by male French citizens in the same jurisdiction. What became called the "second college," although virulently attacked by the settler lobby, was extremely limited in its inclusiveness and its competences. It included only 10.5% of the male Muslim population over twenty-five years of age (some 103,000 electors). See Claude Collot, *Les institutions de l'Algérie durant la période coloniale, 1830–1962* (Paris, 1987), 56.

[51] The Senatus-Consulte and later laws prolonging its naturalization measures resulted in the naturalization of about 1,745 "indigenous" Algerians. By the census of 1931, after the 1919 reform, there were 5,836 "naturalized Muslims" (people from Algeria who had abandoned Koranic civil status and assumed full citizenship and governance by "common law") and 7,817 in 1936; see Kateb, "Histoire statistique des populations algériennes," 199. Refusing naturalization was one of the rare means of elite resistance to French domination, besides armed rebellion. See Kateb, *Européens, "indigènes," et juifs en Algérie*, 208.

[52] See Jonathan Gosnell, *The Politics of Frenchness in Colonial Algeria, 1930–1954* (Rochester, N.Y., 2002). On anti-Crémieux campaigns, see Ageron, *Les Algériens musulmans et la France*, vol. 1, 583–94; Friedman, *Colonialism and After*, 23–25; Prochaska, *Making Algeria*

Until the collapse of the Third Republic, the state continued to deny the overwhelming majority of male French nationals in the Algerian departments most of the rights of citizens, while subjecting them to exigent obligations. This provoked numerous efforts to end the oppression of Algeria's majority, as well as sparking attempts to articulate what this majority had in common. In the years before World War I the "Muslim" group the Young Algerians called for increased rights for Algerians with local status in return for their willingness to assume concomitant duties, such as conscription (which had become obligatory for "Muslims" in 1912). "Indigenous" elites made up this movement, both sons of monied families and those whom French schools or the army had identified as talented and whom they helped prosper. They forged working ties with what French historian of the Maghreb Daniel Rivet calls "liberal bourgeois and progressive republican intellectuals" within Algeria's "European society"; they were in contact with reformers in the metropole and announced their attachment to "science" and progress in very French terms. In one critic's assessment, "Before the war the only word that ever crossed their lips was 'assimilation'." This approach suffered a humiliating blow when the French government offered only the paltry reforms of the Law of 4 February 1919 in return for the enormous sacrifices made by Algerian "Muslims" during the Great War.[53] By the interwar period, demands for cultural and political autonomy for Algeria's majority took on a new visibility. Muslim political organizations developed tactics and strategies to resist colonial rule that differed both from armed struggle—largely abandoned by the early twentieth century (although there were some exceptions)—and passive rejection of French assimilationist claims, which continued.[54] In Algeria, the Association des Oulémas (Islamic Reform Movement), which worked to reform and revitalize Islam and Islamic institutions under the leadership of Sheik Abdelhamid Ben Badis, spearheaded these efforts. "Islam is our religion, Arabic is our language, Algeria is our country" was their motto, a clear affirmation of the need for cultural autonomy, which developed through Scouting and other activities. The Oulémas, like most interwar "Muslim" political movements, worked to develop autonomy under French rule while also fighting for Muslim access to the political rights that were their due as (male) French nationals, including full citizenship.[55] The self-taught working-class militant Messali Hadj and

---

French, 138; and Turpin, "Blue Ticket," 186–248. On the growing sense of "Algerian" identity among "settlers," see Ageron, *Modern Algeria,* 55; Smith, "The Colonial in Postcolonial Europe," 153–55; Lorcin, *Imperial Identities,* 198–212.

[53] On Algeria's belle epoque and the Young Algerians, see Daniel Rivet, *Le Maghreb à l'épreuve de la colonisation* (Paris, 2002), 194; Gilbert Meynier, *Histoire intérieure du FLN, 1954–1962* (Paris, 2002), 46, and *L'Algérie révélée: La guerre de 1914–1918 et le premier quart du XXe siècle* (Geneva, 1981).

[54] On violent resistance up through World War I, see Gilbert Meynier, *L'Algérie révélée,* 591–99; on cultural expressions of resistance, see Rivet, *Le Maghreb à l'épreuve de la colonisation,* 184–85.

[55] See Benjamin Stora and Zakya Daoud, *Ferhat Abbas: Une utopie algérienne* (Paris, 1995).

other Algerian "Muslims" living in the metropole founded the Étoile Nord-Africaine organization in 1926. Linked at its origins to the French Communist Party (PCF), this was the first movement to go beyond a critique of the colonial and racist order in Algeria and to demand national independence for Algeria (1927).[56]

Yet Third Republic politicians did little to respond to these increasing demands. They did not move to permanently exclude Algerian "Muslims" from the potential exercise of citizenship in the French departments of Algeria, as racists on both sides of the Mediterranean demanded. Nor did they offer "Muslims" greater control over their own lives, the exercise of full citizenship, or independence, as called for by various "Muslim" leaders. Officials continued to rely on the excuse of legal exigencies and the maintenance of "local civil statuses" to explain the ongoing juxtaposition of the theory of assimilation with a practice in which coexistence predominated. In the face of racist practices on the ground and despite the availability of alternative models of colonial rule that could have replaced it, France continued to proclaim the goal of assimilation for all inhabitants of its Algerian departments.

Redefining Citizenship and the State in the French Union, 1944–1956

After World War II, the Republic broke with the post-1789 insistence that citizenship be one and indivisible, introducing for what began to be called "Muslim French from Algeria" the possibility of both full political rights and the maintenance of local civil status. The 7 March 1944 Ordinance of the Provisional Government of the French Republic (GPRF), in Algiers, laid out the logic of the new synthesis. While affirming that the same public law governed all French territory, it admitted that a diversity of civil statuses was compatible with a uniform French public law. That is, in civil or personal status questions, French, Koranic, Mosaic, and various customary laws now were theoretically equal.[57] France granted full political rights to a specified list of Algerian elite men (some 65,000 individuals) who also were allowed to maintain their local civil status. (As nationalist organizations had urged,

---

[56] For a description of the Étoile Nord-Africaine's founding, its relationship to the PCF, and its evolving political platform, see Benjamin Stora, *Messali Hadj: Pionnier du nationalisme algérien, 1898–1974* (Paris, 1986), 58–64.

[57] Further, the ordinance reaffirmed that "all other Muslim French are destined for French citizenship." This principle was included in the Constitution of 27 October 1946, where Article 82 in the section founding the French Union states: "Citizens [of the French Union] who do not possess French civil status conserve their personal status as long as they have not renounced it. This status cannot, in any instance, constitute a reason to refuse or limit the rights and liberties attached to the quality of French citizen." In the intervening months, the Law of 7 May 1946 had attributed French citizenship, equal to that of metropolitans, to all French people from Algeria. From then on, all Algerians in the metropole were eligible both to participate fully in the polity and to maintain their local civil status. Commission rélations entre les communautés, "Le regime juridique des statuts privés et des juridictions civiles en Algérie," 2.

about half of those eligible rejected this privilege.[58]) The Law of 7 May 1946 and the Constitution of the Fourth Republic (Article 80) affirmed that all other Algerians with local civil status were French citizens. These texts did not specify what this meant or how it would be applied.

These changes in Algeria were part of an abrupt post–World War II French shift in attitude toward the nonwhite subjects that the French Republic ruled around the world. Legislators proposed both a new federal system to knit together and govern republic and empire and the redefinition of legal statuses in order to create equality between all French subjects. These reforms paralleled but went further than concomitant changes in the British Empire, and both emerged in the same context: the victory of "democracy" over racist fascism, and the desire of metropolitan elites to maintain control of their empires. As the historian of Africa Frederick Cooper argues, "The old claims to colonial authority based on superiority of race and civilization were thoroughly discredited by the experience of Nazism and fascism, whereas universalistic notions of social progress . . . offered a seemingly more plausible basis for assertions of imperial hegemony." Referring to this new vision, in 1948 the governing British Labor Party proclaimed, "Imperialism is dead, but the Empire has been given new life."[59] France renamed its colonies "Overseas France"; the empire became the French Union (modeled on the British Empire's becoming the Commonwealth). The October 1946 Constitution of the Fourth Republic reaffirmed the principle of equality between civil law codes; it also created French Union citizenship, which extended to all French citizens (including all Algerians with local civil status) and colonial subjects, eliminating the latter term altogether from official language.[60] Cooper has called such post-1944 efforts "deracialized imperialism." This juridical revolution produced comparatively significant economic effects (the end of native codes and forced labor) and political reforms in both the "old colonies" (Guadeloupe, Guiana, Martinique, and Réunion became "départements d'outre-mer"—Overseas departments or DOMs) and in other colonial holdings that became "territoires d'outre-mer"—Overseas territories or TOMs. French officials discussed and began to put in place

---

[58] Ageron, *Histoire de l'Algérie contemporaine*, vol. 2, 602–3.

[59] Frederick Cooper, *Decolonization and African Society: The Labor Question in French and British Africa* (Cambridge, 1996), 173. On labor, see Stephen Howe, *Anticolonialism in British Politics: The Left and the End of Empire 1918–1964* (Oxford, 1993), 144. On the importance of Vichy rule in shaping French responses to the postwar situation, see Eric T. Jennings, *Vichy in the Tropics: Pétain's National Revolution in Madagascar, Guadeloupe, and Indochina, 1940–1944* (Stanford, 2001). On British efforts in Kenya, see J. E. Lewis, "The Ruling Compassions of the Late Colonial State: Welfare versus Force, Kenya, 1945–1952," *Journal of Colonialism and Colonial History* 2, no. 2 (Fall 2001), online journal. In addition to his writings, several discussions with Frederick Cooper have shaped my thinking about this period.

[60] While the Lamine Guèye Law of 7 May 1946 appeared to have given French citizenship to most inhabitants of the French Union, only in Algeria did it eventually lead to French citizenship. Elsewhere, it led to French Union citizenship only, a distinct status. See James Genova, *Colonial Ambivalence, Cultural Authenticity, and the Limitations of Mimicry in French-Ruled West Africa* (New York, 2004), 208–11.

forms of federalism to replace their empire and collaborated with newly elected local representatives toward that end.[61]

Throughout the French Union, the post-1944 reforms created confusion about what exactly the texts promised in the way of rights and in terms of possibilities for greater equality. In West Africa, union leaders, political organizations, and French colonial officials worked to determine how such promises could be made real. In Algeria, the texts were even more confusing, but political reaction was clear: nationalist and Islamic organizations as well as representatives of Algeria's "Europeans" wholly rejected them. Although there were numerous discussions about how to introduce forms of federalism into Algeria, there were few concrete results.[62] Earlier "Muslim" proponents of federalism, such as the pharmacist and nationalist politician Ferhat Abbas, increasingly distanced themselves from a policy that proved in practice to be a cover for continued colonial domination. In terms of citizenship, representatives of the "Europeans" of Algeria, as they had during every debate over citizenship or rights for Algerian "Muslims" in the Third Republic, struggled to reduce the effects and the extent of reform. Their efforts succeeded in establishing a new distinction between Algeria and the metropole: "Muslims" now had more rights in the latter. In Paris, after much hesitation, Article 3 of the new statute for Algeria of 20 September 1947 stated that "those Muslims residing in metropolitan France enjoy *there* all the rights attached to the quality of French citizenship."[63]

After 1944, official texts no longer invoked civil status to explain why "Muslims" had fewer rights than other French nationals. Instead, from 1947 until 1958, it was the distinction between Algerian and "European" French territory that legitimized continued restrictions on the rights of "Muslim French from Algeria." The Third Republic, under pressure from French citizens from Algeria, had pursued the "assimilation" of Algerian territory to the metropole, in terms of laws, decrees, regulations, and rules. The Fourth Republic, under pressure from "French citizens from Algeria with common

---

[61] For economic and social effects in French sub-Saharan Africa, see Cooper, *Decolonization and African Society,* 277–322; for political shifts, see Dickens, "Defining French Citizenship Policy in West Africa."

[62] See Ageron, *Histoire de l'Algérie contemporaine, vol. 2 ,* 547–618; Collot's study, *Les institutions de l'Algérie durant la période coloniale,* is unmatched in explaining the complexity of French governance in French-controlled Algeria (see 56–58).

[63] Emphasis added. In an intermediate time, the French government of General de Gaulle, in the Ordinance of 14 March 1945, decided that "Muslim French men and French women from Algeria residing in continental France in a continuous manner since 3 September 1938, can exercise on the continental territory the right of suffrage for municipal and cantonal election in the same conditions as French citizens." This initial reform, convoluted and limited, (1) ignored the newly proclaimed equality of civil statuses; (2) established a new territorial distinction between Algeria and continental France; and (3) refined the classic republican confidence that living in France would produce French citizens to privilege the European continent. Cited in Jacques Beyssade, "Evolution du statut juridique des musulmans," *Documents Algériens: Serie Politique* 25 (Algiers: Service d'information du Cabinet du Gov. General de l'Algérie, 25 October 1950), 6, in CAC/AN 950236/7.

civil status," established a new separation.[64] (This distinction did not reverse previous territorial "assimilation," although it now was open to debate whether Algeria legally remained an extension of the metropole or whether it was comparable to the new Overseas departments.[65]) The Law of 20 September 1947 declared the departments of Algeria and the Southern Territories in the Sahara a "grouping of departments with its own civic personality." This novel administrative unit allowed continued restriction of the political rights of the majority of people from Algeria. In continental France, French citizens with "local" civil status—both men and women, most of them regulated by "Koranic law"—were, in theory, politically equal to French citizens with common "French" civil status. They had the right to vote, and metropolitan authorities (including French courts) were to adjudicate all questions of civil status according to the appropriate "local" legal code. In the new Algerian "grouping of departments," the statute left in place the existing local law court systems.[66] Rather than granting political equality, the statute modestly liberalized electoral arrangements destined to assure the continued dominance of citizens with common civil status.[67] Despite the Ordinance of

[64] For the term, see Louis Rolland and Pierre Lampué, *Précis de droit des pays d'outre-mer, territoires, departments, Etats associés,* 2nd ed. (Paris, 1952), 97.

[65] Jurist Paul-Emile Viard argued the first interpretation, in *Les caractères politiques et le régime legislative de l'Algérie* (Paris 1949), 10–16, Pierre Lampué, the second, in Rolland and Lampué, eds., *Précis de droit des pays d'outre-mer.* Viard makes the important points that the Algerian Assembly, which the Constitution of 27 October 1946 established, was not legally a "parliament," which is to say that it did not exercise sovereignty, and that the territorial entity "Algeria" was not constitutionally defined or recognized by international law, but was a grouping of departments that the National Assembly had voted to recognize in order to facilitate the state's acknowledgement of what Viard calls "their special character, their distance, the sociological difficulties specific to the territory they cover" (23–24).

[66] The Ordinance of 23 November 1944 regulating these statuses largely reproduced the original Decree of 17 April 1889. As with French civil law, French deputies alone had the authority to legislate, reform, or recodify the local legal regimes. French legislators, however, had always been very hesitant to meddle in local civil law. Isolated from other Islamic or North African legal traditions, Algerian local law jurists, French commentators contended, largely camped on precedents and codes unchanged since the nineteenth century (see Doyen Marcel Morand, *Etudes du droit musulman et du droit coutumier berbère* [Paris, 1931]). See "Note récusée par Me. Breive rédige par l'organisation judiciarie" (Paris, 20 December 1960), 1, in CAC/AN 950395/76.

[67] In place of political equality, it reasserted the principle of a double college, to assure the continued dominance of citizens with common civil status. Whereas, after 1919, the "second college," composed of Algerian men with local civil status, voted for up to one-third of each elected body, the reformed system offered male citizens with local civil status more representation. The second college voted separately for two-fifths (in local elections) or one-half (in legislative and Algerian Assembly votes) of those elected. In the Algerian Assembly, the governor general, the Finance Commission, or one-fourth of the members could request and obtain a requirement of a two-thirds vote to approve a stated measure (see *Année politique 1947,* 151). Thus everything was done to limit decision making by Algerian "Muslim" men and to attenuate the fears of "Algerians with common status" (the Europeans, both men and women), except not to reform at all, which is what European representatives wanted. As Charles-Robert Ageron decisively shows, even these minimal advances were cynically sidestepped by Governor General Marcel Naegelen, who after his arrival in 1948 succeeded in manipulating second college elections through the exclusion of all nationalists (candidates associated with Messali Hadj; see n. 56). See Ageron, *Histoire de l'Algérie contemporaine, vol. 2,* 608.

2 August 1945 that guaranteed French women the vote, local officials (the Algerian Assembly) continued to exclude Algerian women with local civil status from even the restricted exercise of suffrage in Algeria until 1958.[68]

Integration in France and Algeria, 1956–1962

What French officials for so long termed "the events in Algeria" began on 1 November 1954. That night, which the Parisian newspaper *Le Monde* promptly christened "le Toussaint rouge," or "Bloody All-Saints," a series of bomb blasts throughout Algeria killed eight people and wounded four. A previously unknown politico-military organization, the *National Liberation Front* (Front de Libération Nationale, FLN) and its military arm, the *National Liberation Army* (Armée de Libération Nationale, ALN), claimed responsibility for these acts. Its members were dissidents from the banned Movement for the Triumph of Democratic Liberties (MTLD), already in hiding from the French police. The statements announcing their claims demanded immediate and unconditional independence, what the manifesto termed "the restoration of the Algerian State, sovereign, democratic, and social, within a framework provided by Islamic principles." The events of 1 November 1954 were highly symbolic: this was the first time since 1830 that a series of coordinated attacks touched all the main regions of Algeria. The targets were clear: institutions and representatives of the French colonial government and of colonialist economic exploitation. The initial declaration twinned the "internal" struggle on Algeria soil with the "external" struggle on the world stage, meant to "internationalize" the Algerian question. The authors announced that the FLN was ready to use "any means" to obtain its goals. Terrorism came to symbolize this willingness.

Nationalist violence aimed at civilians in Algeria, and to a lesser extent in the metropole, outraged even many people who were sympathetic to nationalist demands. In the first months of their action, the frontists claimed that the civilians they attacked were identified "traitors" or colonial agents. In August 1955, however, certain ALN groups of *moudjahidine* (fighters)— whom French authorities named *fellaghas* (bandits) and, later, *hors-la-loi* (outlaws)—began to embrace a new tactic: terrorism aimed at the inhabitants of "colonist centers."[69] The probable strategic aim of this tactic was to encourage or force local "Muslim" inhabitants into a new level of complicity with the rebels. At the 1956 Congress of Soummam, where a small group of FLN leaders agreed on the principles that were supposed to govern their struggle and the future republic, the FLN announced that it

---

[68] The 1947 Organic Law concerning Algeria authorized the vote for Algerian women with Koranic civil status, yet it required the Algerian Assembly to decide by decree how they would participate. The local assembly never published such decrees.

[69] Mohammed Harbi and Gilbert Meynier, eds., *Le FLN, documents et histoire, 1954–1962* (Paris, 2004), 38–44.

would expand its strikes against outposts of the colonial state to include all European civilians. This decision was made in the name of responding to French collective punishment against "Muslims" suspected of complicity with the ALN. In practice, FLN forces killed far more "Muslim" civilians (over 16,300 in Algeria through 19 March 1962) than "European" civilians (over 2,700 in Algeria through 19 March 1962).[70] The French government and other supporters of French Algeria produced photographs and testimonials of FLN terrorism and "savagery"; French and international media fixated on incidents where guerrillas had emasculated or beheaded soldiers or civilians. International and French condemnations of FLN violence reached their height in 1957, after the FLN's massacre of the villagers of Mélouza. The mainstream press presented such "barbarism" as far more despicable than such French army activities as napalming villages, collective punishment, and torture. The almost complete absence of images of such state-sponsored acts facilitated this wartime focus on nationalist atrocities.[71]

The FLN eventually triumphed more through diplomacy, popular support, and political acuity than through military might and tactics. Indeed, the historian Matthew Connelly argues compellingly that FLN representatives pioneered forms of diplomatic maneuvering and negotiation that gave shape to the "post–Cold War world."[72] Yet analysts invariably emphasize the forms of violence that the FLN embraced in conjunction with its ideological combat and diplomatic maneuvers. For numerous authors, inspired by the arguments of the Martinican-French-Algerian revolutionary Frantz Fanon, terrorist violence established the basis for national renaissance and unity, by enabling the colonized to overcome the sense of inferiority and humiliation that colonialism produced, that allowed diplomatic action to bear fruit. Other commentators focus on how the FLN's tactics gave new legitimacy and currency to "terrorism" on the world stage. (Although popular among anarchists at the fin de siècle, this form of political violence had largely disappeared after 1917, as the Communists and Marxist-Leninist analysis—which rejected "blind terror"—marginalized other forms of radical political contestation. The 1940s embrace by right-wing Zionist groups of terrorism, targeting Arab civilians in Palestine and the British, had not

---

[70] Meynier, Histoire intérieure du FLN, 322–23; and Hartmut Elsenhans, La guerre d'Algérie 1954–1962: La transition d'une France à une autre; Le passage de la IVe à la Ve république (Paris, 1999), 210–11 and 430–36. The numbers for civilian casualties are drawn from official French statistics, as cited in Guy Pervillé, Pour une histoire de la guerre d'Algérie (Paris, 2002), 242.

[71] See James D. LeSueur, Uncivil War: Intellectuals and Identity Politics during the Decolonization of Algeria (Philadelphia, 2001).

[72] See Matthew Connelly, A Diplomatic Revolution: Algeria's Fight for Independence and the Origins of the Post–Cold War Era (Oxford, 2002), 276–287; Charles-Robert Ageron, "Postface," in Les archives de la révolution algérienne, ed. Mohammed Harbi (Paris, 1981), 536; and Jean Lacouture, Algérie 1962, la guerre est finie, 2nd ed. (Brussels, 2002), 24.

transformed such tactics into "weapons of the weak" in the way that the Algerian Revolution did.)[73]

There has not been a similar effort to analyze French political efforts to keep Algeria French in conjunction with the government's use of violence. It is morally tempting to focus only on French military and police responses. The scale and effects of French military and police efforts to destroy Algerian nationalism and the terrorism linked to it led directly to the deaths of at least 150,000 (and upwards of 350,000) Algerian "Muslims."[74] Wide in scope, it was the kinds of violence that the French state employed that sparked much controversy, first among intellectual circles in France and then across the world. French armed forces targeted civilians and made regular and frequent use of torture against Algerian "Muslims" and, far less often, "Europeans" whom they suspected of sympathy or collaboration with, or having information about, the nationalist rebellion.[75] But we also need to pay attention to the second element of the French response: an extension of political rights and economic assistance unparalleled in the history of Western overseas imperialism. Efforts that administrators and politicians had blueprinted when they designed the French Union became a way to guarantee that Algeria would remain part of the French Republic. These attempts to enhance the political and economic possibilities for Algerians began in earnest in 1955–56, at precisely the moment when post-1944 French attempts to relegitimize their empire definitively foundered. Redefining the nation-state, rather than the novel federal-imperial structure of the French Union (which withered away when, in 1956, France began to "territorialize" its functions), was the way France attempted to reconcile republican values and imperial conquest. Political reforms played an enormous role in France's Algerian War, and they particularly shaped the new French Republic that Algeria's independence crystallized.[76]

The French decisions between 1944 and 1947 to create "French Union citizenship" and to extend French citizenship to all "Muslim" Algerians—without offering the vast majority of these new citizens the political rights that, since the French Revolution, were associated with this status—had left the very meaning of this seminal category uncertain. The Algerian Revolution forced the French to clarify what French citizenship—and equality—meant. Writing in July 1958, one official noted that "it took the painful events that, since All-Saints Day [1 November] 1954, have disturbed public order in Algeria to make real the formal promises we had made to our Mus-

---

[73] See LeSueur, Uncivil War; Martha Crenshaw Hutchinson, Revolutionary Terrorism: The FLN in Algeria, 1954–1962 (Stanford, 1978).

[74] Pervillé, Histoire de la guerre d'Algérie, 240–41.

[75] See Raphaëlle Branche, La torture et l'armée pendant la guerre d'Algérie (Paris, 2001), and Sylvie Thénault, Une drôle de justice: Les magistrats dans la guerre d'Algérie (Paris, 2001).

[76] On "territorialization" and how it put an end to reforms undertaken by local officials since World War II, see Cooper, Decolonization and African Society, and Cooper, Colonialism in Question: Theory, Knowledge, History (Berkeley, 2005).

lim compatriots." In Algeria, in response to the Algerian Revolution, the French government worked to eliminate all uncertainties about the reality of "Muslim" French citizenship. The same official noted that "equal rights are now presented as the prime imperative behind our Algeria policy." This, he noted, had been a legal imperative since 1944, but "until 1956, the will to achieve equality, although clearly expressed in a series of laws and constitutional articles voted ten years earlier, widely was seen as merely a declaration of what we intended to do, without any effect in practice." The policies this official wanted the government to extend to the metropole were supposed to make clear that formal rights offered real benefits to all Algerians.[77]

Directly challenging French justifications for their rule in Algeria, their Algerian nationalist opponents had rejected formal or legal definitions as meaningless. The FLN took action in the name of the Algerian nation. This nation was not defined in the law but rather by "Berber heritage, Arabic language, and Islamic tradition."[78] Further, the FLN broke with all previous Algerian nationalists by rejecting any discussion with France based in French law. Because of who they were, the Algerian people had the right to rule Algeria and the French did not. This challenge to French claims to sovereignty based in the law was also a challenge to post-1889 republican understandings of the nation, which used the law, and not ethnicity, language, or religious heritage, to define all Algerians as French.[79]

To keep Algeria French, French laws, policies, and, above all, some of the key principles that structured those rules changed. In 1958, the Constitution of the Fifth Republic reasserted and reinforced the juridical revolution of 1944: all French nationals from Algeria—men and women—who had "local civil status" were full citizens who could maintain their civil status, in Algeria as well as in the metropole. Articles 3 and 75 clearly and specifically addressed Algeria as a part of the French Republic, rather than as part of the French Union (unlike the October 1946 Constitution); they (re)established or extended, in attribution of citizenship rights and in all other domains, territorial indivisibility between Algeria and the metropole, which had been sundered in 1947.[80] The French Revolution's promise of universal adult suffrage was fulfilled not when women's suffrage was accepted in 1944 but when the Constitution of 1958 extended full citizenship to all adult Algerian men and women with local civil status.[81]

---

[77] Victor Silvera, "L'accès à la fonction publique des Français musulmans d'Algérie" (Paris, 19 July 1958), in CAC 19960393, 2 and 6.

[78] See Meynier, Histoire intérieure du FLN, 125–26.

[79] See Brubaker, Citizenship and Nationhood, and Weil, Qu'est-ce qu'un Français?.

[80] See the Constitution of the Fifth Republic, Articles 3 and 75. Removed from the section on the "French Community" (placed instead in Title I, "On sovereignty," and Title XII, "On territorial units," which defined no larger unit than the department), this equality was recentered in the Republic. The new constitution also reaffirmed the territorial unity of Algeria and the metropole.

[81] See, e.g., Rosanvallon, Le sacre du citoyen, and the two volumes of La démocratie en France, ed. Marc Sadoun (Paris, 2000).

Beyond establishing formal political equality, French bureaucrats and politicians in the 1950s and early '60s adopted a radical new approach to Algerian difference in the Republic. Starting in 1955, the liberal Gaullist governor general of Algeria, Jacques Soustelle, theorized and pursued policies aimed at "integrating" "Muslims" into the nation. So-called integrationism attempted to break the tight connections between colonial oppression and France's self-proclaimed universalism. Since the 1870s French governments had claimed that everyone in Algeria could become a French citizen—a theory "proven" by the fact that several thousand Algerians with Koranic civil status (and their descendents) had obtained full citizenship by abandoning that status. Those drafting integrationist policies recognized that equal political rights for all, if always a theoretical possibility, had not happened because it could not have happened.[82]

The architects of integration admitted that official failure to grapple with the reality of the mass exclusion of "Muslim" Algerians from citizenship had institutionalized discrimination; that is, more than just failing to efface existing factors that made them different from other French nationals, the state had produced novel distinctions in the guise of pursuing republican universalism. Decades of applied assimilationist theory—which worked to eliminate group "particularisms" in order to create individuals who could be French citizens—had pushed most Algerian "Muslims" farther away from other French people, not closer. French governance also had encouraged new forms of French racism. With these analyses in mind, they looked for ways to hold on to their ideals of equality for all, while coming up with novel ways to allow some differences to be taken into account. These integrationist policies, implemented in response to the Algerian Revolution, reveal a willingness to confront France's history of racist colonial oppression. This willingness was grounded in the belief that France had the capacity to deal with that heritage and, in so doing, to keep Algeria French.[83]

Integration was the policy extension of the post-1944 recognition that French citizenship was compatible with various civil statuses. This meant that legal uniformity was no longer a prerequisite for political equality. Previously, official references to civil status had ascribed differences in treatment between groups to the existence of distinct legal regimes. Integration recognized that civil code status did not simply mirror regrettable but real group differences that impeded the extension of citizenship to all adults in Algeria. Rather, integrationists proposed a historical analysis: since 1830, France had established a system that produced new differences and reinforced the privileges of one group, French with common civil status, over nationals with other civil statuses. Integration policies aimed to reverse the inequalities that this institutionalized discrimination had produced. Integration broke with

---

[82] For a description of this new analysis, see Commission rélations entre les communautés, "Le regime juridique des statuts privés et des juridictions civiles en Algérie,", 11–13.

[83] Ibid.

the tradition of coexistence by accepting that maintaining *particular* relationships between various subnational groups and the French state, expressed via the coexistence of different civil law regimes, need not entail an *unequal* relationship to the nation, expressed through the political rights attached to citizenship, which now were uniform. The Fifth Republic offered the vote to all Algerians while it recognized the possibility that certain groups of citizens could be governed by distinct legal regimes. Integration explicitly recognized, as well, that true political equality demanded the reduction of economic inequalities. Integrationism thus differed from assimilationism because it supported measures that advanced *all three* versions of equality for Algerians: civic, political, and social. It was thus very similar to the arguments for post-1945 social democracy offered by the theorist T. H. Marshall.[84]

Integration did not embrace "Algerian difference" as beneficial or worth encouraging. This was not late-twentieth-century American multiculturalism avant la lettre.[85] The goal of ensuring that all French people would be governed by the same law endured. Instead, integration opened limited possibilities to accommodate some of the existing particularities of a certain population ("Muslim" Algerians) in the pursuit of eventual full and real equality. The policy of integration accepted the equality of different civil statuses enjoyed by French citizens, although this situation was supposed to be temporary. Exceptional measures in the present were necessary to re-create the imagined unity of all French people before the law in the future.

Without accepting FLN claims about the existence of an organic Algerian nation, integrationist policies broke with republican tradition by accepting that France needed to explicitly take "origins" into account. These radical reforms disappeared when Algeria became independent, but the ways that "origin" entered into French law would shape the dramatic changes in French institutions and identity that took place in 1962. The Fifth Republic went beyond the post-1944 recognition of the compatibility of distinct "civil" legal regimes and republican equality. With integration, the Republic no longer was limited to seeking to overcome group particularities (the announced goal of assimilationism); it also could attack the effects of existing perceptions of group particularities: discrimination against "Muslims" from Algeria. In an effort to rectify specific social inequalities affecting Algerian "Muslims" that the history of the French state in Algeria had encouraged or allowed, officials of the late Fourth Republic created a new legal category, which by distancing itself from "civil status," slipped close to what could be thought of as "ethnicity." A 1956 memo clarifying eligibility for Decree 56–273 of 17 March 1956 delineated a new subset of French

---

[84] See T. H. Marshall and T. Bottomore, *Citizenship and Social Class* (London, 1992).
[85] Matthew Connelly is one of the very few historians to have discussed integrationist efforts, but he mistakenly aligns them with "multiculturalism"; see Connelly, *A Diplomatic Revolution*, chap. 9, "A Multicultural Peace?"

people. The decree extended to "Muslim French from Algeria" a five-year waiver on various age limits at which an individual was no longer eligible to apply for a given civil service position. The term and its acronym, FMA, had emerged in the metropole after 1944, ad hoc, in response to the joint recognition of citizenship for all Algerians and the equality of local civil statuses. (Although it lacked a fixed definition, it appeared in various forms in French official documents, for example, "French citizens with Muslim status originally from Algeria.")[86] An official from the secretary of state for the Civil Service, Pierre Metayer, in instructions to his subordinates, provided a definition that all subsequent official documents would adopt:

> The expression Muslim French citizens from Algeria [*citoyens français musulmans d'Algérie*] includes not only all citizens originally from Algeria who have conserved their local civil status, but also those citizens, and their descendants, who have renounced this status in application of the Senatus-Consulte of 14 July 1865, or of the Law of 4 February 1919.[87]

It was their "origin" and not the "civil status assigned at birth" by the state, as a Justice Ministry senior official explained, that determined membership. This new legally recognized category was "not based on current possession of local civil status," which, although "it would have been the simplest criteria" would not have "complied with the legislators' intentions." He identified the "foundation" underpinning membership in the FMA category as "having an ancestor who had Muslim [civil] status" in 1830.[88]

To facilitate state action to help this category, FMA cobbled together and identified a new subgroup of French nationals in both the metropole and Algeria who shared Algerian origins and were not "European." Alien to republican tradition, it closely resembled the Algerian people that nationalists such as the FLN described as "Arabo-Berber in heritage, Islamic by tradition." The French Republic's identification of "FMA" concretized integrationism's break with the old models of assimilation and coexistence and mapped an innovative French approach to grappling with Algerian difference within the Republic.

---

[86] See "Instruction générale rélative à l'Etat civil du 21 septembre 1955," in *J.O.* of 22 September 1955, 9321–9394; also in AN F/1a/5124. The term "Français musulman d'Algérie," according to Guy Pervillé, "Comment appeler les habitants de l'Algérie" (59), began to be used in 1945.

[87] P. Metayer, Secrétaire d'Etat à la Présidence du Conseil chargé de la Fonction publique, "Définition et justification de la qualité de citoyen français musulman d'Algérie: Mémo à MM. les Ministres et Secrétaires d'Etat" (Paris, 27 November 1956), 1, in CAC/AN 950236/7. For subsequent official reliance on this definition, see sous-directeur des Affaires Civiles et du Sceau, chef du Contentieux de la nationalité, Ministère de la Justice, "Note pour M. le Directeur du Centre National d'Etudes Judiciaires" (Paris, 28 April 1959), 1, in CAC/AN 950236/7.

[88] See sous-directeur des Affaires Civiles et du Sceau, chef du Contentieux de la nationalité (28 April 1959), 2.

Between 1956 and 1962 the French Republic relied on this new category to establish an extensive and pioneering program to redress the effects of discrimination on its "Muslim Algerian" minority. Although what the French officially termed "exceptional promotion" (but also referred to as "Muslim social promotion," "exceptional social promotion," or, in de Gaulle's speeches, "Muslim promotion") was more centralized, more sweeping in its aims, and more attached to binding quotas than the U.S. system for redress of racial inequities that began to emerge some time later, it seems fair to call the efforts French "affirmative action." The emblematic government effort was a binding *réserve* for any and every public sector job filled via exam. From mid-1956, quotas starting at 10 percent and going up to 70 percent applied to all government hiring in Algeria (the quotas varied depending on the post, and most increased over time). In October 1958, the government of Charles de Gaulle published a series of decrees and ordinances that extended the policy of "exceptional promotion" for FMAs to the metropole. The categories affected included judges, specified corps of the civil service, and the National School of Administration, among others. Whereas the 1956 decrees creating "exceptional promotion" had been limited to Algeria, those of 1958 and after explicitly included—indeed were concentrated on—the metropole. In 1960 the French Parliament voted to extend these measures—which the executive had established using "exceptional powers" aimed at suppressing the Algerian Revolution—to all levels of the military.[89]

Scholars have ignored these policies; indeed, a number of recent studies reaffirm ideological claims that French practice has always been "color-blind" in order to analyze why "race-conscious" policies are "unimaginable" in France.[90] From 1958 until the measures disappeared in late 1962, 10 percent of all jobs in the metropole in every corps of the civil service—from the highest rankings, including prefects, judges, high functionaries, and the like, to the lowest—were reserved for FMAs and were to be filled through exams open only to FMAs.[91] Measures guaranteed that if the exams did not

---

[89] For examples of such laws, ordinances, and decrees: *J.O. Tables* L. 56–258, "Mise en oeuvre d'un programme d'expansion" (16 March 1956), 2591; D. 56–273, 17 March 1956, 2664; "Acces des citoyens musulmans: Avis concernant le recrutement des Français musulmans dans les emplois publics," 6654, 1956; see also 1957, 820.

[90] See, for example, Erik Bleich, "The French Model: Color-Blind Integration," in *Color Lines: Affirmative Action, Immigration, and Civil Rights Options for America,* ed. John David Skrentny (Chicago, 2001), 270–96, and *Race Politics in Britain and France: Ideas and Policymaking since the 1960s* (Cambridge, 2003); Adrian Favell, *Philosophies of Integration: Immigration and the Idea of Citizenship in France and Britain* (New York, 2001); Peter Fysh and Jim Wolfreys, *The Politics of Racism in France* (New York, 1998); Anne-Marie Le Pourhiet, "Pour une analyse critique de la discrimination positive," *Débat* 114 (March–April 2001). Daniel Lefeuvre does mention that in 1958 de Gaulle called for such quotas in *Chère Algérie. La France et sa colonie, 1930–1962,* 2nd ed. (Paris, 2005), 366. Robert C. Lieberman's article, "A Tale of Two Countries: The Politics of Colorblindness in France and the United States," *French Politics, Culture & Society* 19, no. 3 (Fall 2001): 32–59, challenges the tendency to contrast French "color-blind" and American "color-conscious" policies.

[91] See Ordinance 1270 of 22 December 1958; Ordinance of 20 October 1958, 58–1016;

identify enough qualified FMA applicants to fill the quotas, temporary workers (FMAs) could be hired who would receive training destined to prepare them for the exam.[92] Despite the great difficulty in filling their quotas, officials maintained the obligation (*impératif*) for all government agencies. The heads of several services did ask the prime minister to grant them an exception for key posts, but although some requests were approved (for example, the decision to allow the National Institutions for Deaf-Mutes to temporarily suspend the quota until the next recruitment in the case of "three master trainers"), most were rejected.[93] The new Constitutional Council was asked to decide whether exceptional promotion was a violation of the principle of equality. In one of their very first decisions the council "sages" found exceptional preference to be constitutional.[94]

France's confrontation with the Algerian Revolution accelerated French efforts to define the identities of the people of Algeria and to do so in ways that both guaranteed French rule and coincided with republican principles. Historically, the latter goal had been less important, but still it had mattered: opening full citizenship to a small number of (male) "Muslims"; maintaining the goal of assimilation for all; and avoiding any codification of racial explanations for the exclusion of most. During the Algerian War, French officials continued to pursue these goals, and in doing so they used the categories developed after 1830 and invented new ones, and tried to continue the process of making Algeria French while, with integration, seriously revising republican theory and principles. To achieve these goals in Algeria, officials once again proved willing to rethink the rules and definitions governing all of the French. Such efforts were not limited to definitions of citizenship and nationality.

Illuminating both the weight of France's history in Algeria and attempts at reform, a second important redefinition of terms began in the armed forces, followed by lawmakers, French bureaucrats, and the public. In early 1958, the French armed forces decided to replace the term "Muslim French from Algeria" with the term "French of North African origin" (*français de*

Law of 28 October 1958 concerning *magistrats Français musulmans*. For reaffirmation of the definition, cf. sous-directeur des Affaires civiles et du Sceau, chef du Contentieux de la nationalité, Ministère de la Justice, "Note pour M. le Directeur du Centre National d'Etudes Judiciaires" (Paris, 28 April 1959), 1, in CAC/AN 950236/7.

[92] "Note Objet: Mésures destinées à favoriser l'accès des Français musulman d'Algérie aux emplois publics de l'Etat. Ord. n. 58–1016 du 29 Octobre 1958" (Paris, March–April, 1962), in CAC/AN 19960393.

[93] Joseph Gand (signed), the prime minister, "FP/3 n. 2067" (Paris, 9 June 1959), in CAC/AN 19960393.

[94] The legislators had approved this mechanism before popular approval of the new constitution had established the possibility that the Constitutional Council could exercise constitutional review; "exceptional preference" for Muslim French citizens from Algeria thus was categorized as an organic law governing the operation of the Fifth Republic. For a description of the emergence of a form of constitutional review in the Fifth Republic, see Alec Stone, *The Birth of Judicial Politics in France* (Oxford, 1992).

souche nord-africaine, or FSNAs). The former had been used in official documents to distinguish hundreds of thousands of conscripts, regular soldiers, and officers from their fellows who were simply "French," as well as to identify (after 1954) the large number of auxiliary forces organized to fight the FLN: *harkis* and *moghaznis.* With this new designation, the army also initiated as its pendant a novel term—"French of European Origin" (*français de souche européenne,* or FSEs)—to distinguish a grouping of French citizens that, at least in official terminology, had not previously been identified.[95]

The elaboration of this policy revealed many of the still-important tensions implicit both in the history of French Algeria and among policies premised on assimilation, coexistence, and integration. In November 1957, the minister for Algeria indicated to Gen. Raoul Salan, the armed forces commandant for Algeria (who later became head of the illegal OAS), that "in order to eliminate an artificial distinction between the citizens of the two principal Algerian communities, I have banned the use of the designation 'Muslim French' in reference to French with local status." Predictably, this gesture, inspired by egalitarian principles, was unable to avoid the perceived reality of "two communities." Responding to Salan's inquiry about how— when "necessary"—to distinguish between members of the two communities, the minister proposed that "French with local status" should be used for "Muslim servicemen from Algeria." This would establish, he affirmed, "the desired distinction and the other servicemen could be called 'French with civil status.'" Salan found these terms "unsatisfactory"; they were "debatable for the FMA personnel posted in the metropole" (where the geographic reference "local" took on a different meaning) and, "premised on the question of status," would work against the military's recent effort "to erase all mention of [legal] status within the ranks." Salan suggested that the title "Muslim French" be retained "on a *collective* or *numerical* plane," while, "on the other hand, for individuals, no particular designation appears necessary." He made no mention of the second category. Days later, the general revised his suggestion: "French of North African origin and French of European origin" could signal "the desired distinction" between personnel.

References to ancestral origin replaced links to legal status, geography, or religion, in an attempt to capture a difference that was at the heart of "the events in Algeria." There were "North Africans" and "Europeans," although both could be French. In the beginning of the twentieth century, the

---

[95] I choose to translate *souche* with the term "origin," although it would also be correct to employ the term "roots." Consonant with this choice, throughout the text, I indicate when the French words *origine* and *racine,* infrequently used in the documents I studied, are being translated. The term *harkis* (plural of *harka*) referred to self-defense groups that government officials organized (often through the use of threats or force) and armed to fight nationalist *fellagha. Moghaznis* were groups of guides and scouts recruited among local populations to fight with French army units. The term *harkis,* as I discuss in later chapters, came to refer to all Muslim French citizens from Algeria allied with the French government both in France (before and after independence) and in the Algerian Republic.

term "of French origin" had emerged to distinguish those French whose origins were in metropolitan France from "naturalized" French citizens in Algeria, whose origins were in other European countries. FSE encompassed all of them and extended this term to metropolitans: it now identified "Europeans of France" as a trans-Mediterranean group of citizens defined by European origin. This reformulated official terminology maneuvered between assimilation and coexistence tactics, while attempting to incorporate integrationism's insistence that the path toward equality required recognition of difference. When the secretary of the army finally sought to bring these reconsiderations out of "Secret/Confidential" discussion into public application, he enunciated more sharply what was at stake: the need to acknowledge *perceived* difference flowed from the need to fight *real* discrimination. The memorandum for general distribution "made known that to avoid all appearance of discrimination in comparison with the so-called French 'by origin,' the Ministry of National Defense and the Armed Forces has decided to eliminate the designation 'Muslim French' currently assigned to Muslim French personnel from Algeria." The question of origin, betrayed by this evocation of the idea of "so-called French by 'origin'" was at the heart of the debate. The one-line modification Army Deputy Chief of Staff Pasteur officially appended made clear that what was at stake was how to acknowledge origins in order to fight racism: he canceled and replaced the specification "in the case of a serviceman of mixed descent, the father's origin [*souche d'appartenance*] alone should be taken into consideration," with the instruction that "in all cases the designation *français de souche européenne* will be given to a serviceman of mixed ancestry."[96]

France always had made distinctions between its subjects in Algeria. What the hesitation over assigning the labels FSE and FSNA made explicit was the emergence in official terminology and categories of a still amorphous idea of *origin* that went beyond the *jus soli* recognition that a French father's legal recognition of his child extended French nationality to that child. Without touching on the question of nationality, FSE and FSNA—like the post-1956 category FMA—embraced a *jus sanguinis*–type definition of membership as wholly compatible with French citizenship: this (legally or bureaucratically) codified definition was "ethnic"; its reference to "European" suggests, in important ways, "racialized" ethnicity.

[96] See Colonel Ducournau, "Objet: Appellation nouvelle des Français musulman d'Algérie" (Algiers, 12 November 1957); Général Salan/Colonel Marquet, "Objet: Appellation nouvelle des Français musulmans d'Algérie" (Algiers, 8 January 1958); Général Salan/Colonel Marquet, "Objet: Appellation nouvelle des Français musulmans d'Algérie" (Algiers, 14 January 1958); Général Pasteur, "Objet: Appellation nouvelle des personnels Français de souche et des Français musulmans" (Paris, 21 February 1958); Général Pasteur, "Modificatif n. 1456EMA/IE" (Paris, 24 March 1958), all in Service historique de l'Armée de Terre (hereafter, SHAT) 1H/1392/4. Kateb, "Histoire statistique des populations algériennes" (263) discusses the distinction between naturalized and *d'origine* for French census takers and demographic analysts of census figures between 1901 and 1936.

The evolution between 1954 and 1962 in the colonizers' thinking about the connections between the French and Algerians, and the confusion that shaped this rethinking, differed strikingly from Algerian nationalist positions. The FLN affirmed the existence of a people who had the right, as the Algerian nation, to rule Algeria. FLN actions after 1954, and the international community's eventual acceptance of their assertions, forced the French to redefine their relationship to Algeria, the land and people. This redefinition was abrupt and was accompanied by little explanation. There were metropolitan intellectuals and political activists who accepted nationalist arguments, but they had relatively little effect on the evolution of official or popular understandings of what should be done with Algeria. Instead, as the next chapter explores, French elites referred to world opinion as they acted to exclude Algeria and its people out of French history and into a previously unknown stage of international development: decolonization.

Chapter 2

Inventing Decolonization

Writing in 1962, a high-ranking French official described the "emancipation of overseas territories" as "a very recent development," remarkable for the contrast between "the magnitude of the phenomenon and how rapidly it occurred." For years, French politicians and public opinion had paid little attention, but when they did, he opined, it was like "a veil, which suddenly was ripped apart." As in numerous policies proposed to the French at the war's end, Jean Vacher-Desvernais here evoked an international and explicitly non-French context in order to talk about Algeria. He relied on the orientalist image par excellence of the veil to suggest a jump from obscurantist ignorance to reason-based knowledge: "The notion of decolonization brusquely became commonplace. In this way, a new term was born."[1] What Vacher-Desvernais sought to explain was the abruptness of the French reversal vis-à-vis Algeria between 1959 and 1962: the large-scale abandonment of arguments that "Algeria is France" and the acceptance that "Algeria is a colony that must be decolonized." Yet his depiction of France as an increasingly informed polity embracing a supremely rational interpretation of world events, however vivid, is inaccurate. Even contemporary polling, which suggests that "public opinion" was far more skeptical than leaders of opinion about the legitimacy, the realism, or the cost of keeping Algeria French, does not suggest an accumulation of individuals slowly won over. The critical shift was sudden and definitive: "decolonization" emerged as a structural cause that French people could and did refer to in order to avoid explaining why they now overwhelmingly accepted Algerian independence.[2]

---

[1] Jean Vacher-Desvernais, *L'avenir des Français d'outre-mer* (Paris, 1962), 2–3.
[2] On popular disinterest in the conflict, see Benjamin Stora, *La gangrène et l'oubli: La mémoire de la guerre d'Algérie,* new ed. (Paris, 1998), 115–17. For polling, cf. Charles-Robert

In 1962, a British author affirmed that the French recently had invented "the word *décolonisation*."[3] A Frenchman, in fact, had come up with the word, and it was in reference to Algeria, but Henri Fonfrède's 1836 coinage had disappeared from circulation by the 1850s. What the French historian Charles-Robert Ageron tells us about its early twentieth century reemergence provides a fitting prehistory to what follows. He outlines how, during the interwar period, the word "decolonization" was invested with racist understandings that the world was witnessing the historically inevitable process of Western decadence:

> Invoked as a neutral way to describe the pullback of imperial powers, the designation *Entkolonisierung* was used in Germany after 1930, notably by [Moritz] Julius Bonn. After emigrating to Britain, Bonn translated it into English as "Dekolonization." This scholar even predicted in his book *Crumbling of Empire* that very soon we would witness not only the crumbling of the British Empire but that of all colonial empires. After 1918, numerous German intellectuals [like Bonn] believed in the "decline of the West," to quote the supposedly prophetic title of Oswald Spengler's book; others ruminated on "the rising tide of color against white world-supremacy" ([by the American scholar] Lothrop Stoddard); still others on "Islam's awakening," Asianism, and even Pan-Africanism.[4]

Through the 1950s, European political scientists continued to use the term as a technical description of shifts in sovereignty over specific territories: after World War II, numerous colonized areas experienced such transitions.

"A Ring of Fire Burning All along the Tropics"

During World War II and after, a growing clamor from political parties, labor movements, intellectuals, and local elites in the colonies demanded an immediate end to Western states' continued political and economic control

---

Ageron, "La guerre d'Algérie et les Français: Avis de Recherche," *Vingtième siècle* (July–September 1989): 123.

[3] Charles E. Carrington, "Decolonization: The Last Stages," *International Affairs* 38, no. 1 (January 1962): 29.

[4] Charles-Robert Ageron, "Décolonisation," in *Encyclopedia Universalis*, Corpus 7 (Paris, 2004), 11. An example from journalism, the *Times* of London, indicates how the term became popular in the 1950s and took its meaning from the Algerian Revolution. The *Times* first used the term "decolonization" in the article "Development of Colonies: Native Advance to Self-Government," June 14, 1927, p. 15, in a report on a speech by the Belgian scholar Henri Rolin at the meetings of the Nineteenth Congress of the International Colonial Institute. The second time the term appeared in the *Times* (placed in quotation marks) was thirty-one years later, in "Belgian Policy of 'Decolonization'," August 20, 1958, p. 7. The term appeared in seven articles between then and December 1960. From December 1960 until December 1963, it appeared in forty-two articles. Although almost all the articles in the first years that used "decolonization" were about France and Algeria, by mid-1961 the term appeared in articles that touched on many nations (*Times* Digital Archives, 1785–1985). Searches of other scholarly and popular periodicals reveal a similar development. "Decolonization" first appeared in a *New York Times* article in two articles published in 1959. Between 1960 and 1963 the *New York Times* used it in ninety-nine articles (the verb "to decolonize" was not used until 1963).

of overseas territories. Foundational texts for the postwar international order proposed the independence of colonized peoples as a goal, agreements such as the Atlantic Charter, which Winston Churchill and Franklin Roosevelt signed in August 1941, and the United Nation's Charter of 1946, which committed signatories "to develop self-government." More important, nationalist movements succeeded in forcing the British to hand over control of India (1947) and Palestine (1948), and the Dutch to free Indonesia in 1949.

French officials and chattering classes, however, did not see these developments as having any particular meaning or lesson for what, in these same months, the government renamed Overseas France, and then the French Union. French officials interpreted the UN Charter as a call "to develop the ability of colonized peoples to administer themselves," not to move toward independence.[5] Rather than independence, they sought to build institutions that would lead colonized peoples to embrace the new French Union. Between 1944 and 1956 French diplomats and politicians in Paris, as well as officials in the colonies, worked to keep international institutions, such as the UN, and other countries from interfering in French "internal" affairs.[6] Meanwhile, French newspapers explained what they referred to as the "end of the British Empire" in India as a result of the failure of the "British model": the conjoined effect of the "indirect" form of colonial rule and Britain's historical incapacity to respond to popular demands for liberation. The "French model"—in which a revolutionary heritage at home shaped direct rule of overseas possessions—had lessons to give, not to receive. The restored French Republic unleashed brutal crackdowns in 1945 in response to V-E Day protests against French rule in Sétif, Algeria, and in Damascus, Syria; in 1947, there was an even greater bloodbath against proindependence protests in Madagascar.[7] In Indochina, France fought an aggressive military campaign to crush Viet-Minh activity, from Ho Chi Minh's proclamation of independence on 2 September 1945 until the nationalists defeated French forces at Dien Bien Phu in May 1954.[8]

In 1955, most of those who had led their states to formal independence, or broken with Western domination of their homelands (including Egypt's Gamal Abdel Nasser and China's Zhou En-lai) gathered in Bandung, In-

[5] The quoted translation of the United Nations Charter is from Louis Rolland and Pierre Lampué, *Précis de droit des pays d'outre-mer, territoires, departments, Etats associés,* 2nd ed. (Paris, 1952), 25. See John D. Hargreaves, "Habits of Mind and Forces of History: France, Britain and the Decolonization of Africa," in *Imperialism, the State and the Third World,* ed. Michael Twaddle (London, 1992), 216.

[6] John Kent, *The Internationalization of Colonialism: Britain, France, and Black Africa, 1939–1956* (Oxford, 1992), 287.

[7] Cf. Kate Marsh, "The End of the British Raj: Representations of the Decolonization of India in French-Language Journalism (1923–47)," *Journal of Francophone Postcolonial Studies* 3:1 (2005), 43–55 and Jean-Charles Jauffret, ed., *La guerre d'Algérie par les documents,* vol. 1, *L'avertissement, 1943–1946* (Vincennes, 1990).

[8] See Alain-Gerard Marsot, "The Crucial Year: Indochina 1946," *Journal of Contemporary History* 19, no. 2 (April 1984): 337–54.

donesia to trumpet the existence of a new, independent force in world politics. They proclaimed that the "Third World" included all countries that had
been—or still were—colonized or dominated by Western powers, and that
it was unified in its demands and needs, including that of independence. Imperial authorities wholly rejected such a vision.[9] Like the French, the British
sought to hold on to their empire, even after leaving their South Asian and
Middle Eastern colonies.[10] Historians of the British Empire and of various
anti-imperialist movements still discuss whether Britain "pushed" or was
"pulled" toward granting particular colonies independence. The most be-
nign interpretations of British actions after 1947 highlight a "conscious effort to meet, at first to contain, if possible to collaborate with, and ultimately
to transfer power to the accelerating force of . . . nationalism."[11] What is
undeniable is that British officials rejected any systematic approach to dealing with their overseas possessions, even after they were forced to "transfer power" in West Africa and the Caribbean. They had insisted that the differences between "Asian" and "African" colonies meant that the independence of the former had little to teach officials in the latter. When the Gold
Coast (which became Ghana in 1957) and then other British colonies in
Africa obtained independence, British colonialists, like their French counterparts, refocused their arguments on how different their "settler colonies"
were from their other African colonies. As the British historians D. A. Low
and John Lonsdale affirm: "In most British minds these [other] precedents
offered no guide to the future of East—or Central—Africa: on the contrary,
their European and Asian minorities made these areas entirely different."[12]
There were multiple colonialisms and thus multiple paths out of the current
situation.

Western officials during the 1950s denied that there was a necessary
corollary between what had been done in some former colonies and what
should be done in those that remained. Yet there was one unity they did per-
ceive throughout the colonized territories, one premised on race. This vision of what was going on in the colonies spread, mostly behind the scenes,
among Western diplomats and politicians who shared many of the concerns that Ageron attributes to certain interwar-period German intellectu-

[9] Ibid.

[10] See R. F. Holland, "The Imperial Factor in British Strategies from Attlee to Macmillan,
1945–63," in Perspectives on Imperialism and Decolonization: Essays in Honour of A. F. Madden, ed. R. F. Holland and G. Rizvi (London, 1984), 165–86.

[11] John W. Cell, "On the Eve of Decolonization: The Colonial Office's Plans for the Transfer of Power in Africa, 1947," Journal of Imperial and Commonwealth History 8, no. 3 (May
1980): 235. For this "Whig" interpretation, following John Darwin, see also Ronald Robinson,
"Andrew Cohen and the Transfer of Power in Tropical Africa, 1940–1951," in Decolonisation
and After: The British and French Experience, ed. W. H. Morris–Jones and Georges Fisher (London, 1980). For the critique, see, e.g., John Darwin, "British Decolonization since 1945: A Pat-
tern or a Puzzle?" Journal of Imperial and Commonwealth Studies 12 (1984): 187–209.

[12] D. A. Low and John Lonsdale, introduction to Towards the New Order, 1945–1963 (Oxford, 1976), 2.

als. It evoked a "tide of History," in which "nonwhite" peoples, driven by their increasing numbers, were rising up to challenge "white" civilization. Throughout the 1950s, as the diplomatic historian Matthew Connelly shows, numerous Western officials and scholars used references to "the current of history" to describe what they saw as the new challenges non-European or non-Western peoples posed to the West. These challenges included both anticolonial nationalism and, most saliently in Connelly's analysis, the worldwide surge in the number of "non-Europeans." European and American commentators and officials worried about "nonwhite" peoples swamping the West. The 1961 and 1962 correspondence between British prime minister Harold Macmillan and Australian prime minister Robert Menzies highlights the central role racial fears played in contemporary discussions of "decolonization" among Western officials. Both men saw the independence of certain former British colonies as the result of the declining prestige of "whites" and the "revolt" of what Macmillan calls the "yellows and blacks." Certain contingencies and unwise decisions by European leaders (Macmillan particularly had in mind the Holocaust) made these challenges more pressing and difficult to overcome, but there was nothing inevitable or unstoppable about this current of history.[13]

The inventor of the term "Third World," the French demographer Alfred Sauvy, famously concluded his 1952 article on the "Three Worlds"—industrialized capitalist states; industrialized socialist states; the rest—with the claim that "this ignored, exploited, and distrusted Third World, just like the Third Estate, wants to be something." Sauvy's reference to the French Revolution has usually been understood as calling for a political understanding of and response to what was happening across the world.[14] Yet, his article also connected the "Third World" with the pseudoscientific idea, elaborated in the 1920s and 1930s to advance racist ends, that racially distinct "populations" existed and that the ways they grew or shrank shaped world history. Sauvy himself had played a key role in the elaboration of the Vichy-based French state's pronatalist "population" policies. In the midst of a post-1945 "baby boom" across the West—which raised questions about the utility of pronatalist policies, as well as the predictions of demographers—his famous article shifted natalist concerns away from "how to reverse" declining European "populations" to "how to respond" to surging non-European "populations."[15]

[13] See Matthew Connelly, *A Diplomatic Revolution: Algeria's Fight for Independence and the Origins of the Post–Cold War Era* (Oxford, 2002), esp. v–xiii, 48, 85–90, and 276–87. See Chris Waters, "Macmillan, Menzies, History and Empire," *Australian Historical Studies* 119 (2002): 93–107; 100.

[14] For the ideological interpretation, see Robert Malley, *The Call from Algeria: Third Worldism, Revolution, and the Turn to Islam* (Berkeley, 1996), 78.

[15] Alfred Sauvy, "Trois mondes, une planète," *Observateur* 118 (14 August 1952): 14. On definitions of the "Third World," see B. R. Tomlinson, "What Was the Third World?" *Journal of Contemporary History* 38, no. 2 (April 2003): 307–21. On Sauvy, see Sandrine Bertaux, "En-

Sauvy's article also highlighted the ongoing cold war between the United States and the Soviet Union. He argued that both sides should alter their ideological understandings of their mutual conflict, in order to respond to the demographic problem posed by the growing Third World. The Soviets in fact did so, increasingly embracing struggles they had previously dismissed as merely "nationalist" or "bourgeois." In the early 1960s, Nikita Khrushchev waxed enthusiastically about what historians Vladislav Zubok and Constantine Pleshakov term the "wave of national liberation in Asia, Africa, and Latin America," and reoriented Soviet foreign policy (and assessment of revolutionary status) in their direction. Soviet shifts made U.S. attempts to woo the Third World more difficult.[16] U.S. diplomats invoked their country's history since 1776 to prove their anticolonial bona fides; however, the U.S. tendency to assess anticolonial movements in terms of their relationship to Marxism, while ignoring questions of race and racial injustice, hampered this effort. Indeed, if there was one issue that the country that still had Jim Crow laws wanted to avoid bringing up in international discussion during the 1950s it was racial injustice.

The invention of decolonization made the distinction between anticolonial movements and the U.S. civil rights movement obvious: one was about state sovereignty, the other about racism. Yet at the time a number of people made clear connections between the two struggles. Connelly's study of diplomatic sources hints at how U.S. secretary of state John Foster Dulles, formed by his experience growing up in the American South, both perceived the Algerian War in racial terms and sought to avoid such comparisons when characterizing events on the world stage. A number of French writers did just that: the historian Frank Costigliola notes that defenders of French Algeria answered American criticisms of France's fight to defeat the FLN by "pointing out that Europeans had emigrated to both North Africa and North America. In North Africa, French settlers had civilized the inhabitants; in North America, the pioneers had annihilated them." Self-serving comparisons between French efforts to "integrate" Algerians in the face of terrorism and the ways that U.S. authorities responded to the nonviolent civil rights movement were constants in mainstream and right-wing French

tre ordre social et ordre racial: Constitution et développement de la démographie en France et en Italie, de la fin du XIXe siècle à la fin des années cinquante," PhD diss., European University Institute, 2002. On uses of demography in the twentieth-century British Empire, before and after World War II, see Karl Ittmann, "Demography as Policy Science in the British Empire, 1918–1969," *Journal of Policy History* 15, no. 4 (2003): 417–44.

[16] Vladislav Zubok and Constantine Pleshakov, *Inside the Kremlin's Cold War: From Stalin to Khrushchev* (Cambridge, Mass., 1996), 206.

[17] See Connelly, Diplomatic Revolution; see also Mary L. Dudziak, *Cold War Civil Rights: Race and the Image of American Democracy* (Princeton, 2000); Brenda Gayle Plummer, *Rising Wind: Black Americans and U.S. Foreign Affairs, 1935–1960* (Chapel Hill, 1996); Plummer, ed., *Window on Freedom: Race, Civil Rights, and Foreign Affairs, 1945–1988* (Chapel Hill, 2003); and Penny Von Eschen, *Race against Empire: Black Americans and Anticolonialism, 1937–1957* (Ithaca, 1997); Frank Costigliola, *France and the United States: The Cold Alliance*

media.[17] Other commentators who criticized both the French and the Americans highlighted how racial injustice necessarily was linked to imperialist and capitalist injustices.

Radical intellectuals from the colonized world developed the other important vision of "decolonization" in the 1950s and early '60s. Like Western diplomats and politicians, they relied on historical interpretations to describe widespread and increasingly pressing demands to end or redefine colonial relationships between European states and their overseas possessions. They, too, presented these phenomena as at once inextricable from questions of race and as fundamentally the result of contingent rather than structural processes, as part of the realm of choice and historical action rather than historically inevitable. The Martinican-French writers Aimé Césaire and Frantz Fanon, in particular, sought to articulate the ways diverse demands for "decolonization" posed political and epistemological challenges to Western humanism. Césaire was born in the French colony of Martinique. In the 1930s, while studying in Paris, he became one of France's most well-known poets and elaborated, along with Léopold Sédar Senghor and Léon Damas, the idea of negritude. Césaire's understanding of negritude (unlike Senghor's) was profoundly historical, encompassing both the specificities of an experience formed by oppression and exploitation, which all people with origins in "Black Africa" shared, and a deep connection to universal humanity. As he wrote in his seminal poem *Notebook of a Return to the Native Land:*

> entrenched as I am in this unique race
> you still know my tyrannical love
> you know that it is not from hatred of other races that I demand a digger
>   for this unique race
> that what I want is for universal hunger
> for universal thirst.

He worked to make his poetics of blackness speak to other experiences of oppression as well as to awaken people who denied the humanity of those, such as Africans, whom they oppressed.[18]

---

since World War II (New York, 1992), 112. On estimates of the large percentage of indigenous Algerians who died as a result of the French conquest, see Kamel Kateb, "Histoire statistique des populations algériennes pendant la colonisation française, 1830–1962," PhD diss., Ecole des hautes études en sciences sociales, 1998, chap. 2. For an interesting analysis of "liberal" U.S. public opinion on the French in Algeria (and Tunisia and Morocco), see Martin Thomas, "Defending a Lost Cause? France and the United States Vision of Imperial Rule in French North Africa, 1945–1956," *Diplomatic History* 26, no. 2 (Spring 2002): 215–47.

[18] Aimé Césaire, "Notebook of a Return to the Native Land," in *Aimé Césaire: The Collected Poetry,* trans. Clayton Eshleman and Annette Smith (Berkeley, 1983), 32–85, 71. On Césaire's humanism, see Maria De Gennaro, "Fighting 'Humanism' on Its Own Terms," *differences: A Journal of Feminist Cultural Studies* 14, no. 1 (2003): 53–73. On his use of history, see Albert Owusu-Sarpong, *Le temps historique dans l'oeuvre théâtrale d'Aimé Césaire* (Paris, 2002).

In Césaire's estimation World War II had confronted Europeans with the types of inhumanity that they had depended on to rule their colonies. His reading contradicted that of Western leaders and diplomats who bemoaned how the war had fatally weakened the colonial powers of Europe, sapping not just the material but the moral force they had relied on to rule empires. The history of Western imperialism, for Césaire, demonstrated the modern West's immorality and had led inevitably to Hitler: "The very distinguished, very humanistic, very Christian bourgeois of the twentieth century . . . has Hitler inside him. . . . Hitler is his demon." The challenge that Césaire believed the colonized needed to pose to colonialist barbarism would offer new possibilities to the world. He called on the colonized "not to follow Europe's footsteps, and not to go back to the ancient way, but to carve out a new direction altogether."[19]

Fanon, the psychologist and political theorist, proposed perhaps the most well-known analysis of decolonization. He also was born on Martinique. He studied in metropolitan France and practiced medicine in French Algeria, and then worked for Algerian independence in Tunis and Ghana. His numerous writings moved constantly between questions of race and colonialism. He argued that each of the multiple "decolonizations" needed to be struggled for, and struggled for violently. He rejected structural interpretations of these phenomena: "It is rigorously false to pretend and to believe that this decolonization is the fruit of an objective dialectic which more or less rapidly assumed the appearance of an absolutely inevitable mechanism." Such an understanding was wrong because it denied the emergence of the colonized masses as historical agents, and dubious because it opened the way for local elites to betray the masses' goals and expectations. Fanon analyzed this betrayal, envisioning "national elites" using nationalism to take control of newly independent states and ignoring demands for justice and a "new humanism." Unlike Césaire, who employed a violent language that aimed to awaken both colonized and colonizers to injustice but avoided calling for armed struggle, Fanon advocated violence as a way to create the basis for a new humanism, by which he meant that truly universal human values would become apparent and meaningful only after the colonized had exposed and destroyed the Manichean divisions on which Western "civilization" depended. This, rather than any supposed reverse racism, is why he addressed himself almost exclusively to the colonized. Still, it was the analytic framework of Fanon, rather than Césaire, that most shaped the efforts of certain metropolitan intellectuals and militants to think about what the Algerian Revolution meant for the West.[20]

---

[19] Aimé Césaire, *Discourse on Colonialism*, trans. Joan Pinkham (New York, 2000), 2, 27.
[20] *Towards an African Revolution* (New York, 1967), 179.

A Shared Prescience: Raymond Aron and Jean-Paul Sartre

Between the 1954 explosion of the FLN onto the world stage and 1959, only a scattering of (metropolitan) French people came out against keeping Algeria French. These arguments for Algerian independence received a fair amount of attention, even though very few people in France shared them, for they were identified, respectively, with two iconoclasts of the mid-1950s intellectual scene: the philosophers Jean-Paul Sartre, the far-left trouble-maker, and Raymond Aron, the often-lonely Gallic defender of classic liberalism. The first offered a metropolitan revision of "colonial" radicals such as Fanon, the latter pursued the racially charged vision of Western diplomats to what he saw as its logical conclusion. Their shared, early, and clairvoyant opposition to French Algeria revealed a number of affinities between Sartre and Aron, men usually presented as intellectual and political adversaries. Each placed his analyses of the evolution of French/Algerian relations within an ongoing philosophical interrogation of the meaning of History. Each relied on an understanding of History to explain why Algeria should be granted independence. Neither of their arguments for Algerian independence relied primarily on the traditions or ideology of French republicanism, Aron preferring a "realistic" liberalism, while Sartre developed a revolutionary radicalism. The philosophers' antirepublicanism allowed them to articulate clearly their shared understanding that French people and Algerian people were different. Sartre and Aron's joint minimization of republican references explains in large part the political and intellectual isolation of their arguments for independence until well after the war's end.[21]

"Colonialism Is a System": Sartre and the *Temps Modernes* Group

Between the Liberation in 1944 and the beginning of the FLN's public activity in late 1954, *Les Temps Modernes*, the journal Sartre and fellow philosopher Simone de Beauvoir founded in 1945, had been one of the few metropolitan forums to present arguments favorable to Algerian independence. Among these early articles, the most influential was Francis Jeanson's analysis of Algerian nationalism. The young philosophy teacher described this movement as a historically determined struggle for human liberation.

---

[21] Scholars describe the 1950s as a moment of exhaustion with exegeses premised in historical reasoning, which Michael S. Roth terms "Hegelianism," among French intellectuals. Until this exhaustion, Roth states, history served most French philosophers "as the source of truths and criteria of judgment . . . providing insight into how that world might be changed for the better." See *Knowing and History: Appropriations of Hegel in Twentieth-Century France* (Ithaca, 1988), ix. On Sartre as the last major French intellectual to propose "[the] Hegelian possibility of the end of alienation and the creation of a world of free subjects," see Mark Poster, *Foucault, Marxism, and History* (New York, 1984), 21.

This conception of a liberatory, anticolonial nationalism, developed in the language of Sartrean existentialism, provided the theoretical foundations for the *Temps Modernes* group's embryonic support for Algerian independence.[22] After the war had started, Sartre himself sought to amplify this analysis. In a January 1956 speech intoned before the Comité d'Action des Intellectuels contre la Poursuite de la Guerre en Afrique du Nord (Action Committee of Intellectuals against the Continuation of the War in North Africa), in a packed Salle Wagram, he began with a historical exegesis of French colonialism in Algeria. He told the crowd, "We, we have only one lesson to draw from these facts: colonialism is destroying itself." Yet, the famed thinker continued, this fateful certainty should not inspire satisfaction in any individual. Colonialism "pollutes the atmosphere: it is our shame, it mocks our laws or deforms them; it infects us with its racism." The role of French militants and intellectuals "is to help it die . . . the only thing we should and must attempt—yet today this is the essential—is to struggle alongside [the Algerian people] in order to deliver simultaneously the Algerian and French peoples from colonial tyranny." As the title of a subsequent article evidenced, Sartre here proposed that "colonialism is a system," a system he actively rejected and reviled.[23]

Sartre's support for Algerian nationalism sharply distinguished the *Temps Modernes* tendency from the republican Left, which encompassed both the established political parties and the emerging "new left" (not to be confused with the New Left of the late 1960s). In the mid-1950s, the Radical Party, the Socialists (French Section of the Workers' International—Section Française de l'International Ouvrière or SFIO), as well as the left-wing "clubs," were fully committed to maintaining French Algeria. Between 1954 and 1958 left-wing governments twice directed this defense, first under the leadership of the Radical Pierre Mendès-France, then of the Socialist Guy Mollet. Harshly critical of "colonialist" French attempts to block Indochinese independence and responsible for abandoning French control of Morocco and Tunisia, these left-wing politicians explicitly rejected Algerian independence. They did so in the name of the Republic. As Mendès-France, prime minister at the time of the FLN's first public actions, asserted: "We do not negotiate when it comes to defending the internal security of the nation and the integrity of the Republic. Between Algeria and the metropole, secession is unthinkable."[24] The non-Communist Left, an integral part of the Fourth

---

[22] See Francis Jeanson, "Logique du colonialisme," *Les Temps Modernes* 82 (1952), 2213–2229. On the role of *Les Temps Modernes* during the Indochina war, see David Drake, "*Les Temps modernes* and the French War in Indochina," *Journal of European Studies* 28, nos. 109–110 (1998): 25–41.

[23] See *Situations V*, 47–48; *Les Temps Modernes* (March–April 1956). On the Comité in general and this meeting in particular, see James LeSueur, *Uncivil War: Intellectuals and the Decolonization of Algeria* (Philadelphia, 2001), 28–54.

[24] *J.O.*, 12 November 1954.

Republic's political establishment, although sporadically seeking to reform French Algeria did not countenance or even begin to think about independence for Algeria until well after de Gaulle's 1959 call for self-determination. Indeed, they supported, and when in power initiated, measures aimed at crushing the armed rebellion. Besides backing a muscular military response, the Left also affirmed its commitment to realizing the long ignored promises of France's "civilizing mission."[25] The Fourth Republic and its leftist politicians advanced in Algeria with the tried and trusted tools that the Third Republic had used to make the metropole French: more schools and further extension of Algerian "Muslim" participation in the army. Despite the increasing skepticism directed at the concept of the "civilizing mission" over the course of the 1950s, and despite the crisis of the republican army, for the parties of the Left the army and education remained the primary vectors of reform in the Algerian departments. In the face of an armed and internationally credible rebellion, the main parties of the Left continued to see making Algeria more French as the way to solve the Algerian crisis.[26]

Historically, the Left had missed a number of opportunities to extend equality to the "Muslims" of Algeria, beginning in 1936, when the Popular Front's Blum-Viollette reform collapsed in the face of the mass resignation of Algerian mayors. In 1944, the Provisional Government of the French Republic made only limited changes in rules restricting the vote of Algerians with local civil status (Ordinance of 7 March). In 1945, the SFIO and PCF, each of which had ministers in the government, actively supported the brutal repression and subsequent political clampdown that followed an outbreak of nationalist violence in Sétif. In 1954, Radical prime minister Pierre Mendès-France chose domestic accommodation over decisive reforms. In 1956, Socialist prime minister Guy Mollet—after a hail of tomatoes greeted his visit to Algiers—agreed to replace Governor General Jacques Soustelle with the resident minister, Robert Lacoste, a strong supporter of "integration," rather than the more skeptical General Georges Catroux.[27] In each instance, the French Left's attempts to think through and act on "when" and "how" Algerian "Muslims" would become wholly equal were crippled by the consideration given to those in Algeria who already had the vote: the "Europeans."

Although the republican Left continued to believe that the assimilation of Algerian "Muslims" was possible, its members were unable, at any point, even to make this future possibility an immediate *legal* reality. This failure arose, in part, from the political instability inherent in the coalition building needed to form parliamentary majorities in the Third and Fourth Republics.

[25] Etienne Maquin, *Le parti socialiste et la guerre d'Algérie* (Paris, 1990), 233.

[26] On the importance of Algerian "Muslim" participation in the army, see Anthony Clayton, *France, Soldiers, and Africa* (London, 1988).

[27] On Catroux, see LeSueur, *Uncivil War,* 269 n. 60.

It resulted, as well, from the inability of a Left historically wedded to the fight for secularism to respond convincingly to "European" arguments that the supposedly profoundly religious "Muslim" Algerians were not yet ready for full citizenship.[28] The Fourth Republic's failure to offer full suffrage to all but a tiny minority of Algerian "Muslims" was emblematic of the incapacity of both Radicals and Socialists to articulate effective responses to the pressing problems raised by the Algerian conflict. Their ineffectiveness opened the door to the return to power of Charles de Gaulle and the rise of the French "new left."

On the margins of the left-wing political parties, a growing metropolitan clamor responded to the events in Algeria, mostly concerned with all too accurate accusations of torture. The French military and police stood accused of systematically violating the most basic human rights of detainees suspected of FLN militancy or of withholding information. Claude Bourdet's "Your Gestapo in Algeria" appeared in *France-Observateur* the same week in January 1955 as François Mauriac's "The Question" was published in *L'Express*. The first widely noted metropolitan challenges in the wake of 1 November 1954 to the government's aggressive policy south of the Mediterranean, both articles asserted that French forces were using torture in their three-month-old fight against the FLN. In subsequent years, the left-Christian reviews *L'Esprit* and *Témoignage chrétien* revealed accusations of torture, while intellectuals united in the Comité Audin, a group that first organized to demand information about the disappearance of the young doctoral student in mathematics and Communist Party of Algeria member Maurice Audin, who died in police custody, investigated such charges. On the rare occasions when officials, politicians, or intellectuals who supported the army admitted to the use of torture, they made their defense in the name of French national interests, or *raison d'Etat*.[29]

Almost all of the periodicals and writers who challenged the use of torture belonged to what was emerging as the "new left" of the late 1950s and early 1960s. The U.S.–style newsweekly *France-Observateur* showcased the coming together of a group of small leftist organizations committed to pursuing a "third way" between the (Stalinist) PCF and the (socialist) SFIO (which they saw as more committed to holding power than advancing left-wing projects). These groups were inspired by Marxism, neither Stalinist nor Trotskyist, and open to left-wing Christians. The late 1954 birth of the National Committee of the New Left aimed to organize this current. Three

[28] See Rabech Achi, "La laïcité en situation coloniale. Usages politiques croisés du principe de separation des Eglises et de L'Etat en Algérie," in *La justice en Algérie* (1830–1962) (Paris, 2005), 163–176.

[29] *France-Observateur* 244 (13 January 1955), 6–7; *L'Express* 86 (15 January 1955), 16.

weeks later, the other U.S.-style weekly newsmagazine, *L'Express*, announced the existence of what it termed the "new left."[30] This "new left" was liberal, particularly in its emphasis on reforming capitalism. They sought to liberalize state and society in order to create the conditions for the realization of left-wing values. Their emblematic figure was Pierre Mendès-France. Both "new left" groups wanted to redefine the political landscape: to reduce, but not eliminate, the role of the Communist Party in order to create conditions that would bring a new left-wing (or left-centered, for *L'Express*) political coalition to power. The "socialist new left" sought to revive the Popular Front of the 1930s, which had brought together left-wing parties (the PCF, the SFIO, and the Radical Party) and had governed, under socialist Léon Blum, in 1936–37. The "liberal new left" held out the hope of a New Deal *à la française*.[31]

In the first years of the war, new left critics, unlike Sartre's coterie, situated their campaigns against torture within their larger vision of republicanism, in what they presented as a particularly French tradition of the defense of the Rights of Man. They formed what the classicist Pierre Vidal-Naquet (himself a prominent campaigner against torture during the war) calls the "Dreyfusard" tendency of antiwar engagement. This moniker captures the new left's self-fashioned descent from the fin-de-siècle defenders of Alfred Dreyfus, such as Emile Zola, who had protested against the treason conviction of the officer of the French army's general staff, which was a result of anti-Semitism, traditionalism, and bigoted patriotism rather than evidence. The history of this epochal confrontation—between Left and Right, tradition and modernity, justice and *raison d'Etat*, Republic and Reaction— framed the new Dreyfusards' primary argument: that the Algerian War, which entailed constant violations of republican values, posed a danger to the Republic.[32] These "defenders of the Republic" hesitated to take a clear position on Algerian independence or in support of the FLN. They focused on what French conduct was doing to Algerians and what this meant about France. It was not until after 1959 that most spoke out about whether Algeria should remain French. The Dreyfusards who had saved French honor and the Republic inspired what the historian Raoul Girardet (himself jailed for pro-OAS activity) termed an outspoken if inefficacious "moral refusal" of what the government was doing to defend French Algeria.[33]

[30] In 1961, the RG described *L'Express* as the magazine of the "bourgeoisie gauchisante," although the magazine claimed to be targeted at the left-leaning middle classes, "intellectuals or not." Its weekly circulation was around 220,000. The RG classified *L'Express*, along with *France-Observateur* (circulation 85,000) and *Témoignage chrétien* (circulation 48,000), under the rubric "left progressive weeklies." See Section "Presses," Direction des RG, "La presse politique hebdomadaire" (December 1961), 27, and 3–4, in CAC 940560/01.

[31] See Jean-François Kesler, *De la gauche dissidente au nouveau Parti socialiste: Les minorités qui ont rénové le P.S.* (Paris, 1990), 214–21.

[32] See Pierre Vidal-Naquet, "Une fidélité têtue," *Vingtième siècle* (April–June 1986).

[33] Raoul Girardet, *L'idée coloniale en France, 1870 à 1962* (Paris, 1972); see also Paul Clay Sorum, *Decolonization and French Intellectuals* (Chapel Hill, 1977), 15–16.

Sartre and de Beauvoir spurned such an explanation for their engagement, despite what the latter termed her "outrage" at "the burns on the face, on the sexual organs, the nails torn out, the impalements, the shrieks, the convulsions." Both argued that torture was not an "excess" but a result of the (French) imperialist system. They refused to let anguish guide their arguments and action. De Beauvoir wrote in 1962, "To protest [torture] in the name of morality against excesses or abuses is an error which hints at active complicity." Only a dialectical analysis of the actually existing historical situation, she argued, could grasp what was at stake. "There are no abuses or excesses here, simply an all-pervasive system." She also noted how isolated they had been, even on the Left, just a few years earlier: "The word 'independence' was so unpopular that even in *Les Temps Modernes*, which wanted it and considered it inevitable, we avoided calling it by its real name."[34]

Raymond Aron's National Liberalism

Like Sartre and de Beauvoir on the Left, the right-wing philosopher Raymond Aron relied on historical inevitability to explain his pro-independence apostasy in *The Algerian Tragedy* (1957). It was a position he continued to develop in subsequent books (although not in *Le Figaro*, whose editors, once they became aware of his position on the Algerian question, refused to let him write about Algeria in its pages).[35] His reasoning was broadly similar to that of Raymond Cartier, publisher of the popular photo-weekly *Paris-Match*. Both (the man and the magazine) purveyed blandly mainstream right-wing populism. Cartier, like Aron, had surprised his usual readers by advocating French "decolonization" (of sub-Saharan Africa) in a series of columns during August and September 1956.[36] At odds with the Sartrean critique of France and the West, Aron and Cartier based their support for abandoning Algeria on an economic conception of French national interest. As Cartier asked after traveling in French Sub-Saharan territories, "Black Africa for us is, like everything, a ledger. What is it worth? What does it cost? What does it offer? What hopes does it inspire? What sacrifices is it worth?" He eventually extended these interrogations to Algeria.[37]

[34] Simone de Beauvoir, *La force des choses* (Paris, 1986), 389–90; and Gisèle Hamini, *Djamila Boupacha* (Paris, 1972), 19, cited and translated in Kristin Ross, *Fast Cars, Clean Bodies* (Cambridge, Mass., 1995), 216; de Beauvoir, *La force des choses*, 362.

[35] For more on Aron's isolation on Algeria and the shifting position of Pierre Brisson, editor in chief of *Le Figaro*, see Aron, *50 ans de reflexion politique: Memoires* (Paris, 1983), 218; 355–91.

[36] Section Presse/Dir. des Renseignements Généraux, "La Presse politique hebdomadaire" (December 1961), 1, in CAC/AN 940560/01.

[37] On the congruency of the positions of Cartier and Aron, see Girardet, *L'idée coloniale en France*, 231.

The national liberalism of these proposals met with shock. The pro–French Algeria Right publicly disdained them as "doctrines of accountants." From the reformist Left Jean Daniel criticized Aron's "crossover from conservatism" to what the young writer termed "economic defeatism, which consists in calling for the abandonment of a territory as soon as the colonial pact no longer pans out and the colony is no longer a 'sweetheart deal.'" This attitude, Daniel argued, "is as grave in the Algerian case as the worst colonialism."[38] Skepticism toward continued French intervention overseas grounded in a cost-benefit analysis never rallied much support, even when accompanied by Aron's exegesis of the dangers for France of the contemporary world-historical situation. Before 1961 the political and cultural Right and Center in the Fourth Republic, which stretched from the far right to the vast majority of Gaullist militants, overwhelmingly supported the continuation of French Algeria. Further, even when acceptance of Algerian independence became widespread, Aron was never widely (nor even privately) cited. Instead, the element of Aron's argument that eventually was adopted in public utterances was that most aberrant in the context of his oeuvre: historical determinism.[39]

When Aron made his Algerian argument, what his critics most remarked in this proindependence stance was the use of History. As a polemicist and scholar, Aron became famous for his opposition to History. In the debates about historicist reasoning that consumed French critics such as Sartre, Alexandre Kojève, and Jean Hyppolite in the 1940s and '50s, Aron almost alone rejected Marxian theories of history. Instead, Aron replaced a rational dialectic, which he found in Marxism, with a "dialectic of the real." Theories that depended on History, he argued, were flawed genuflections to the "last idol of our faithless century."[40] The rigorous rejection of historical determinism that Aron had deployed polemically against PCF-aligned intellectuals inspired wide admiration for Aron among anti-Communists. When the philosopher relied on "a historical perspective" to insist that decolonization was inevitable—in Algeria, as in Africa, "what is happening," Aron advanced, "is part of a wave of history"—his erstwhile allies accused him of hypocrisy. The Gaullist intellectual and former governor general of Algeria Jacques Soustelle responded in 1957 that "M. Aron finds himself in perfect agreement with that which he denounced in *The Opium of the Intellectuals*" (1955). With irony and malice, Soustelle wrote that "now it is he who kneels in turn before the Moloch of historical fatalism." Gaullists such as Soustelle,

[38] Nicolas Baverez, *Raymond Aron: Un moraliste au temps des idéologies* (Paris, 1993), 320; Jean Daniel, "Des vacances algériennes," *L'Express* (1 June 1957). For details on private and public reactions to Aron from defenders of French Algeria, see LeSueur, *Uncivil War*, 141–45.

[39] Baverez, *Raymond Aron*, 358. On attitudes on the Right, see Girardet, *L'idée coloniale en France*, 263; see also René Rémond, ed., *Les droites en France* (Paris, 1983), and Richard Vinen, *Bourgeois Politics in France, 1945–1951* (Cambridge, 1995).

[40] See Sylvie Mesure, *Raymond Aron et la raison historique* (Paris, 1984), 18–21; Raymond Aron, "Superstition de l'histoire," in Raymond Aron, *Polémiques* (Paris, 1955), 167.

who fought for French "grandeur," and center-right politicians such as former prime minister Georges Bidault attacked Aron's move as denying the historical lessons and ideals of France and the republic.[41]

Recognizing Algerian Difference

Aron and Sartre, in responding to the Algerian War, proposed solutions premised in twin beliefs that would be shared widely at the war's close. We have seen how each deployed the "tide of History" or "decolonization." The two philosophers were also among the first to "recognize" publicly that inarguable differences between the French and Algerian peoples necessitated separate states. In the 1950s, belligerent attacks from the Left and the Right identified and denounced both theses in Aron's writings on Algeria. They identified his dismissal of the policy of "integrationism," begun in 1956, as exemplary of his antirepublicanism. Aron's attack on integration was clear: "Integration, whatever meaning we give to this word, is no longer practical." His reasoning took up the concerns about a rising tide of nonwhite peoples that Western diplomats and politicians also worried about: "The rate of demographic growth is too different on the two shores of the Mediterranean to allow these peoples, racially and religiously different, to be part of a single community."[42] It was thus unsurprising that Jacques Soustelle would so oppose him, for as governor general of Algeria he had trumpeted the policy of integration and, as a key player in de Gaulle's return to power, he helped effect the extension of full citizenship (including the vote) to all Algerians.

But Aron's rejection of integration also reflected his rejection of republican universalism. In discussing Algeria, Aron slipped from a position "*outside*" of republicanism, to reverse the frame in which the British historian Julian Jackson locates his early writings, to a position "*against*."[43] Integra-

---

[41] Jacques Soustelle, *Le drame algérien et la décadence française: Réponse à Raymond Aron* (Paris, 1957), 14; Baverez, *Raymond Aron*, 359. James LeSueur analyzes this exchange in *Uncivil War*. LeSueur evokes how, as he terms it, "some of Aron's conclusions had a troubling if not openly xenophobic quality" (137). For an extremely sympathetic portrayal of Aron's liberalism and critique of French intellectuals' rejection of this political philosophy, see Tony Judt, *Past Imperfect: French Intellectuals, 1944–1956* (Berkeley, 1992), chap. 12. For a wholly different reading of Aron's analyses of the Algerian situation from my own, see Tony Judt, *The Burden of Responsibility: Blum, Camus, Aron, and the French Twentieth Century* (Chicago, 1998).

[42] Aron, *La tragédie algérienne* (Paris, 1957), 25. For an analysis of how "integrationism" differed from previous French policies premised in either "assimilationism" or "associationism," see chapter 1. For the classic description of "assimilation" and "association," see Raymond F. Betts, *Assimilation and Association in French Colonial Theory, 1890–1914* (New York, 1961). For the most important recent analysis of their importance in French late imperialism, see Alice L. Conklin, *A Mission to Civilize: The Republican Idea of Empire in France and West Africa, 1895–1930* (Stanford, 1998).

[43] Julian Jackson suggests this reading of the political imaginary of many young elites of the 1930s. See "The Long Road to Vichy," *French History* 12, no. 2 (June 1998): 221.

tion, he argued, was one of the foundering French Republic's "'flailing cuts' without effects" because, as his biographer summarizes, "it no longer disposes of either the capacity for violence or of the universalist ideal which could still animate the Soviet Empire."[44] Convinced that French republicanism was ideologically exhausted, Aron proposed liberalism as an alternative. Certain that the Algerians were not like the French, he asserted that France should stop trying to make them French. Confident in his rejection of contemporary French pretensions to universalism, and thus of the necessary failure of assimilation, Aron argued that Algeria was not part of France. Algeria was a colony and therefore historically fated to experience decolonization. Almost no one in France took up such explanations with their wide-ranging implications. Only Aron's historical determinism was openly embraced in 1962.[45]

Sartre, too, rejected outright French pretensions that Algeria could ever be French. He embraced the FLN's claim that Algerians were a people separate from the French. Yet while accepting the boundaries of the Algerian people that the FLN outlined, he projected a very distinct definition of what made them different: only in relation to the French colonizer had the Algerian nation emerged. Against FLN invocations of Berbers, Arabs, Arabic, and Islam, Sartre presented an Algerian identity that had no organic existence based on ethnicity or religion outside of that historical encounter. Sartre conceived of the Algerian nation's recognition of its shared oppression and its struggle to free itself as historically inevitable. In this recognition he celebrated an existential choice that could potentially offer a model and an inspiration to their colonial masters as well as the rest of the world. For Sartre, the embrace by Algerian nationalists of Algerians' specificity allowed new insights into the tide of History; the Algerian Revolution was a historical event that offered novel possibilities to change the world for the better.

By the early 1960s, Sartre was at the hub of a small yet very visible constellation of intellectuals and militants. Unlike Aron, whom his habitual allies ostracized as a hypocrite, Sartre's announced philosophical project and his political engagement in favor of Algerian independence (a rapport he worked to make more evident in *The Critique of Dialectical Reason* [1960]) were congruent, to some extent explaining why there was growing public attention in late 1960 and 1961 to the "Sartrean critique."[46] The two vital moments were the trial of the so-called suitcase carriers, a trial accompanied by the "Manifesto for the Right to Resist the Algerian War," often referred to as the "Manifesto of the 121" (a one-two proindependence punch in September 1960), and the landmark publication of Fanon's *The Wretched of the*

[44] Baverez, *Raymond Aron*, 522. See Aron, *Espoir et peur du siècle: Essais non partisans* (Paris, 1957), 347.

[45] Baverez, *Raymond Aron*, 522.

[46] *La critique de la raison dialectique, précedé de question de méthode*, vol. 1, *Théorie des ensembles pratiques*; vol. 2, *L'intelligibilité de l'histoire* (1960).

Earth with a preface by Sartre (1961).[47] In the trial, the government sought to convict several important participants in a network of "European" French metropolitans—the "suitcase carriers"—who transported funds collected within the metropole for the FLN to contacts in Switzerland. Their discovery and capture led to the court case; this in turn inspired the (censored) publication of the "Manifesto." This media event provoked a divisive and defining public contest. A coterie of intellectuals supported the controversial defense strategy of the accused, *insoumission:* the right of French citizens to resist their government, even to assist its enemies, in defense of universal values.[48]

The trial, the Manifesto, Fanon's book, and Sartre's preface, each a direct response to the Algerian Revolution, together articulated an analytic description of decolonization as an international and deeply political process. Support for the FLN now was presented in relation to other "struggles" (e.g., Castro's Cuba, Mao's China) through a new concept: *tiers-mondisme* (Third Worldism). Sartre's preface to *The Wretched of the Earth* catalyzed tiers-mondisme: a Western rethinking of Marxism, in light of "decolonization," "nonalignment," and anti-imperial movements and writings, which placed the relationship between colonizer and colonized at the center of radical political theory and praxis. Tiers-mondisme looked to "the colonized" much as Marxism looked to "the working class." Metropolitan militants embraced Fanon's analytic strategy of moving from the Algerian situation to the universal struggle between colonized and colonizer. This inadvertently set the stage for decolonization's reinvention not as an analysis but as a cause that required submission—not further explanation or examination.[49]

Sartre and his comrades subsumed the "colonized" into a universal, if binarized, category in which colonialism shaped them along with the colonizers; Aron worked to exclude Algerians from any understandings of France. Aron, liberal defender of French national interests who assumed that Algerians and French were different, supported Algerian independence so that France could take back control of its destiny. He acquiesced to historical determinism, while presupposing ethnic difference in order to restore freedom of action to the French. Independence for Algerians was incidental. The Sartreans, on the contrary, imagined their support for the struggle of Algerian nationalists as potentially provoking a dialectical exit from the oppressive binary of colonizer-colonized. Sartre argued in his preface to Fanon's book that "it is enough that [the victims of European colonialism] show us what we have done to them for us to understand what we have done to ourselves." Algerian liberation, the argument went, was a necessary condition

---

[47] See Nourredine Lamouchi, *Jean-Paul Sartre et le tiers monde: Rhétorique d'un discours anti-colonialiste* (Paris, 1996).

[48] On this moment, see Pierre Vidal-Naquet, "Une fidelité têtue," *Vingtième siècle* 12 (April–June 1986): 16.

[49] Sirinelli, *Deux intellectuels,* 141.

for the very possibility of French enlightenment; an opening, perhaps, to liberation from what Sartre and Fanon saw as the current hegemony of Manichean thinking—in which terms such as *native, colonizer, colonized, white,* or *black* confined people to polarized identities—and to possibilities for more complex, and more fully human, understandings and relationships.[50]

The Algerian Revolution did, as Sartre and others had hoped, provoke major changes in French understandings of themselves. Very soon after 1 November 1954, the Algerian Revolution became an international symbol of resistance to imperialism in its dominant "bourgeois" Western variant. From delegates to the 1955 Bandung Conference of African and Asian States to broadcasts from Nasser's Egypt of "The Voice of the Arabs," other peoples and leaders who continued to struggle against European colonialism, or who lived in states that had decolonized, carefully followed developments in what the French proclaimed were the French departments of Algeria.[51] Despite the argument from Paris that this was a domestic problem, the FLN succeeded in internationalizing the conflict, as it was taken up by the United Nations and became a tense issue in relations between France and its most important ally, the United States. In addition, international condemnation of French rule in Algeria and French efforts to end the revolution brought to the fore the issue of colonial violence, historical and ongoing.[52] The international context that the Algerian Revolution helped create forced the French to change. By the early 1960s, a novel proindependence consensus in France replaced the isolation of the early proponents of Algerian secession, a shift strikingly visible in the two political forces that dominated political debate and the popular vote in the early years of the Fifth Republic: first, Charles de Gaulle and his coterie; second, the PCF.

De Gaulle and the Abandonment of French Algeria

It was from Algiers that General Charles de Gaulle retook the heights of the French state in May 1958. This was a markedly different situation from May 1943, when the leader of Free France and the embodiment of republican legitimacy arrived in the city en route to recapturing the metropole.[53] In 1958, cries of "Algérie française!" summoned him from retirement in Colombey-

[50] Jean-Paul Sartre, preface to Frantz Fanon, *Les damnés de la terre* (Paris, 1991), 43.

[51] See Malley, *Call from Algeria* and Jean-Charles Jauffret, "Algérie 1945–1954: les exemples de la décolonisation vues par les services de renseignments français," in *Décolonisations européenes. Actes du colloque international "décolonisations comparées"* (Aix en Provence, 1995), 41–53.

[52] On the revolution's impact, see Mohamed Touili, ed., *Le retentissement de la révolution algérienne* (Algiers, 1985); on diplomacy, see Irwin Wall, *France, the United States, and the Algerian War* (Berkeley, 2001) and Connelly, *Diplomatic Revolution.*

[53] On de Gaulle's arrival in Algiers on 30 May 1943, see Eric Roussel, *Charles de Gaulle* (Paris, 2002), 364.

les-deux-Églises to stand before a crowd of Algerians mobilized to fight off any compromise of French sovereignty in their homeland. The "May Days" began on 13 May 1958, when a public march in memory of three French soldiers—executed by FLN troops on Tunisian territory in response to the French government's execution of seven prisoners accused of FLN activities—degenerated into a riot, which led to the sacking of the seat of the highest civilian authority, the General Delegation. The same day, in Algeria, Gen. Jacques Massu announced the formation of the Committee of Public Safety, composed of officers and civilians. News reports suggested that French armed forces units based in Corsica planned to land in continental France, aiming to guarantee the goals announced in Algiers: to keep Algeria French. On 15 May, Gen. Raoul Salan, head of French armed forces in Algeria and a member of the Committee of Public Safety, concluded his address to the massive crowd of "Europeans" and "Muslims" gathered in the Forum of Algiers with the words "Long live France! Long live French Algeria! . . . Long live de Gaulle!" Two weeks later, President René-Jules-Gustave Coty named de Gaulle prime minister.

De Gaulle assumed power amid scenes of a popular uprising and in a context heavy with the possibility of an armed forces putsch. The general insisted that his moves were legal. Many others, however, posed trenchant questions, or expressed their outrage; François Mitterrand famously characterized those moves as a "coup d'état." For in agreeing to lend his personal legitimacy to the French Republic, de Gaulle demanded and received guarantees from leading notables of the Fourth Republic that the constitution would be rewritten and the division of powers rearranged, both according to his specifications. On 28 September 1958, a resounding popular vote in favor of this constitution—by French voters on both sides of the Mediterranean, "Europeans" and "Muslims," Algerians and metropolitans—led to the establishment of the Fifth Republic.

On 8 January 1959, de Gaulle became the first president of the Fifth Republic. He ended his acceptance speech with the exhortation: "Long live the Community! Long live the Republic! Long live France!" The Community had replaced the French Union, its ambitions greatly reduced. Michel Debré, a de Gaulle loyalist and the former editor of a virulently pro–French Algeria periodical who had overseen the writing of de Gaulle's constitution, became the new republic's first prime minister.

For Charles de Gaulle, May 1958 was an opportunity to assume and to rehabilitate the power of government and the unique *grandeur*—or greatness in reputation, ambition, and potential—of the French state, which he and others believed the leaders and institutions of the Fourth (not to mention the Third) Republic had lost. He had fully prepared this effort during the years that followed popular rejection of, first, his proposed constitution in 1946, and then, second, his political movement, the Rally of the French People (RPF). He originally had achieved international legitimacy when, speaking from London on 18 June 1940, he called on all French people to reject capitulation to the Germans and to resist. Crowds and politicians greeted him as the nation's savior when he returned to Paris in 1944 at the head of the Free French forces he had organized. In the years that followed, he had believed that his history-making role—in France he is still known as "the Man of 18 June"—would guarantee the success of his political vision. He was wrong. In 1953 repeated electoral rebuffs led de Gaulle to retreat from active involvement in politics, his "desert crossing."[54]

The events of May 1958 may have been the perfect pretext to implement his "predestined" return, yet inarguably de Gaulle's assumption of power occurred in a moment that ardent defenders of French Algeria produced. Four years later, despite this debt, Charles de Gaulle would announce that the Fifth Republic was now ready to grant Algeria independence. His decision, he explained, was a recognition of the "tide of History," the worldwide phenomenon of decolonization. For de Gaulle, a man of many paradoxes, a reliance on historical determinism allowed him to further his reputation as a maker of history.

De Gaulle rarely explained publicly his understanding of the rapport between Algeria and France, or of how to resolve the Algerian crisis. One major exception was his September 1959 announcement in support of Algerian "self-determination." He expounded on his position with three speeches in the lead-up to the 8 January 1961 referendum, in which a large majority (75.26% voted "Yes") supported offering Algerians several options, including self-government.[55] From 5 September 1961, when de Gaulle announced that his negotiators with the FLN would no longer insist on maintaining French sovereignty over the Sahara, the president explained his decisions about Algeria's future in terms of the "inevitability" of independence, as part of the "process of decolonization." At no point after September 1961 did de Gaulle respond, except with disdain, to the proposals and pleadings of those who continued to pretend that Algeria should remain French. This allowed de Gaulle to avoid having to explain which "historical conditions" made Algerian independence necessary, and which made it possible to exclude certain groups of (legally) French people from the nation.[56]

De Gaulle simply did not believe the Algerian people were French. As he exclaimed to Gen. Marie-Paul Allard in 1959, "You cannot possibly consider that one day an Arab, a Muslim, could be the equal of a Frenchman?"[57]

---

[54] On this period, see Jean Charlot, *Le gaullisme d'opposition, 1946–1958* (Paris, 1983); Serge Berstein, *Histoire du gaullisme* (Paris, 2001); Henri Rousso, *The Vichy Syndrome: History and Memory in France since 1944*, trans. Arthur Goldhammer (Cambridge, Mass., 1991).

[55] See his televised speech on 4 November 1960, his announcement of the referendum on 20 December 1960, and his televised remarks on 31 December 1960 and 6 January 1961.

[56] See Richard Vinen's analysis of the incentives that push French historians to privilege biographical interpretations of contemporary French history, in Vinen (1995), 15.

[57] Cited in Maurice Faivre, "Les Français musulmans dans la guerre d'Algérie: 1—de l'engagement à la mobilisation," *Guerres Mondiales et conflits contemporains* 177 (January 1995):

Between 1958 and 1962, the Fifth Republic's policy of integrationism pursued the most coherent and aggressive effort in French history to make Algerian "Muslims" equal to other Frenchmen. Yet de Gaulle himself appears
never to have accepted the claims of integration, and he came to reject the
traditional republican policy of assimilation. His minister of information,
Alain Peyrefitte, recorded the general's October 1959 dinnertime dissertation
on the history of the Third Republic:

> We have premised our colonization, since the beginning, on the principle of as-
> similation. We pretended to turn negroes [nègres] into good Frenchmen. We
> had them recite: 'The Gauls were our ancestors' [Nos ancêtres les Gaulois]. . . .
> [That] was not very bright. That is why our decolonization is so much more
> difficult than that of the English. They always admitted that there were differ-
> ences between races and cultures.

Observing his speech, Alain Peyrefitte "noted that his rejection of [the policy of] 'integration' was hardening."[58]
There is, as a number of historians note, ample evidence of de Gaulle's antiracism. Pierre Portier argues that "de Gaulle does not refuse difference,"
highlighting the important break the young officer had made from the traditional Catholicism and militarism of his upbringing: "Nothing is more foreign to him than the discourse of exclusion proffered by [Charles] Maurras
[leader of Action Française] and his henchmen." During World War II,
speaking from his provisional capital of Algiers, de Gaulle proclaimed, in
Porter's words, that "France is rich with her diverse spiritualities and ethnic
cultures: her 'métissage' [racial blending] was fortunate."[59] De Gaulle's conception of France was somewhat cosmopolitan. It was in this acceptance of
visible and marked difference that he differed strikingly from the Charles
Maurras/Maurice Barrès (fin-de-siècle thinker known for his rejection of the
déracinés, or rootless cosmopolitans) brand of xenophobic nationalism. As
he stated to Peyrefitte, "It is all very well that there are yellow French, black
French, brown French. They demonstrate that France is open to all races and
that she has a universal mission." In his view, however, the sine qua non of
this vision was that "they stay a small minority. If not, France will no longer
be France. We are, in any case, above all a European people, racially white,
culturally Greek and Latin, and religiously Christian." It must be emphasized, as well, that the end of the Algerian War confronted him and his coun-

244; Faivre extends this remark in Les combattants musulmans de la guerre d'Algérie: Des soldats sacrifiés (Paris, 1995), 107 n. 24; cf. Jean Lacouture, De Gaulle, vol. 3 (Paris, 1986), 49,
142, 149.
    [58] Alain Peyrefitte, C'était de Gaulle, vol. 1, La France redevient la France (Paris, 1994), 54,
56.
    [59] Pierre Portier, "Le général de Gaulle et le catholicisme: Pour une autre interprétation de
la pensée gaullienne," Revue historique 602 (April–June 1997), 535; cf. "Alger 30 octobre
1943," in Discours et Messages, vol. 1 (1970), 334.

try not with random "yellows," "blacks," or "browns," but rather with Algerian "Muslims," a group he perceived as wholly different from the French. "The Muslims, have you gone to see them?" he asked his minister of information. "Have you watched them, with their turbans and their jellabas [robes]?" In deciding the future of these French citizens, he rejected the policy of integration, the early Fifth Republic's efforts to overcome the limits of assimilation, stating that "those who push for integration are pea-brained, despite their grand education . . . [Algerian] Muslims could not be French. Try and combine oil and vinegar. Shake the bottle. After a minute, they separate again. Arabs are Arabs, French are French." He paused in his demonstration, Peyrefitte tells us, to pursue a line of argumentation drawn more from demography (or virology), asking: "Do you think the French body politic [*corps français*] can absorb ten million Muslims, who tomorrow will be twenty million and after that forty?" De Gaulle did not, as his actions at the end of the war make clear.[60]

Few critics have been able to pursue what the French sociologist Dominique Colas calls the paradoxical embrace by de Gaulle of both republicanism and an ethnic vision of the nation: "Let us insist on the ethnic dimension in de Gaulle's conception of the nation, for it seems as far as can be from republican ideology, thoroughly opposed to the ideals established in 1789 and completed in 1946, and as inscribed in the preamble to the Constitution of 1958." De Gaulle, Colas suggests, could offer both "an affirmation of races at the same time as a rejection of racism." Although Colas does not refer to Algeria, I would suggest that de Gaulle's reliance on the "tide of History" allowed him to avoid explaining—or, in Algeria, having to act on—this paradoxical understanding.[61]

For de Gaulle, Algeria could be abandoned to the tide of History because Algeria and Algerians were not and had never been French. De Gaulle, in extricating France from its seemingly intractable overseas troubles, corrected what he viewed as the mistaken assimilationist vision, which had always predominated in explanations of France's imperial project. At the moment he agreed to abandon the French Empire, he replaced it with one congruent with that of the British Empire. Unlike with British "indirect rule," however, French assimilationism was a central tenet of domestic policies as well. When de Gaulle refocused his (and French) ambitions from the empire to the Republic, he pretended that this concurrent ideological shift would have no effect on France or its democracy.[62]

---

[60] All citations in this paragraph are from Peyrefitte, *C'était de Gaulle*, vol. 1, *La France redevient la France* (1994), 52.

[61] See Dominique Colas, "Portrait de la République selon Charles de Gaulle," in *De Gaulle et son siècle*, vol. 1, *Dans la mémoire des hommes et des peuples* (Paris, 1991), 196–97. On de Gaulle's attachment to an ethnic vision of the French nation, see also Serge Berstein, *Histoire du Gaullisme* (Paris, 2001), 20.

[62] For the long battle in France over assimilation cf. Eric T. Jennings, "Monuments to French-

Stalinist Somersaults or Dialectical Dead End?

Almost all of the political Left and most of the Right supported de Gaulle's moves toward granting Algeria independence. Their reasons varied widely, yet all shared two fundamental assumptions: historical inevitability and inassimilable difference.[63] The evolution of the French Communist Party from pro–French Algeria to supporter of Algerian independence was at once the most blatant and most subtle of these partisan shifts. On the one hand, leftist critics from within and without constantly criticized and commented on the party's Algerian policy, while revisions were printed in PCF publications. On the other hand, "minor" changes followed one another, building on previous reorientations to avoid the appearance of an about-face. All the while, party leaders insisted on the line's coherency and continuity.[64]

The Algerian War provoked fissures between left French activists and the party.[65] Those engaged in leftist politics during the war—whether against torture or imperialism, or for civil disobedience (*insoumission*) or Algerian independence—were disturbed, even disgusted, by what seemed the party's hesitant positions toward Algeria. The PCF's support for Algerian independence was tardy. Its inability once again to offer an incisive response to the political exigencies emanating from French leftists aggravated an already simmering revulsion over the party's pro-Moscow orientation.[66] Indeed, the PCF's unequivocal support for the FLN's liberation struggle coincided with the USSR's 1960 recognition of the Tunis-based Gouvernement Provisoire de la République Algérienne (GPRA), after six years of combat.[67] Yet, as Raoul Girardet compellingly demonstrates, the PCF's reversal can only be understood in conjunction with the shift among all the major French political "families"—Christians, Gaullists, socialists, syndicalists—from being pro–French Algeria to supporting Algerian independence. However preponderant the role of Moscow in party decisions in general, it was French developments that produced this Communist position. The decision maker who provoked the party to articulate its struggling evolution was the French pres-

---

ness? The Memory of the Great War and the Politics of Guadeloupe's Identity, 1914–1945," *French Historical Studies* 21, no. 4 (Fall 1998): 561–92; Alice Conklin, "Democracy Revisited: Civilization through Association in French West Africa, 1914–1930," *Cahiers d'études africaine* 145 (1997): 59–84. On the uses of direct rule and indirect rule in, respectively, French and British discussions, see Véronique Dimier, *Le discours idéologique de la méthode coloniale chez les Français et les Britaniques de l'entre-deux guerres à la décolonisation (1920–1960)* (Talence, 1998).

[63] Important works analyzing the shift in French attitudes include Sorum, *Decolonization and French Intellectuals* , Girardet *L'idée coloniale en France,* and LeSueur, *Uncivil War.*

[64] Unlike most other French parties, the PCF's claim to act in accordance with the dialectic (and thus scientific truth) provide easy evidence for its zigzagging political positions.

[65] See, e.g., Hervé Hamon and Patrice Rotman, *Generation* (Paris, 1987).

[66] On how the PCF directly shaped Soviet policy toward Algeria, see Yahia Zoubir, "The United States, the Soviet Union, and Decolonization of the Maghreb, 1945–62," *Middle Eastern Studies* 31 (1995): 58–84; 59–60.

[67] Emmanuel Sivan, *Communisme et nationalisme en Algérie, 1920–1962* (Paris, 1976).

ident, not the Soviet secretary-general. If anything, as Matthew Connelly argues, it was choices made in Washington that provided the context in which all French parties, including the PCF, acted. The Communists' particularity among French parties was their effort to offer an explanation for their flip-flop: the other groups, following de Gaulle, remained silent.[68]

The PCF's slowly developing position on Algeria's political status is most fully explained by the PCF's doctrinal exegeses of Algeria, its people, and their relationship to the French nation. In these explanations, the role of republican understandings and examples from French history were crucial. Their very French republicanism—not "foreign" Bolshevism—was what made the process so difficult.[69] In February 1939, speaking in Algiers, Communist leader Maurice Thorez enunciated a theory of an Algerian "nation in formation": nationhood, argued the French Communist, was a historical achievement, not a given. This formulation, while recognizing local specificity, or "Algerian-ness," buttressed the party's contemporaneous decision to no longer support immediate French withdrawal from the Algerian departments. The PCF instead would support "liberty" for Algeria, a call renewed on 8 November 1954 just after the FLN's first actions. "Liberation" did not equal independence.[70] The PCF's conception of the French nation explained why Algerian "liberation" could best develop in the French Republic. Between the Algerian War's opening shots and 1957, the PCF's call for liberty not only impeded it from supporting independence but also prevented it from evaluating the FLN in a positive way. The party saw the FLN's advancement of Algerian nationalism as wrong-headedly defending a national identity that did not (yet) exist as well as being dangerously linked to Islam. The PCF, following Lenin's condemnation of "blind terror," also refused to support the methods adopted by the FLN.[71]

Early 1957 saw a sea change in the party's approach, which Thorez sought to present as a carefully honed theoretical evolution. Arguing that his theory of "Algerian-ness" had proved prescient, the Communist leader asserted that, as a result of their revolution, an Algerian nation now existed (*le fait national algérien*). For Thorez, in February 1957, this "nation" was composed of "Algerians of European origins: French, Spanish, Italians, Greeks . . . who, over the course of time, have been added on to Berbers, Kabyles, and Jews installed for centuries." The emergence of the Algerian nation, Thorez insisted, "rests on the fusion of elements from diverse origins." This

---

[68] Connelly, *Diplomatic Revolution*.

[69] For a discussion of the widespread silence of most parties and intellectuals on the subject of Algerian independence at the war's close, see chapter 3.

[70] Danièle Joly, *The French Communist Party and the Algerian War* (London, 1991), 70.

[71] On the Communists' refusal of "blind terror," see Sivan, *Communisme et nationalisme en Algérie*, 243. French historian Sylvain Boulouque argues that a similar suspicion of blind terror shaped the reticent response of most French anarchist organizations to the FLN's struggle. See "Les anarchistes et les soulèvements coloniaux," *Homme et la société* 123–124 (1997): 105–17.

position did not reflect the "Arabo-Muslim" thesis proposed by Algerian nationalists.[72]

The PCF's refusal to understand the Algerian nation in ethnic or religious terms resonated with the party's appropriation of republicanism. Several historians have detailed the PCF's embrace of the regalia and history of French republicanism as part of the Popular Front, an adaptation that accompanied its emergence as a potent political force in the 1930s. After World War II (and the dissolution of the Comintern in 1943), the party relied on its nationalist and republican credentials, newly enhanced by its preponderant role in the Resistance, to consolidate an impressive position in French politics—it had more militants and received more votes than any other party in the Fourth Republic.[73] A number of developments in 1958 reinforced this attachment to republicanism. In their response to de Gaulle's claims to embody a certain idea of the nation, the PCF (along with other French parties) sought, as historian Pierre Nora remarks, "to incarnate France, true France."[74] Faced with the challenge of Algerian nationalism, the PCF was slow to drop its republican credentials and its self-proclaimed descent from the Revolution of 1789, the sans-culottes, 1848, the Commune, or its "70,000 martyrs" of the Resistance. Why should they support a nationalist rebellion that was neither Marxist-Leninist nor explicitly pro-Soviet, and one that rejected a series of republican principles the party had made its own? The PCF's enthusiastic (if for many hypocritical) assumption of a republican heritage clearly shaped the party's policies and doctrines about Algeria.

When in 1958 the PCF recognized the FLN "as the sole representative body of the Algerian people," the party's definition of "people"—territorially based, formed, as Thorez had outlined, by a shared and continuing historical development—remained republican. For the PCF, the concept "people," like "the nation," was consonant with republicanism.[75] The PCF continued to reject the understanding of the nation, presented in ethnic or religious terms, that the FLN proposed. The Algerian Communist Party (PCA), controlled by the PCF until the mid-1950s, broke with its metropolitan "big brother" on this point. The PCA posited that "the nation is made up of Algerian autochthons. It does not include the Europeans of Algeria."[76]

As the conflict continued, violently in Algeria, increasingly contested in

---

[72] Sivan, *Communisme et nationalisme en Algérie*, 245–57.

[73] On pre-1930s conflicts between French Marxists and republicanism, see Robert Stuart, "Marxism and Anticlericalism: The Parti Ouvrier Français and the War against Religion, 1882–1905," *Journal of Religious History* 22, no. 3 (October 1998): 287–303, and *Marxism at Work: Ideology, Class, and French Socialism during the Third Republic* (Cambridge, 1992). On the PCF's close, if incidental, engagement in the integration of "ethnically" distinct groups into the French nation, see Gérard Noiriel, *Longwy: Immigrés et prolétaires, 1880–1980* (Paris, 1984).

[74] Pierre Nora, "L'historien devant de Gaulle," in *De Gaulle et son siècle*, vol. 1, *Dans la mémoire des hommes et des peuples* (Paris, 1991), 177.

[75] Laurent Casanova, *Humanité* (22 January 1958).

[76] Sivan, *Communisme et nationalisme en Algérie*, 250; *Réalités algériens et marxisme* 2, 3–35; *Cahiers du communisme*, supplement (August 1958).

the metropole by the budding new and radical Lefts, the PCF again redefined its terms. By 1960, the party began to synthesize the terminology of Algerian nationalists and Communists. The historian Emmanuel Sivan shows how this change appeared in the party publication *Réalités de la nation algérienne:* whereas in the 1957 edition "Europeans" and "Muslims" are equally Algerian, in the 1961 revision Algerian national culture "is presented as 'Arabo-Muslim,' with the Europeans as a 'minority' headed toward fusion."[77] Unlike those on the French Left and elsewhere in the world who wholeheartedly supported nationalist theses about Algerian identity, the PCF continued to maintain that the definition of the "Algerian people" need not be determined by blood ties to pre-1830 North Africa. In Algeria, apparently, assimilation was still possible.

This was, at the war's close, no longer the case in the French Republic. The party now excluded Algeria, the territory and its people, from its historical vision of France and the Republic. What is more remarkable was the PCF's bracketing, in regard to Algeria, of its own voluntarist vision, which saw in French history a privileged march toward socialism. For the PCF, unlike the tiers-mondistes, the French Republic (even the Fifth) still remained at the forefront of history and the march toward socialism: French national interests remained congruent with those of the French proletariat. Yet "Algerians," even those working in France, no longer belonged to either. The PCF, like Charles de Gaulle, did not articulate publicly what it was that made "Algerians" different, not French. In chapter 3 I analyze how understandings of decolonization as a "tide of History" uncoupled from any clear explanation of why Algerians were different shaped the ways that France sought to end the war.

[77] Sivan, *Communisme et nationalisme en Algérie,* 257; Marcel Egretaud, *Réalités de la nation algérienne* (1957), 159–60; (1961), 54.

Chapter 3

The "Tide of History" versus the Laws of the Republic

In late 1961 and 1962, to justify their acceptance of Algerian independence, French leaders invoked the mantra "le courant de l'Histoire" ("the tide of History") without further elaboration. "History" was no longer to be debated; its demands needed to be applied and Algeria "decolonized." A large majority of French voices, the disparate figures and factions that had come to take for granted the inevitability of an "Algerian Algeria," shared a strikingly similar reliance on a form of historical reasoning to respond to the events of the war's close.[1] De Gaulle's "certain vision of France" and various Marxist dialectics about decolonization and struggle all depended on the supposed exigencies of historical development to prescribe French actions vis-à-vis Algeria. Each claimed to recognize in the tide of History—some resignedly, others with revolutionary or reforming fervor—proof that Algeria and France were not, could not be, and had never been one. The "tide of History," was the phrase politicians like Michel Debré or Guy Mollet, journalists like Philippe Hernandez or Françoise Giroud, and intellectuals like André Malraux or Pierre Nora repeatedly intoned to refer to "decolonization." The "tide of History" was not summed up in a single key speech or text; nor did it become the subject of any extended public explanation. There was nothing like British prime minister Harold Macmillan's famous "Winds of Change" speech, which he delivered in February 1960 before the parliament of the Union of South Africa. In that programmatic address, he an-

---

[1] I term the "war's close" a period roughly situated between late 1961 (see chapter 5) when, cautiously, preparations for the effects on France of Algeria's potentially imminent independence began to be publicly debated, and early 1963, when the final extraordinary executive decrees claiming to regulate the unexpected exodus of hundreds of thousands of people from Algeria to metropolitan France were implemented.

nounced and laid out rationales for the end of Britain's support for white minority rule of territories in its Commonwealth and for the decolonization of all colonized territories. (In more informal discussions, he referred to Algeria as the model for what would happen in British Central Africa if independence was delayed.) The "tide of History" mantra that French public figures recited made Algerian independence inevitable. They offered no further details. Those metropolitans who had early supported independence—Raymond Aron and Raymond Cartier, on the Right; the *Temps modernes* group, on the Left—had joined their historicism with an explanation of why Algerians were not French; the majority that now accepted the inevitability of independence did no such thing. This approach left many questions unanswered.[2]

Against these understandings, the minority who still supported a French Algeria looked to the law, to the juridical codes and the legal tradition of the French Republic. Through legal arguments, they advanced their interpretation of how France should respond to Algerian nationalist demands. The laws of the Republic, they insisted, formed by French history in reference to universal principles, defined who was French and what land was France, as well as outlining what French governments could and could not do. They argued that rejecting Algerian independence was vital to the very existence of France and the Republic. This was the only path of action, they contended, that hewed to the principles of liberty, equality, and fraternity, and the Rights of Man.

The ideological confrontation at the war's close, then, can be understood best not in commentators' usual terms, of "republican" versus antirepublican, far right, or "fascist." Rather, the primary clash was between those who relied on historical determinism and others who looked to republican legalism. In highlighting this confrontation, I do not seek to deny the key influence that the members, organizations, and even the ideas of the French Far Right exercised within groups that supported French Algeria. Nor do I wish to blur the genealogical ties between the post-1962 French Far Right and the defense of French Algeria that recent scholarship has begun to unravel. Attending to law and history, however, reveals the importance of this ideological struggle for France, as well as for what it meant to be French.

To Fight Fascism

In early 1962, few French people could imagine how the Algerian conflict would end. Almost everyone came to agree, however, that "History" was on

---

[2] On the "Winds of Change" speech, see Frank Myers, "Harold Macmillan's 'Winds of Change' Speech: A Case Study in the Rhetoric of Policy Change," *Rhetoric & Public Affairs* 3, no. 4 (2000): 555–75; on Macmillan and Algeria, see Wm. Roger Louis, "Introduction," in *The Oxford History of the British Empire*, vol. 4, *The Twentieth Century*, ed. Judith M. Brown and Wm. Roger Louis, (Oxford, 1999), 1–46, 29.

the march. All the better, as most French people had other things to do. In the photo-weekly *Paris-Match*, the year's first editorial, "Snow and Fascism," sought in an insouciant tone to speak for the sentiments of the French everyman. It told of a nation "under violent siege and surrounded by contradictory propaganda." Yet, with a knowing wink to the widespread feeling that it was time for France to move on, the author continued, "between Christmas and these first days of January, 900,000 Parisians put on hold their rendez-vous with History and rushed off to the slopes!" Confident that things would turn out as they should, the vacationers remained—as they were right to do, the editorial suggested—"deaf to the shouts of prophets accusing them of political desertion and threatening them with fascist enslavement." Algerian independence would come, that was certain. Until then, the French would have to deal with those who argued otherwise: from the far left, imploring "prophets," who thought the battle not yet won, and, on the other side, spreading "hopelessness and hate," the article warned, those who fought to keep their struggle from being lost: the "fascists."[3]

In the final months of 1961, French politicians hesitantly had begun to prepare for the aftermath of Algerian independence. They did so in the privacy of parliamentary corridors, however, neither seeking nor receiving much echo in the public sphere. The minimal coverage the mainstream press now accorded Algeria was occupied by a fierce debate over the merits of splitting Algeria into ministates, one "francophile," one "nationalist," with a third for the Sahara;[4] some discussions took place about whether the 10 November 1961 vote of eighty deputies for the so-called Salan amendment could be considered treasonous.[5] In the low-circulation journals that were their mouthpieces, the sparse forces of pro-FLN leftists and human rights activists sought to spark national outrage at the brutal repression of Algerian "Muslims" that took place on 17 October 1961. Their efforts met with little success, although demonstrations held in Paris in late November and early December drew more people than anyone expected.[6] Algerian "Muslims"

---

[3] "Neige et Fascisme," *Paris-Match* 665 (6 January 1962), 13. The most evocative depiction of this metropolitan lassitude concerning events in Algeria is Chris Marker's documentary of life in Paris in May 1962, *Joli Mai* (1962).

[4] This was a proposal Minister of Information Alain Peyrefitte had put forth in June and continued to elaborate. See Alain Peyrefitte, *Faut-il partager l'Algerie* (Paris, 1961).

[5] A deputy proposed an amendment to the defense budget to reduce the length of military service for draftees to eighteen months while drafting "eight age cohorts" of eligible young men living in the Algerian departments. This amendment, as other deputies and the press immediately remarked, reproduced a proposition that the head of the OAS, Raoul Salan, had made in an 11 September 1961 letter addressed to all deputies and senators. It was rejected on a 383–80 vote.

[6] On that night, a protest called by the French Federation of the FLN against a "voluntary" (yet strictly enforced) curfew on Algerian "Muslims" in the Paris region was met with massive police violence. Reports claimed that some two hundred had died, while Paris Prefect of Police Maurice Papon eventually admitted to two deaths. Since the late 1990s, the events of 17 October 1961 have become a political issue and a question of memory, with several scholarly studies offering starkly different evaluations of police actions and the number of dead. See Joshua

and, less frequently, "Europeans" as well as French soldiers continued to die in what still was not officially the Algerian War. Yet in the metropole most people, rather than protest, simply waited for it all to end.

On 29 December 1961, President de Gaulle broke this silence in his New Year's address. He announced to those listening that the year ahead would see the end of French Algeria "one way or another"; 1962, he intoned, "will be the year the army will be regrouped in Europe." Pro–French Algerians greeted the speech with "extreme shock." Military Intelligence remarked on a sense of abandonment among Europeans, whose future de Gaulle mentioned not at all, and recorded the first public demonstration for "Algérie française" by "francophile Muslims" in many months.[7]

The quiescence de Gaulle shattered gave way to an intense period of widespread activity and argument in the metropole as well as in Algeria. Paradoxically, events on both sides of the Mediterranean soon would inspire new hope in those Algerians who opposed independence as well as in all people who had long supported it. These were the months when the "Algerian events" no longer appeared as a fight between the French government and the FLN, but between two visions of France.

In the metropole, the New Year saw an increase in OAS attacks on left-wing targets. During the evening of 5 January armed men assaulted the national headquarters of the French Communist Party, capping a string of strikes against the PCF. In previous months the OAS had expanded its use of terrorist tactics from civilian targets in Algeria to the metropole. In response to the early 1962 attacks (and at long last, in the view of those who for years had been organizing in support of Algerian independence), the forces of the French Left began to mobilize. In newspapers, on the airwaves, in meetings, and on the streets, they spoke and acted against the OAS, against "fascism," and for the Republic. The Gaullist government was unable or unwilling to engage this combat: this interpretation took on new force weeks later. On 8 February, near the Charonne métro station in Paris, police violence against anti-OAS demonstrators resulted in the death of eight Communist militants. The historian Jean-Pierre Chanteau presents the political engagement in the days that followed Charonne as "a veritable catharsis . . . when the Left washed away eight years of hesitations, division, and cowardice." Days later, hundreds of thousands—workers, students, militants, intellectuals—gathered to commemorate this martyrdom. Together, Communists, Socialists, "progressives," and democrats of all stripes, rediscovered the French Left's hallowed marching grounds, from the Place de la République to the Place de la Nation; final destination, the Mur des Fédérés, the mass grave and memo-

Cole, "Remembering the Battle of Paris: 17 October 1961 in French and Algerian Memory," *French Politics, Culture & Society* 21, no. 3 (Fall 2003): 21–50.

[7] "French Algeria." Colonel Cavard, chef d'Etat-major-2ème bureau, Corps d'Armée d'Alger, "Bulletin hebdomadaire de renseignement psychologique; n. 97/RT/CAA/2.SC (semaine de 3–9/1/62)" Secret (Algiers, 11 January 1962), in SHAT 1H/2549/2.

rial for thousands of 1871's murdered Communards. Meanwhile, the government discussed with growing concern, and writers on the Left with unabashed excitement, the potential formation of a new "Popular Front," like the alliance of Socialists and others on the political Left with the PCF that had existed and briefly governed France in the mid-1930s. In cabinet meetings and in the officers' mess, "men of order" nervously evoked the possibility of a civil conflict between the OAS and the Communists.[8]

Concurrently, the OAS-led struggle to keep Algeria French mobilized thousands in the streets of Algeria to mount strikes, shut down cities, loudly honk car horns, and bang pots in the quick catchphrase of their defiance, "Al-gé-rie, fran-çaise!" But mass mobilization, wrapped in the tricolor and singing the "Marseillaise," was not what publicly defined this movement in the metropole. They were terrorists, targeting innocents. What most French people understood about the last-ditch fight to keep Algeria French was a photo of four-year-old Delphine's blood-covered face, when she was blinded by an attack directed at the apartment of her neighbor, André Malraux, and Brigitte Bardot's angry denunciation of OAS efforts to blackmail her and others. It was the hundreds of "Muslims" killed, often without even the pretense that they were involved in the rebellion; between the first murder on 31 May 1961 until 20 April 1962, the OAS had killed over sixteen hundred people in Algeria.[9] The press reported on the new dangers French conscripts now faced, taunted, harassed, even shot at in the streets of Algiers and Oran, by the very pieds noirs whose homes and lives the French Army had protected at high human cost. Scandalized or enraged by the terrorism of the OAS, most metropolitan French agreed that "those people"—the OAS and their supporters—were dangerous and criminal.

The OAS's cruel and bloody exactions against people in both Algeria and the metropole, however, do not by themselves explain the refusal of the French political establishment and general public to respond to the claims that those associated with the so-called activists made for the defense of French Algeria. Quite simply, most French people in 1962 as well as most French political actors and commentators considered all of these acts—street protests as well as random violence—to be futile and blind: Algerian independence was inevitable. Perceived as lacking any logical explanation or attainable goal, actions taken to defend French Algeria were merely hateful and, since they bucked the tide of History, irrational. They could only increase the difficulties of pieds noirs in an independent Algeria. More men-

---

[8] Jean-Pierre Chanteau, "17 octobre 1961: Le deuil impossible," *Cahiers de l'Institut du temps présent* 2 (1995): 103–4. On the Mur des Fédérés and the French Left, see Danielle Tartakowsky, *Nous irons chanter sur vos tombes: Le Père Lachaise au XIXè et XXè siècles* (Paris, 1999). See Etat-major, poste de la Sécurité Militaire en Algérie; Dir. de la Sécurite Militaire/Ministère de l'Armée, "Fiche d'ambiance en milieux civils et militaires. Semaine du 9 au 15 février 1962" (SP 87.265, 17 February 1962), in SHAT 1H/1254/4.

[9] On the beginnings of the OAS, see Sylvie Thénault, *Histoire de la guerre d'indépendance algérienne*(Paris, 2005), 214–18.

The march in memory of eight Communist Party militants killed by the police during an anti-OAS demonstration, Paris, February 1962. Reprinted by permission of *L'Express*.

The threat of civil war? "Pieds noirs" in the streets of Algiers, September 1961. Reprinted by permission of *L'Express*.

acingly, their actions might threaten the Republic. This was the conception of both metropolitans marching against the OAS (even those on the far left who hoped to provoke the "next act" of a drama that opened with the French Revolution) and those in the government and the military (rather pleased with the existing order) whom "anti-fascist" activity unnerved.

"Fascism," in the pages of *Paris-Match* as well as PCF pamphlets, now described those who fought to keep Algeria French. First and most feared was the OAS, the underground, armed, and violent grouping formed in late spring 1961 that operated both in Algeria and in the metropole. Deserters from the French military had taken over the leadership of the OAS. Second came those who were objective allies of the activists: the deputies who made up the National Rally for the Unity of the Republic (RNUR) parliamentary group—primarily former Gaullists joined by others from the far right (the eighty deputies who had voted for the Salan amendment)—and the senators and lesser politicians who continued to defend French Algeria, despite de Gaulle's late 1959 call for self-determination. Finally, there were the supporters of fascism, the vast majority of the pieds noirs, the non-"Muslim" population of Algeria, as well as their metropolitan allies. These representations painted the pieds noirs as deeply racist and fundamentally irrational: ideologically incoherent, oblivious to reasoned discussion, at home only in the crowd, prone to loud, ultravirile displays—in short, "Mediterraneans."[10] Popular opinion as well as secret official assessments presumed that metropolitans who still defended French Algeria were organized by or active in royalist, Vichyite, pro-fascist, or traditionalist movements. All were thought ripe for the worst temptations of the "Far Right," for they supported a cause that was perceived as rejecting both progress and rationality. This schema still dominates critical commentary of the period.

In 1962, against what they conceived of as the most recent avatars of the Republic's blood foe, the French Left and the French government proved more than capable of action. Within six months the OAS in Algeria was crushed, the defenders of French Algeria in the metropole were ostracized from political life, and, as de Gaulle had foretold, Algeria was independent and the French Army was in Europe. These achievements are the measure of their success. France had not missed, despite the best (or worst) efforts of a small minority, its "rendez-vous with History."

Alongside this history of progress, it is equally important to understand the confrontation that did not take place, a conflict manqué between ideas, not flesh and bullets or mass demonstrations and Semtex explosives. By the early 1960s a late-blooming metropolitan consensus embraced an argument that ever since has functioned as a fact: Algeria was not France but a colony, and thus it deserved and would obtain independence.[11] Gaullists and most

---

[10] See Pierre Nora, *Les Français d'Algérie* (Paris, 1961), discussed in chapter 6.

[11] See Charles-Robert Ageron, "La guerre d'Algérie et les Français: Avis de recherche," *Vingtième siècle* (July–September 1989): 123.

on the left, political parties and figures who long had defended the justice and inviolability of French Algeria, all embraced historical determinism. With this interpretation, they at once could explain their support for Algerian independence and refuse to respond to the substantive arguments proffered by those who resisted. Against historical inevitability, a minority of people in France, many of them living in the fifteen departments of Algeria and the Sahara, continued to maintain that Algeria in 1962 was in fact, and should remain, French. For them, the early months of the year were full of drama and would end in disaster. As one summons to keep up the resistance exclaimed at the mid-June 1962 height of departures from Algeria: "This movement of History is the greatest catastrophe of all times."[12] Their rejection of Algerian independence was not articulated, however, as a rejection of progress: despite the claims of their critics, only rarely did anyone put forward merely a sentimental defense of "Algérie de Papa" (the Algeria of yore).

The OAS and Marianne

A study of the propaganda, available internal OAS documents, pro–French Algeria publications and recorded arguments in the final months of the Algerian War suggests that the primary reference for this congeries of activists, terrorists, thinkers, ordinary people, and politicians was "the Republic," as they invoked its ideals, principles, methods, and myths. Republican values—and not themes and analyses associated with the French Far Right—shaped and exemplified this political current. The French Algeria camp claimed to be defending republican principles (the territorial inviolability of the Republic, the irrevocability of citizenship), republican ideals (the policy of assimilation, secularism), and republican methods (respect for the constitution and the laws).

Rejecting historical inevitability, at the war's close defenders of French Algeria hurled accusations of illegality, anticonstitutionality, and a fundamental disrespect for the law at those who supported French disengagement from North Africa. Whether in parliamentary debates or in publications ranging from anonymous tracts to weighty tomes, from men exiled in Spain or underground in the Ouarsenis, a constant and consistent series of speeches, legal briefs, and letters to magistrates—both pleading and threatening—explained that Algeria was legally France and that French law and legal tradition offered no possibility of changing this reality.[13] From this it followed

---

[12] "Les associations de rapatriés en France (1ère partie)," *Bulletin de documentation de la direction des Renseignements Généraux* 78 (September 1962), 5, in AN F/7/15581.

[13] See, for example, the letters from Les détenus politiques de la Prison de la Santé . . . /Reseau Diamant, "Monsieur le Juge" (1962), 2, in AN 78aj32; Un groupe de professeurs du Département d'Alger, "Lettre aux enseignants de la Métropole" (Algiers, 13 March 1962), in SHAT 1H/1735/1.

that the referendums were illegal, the Evian Accords were illegal, the exclusive control claimed by the executive branch was illegal: these so-called fascists deployed the law and the constitution of the Republic to defend their positions.

Born and shaped by the struggles of French history, the Republic, they insisted, was the legally ordered expression of the will of the nation. Within this narrative, they argued that true progress toward equality was possible. One anonymous booklet presented "M. Dupont," a French everyman, exclaiming, "The time for colonies has passed, there is nothing we can do about it, it's the evolution of History," and the other speaker, "the Activist," responding: "It is all a question of will. Behind the events of the last fifteen years, there are no obscure forces, or historical determinism, as Marxist intellectuals call it, rather there is intelligence, astuteness, and resolve."[14] This pro-OAS script insisted that the French Republic's laws and history opened political possibilities to respond to the challenge of decolonization. Another pro-OAS tract presented the French Algeria cause as responsive to present-day events. It proposed that "*Decolonization* can be achieved in its highest form" not through independence but "by the *adoption* of Algerians into the family of France." Against prevailing metropolitan and world opinion, the handbill's author asserted that "the Muslims wish it" and "the French of Algeria are not opposed," a historically recent agreement that emerged "in the enthusiasm of the May Days [1958]. It is what *Maréchal* Jean *De Lattre de Tassigny*," a hero of the Free French forces who fought Vichy and the Nazis, "has termed *la victoire de mai*." For French Algeria diehards, the "victory of May" had meant much more than the end of the Fourth Republic and the return to power of Charles de Gaulle. They presented the 1958 May Days as a new revolutionary moment that, like the 1830 July Days, which brought the Restoration monarchy to an end, and 1848's June Days, in defense of the "social republic," signaled the march of progress and the revitalization of fraternity, liberty, and equality.[15]

In late 1961 and 1962, defenders of French Algeria placed their efforts in a lineage of republican struggles. They invoked the French Revolution, the Commune, the Resistance. In his banned comic book, *Prisoners of the Bastille*, Coral, whom the preface notes was writing from a prison cell, compares de Gaulle to King Louis XVI as well as Napoleon, while the OAS, seeking to save Marianne, is rendered as sanculottes, chanting "Ça ira" from the revolutionary hymn "La Carmagnole."[16] In such tales, OAS sympathizers celebrated republican antecedents that had shaped and changed history. The struggle for Algeria, in their telling, was a worthy continuation of this heritage.

[14] Anonymous, *L'Activiste* (1962), 52, in AN 78AJ/31.
[15] Anonymous, "*Un Million de Français*" (1962), in AN 78AJ/31.
[16] Coral; preface by Gen. Jacques Faure, *Journal d'un embastillé sous la Vème République* (1962 [censored 20 December 1962]), in AN 78 AJ/31.

They insisted that a new French revolution had transfigured Algeria, one born not on the tennis court of Versailles in 1789, but at the Forum of Algiers in 1958. Another flyer presented the events of May 1958 as a change of regime: "*In Paris*, the men hoping for the abandonment, more or less camouflaged, of Algeria, or who were pushing for it, were removed from power." This had been accompanied, in Algeria, by "fraternization that erupted in every public space in a spontaneous and breathtaking rush." The result of this new revolutionary fraternity was "the two communities reconciled; establishing, as well, the bases for a generous political settlement based in equality between men." From this new beginning, the OAS argued, the horrors of colonialism in the Algerian departments now could be overcome.

A tract the OAS published in late January urged "Europeans" to act on the organization's call for "sincere gestures of fraternization toward Muslims. . . . Remember the power of the fraternization of 13 May." A book published the following month described and celebrated the historical transformation of that intense moment. With the OAS having refused simply to abandon Algeria without a fight, "History undoubtedly will say that it was in a difficult and sad period of insecurity and of terror that Algeria most transformed itself and that it began to take on the look of a French province, characterized by a population made up of different communities." The "History" that defenders of French Algeria turned to was one in which French genius, reflected in French precedents as well as present-day French voluntarism, was greater than any abstract force. France, they proposed, was still ready to sail, even against the tide.[17]

By consistently and insistently foregrounding the law and the constitution, the OAS and its fellow travelers sought to legitimate their cause—and thus the violence they employed to advance it—as a fight for "Justice" and "the Republic." Military Intelligence in Algeria, in reports the Renseignements Généraux (RG), the French equivalent of the FBI, sent to French government offices in Paris, reported the distribution of legalistic propaganda by the OAS. In June 1962, for example, they reported that "flyers have been distributed that challenge the juridical foundation of the Evian Accords, with others deploring the activities in Algeria of French troops."[18] Although it varied enormously over time and in different regions of Algeria, OAS propaganda in late 1961 and early 1962 almost always cited or elaborated legal arguments as the justification for their actions. The military, the government, and French media, followed by later commentators, have analyzed this as blather, background noise to be dismissed.[19] For the military it cam-

---

[17] Copies collected at Maison Carrée, 29 and 30 January 1962, in SHAT 1H/1735/1; Jean-Marie Millet, *La Coexistence des communautés en Algérie* (Aix-en-Provence, 1962), 289.

[18] Direction centrale des Renseignements Généraux, "Sommaire général" (Paris, 8 June 1962), 1, in CAC/AN 800280.

[19] For the military, see Colonel Guerin, "Bulletin de renseignement hebdomadaire. Semaine du 31 décembre 1961 au 7 janvier 1962" (Constantine, 10 January 1962), in SHAT 1H/2836/3.

ouflaged changes in activist tactics, for the others, the organization's true nature. But if we attend to what was spoken and recorded, there was a coherent argument: French Algeria partisans identified in the law of France not a code that politics must not tamper with à la Dicey but the written expression of the Republic and of justice. The law, they asserted, undeniably prohibited any separation of France or the French from Algeria and the Algerians. To allow this in the name of historical necessity would not only violate French law but also the lessons of French history. Rather than a conservative defense of tradition, or a call for a "republic run by judges," they proposed that France, instead of submitting to History's will, could make a new Algeria, to be sure freed of colonialism and racism, but French.

More than simply propaganda, the OAS's advancement of republican legalism in the final months of the war shaped all elements of their struggle. Critically, the organization stopped trying to replay de Gaulle's taking of power in 1958, a maneuver that elements of the Left (the PCF, the "new lefts," François Mitterrand) had criticized strongly as a coup d'état and had compared with earlier antirepublican machinations. A little-remarked yet crucial reversal of its military strategy signaled this new tack. Internal OAS documents captured by the French military, among them the so-called Plan Salan of February 1962, reveal that the OAS leadership now sought to avoid a repetition of the military putsches—the first successful, the others not—of 1958, 1960, and 1961. Following the Evian Accords, and despite supporters' angered urgency, the OAS's revised "Plan d'Action" reaffirmed that they had no plans to foment a military coup d'état.[20]

Informed by republican precepts, the OAS in Algeria now looked to another precedent for taking power that included armed struggle. They worked to reproduce a pre-1958 history of de Gaulle, one wrapped in republican legitimacy, model 18 June 1940, when the general spoke from his exile in London to call on all French people and forces to resist, to reject collaboration and the government of Marshal Pétain, until the defeat of the Nazis and the collaborators. They now intended to put forward what the Plan d'Action termed the "myth of the Resistance," through which the French people would come to see the OAS as defending the Republic against its usurpation by de Gaulle and the Fifth Republic. In their vision, after the Gaullists failed to impose Algerian independence they would be destabilized and the people and other parties would rally to the OAS as a "pole of order" against the Communists. The extremist Gaullists and Communists, the two groups that had opposed the (Fourth) Republic, would be isolated again. French Algeria, and therefore the Republic, would be safe.[21]

[20] Etat-major, poste de la Sécurité Militaire en Algérie, "Fiche d'ambiance en milieux civils et militaires. Semaine du 9 au 15 février 1962" Secret (SP 87.265, 17 February 1962), in SHAT 1H/1254/4; Général de Brigade Hublot, chef d'état-major, 2ème bureau, "Note d'information. Plan d'Action de l'OAS" (SP 87.000, 27 March 1962), in SHAT 1H/3164/3.

[21] On pro–French Algeria and OAS connections to the Resistance, see Benjamin Stora, *La*

The OAS thus abandoned what had seemed its most potent military option. The attempted putsches of 1960 and 1961 had led to the birth of the organization and brought into its ranks the officers and soldiers implicated in these actions who now led the pro–French Algeria underground. Further, the absence of a new putsch, to paraphrase Jean-Paul Sartre, disappointed Bab-el Oued, that is, the working-class heart of pied noir Algiers. In the days following the announcement of the Evian Accords, military intelligence described how the "failure" of this seemingly annual event to take place led to general incomprehension among OAS supporters.[22] For the metropolitan press, the absence of a new putsch revealed the OAS's military weaknesses. *France-Observateur* and others on the Left weighed in on the cowardice of Algerian Europeans. Unlike the valiant "Muslim" population, the Europeans were blowhards: all talk, no action. Because they were seen to be fascistic and irrational, only incapacity, operationally and morally, could explain why the OAS did not pursue the strategy it had now abandoned. The most salient consideration, then, affecting the political effectiveness of the strategies proposed in the Plan Salan or the Plan d'Action was that which popularly discredited all legalistic claims about the meridional departments: for most French people in 1962, Algeria was not France.

Ex-general Raoul Salan—former commander of the French forces in Algeria who had joined Generals Challe, Jouhaud, and Zeller in the failed April 1961 Algiers coup d'état and had then taken command of the OAS—embraced tactics that revealed an attention to the law, the constitution, and republican precedents. The OAS claimed that it was forced into illegality and violence in order to defend republican legalism, which official acceptance of Algerian self-determination was destroying. Having aligned their rhetoric, arguments, and strategy with the principles of republican legalism, opponents of Algerian independence in the spring and summer of 1962 constantly appealed to those institutions and individuals charged with guaranteeing the laws of the Republic. Criticism of the illegality of the Evian Accords—and other "assaults" on French territorial integrity—was ubiquitous, and not only in clandestine tracts. Attacks on the contents of the accords, which were said to jettison French departments and to cast doubt on the citizenship of French nationals, were joined with indictments of their promulgation, via a referendum said to be unconstitutional in form and process.

The 8 April 1962 referendum was an up or down vote open to all French citizens living in metropolitan France. The "Yes," granting the government

---

gangrène et l'oubli: La mémoire de la guerre d'Algérie, new ed. (Paris, 1998), 109–13. On the post-1945 "Gaullist" elaboration of this "history," see Henry Rousso, *The Vichy Syndrome*, trans. Arthur Goldhammer (Cambridge, Mass., 1991). For a description of how pro–Algérie française deputies advanced these arguments, see Michèle Salinas, *L'Algérie au Parlement, 1958–1962* (Toulouse, 1987), 64–65.

[22] See Général de Brigade Hublot, "Bulletin de renseignements mensuel. Mois de Février" (SP 87.000, 13 March 1962), 14, in SHAT 1H/1428/1.

the right to implement the agreements reached with Algerian nationalists, won a massive majority (91%) of the vote. Yet, in the French Parliament, those who opposed Algerian independence continued to hammer at the Evian Accords and other government actions relating to Algeria as unconstitutional and antirepublican.[23] Senator Gil Paulian, defending his proposition that the enactment of the Evian Accords required the approval of both French assemblies, asserted that "the unconstitutional nature of the Law of 13 April 1962 . . . is recognized by virtually every single jurist as well as by qualified representatives of the political parties." The statement was accurate. To give one example, documents from the Constitutional Council, charged with overseeing the application of the Constitution of 1958, reveal that the majority of its members viewed the 8 April referendum ratifying the Evian Accords as illegal.[24]

In the question posed to voters on 8 April 1962, support for the government's declaration of 19 March 1962 concerning Algeria was twinned with a second clause that granted the executive full legislative powers to decree any measures the executive itself deemed necessary to implement these accords. Denouncing what he characterized as illegality, Senator Paulian deplored that "the most determined partisans of the actual government do not even bother to deny this." Instead, he argued, "they seek justification in the name of opportunity and the needs of public order." Against these necessities, Paulian warned that "Article 3 of the Law of 13 April 1962," did more than simply make the Evian Accords law. It also extended "the most extreme, the most complete, and the most exorbitant delegation of powers in our history."[25] This concern was widespread even among jurists and politicians who supported the referendum.

Against the "tide of History" and a popular plebiscite, Paulian offered the lessons of French history: the Republic cannot depend on "the whims of one man or of the exceptional tribunals that he establishes." Referring to new judicial institutions and rules that the government, with the referendum's authorization, was preparing to put in place to pursue OAS activists, he warned that "no threat" should allow the establishment of procedures that "offer no possibility for appeals, not even appeals based in the fundamental guarantees of the rights of the individual." The boilerplate of French republicanism, formed in the rejection of Bonapartism and Boulangism, resonated dully in the face of charges that the far-right terrorists of the OAS, and not the abandonment of due process, was the true and imminent menace to the republic.

[23] See chapter 4.

[24] The Law of 13 April 1962 registered the measures approved by the 8 April referendum. See CAC/AN 91011/12. For further discussion, see chapter 4.

[25] Sénateur Gil Paulian, "Proposition de loi [n. 205] tendant à modifier la loi n. 62–421 du 13 avril 1962 . . ." (25 May 1962), in CAC/AN 950395/76; René Schmitt, "Les parlementaires de la Manche et le referendum," *La Presse de la Manche* (3 April 1962), clipping in AN F/1cII/640.

In addition to speeches and failed parliamentary propositions invoking the law and the republic, opponents of Algerian independence sent letters and petitions to numerous judges. Court cases and appeals to the Council of State reinforced such efforts. The summer of 1962 saw Ministry of the Interior functionaries preparing a response to the separate (although remarkably similar) complaints that two plaintiffs had presented to the Council of State. Both sought the annulment of Decree 62–315 of 20 March 1962, "On the Organization of a Referendum" to ratify the accords. By excluding voters in the departments of Algeria and the Sahara, the plaintiffs argued, the accords were "null and void due to abuse of authority." Government experts, unable or unwilling to respond to the legal content of the complaint, argued for the preeminence of "the facts of the existing situation." In the end, both challenges were dismissed because, an Interior official noted, the effects of the referendum were, in any case, irreversible.[26] One pro–French Algeria group bitterly remarked that their supporters now could be imprisoned "for having asserted an idea that appears in the [1789] Declaration of the Rights of Man and Citizen."[27] Among the many trials of OAS terrorists, several cases, most notoriously that of OAS leader Raoul Salan in May and the October 1962 trial of André Canal ("the Monocle") a key figure in OAS violence in the metropole, ratified elements of the pro–French Algeria legal critique of French policy.[28]

"History Cannot Be Changed When History Has Already Been Written"

The laws of the Republic and the Constitution of 1958 framed the arguments of those who defended French Algeria. Their republicanism was not merely trompe-l'oeil. It relied on republican historical precedents and defended republican ideals, principles, and methods. Yet the large majority of politicians and pundits felt no need to respond to the republicanism the defenders of French Algeria put forth. The opposition between a "legal" and a "historical" argument that the final months of the Algerian War witnessed was at once novel, temporary, and deaf to the arguments the other side offered.

At the war's end, virtually no one was able to recognize the implications, implicit or obvious, of both of these seemingly opposed logics. The French Algeria camp, with its fixation on the revolutionary changes wrought by the

[26] Yves Bourges, in a letter to the prime minister, "*Moyens Developpés par le Requérant, Avis,* Réponse à Barreau" (15 June 1962), in AN F1cII/647. My request for access to Conseil d'Etat archives on this case was denied.

[27] Referring to General Vanuxem, in AN 78aj/32, 6–7.

[28] See chapter 4. These judicial decisions did more than outrage President de Gaulle: the recently opened archives of the interministerial committee and of the Council of Algerian Affairs reveal that overturning these decisions was virtually the only subject that de Gaulle insisted must be addressed in the months following the Evian Accords. See MAE 117.

May Days, proved incapable of seriously addressing how racism and French imperialism structured all facets of life in Algeria. They presumed that France simply could ignore the criticisms of Algerian nationalists and international observers.[29] Those who accepted Algerian independence did not pause to interrogate how legal quibbles with their positions could reveal alternate understandings of history and its lessons. They dismissed calls to address the risks inherent in ignoring the constitution, various laws written to protect the Republic, or procedures put in place to promote justice. Just as they ignored the challenges that the Algerian Revolution posed to French pretensions to universalism, they ignored pro–French Algeria pretensions that the revolutionary heritage of France was at stake.

As evidenced in the fall 1961 parliamentary discussion of repatriation and the president's New Year's message about Algeria, De Gaulle and his government abstained from engaging in any sustained explanations or discussion of why Algeria should be independent. French historian Michèle Salinas, in her study of the French Parliament during the war, notes the deafening silence of supporters of the Evian Accords. To read records of the debates about French policy in Algeria in 1962 "would lead one to think that a strong opposition to the Elysée's policies existed" when, in fact, at every moment opponents "were a numerical minority." With rare exceptions, only the small minority that still defended French Algeria ever raised the issue.[30] Avoiding any discussion or debate in the parliament about Algeria was a goal of de Gaulle's government:

> The debates [nine between March 1958 and April 1962 in both Senate and Assembly] were always provoked either by a declaration of the President of the Republic, or by events. In fact, not once did the Government independently seek to bring the Algerian question before the representatives of the nation.[31]

On at least one occasion, Prime Minister Michel Debré agreed to make a declaration concerning Algeria before the French assemblies only on the condition that it not be followed by a debate.[32]

In 1958, the majority of the National Assembly had run on a platform of support for French Algeria and for intensified efforts toward integration. Yet, in 1962, another large majority formed among the class of 1958, with a

---

[29] See, for example, Marcel-Edmond Naegelen's novel, *L'Hexagonie: Essai fantaisiste d'histoire contemporaine* (Paris, 1963).

[30] Salinas, *L'Algérie au Parlement*, 130. The presence of a mere handful of PCF deputies and senators contributed to this silence. Yet even PCF interventions touching on Algeria had less to do with Algeria's future than with the fight against Algérie française "fascism." See also François Goguel, "Les circonstances du référendum du 8 avril 1962," in *Chroniques électorales 2, Les scrutins politiques en France de 1945 à nos jours*, vol. 2: *La Cinquième République du général de Gaulle*, p. 190.

[31] Salinas, *L'Algérie au Parlement*, 28.

[32] On 27 June 1961, see Jean-Paul Brunet, *Gaston Monnerville: Le républicain qui défia de Gaulle* (Paris, 1997), 212.

slightly different political contour: the very few Communists were in it, the minority of former Gaullists who had joined the RNUR and their allies were out. This large majority consistently voted in favor of the Algerian policies proposed by President de Gaulle. Most of them, however, did not explain why.

Their silence reflected an inability to articulate their attachment to French republicanism along with their support for Algerian secession. By relying on historical determinism, the Gaullists and most of the French Left could avoid explaining their acceptance of Algerian independence. The widespread assumption that "History" was at work authorized this silence and, in fact, necessitated it: "History" was beyond the control of the French. There thus was no need to attempt to explain what to do with Algeria. Yet French politicians and French understandings of their nation rejected the very idea that the French Republic could not intervene. "History," most supposed, already had decided the question of Algeria's future relationship with France. Yet, this position did not lead to the explicit abandonment of references to republicanism, nor did those who embraced it accept the republicanism of those who still defended French Algeria. Instead, the defense of "the Republic" against its hereditary enemy once again rallied significant numbers. By *not* articulating a republican explanation to justify Algerian secession—by leaving it to History—those who accepted this arrangement were able to focus the question of the Republic on "for" or "against." They positioned those who continued to defend French Algeria as "against" and defined them as "fascists."

In rejecting as wholly alien the traditional republican project of making Algeria truly French, republicanism once again aroused the passions and allegiance of new generations of politically engaged French people. This was the paradox of the war's close.[33] Surfing on the tide of History, proponents of Algerian independence were able to ignore the interpolation of juridical arguments against abandoning French territory and the French citizens, "Muslim" and "European," of Algeria. They set aside republican tradition, ideology, and texts. In place of them, they transformed French popular acceptance of Algerian secession into a twinned struggle: first, by the French people with the Algerian people for liberty, equality, and fraternity among peoples, against those defending colonial oppression and racism; second, by the French nation in defense of the Republic and against the reborn forces of the counterrevolution.

By consigning die-hard defenders of French Algeria to the ideological tradition opposed to republicanism, to the Far Right, they could be and were opposed for what they were said to be—a threat to the Republic—and not for what most of them actually said, which was republican. A reliance on the

---

[33] On republicanism's reputation after 1945, see Mona Ozouf, "L'idée républicaine et l'interprétation du passé national," *Annales HSS* (November–December 1998): 1075.

tide of History also allowed most French people to ignore the radical implications for republican citizenship and the nation that the pro–French Algeria "legal" argument contained. For the contention that in republican ideals and, since 1946, in law all eight-plus million Algerians with Koranic civil status were fully French posed moral, monetary, and political demands on France. The policies of "integration" offered novel approaches to making equality a reality for Muslim French citizens from Algeria. By late 1959, when President de Gaulle first proposed Algerian self-determination, these exigencies appeared to be at once extravagant and doomed to failure. As an editorial in one mass-market weekly magazine asserted, "History cannot be changed when History has already been written."[34] Summoned by proponents of keeping Algeria French to implement the republican rhetoric that for 131 years had explained French domination of Algeria, most French people, politicians, and intellectuals refused to respond.

The government and most of the parties represented in parliament ignored the claims the OAS advanced. Outside these institutions, different elements of the self-proclaimed "new left" asserted noisily and repeatedly that it was hypocrisy, indeed the surest proof of racism, to allege that "Muslims" could be French. Yet like those who merely accepted Algerian independence, these strong supporters of Algerian nationalism also relied on historical determinism. *Les Temps Modernes*, the journal that had waged a lonely campaign in favor of the FLN during the war's early years, denied any validity to the antiracist language of the OAS. As one article analyzed, "That is what they write." Yet, it continued, "There is no doubt that it is not what they believe." As for why they pretended, the author suggested, "maybe it is what they think they believe, it is certainly what they would like to be believed." The conclusion was obvious: "So they lie: whether, if I dare, straightforwardly, or by omission, or by choice, even, sometimes, with big dumb ingenuousness."[35]

In this lens, to truly understand late-war pro–French Algeria ideology, one had to put aside its claims. It was necessary to dig through the layers of republican phraseology and prointegration rhetoric to find what was underneath. Claude Bourdet, editor of *France-Observateur,* covering the trial in May of General Salan, remarked that it was the old-timers who gave up the charade: "From time to time, a word betrays their generation. General Touzet du Vigier, for example, still speaks of 'natives.' This is obviously a faux-pas the ultras of 1962 no longer make. The vocabulary of colonial pillage has gradually acquired manners."[36] From this left perspective, "French Algeria" offered no new—or at least positive and progressive—historical

---

[34] Editorial, "La France et l'Histoire," *Paris-Match* 671 (17 February 1962), 21.
[35] Jacques-Laurent Bost, "Les cours des choses," *Temps Modernes* 192 (May 1962): 1774–80.
[36] *France-Observateur* 629 (24 May 1962).

possibilities. May 1958 had changed nothing. Only the march of History, which the fight to overcome colonialism then embodied, could be antiracist.

The new left was the most explicit among those who relied on history in denying that other possibilities existed. Its assessment articulated what was widely assumed: to reject Algerian independence in 1962 was irrational. Philippe Hernandez, a journalist for *France-Observateur*—himself originally from Algeria—defined the political program of the OAS as: "no independence; no partition; no association; no negotiations with de Gaulle; no negotiations with the 'emigrants in Tunis'; French Algeria, which is to say 'within France'." It was not a program, he continued, but "five negations and one affirmation that is no more than a slogan expressing nostalgia for the past." It was a politics of "nihilism" the pied noir writer continued, for "at heart, nobody still believes in French Algeria." His analysis was that "the pieds noirs are without hope and have confidence in no one. They hate de Gaulle who cheated them at the time of 13 May and who treats them like faggots." This, for Hernandez, explained their refusal to "turn toward the future and help to build it"—an independent Algeria, that is.[37] French Algeria was thus neither rational nor political, because it ignored reality. By placing the rejection of decolonization in Algeria outside of History, this presumption could dismiss the republican form and content of the actual arguments (and thus ignore any potential effects independence might have on the republic). Now conceived as congruent with the Far Right, the defense of French Algeria could be reduced to a reactionary agenda: the refusal of self-determination; the defense of colonialism and the history of exclusion of Muslims from full citizenship; racism; and the shameful conduct of a war engaged to protect this heritage. Like that of Hernandez, the list is one of rejections, plus a malignant nostalgia.

This abridgment, which presented "French Algeria" as the embodiment of values and practices antithetical to republicans, necessitated ignoring the history of France in Algeria. Dismissing pro–French Algeria claims that what was as stake was the Republic, which is to say the legal and institutional framework meant to embody France's revolutionary heritage, made this possible. I insist that whether or not certain (or even most) defenders of French Algeria were hypocritical, as many on the Left cogently argued, does not change the importance, or the effects, of this development: not having a discussion about what the end of French Algeria meant allowed a restructuring of institutions that neither the Left nor the French Algeria diehards supported. The next chapter details how this forgetting dominated both discussion of the Evian Accords and the ways that the French government implemented them.

[37] "Voyage en Algérie fasciste (II): Les pieds noirs à l'heure du désespoir," *France-Observateur* 611 (18 January 1962), 12–14.

Chapter 4

Forgetting French Algeria

In a national broadcast on 18 March 1962 President de Gaulle announced "the conclusion of a cease-fire in Algeria" between the French government and the forces of the FLN, ending more than seven years of undeclared war. De Gaulle explained that this agreement included "projects adopted so that the populations can choose their destiny." These would allow for "the birth of an independent Algeria, cooperating closely with us." The result, the general intoned, "will make sense to France." The announcement was not a surprise. For weeks beforehand, French and international journalists reported on the progress negotiators were making. On 17 March, a military intelligence summary began "yet again Algeria held its breath in anticipation of the proclamation that will end the fighting." Algerian independence, which the French government had resisted with all the political and military tools available—including, as the world had discovered, the systematic use of torture—and which most French politicians had long derided as unimaginable, now "made sense to France."[1]

The day after de Gaulle's announcement, an 11 a.m. news flash on "Europe 1," the metropole's most popular radio broadcast, told of a "European car shot to pieces in Algiers" and of "the pursuit by Europeans of a general strike." Inhabitants of continental France, which people were just beginning to call "the Hexagon," also learned that "calm reigns in the Muslim neighborhoods." "Twelve Noon Europe" let its listeners know that "the large cities of Algeria shun the cease-fire, by order of the OAS." Throughout the

---

[1] The cease-fire agreement, unsigned and undated, appeared in the *J.O.* of 20 March 1962 along with a general declaration, a declaration of guarantees, and six declarations of principle concerning Algeria. Lt.-Colonel Cousin, "Bulletin hebdomadaire de renseignements. Semaine du 10 au 16 mars 1962" (SP 87.000, 17 March 1962), in SHAT 1H/1436/D(1).

day, the news broadcast resonated with recordings of the now familiar sound of banging pots, the "casserole concert," and the honking "ta-ta-ta, ti-ti," that punctuated popular demonstrations for Al-gé-rie fran-çaise. In Algiers, they had "lasted more than an hour" after the official announcement of the Evian Accords on the 18th. Only the arrival of military police units had brought the peaceful protest to an end. The clanging, however, started again as soon as French security left the scene.[2]

The Algerian War of Independence was over. As if to reassure metropolitans of that fact, a news brief signaled that Radio France in Algeria, as of that morning, now broadcast official announcements in both French and Arabic. Now a new struggle brought together former enemies, Algerian nationalists and French leaders, to ensure that a recalcitrant minority in Algeria—the "Europeans"—did not endanger the peace. The 11 a.m. news flash quoted Ahmed Ben Bella, the nationalist hero and FLN leader, who the day before had been released from five years of French imprisonment. He described the main goal of the coming days as ending anti-independence violence and lauded the strict application by both signatories of the accords. These measures, he proclaimed, would "guarantee entente and cohabitation between the communities," by which he meant "Muslims" and "Europeans."[3] Addressing the "people of Algiers," Algeria's governor general Jean Morin begged them "not to let your pain blind you. This is not the solution you wanted, but it is the realistic solution." In the same breath, he called on "Muslims" to "demonstrate their good judgment" by remaining calm.[4]

On the "Muslim" side, reason—on the "European," stubborn and violent irrationality, both distinct from the "French." The "Twelve Noon Europe" announcer detailed the stark difference between the calm that reigned in the "Muslim neighborhoods" and the situation in Bab el-Oued. The voice told of graffiti on the walls of the legendary working-class "European" neighborhood of Algiers reading "OAS" and "insulting the Head of State." All the official posters that had appeared that night, some proclaiming "Peace"—with an image of two smiling young children, one a blond boy, his arm over the shoulder of a younger, curly-haired, brunette girl with dark skin—others announcing "The End of Fighting" or "Cease Fire!" were "shredded by 9 a.m." The speaker compared this to "Muslim areas," where some of these same posters had, "superimposed, the spray-painted image of a soldier with a National Liberation Army [ALN] armband," a seemingly complementary juxtaposition. In Constantine, the man continued, the "Muslim" areas were largely deserted, but the few passers-by "stopped for several moments in front of the posters." The hopeful broadsides the "Muslims"

[2] "Radio Europe 1 Flash de 11h, 19 mars 1962," 1–2, in SHAT 1H/1784/2. On the new popularity of references to "the Hexagon," see Eugen Weber, "L'Hexagone," in Les lieux de mémoire, vol. 2, La nation, ed. Pierre Nora (Paris, 1986), 97–116.

[3] "Radio Europe 1 Flash de 11h, 19 mars 1962"; "Radio Europe 1 Flash de 10h, 19 mars 1962," 1–2, in SHAT 1H/1784/2.

[4] "Radio Europe 1 Flash de 10h, 19 mars 1962," 1–2, in SHAT 1H/1784/2.

French boy in Algiers looks at a post–cease-fire poster announcing "Peace in Algeria," France, March 1962. Reprinted by permission of Central Press/Hulton Archive/Getty Images.

contemplated were, the voice explained, "one of the first elements of the psychological war. Over the next two weeks, planes will drop tracts on Algeria's principal cities and numerous radio discussions will focus on explaining the Evian Accords." If "Muslims" had reached an understanding with the colonial power, the "Europeans," it was clear, would need all the persuasion that France could muster.

Leaving Algeria and its cities behind, the announcer finished by reporting

After Evian: Raoul Salan (leader, OAS), Benyoucef Ben Khedda (president, GPRA), and Ahmed Sékou Touré (president, Guinea). Reprinted by permission of *Le Nouvel Observateur*.

that "for France, the cease-fire brings hopes of playing a greater role in Europe and the world." "Yes" to the accords and "No" to the OAS—this was what metropolitans heard in March 1962, and what they voted for in overwhelming numbers on 8 April. France would work hand in hand with Algerian nationalists on the basis of the Evian Accords to establish an independent nation for all Algerians, "Muslims" and "Europeans." This was part of France's responsibility to Algeria, yes, but, more important, it reflected the nation's place "in Europe and the world." The French Republic could reaffirm a leading role in both now that, under the leadership of General de Gaulle, it was freed of its former empire and out of Algeria. Yet as the confusion on the ground in Algeria and about the relationships between "Europeans," "Muslims," and "French" even then made clear, the Evian Accords were not the end of the "events in Algeria." The Algerian Revolution had won independence. For France, many of the most critical issues raised by its Algerian Revolution would be settled during the next several months, questions that neither the fighting nor the negotiations had resolved.[5]

The End of the History of France in Algeria

Those who fervently resisted the agreement with the FLN included pro–Algérie française deputies, militants in OAS cells in Algeria and the metropole, and large segments of the French citizenry in Algeria. Their representatives angrily argued that the arrangements agreed to at Evian would alter France and French institutions. In challenging what made sense to the French, they also sought to expose how their future both as French people and as inhabitants of Algeria was threatened.

During the extraordinary session of the National Assembly held to discuss de Gaulle's 18 March announcement, Pierre Portolano, deputy from Algiers, took the tribune after Prime Minister Michel Debré's opening remarks. Portolano invoked ancient histories—the West, "our civilization"—and, focusing on the Rights of Man, the more recent histories of the French and the Fifth Republics. Gesturing to his fellow Algerian representatives in the chamber, he asserted:

> These deputies, elected to ensure the just and humane advancement of Algeria in the framework of the French Republic, abiding by the most solemn promises that gave birth to the Fifth Republic, denounce before the French nation and the free world the violation of promises and inalienable rights that are at the base of our civilization. . . . For the first time in the history of the free world, a Western government has freely abandoned guarantees of domestic liberty and the rights of man.

Portolano's words evoked the coming of an apocalypse that threatened both France and Western civilization, but one that men—namely, deputies— could grasp and prevent. He challenged the government's right to agree to the accords: "France, thanks to her army, which remains our best hope, has not suffered violent attacks [from abroad], no such excuse exists." That the situation was neither 1871 nor 1940, not abject defeat at the hands of an invading army, should make it crystal clear, he pleaded, "why the nation can-

<hr />

[5] "Extraits du journal parlé 'Europe Midi'" (19 March 1962), in SHAT 1H/1784/2.

not in any way consider itself as bound by these illegal acts."[6] Pro–French Algerian deputies repeated this opening rhetorical strategy, moving from arguments based in history to legal facts to military viability to moral pleadings, as they struggled to force a debate that might crack their opponents' consensus in support of Algerian independence.

Pro–Algérie française deputies tried again and again to place Evian and its effects within a historical narrative of the Republic and its travails. Portolano pointed to "the deputies from Alsace-Lorraine to whom we link ourselves. Their pathetic call"—after defeat by the Germans and in the face of the Third Republic's acquiescence to a treaty that ceded their homeland to the victors—"remains our charter." Summoning the glorious return of those provinces to the *patrie* in 1918, he reminded his listeners that the memory of the previous century's defeat—and its denouement—was "our reason for hope." Other deputies referred to prerevolutionary strictures against the abandonment of any French territory by France's rulers (Salic law); 1789; and the German takeover in 1940. These attempted contextualizations, which all wrote Algeria into the history of France, did not convince many people. If we look only at the record of the debates, it is difficult to understand why that was so.[7]

Evian's supporters rarely responded to their opponents' claims. At best, they rejected them as hypocritical: the defense of republican values by the far-right deputy Tremolet de Villers, his call for "the application of the principles engraved at the front of our monuments—Liberté, Egalité, Fraternité"—was dismissed with ironic shouts of "Travail, Famille, Patrie!," the triptych mantra of Pétain's Vichy government.[8] Those few who did react offered different historical interpretations, histories that assumed that Algeria was not French. Gaullists returned again and again to the idea that events in Algeria were part of an "evolution" beyond French control. As Prime Minister Debré announced when he opened the session, Evian was the result of "more than the length of the rebellion, it was the evolution of Algeria, the tendencies of the young generations, the general state of Africa." All of these changes "made it necessary to have discussions of a political nature." President de Gaulle, his parliamentary allies announced, had understood this evolution and done what was necessary for France.[9] Evian's supporters on the left, while embracing the idea of historical evolution, rejected the centrality his allies ascribed to de Gaulle. The Communist Waldeck Rochet argued that "having long called for negotiations, our militants and all the partisans of peace have for years been fighting governmental repression . . . this peace is above all the result of a long hard struggle . . , not

[6] J.O. (1962), 458.
[7] Ibid, 458. Imperial Germany conquered the province of Alsace and part of Lorraine in the 1870–71 Franco-Prussian War.
[8] Ibid., 471. Tremolet de Villers had served in Pétain's government.
[9] Ibid., 453.

the gift of [de Gaulle's] personal power." Accepting the Evian Accords and the referendum that the president of the Republic proposed in order to separate France and Algeria, they argued that "the people" had forced this political development.[10]

Most deputies and most French rejected the claim by Evian's opponents that the accords were a radical disjuncture in (French) history or a violation of "natural" or national law. In their tacit agreement, France would remain France without Algeria. A corollary question proved more troubling: If Algeria would no longer be French, could Algerians be? Throughout numerous debates, supporters of Evian insisted that the answer was yes. As Louis Joxe, secretary of state for Algeria, recalled: "The prime minister has said since the first session that French nationality can be kept by anyone who does not renounce it. Thus, the principle is that anyone who has been French, who is French, can remain French." One deputy's cry encapsulated the oppositional position: "Not in Algeria!" The utterance recalled a familiar lesson from French history and law: membership in the French nation was wedded closely to territorial questions.[11]

In the protocols signed with the FLN, the French government agreed that Algerian self-determination would establish Algeria and France as two separate territorial entities. They agreed that independent Algeria would have a separate nationality and citizenship from France. The accords also promised that no one would lose French nationality or citizenship against her or his will. Demanding to know how this was possible, the French Algeria ultra Pascal Arrighi warned:

> Citizens with civil status under common law ["Europeans"] will thus be able to become "Algerian" while holding on to their French nationality, but what can we say about this accumulation of nationalities? Raymond Aron wrote: "None can claim the right to a double citizenship as the essence of being a citizen is obedience to the commands of a state and above all its military obligations."

What was being proposed, the speaker argued, was rooted in neither French history nor French law. Opponents of the accords, in seizing on the question of double nationality, grasped that the government's proposal broke with all previous French discussions of French nationality and citizenship since the Revolution.[12]

---

[10] Ibid., 453 and 467–68.

[11] Ibid., 469. Rogers Brubaker has made the strongest argument for the centrality of this relationship, linked to the notion of *jus soli*, but Patrick Weil's research greatly qualifies his claims. See Brubaker, *Citizenship and Nationhood in France and Germany* (Cambridge, Mass., 1992), and Patrick Weil, *Qu'est-ce qu'un Français? Histoire de la nationalité française depuis la Révolution* (Paris, 2002).

[12] *J.O.* (1962), 460. On the historical link between citizenship and national exclusivity, see Peter Sahlins, *Unnaturally French: Foreign Citizens in the Old Regime and After* (Ithaca, 2004).

Responding to Joxe's assurances about the soundness of proposed guarantees, the Corsican deputy posed a sharp challenge: "Lying propaganda seeks to prove that real guarantees were made for the French of Algeria." Against Joxe's and the prime minister's "principle," Arrighi warned of hidden dangers. He insisted on an inevitable connection of territory and nationality:

> The Europeans and the assimilated [Muslims], at the end of three years, must choose between Algerian nationality or foreigner status in Algeria; they will not, they cannot, at one and the same time, both remain French and live in the land of their ancestors.[13]

He protested against the limitations of the government's guarantees "for those French Algerians qualified as citizens with civil status under common law." This term, he explained, "includes Algerians of European extraction, Israelites, and those Muslims who opted for civil status under common law." But beyond the insufficiency of these guarantees, Arrighi challenged the exclusion of "all the rest of the Muslims," for whom "no institutional guarantees are planned."[14] His litany of terms was legally and historically accurate. More than that, it gave voice to pro–French Algeria worries that the complicated guarantees of Evian masked a French desire to simplify the terms of French identity.

"European" Algerians had been aware of the double nationality proposal for some time and, as the French government knew, emphatically rejected the idea. The General Delegation in Algeria had reported that "double nationality is refused by 99 percent of the senior civil servants," while a more wide-ranging sociological study reported that "double nationality evoked epithets: Stupid! Utopian! Idiocy!" Their refusal, the sociologist Suzanne Frère detailed, was more than a knee-jerk reflex. She quoted one respondent asking, "What is the meaning of this double nationality on the domestic and international scene?" before adding "a concept lacking content." A teacher remarked that it was "a priori an interesting hypothesis, but practically . . . ? They want to take away one to give us two?"[15]

Two seemed necessary, because now Algeria and France together had become an untenable concept. As Arrighi suggested, "The nation wants to reject not only the idea but the very term of 'French Algeria'." From an internationally recognized, juridically sound fact, it was "now officially turned into a myth." He noted ruefully that it now seemed "as if the two words conjoined of France and Algeria pose both to the heart and the spirit a certain je ne sais quoi of contradiction and dishonor."[16] Algeria was French

[13] Ibid.
[14] Ibid.
[15] Affaires politiques, Délégation générale en Algérie, "Sondages d'opinion dans les milieux européens d'Alger" (1961), 1, in MAE 92; Suzanne Frère, "Enquête sur les garanties de la minorité en Algérie" (Rocher Noir, 20 November 1961), 19, in MAE 97.
[16] J.O., 462.

and all Algerians, since 1946, were French citizens. The "heart and the spirit" of most French voters, however, did not accept this: it was this new, yet seemingly obvious, reality that Arrighi and his fellows—invoking French law and history—were trying to change.

The diverse statuses that pro–French Algeria speakers so cherished evoked the policy of integration, the novel attempt to reconcile equality and the recognition of difference that the Constitution of the Fifth Republic had embraced. Most French deputies, like most French people, had no more patience for integrationist rhetoric and its complicated vision of French identity; they preferred a set of other, simpler definitions of the people of Algeria. The previous year, Minister of Information Alain Peyrefitte offered one such depiction. In defense of his proposal to divide Algeria into three states, he reiterated the French canard that "there has never been Algerian unity." As proof, he outlined a mosaic of "Cordovan Arabs and Oriental Arabs, Kabyles and Chaouias, Mozabites and Israelites, Andalusians and Neapolitans, of Catalans and Maltese, of Alsatians and Corsicans, Greeks and Lebanese," who "perhaps could have formed a unique Mediterranean type." He regretted, though, that "seven years of combat have given birth to two units: the unity of the Muslim populations . . . [and] the unity of the non-Muslim population." "There never was," he reiterated, "an Algerian entity: there are now two—two peoples, equally at home there, un-uprootable."[17]

A far less nuanced "two populations of Algeria," subsuming Jews and others into a community of "European origin" in tandem with an Arab, Berber, and other community of "Muslim origin" also appeared in the debates over Evian, embraced by pro-government and/or centrist deputies. Another idiom, which deputies from the PCF, in particular, preferred, contested the government invocation of "two populations of Algeria." Here, the reference contrasted and balanced two bodies, "Algerian people" and "French people." As Waldeck Rochet declared, "This peace . . . is the common victory of the people of Algeria and the people of France."[18] The PCF, through their presentation of "two peoples in struggle," sought to profit from their recently arrived at theory in support of Algerian independence, in order to advance electorally in France. Along with the Gaullists, marching in lock step behind their general, the Communists unhesitatingly defended the changes in Algeria and sought to take credit.[19]

---

[17] The young minister, in deference to the certainties of assimilation, was careful to append to his categorization of the second group—"who fear they will be oppressed in a Muslim Algeria"—that they were "united with those Muslims who wish to remain French." Alain Peyrefitte, *Pour sortir de l'impasse Algérienne* (Paris, 1961), 7.

[18] *J.O.* (1962), 468. The Communists, as I discussed in chapter 2, had admitted that the FLN represented the Algerian people, although this was, in their view, considerably different from their own role as the Leninist vanguard.

[19] See, for example, the analysis in Maurice Papon, "Elections municipales partielles dans la commune de Saint-Maur-des-Fosses" (23 May 1962), 3, in AN F/1cIV/678, "Seine."

What all of these attributions of identity shared was an easy alignment with the eventual division of territory: "European" meant French; "Muslims" meant Algerians. The Algérie française synthesis of *pays* and identity, on the contrary, was confronted with the contradictions its own defenders had predicted from the first debates. Indeed, as they advanced their positions and, soon after, as they saw the failure of their arguments to convince, French Algeria partisans offered a succession of wordy and overdetermined identifications to name those they claimed to defend. Before the announcement of the Evian Accords they most commonly had referred to people living in or from Algeria as "Algerians," often, but not always, joined with either the qualifier "of Muslim origin," "of European origin," or occasionally "of French origin." Algerians—like Bretons, Alsatians, and Provençals this denomination worked to affirm—were all Frenchmen. They inhabited a region that, like the old provinces, had its own particularities and stories but was now, obviously, French. The announcement of the Evian Accords provoked a striking shift in terminology: within a matter of days, references to "French of Algeria" replaced "Algerians." Under the duress of becoming "officially a myth," in Arrighi's phrase, they were forced to give more certain definition to the people in whose name they spoke. Pro–French Algeria deputies layered on increasingly complicated terms to synthesize knotty and interrelated needs. They returned repeatedly to Arrighi's convoluted description, mixing and matching "local status," "common civil status," "European (origin)," "Muslim (origin)," "Israelite," "citizens," and "French at heart." Such naming worked to reaffirm that all Algerians were French and to locate the desire for continued French rule of Algeria in Algeria. Through this play of words, parliamentary speakers claimed that the "French of Algeria" appellation was meaningful for a whole range of people, pretending that because Algerians were French they necessarily wanted to remain French. They reiterated, from the galleries of the Palais-Bourbon, what the OAS insistently announced in its propaganda. The deputies' rhetoric was no more convincing than OAS terrorism.[20]

After the announcement of the accords, in a televised address to French Algerians on what he termed "this evening of confusion and fratricidal struggle," the secretary of state for Algerian affairs told them: "Know that anything in your favor that it was even possible to conceive of has been examined, considered, proposed."[21] In a series of radio interviews, a gov-

---

[20] The same shift appears in a collection of private and pastoral letters and addresses made during the war by the archbishop of Algiers. As the war progressed he moved from placing "of European origin" and "of Muslim origin" in scare quotes to writing them as free-standing descriptions. Only late in 1961, in reference to Algerian *rapatriés*, did he begin to refer to the "French of Algeria." See Léon-Etienne Duval, archbishop of Algiers, *Au nom de la verité: Alger, 1954–62* (Paris, 1982), 160. In a parallel development, there were also the first references in the *J.O.* of April 1962 to individuals "of Algerian origin," which clearly referred only to "Muslims," "Arabs," or Berbers.

[21] Louis Joxe, "Allocution télévisée" (23 March 1962), 4, in SHAT 1H/1123/1.

ernment spokesperson brushed off critics who questioned the guarantees promised by the accords and the French government. According to this official, those who doubted France's commitment to the French of Algeria "know quite well that their critique has no basis in the law"; French "Muslims" and "Europeans" "have the right to retain [their French nationality]. No one can be deprived arbitrarily of their nationality, states the Universal Declaration of the Rights of Man." The phrase that followed went to the heart of both opposition concerns and the tension between the juridical and the political. "France," the radio voice claimed, "neither wants nor can take [nationality] away from them and her decision is supreme [*souverain*] in this area." It was further explained that "the Republic is going to guarantee [*maintiendra*] French nationality for all Europeans or Muslims in Algeria who now possess it and who do not demonstrate a desire to renounce it." There could be no doubt that "they will remain French, and their children, already born or to be born, will remain French as well."[22] Yet, the sovereign Republic, the decision to withdraw from Algeria made clear, could and would ignore French law in the name of the tide of History. The authority of the Evian agreements existed only in French law, not in international law (the government's representatives had refused to sign documents negotiated with nationalist interlocutors to whom France recognized no official status or legitimacy).[23] Thus the paradox: the French government's constant invocation of the law and of legal guarantees was conjoined with blatant disregard for the constitution and the legal system when they stood—as they did—in the way of separating off Algeria.

The 8 April 1962 Referendum and the "Reserved Domain"

In presenting the protocols initialed at Evian to be debated by "the representatives of the Nation," the prime minister announced that on 8 April 1962 they would be submitted via referendum for the approval of the French people, excepting those who lived in Algeria. At this announcement Deputy Olivier Lefèvre-d'Ormesson predicted "the French people will ratify them by an enormous majority." He added a barbed qualification, "This is possible. After Munich, the majority would also have been considerable."[24] His prediction, if not his historical parallel, resonated with the desires of the met-

[22] Transcripts, Radiodiffusion Française. Answers by Philippe Thibaud, "Texte de l'émission diffusée au Bulletin de France II (13h) le 7 avril 1962: Comment pourra-t-on être algérien et français?" (7 April 1962), 1, and "Suite" (10 April 1962), 2, both in AN F/1a/5055.

[23] The so-called Evian Accords were officially termed "protocols," not treaties; instead of signing them, French envoys merely initialed them. This is why Michèle Cointet's disdainful summary of GPRA negotiators' reaction to legal language is flawed: despite her assertion, international law was not yet in play; French legalism was. See *De Gaulle et l'Algérie française, 1958–1962* (Paris, 1995), 246–54.

[24] *J.O.* (1962), 465.

ropolitan French. There was a 65 percent turnout of registered voters, of whom 90.7 percent cast "Yes" votes. In other words, an absolute majority of all voters in continental France approved the accords.[25]

If independence now seemed obvious to most metropolitans, the actual referendum question triggered a vigorous debate. The first clause, accepting that the Evian Accords would regulate the future relations of an independent Algeria with the French Republic, codified what most people already believed to be true. Yet the referendum was not only about recognizing that Algeria was a foreign country. The second clause authorized the government to establish via decree any law it deemed necessary to enact the accords. Neither the legislature nor anyone else would have a say in this novel appropriation by the executive of legislative power. (Novel, that is, in the metropole: A similar authority, limited to the Algerian departments, had been given to the executive by the National Assembly's 16 March 1956 vote of the "Special Powers" law.)[26] Critics repeatedly mocked the way the question was posed. After the referendum received overwhelming support, a writer in Les Temps Modernes compared the collapse of two topics into a single question with asking "Are you hungry and would you like head of veal?" A right-wing deputy remarked that "a single response" was to be given "to two questions (1) To approve a policy for the present; (2) All power for the future." The government dismissed such attacks as partisan criticisms.[27]

Far more difficult to ignore was the fact that the Council of State had rejected the referendum project that the government submitted to it. Housed in the Palais-Royal, founded by Napoleon, and made up of top graduates of the nation's most well-respected schools, the Council of State remains the preeminent guarantor of the legality of state procedures and bureaucratic actions. Since the Ordinance of 31 July 1945, all acts that the government or parliament intends to propose must first be submitted to the council, although its rulings do not bind the legislature or the executive. (This reestab-

---

[25] In total, Année Politique 1962 (1963), 38.
[26] The text of the referendum reads:

First Article. The President of the Republic can conclude all agreements needed in conformity with the governmental declaration of 19 March 1962, if the Algerian populations, consulted by virtue of the Law of 14 January 1961, choose to constitute Algeria as a State in cooperation with France.

Second Article. Until the establishment of the new political organization eventually resulting from the self-determination of the Algerian populations, the President of the Republic can ordain, via ordinances or, according to the case, via decrees taken in the Council of Ministers, all legislative measures relative to the application of the governmental decrees of 19 March 1962.

On the 1956 law, see: Sylvie Thénault, Histoire de la guerre d'indépendance algérienne (Paris, 2005) 58–59.

[27] Jacques-Laurent Bost, "Le cour des choses," Les Temps Modernes 192 (May 1962): 1774; Declaration by Pierre Henault, député CNIP de la Manche, "Les parlementaires de la Manche et le référendum," La Presse de la Manche (5 April 1962), 1.

lished a responsibility that the Third Republic had eliminated with the Law of 24 May 1872.) Despite rules of confidentiality, this particular rejection was widely known. One referendum opponent summarized the decision of the Council of State as "declaring that the referendum was at once anticonstitutional, illegal, and illegitimate." Much trumpeted by those who opposed Evian, commentators have interpreted this rebuff as another example of the conservative nature of councillors of state: they opposed progress in general and decolonization in this instance. The reading follows that of de Gaulle, whose *Memoirs* acerbically advance this view of the body.[28]

Although the Palais-Royal archives remain closed, documents kept by the prime minister's office strikingly nuance these opposing interpretations. There was no clear disavowal of the proposed referendum. The Council of State agreed with a number of elements that other commentators argued were undeniably unconstitutional; two examples were whether part of the national territory could be abandoned and whether citizens living in Algeria could be excluded from the poll. The councillors accepted the premise of the first clause: Algeria was not France, despite the constitution. What they primarily sought to attenuate was the reach of the powers that the proposed second clause granted. The Council of State informed the government that it "was unable to adopt in its present form the second article of this project, which it judges contains a delegation of legislative power that is not in conformity with Articles 11 and 38 of the constitution." From the unpublished drafts forwarded to the prime minister's office, it appears that the council had suggested a different wording for the second article. More restrictive than the one eventually submitted to the voters, this proposal would have authorized only ordinances or decrees "decided in the Council of Ministers" as well as "concerning Algeria and concerning the governmental declarations mentioned in the first article." De Gaulle's government rejected these suggestions and maintained the original wording, which authorized the president of the Republic "by decrees in Council" (announced but neither discussed nor formulated) to implement "all regulatory measures necessary for the application" of the accords.[29]

Imposing the original formulation guaranteed that the executive could exercise its new prerogatives without any need to prove any direct relationship to Algeria. Commentators have focused on the tactical meaning of this maneuver, suggesting, for instance, that de Gaulle sought to force some supporters of Algerian independence to oppose the referendum on procedural terms, so that he could consolidate his claim to be uniquely responsible for peace. Such an interpretation places this maneuver in the context of earlier

[28] Edouard Lebas, deputé CNIP de la Manche, "Les parlementaires de la Manche et le référendum," *La Presse de la Manche* (7 April 1962), 1. See *Le Conseil d'Etat: Son histoire à travers les documents d'époque, 1799–1974* (Paris, 1974), 843.

[29] Conseil d'Etat, "Note n. 284.876. Séance du 20 mars 1962," in CAC/AN 780058/206 [F/60/01982].

divide-and-conquer tactics on the part of the president.[30] Rather than tactical, however, the executive's rejection of the Council of State's proposals reveals that the 8 April referendum was a continuation of the Gaullist strategy
of imposing presidential primacy over and above parliamentary, legal, or
constitutional limits. This strategy had already been obvious, for example,
in de Gaulle's famous 16 September 1959 speech, in which he called for "a
peace of the brave" with the FLN and embraced the previously taboo idea
of Algerian self-determination. While the substance of de Gaulle's speech was
critically important, equally significant was the way in which the speech expanded the power of the presidency. As the political scientist François Goguel
perceptively remarks, the speech "determined what from then on would be
national policy in Algeria." Neither the Constitution of 1958 nor republican
practice assigned such authority to the president of the Republic. This speech
inaugurated what Jacques Chaban-Delmas, the Gaullist president of the National Assembly, termed the "reserved domain" of foreign policy. In the National Assembly, critics contested this claim to presidential primacy in
Algerian policy on procedural grounds. In a parliamentary debate on 15 October 1959, an opponent of self-determination for Algeria insisted that he
had no constitutional right to approve or disapprove the general's statement.
According to this critic, the National Assembly, not a presidential pro-
nouncement, was where policy should be articulated. His fellow deputies,
however, chose content over form. They approved of the move toward self-
determination for Algeria; they thus allowed the president's claim for control over questions related to Algeria.

This precedent proved foundational, since it reaffirmed presidential primacy in foreign policy and beyond. Algeria, however, was not yet foreign.
As long as this remained legally the case, those struggling to maintain French
Algeria consistently challenged what they argued was an unconstitutional
usurpation of power by General de Gaulle. Parliamentary supporters of letting independence happen were unwilling to insist that the government explain what, how, and why it was moving toward this goal or to specify what
measures they believed were needed to effect the separation between Algeria and the Hexagon. In this silence, institutional developments took place
that would outlast the end of French Algeria. The consolidation of presidential primacy in foreign affairs highlights how such restructuring relied on
concerns about Algeria, although the changes imposed had little to do with
resolving the crisis Algerian nationalism provoked.

De Gaulle already had utilized popular and political fatigue with the conflict in Algeria to stake out presidential primacy in the Fifth Republic's first
referendum in January 1961. In late 1960, growing opposition to many of

---

[30] On possible electoral tactics, see François Goguel, "Les circonstances du référendum du
8 avril 1962," in *Chroniques électorales . . . la cinquième république du général de Gaulle: Les
scrutins politiques en France de 1945 à nos jours* (Paris, 1983), 195.

his other policy initiatives, such as proposed agricultural reforms, attempts
to distance France from the United Nations and the North Atlantic Treaty
Organization, and a project to develop an independent nuclear "strike force"
(*force de frappe*) threatened to combine with criticisms of his initiatives in
Algeria and isolate him politically. Bolstered by popular acclaim, he summoned the nation to vote via referendum to approve Algerian self-determination. Supporters of Algerian independence on the Left, notably the PCF
and the new left, as well as those who continued to defend French Algeria,
immediately called on voters to reject the initiative; the former denouncing
the maneuver by de Gaulle to delay independence, the later rejecting any
change in Algeria's relationship to the Republic. On 8 January 1961, overwhelming approval of the question solidified de Gaulle's claim to speak le-
gitimately for the French people. The president of the Republic successfully
split his opponents into multiple camps, isolating critics of his Algerian policies, whether they described the proposal as too much or not enough, and
silencing those who contested his policies in other areas.[31]

Given what the debates preceding the referendum of 8 April 1962 indicate, it is necessary to extend Goguel's comment, apropos of the 1959 parliamentary discussion of self-determination, that French Algeria's partisans
"defend on this occasion the traditional norms of parliamentary government
à la française."[32] Defenders of French Algeria were, in fact, consistent in this
defense. Only after Algerian independence did their ongoing affirmations of
what they characterized as the principles of republicanism against Caesarism
become a widely shared leitmotif for non-Gaullist parliamentarians.

The widespread unwillingness of most politicians, intellectuals, or journalists to engage in further public debate over Algeria opened an impressive
margin for government maneuvering. After the announcement of the Evian
Accords, pro-government propaganda and arguments worked to align public support for peace and popular approval for the man who achieved it:
Charles de Gaulle. The president's allies moved astutely to present the agreement as the definitive end of French involvement with Algeria. President de
Gaulle had brought peace to the French in the form of a cease-fire with the
FLN. Alongside the cease-fire, the government presented the protocols that
accompanied the announcement of peace quite differently: official descriptions emphasized that their contents concerned Algeria and not France. The
state radio's special program "Who Is Affected by the Evian Accords?"
opened with the question "How will these accords affect each inhabitant of
Algeria?"[33] The legalistic formulas of the accords were for Algerians; the ref-

---

[31] Ibid.

[32] François Goguel, "Les circonstances du référendum d'octobre 1962," in *Le référendum
d'octobre et les élections de novembre 1962* (Paris, 1965). Concerning the agricultural crisis,
see esp. p. 20; for 1959, p. 16.

[33] The Ministry of the Interior printed two pamphlets in conjunction with the announcement
of the Evian Accords. The first, "L'Algérie à l'heure de la paix" (Algeria at the Hour of Peace),

erendum of 8 April, limited to metropolitans, was only about peace. From this perspective, in which the reasons why Algeria should not be French went unstated, neither the referendum nor the transitional period could pass quickly enough. Three weeks would be scheduled to debate the former. Meanwhile, far from representing a genuine chance to consult the "populations" concerned, the so-called transitional period was, in fact, merely preparatory for the twin plebiscites, one in the metropole on 8 April, the second in Algeria on 1 July, designed to approve the formula agreed to by the French government and the FLN. One Socialist supporter of the accords wrote that "we are no longer talking about self-determination, but predetermination."[34] The vote seemed a mere formality, a formal acknowledgment of the "reality" that Algeria was not France. As such, the transition period, which when first announced was to last for more than a year, quickly shrank to three months and several days.[35]

Concern about the implications—beyond peace in Algeria—and the unconstitutionality of the 8 April referendum troubled the campaigns of all of the political parties, Gaullists excepted, which supported a "Yes" vote. In particular, some on the traditional non-Communist Left hesitated to approve de Gaulle's two-part referendum question. In his local newspaper, a Socialist deputy who supported a "Yes" vote expressed his "annoyance and unease at the way the [government] has posed two questions to which a single response should be given." He admitted that he was "personally hostile to this hypocrisy," which used the desire for peace "to try and make democrats swallow something more than support for the Evian Accords."[36] The Toulouse-based daily *Dépêche du Midi,* the dominant media voice in its region and ardent supporter of what remained of the Radical Party, called on its readers to cast blank or invalid ballots.[37] Yet, without explaining how it envisioned Algeria's independence—why it was necessary and how it should take place—the non-Communist Left could not find the grounds to explain what was wrong with the methods de Gaulle had chosen.

---

was reserved for "under-prefects, high civil servants, and local personalities." The second, to be widely distributed, was L'Algérie de demain" (The Algeria of Tomorrow). Yvon Bourges, Cabinet du Ministre de l'Intérieur, "Circulaire n. 184: Diffusion de deux brochures sur l'Algérie" (Paris, 20 March 1962), 1, in CAC/AN 770346/03. The first was produced by the Ministry of State for Algerian Affairs, the second by the Ministry of Information.

[34] René Schmitt, "Les parlementaires de la Manche et le référendum," *La Presse de la Manche* (3 April 1962).

[35] Foreign Service archives reveal that, while publicly accepting and taking advantage of the assumption that independence was almost a formality, de Gaulle made sure that every detail of the transition was juridically sound, never admitting that French sovereignty in Algeria would be undermined until the correct formulas were fulfilled.

[36] Schmitt, "Les parlementaires de la Manche."

[37] On the important echo the *Dépêche du Midi*'s summons received, see Préfet de la Haute-Garonne, "à M. le Min. de l'Intérieur/ref: circ. 206 du Bureau des élections" (27 March 1962), in AN F/1cII/640; Direction centrale des Renseignements Généraux, "Sommaire général" (Paris, 18 April 1962), 7, in CAC/AN 800280, article 216; Ministère de l'Intérieur, "Note à l'attention de M. Bonis-Charancle" (2 May 1962), 3–4, in AN F/1cII/634.

In the parliamentary debates there had been near silence from those who later called for voters to approve the accords, although some wordlessly expressed their reservations by applauding the extended speeches of those deputies who ardently rejected the agreements.[38] Supporters of the "Yes" vote also proved taciturn on the campaign trail. One week before the vote, the RG reported, the Gaullists and the Communists were the "only notably active political formations." (This phrase contradicts the report's next paragraphs, which detail the intense efforts of those who called for a "No" vote.)[39] The last three days of the campaign did see a marked increase in political party activity in support of a positive response, limited, the RG remarked, to "tracts and posters," with few appearances by local notables. The activists joined in the National Rally to Vote "No," meanwhile, "visibly accentuated" their already frenzied propaganda efforts, which, one summary enumerated, included the distribution of "one hundred thousand copies of a poster on the 'illegal nature' of the referendum and five hundred thousand tracts calling for a 'No to de Gaulle'."[40]

Largely ignored in the metropole, the campaign moved people in Algeria to action, despite the official exclusion of voters living there. Members of parliament who spoke in the name of Algeria amplified popular anger and apprehension among "Europeans" in the trans-Mediterranean departments. Military intelligence in Algeria reported, first, that even in the untroubled small villages of the east, "French people of European origin are irritated at having been excluded from the forthcoming referendum." A report on the Algiers area remarked "signs of bitterness following . . . the decision to exclude the 'pieds noirs' from the April referendum." In this context, pro–French Algeria "declarations made at the tribune of the National Assembly," although in fact ignored in the metropole, "offered Europeans the impression that the parliamentary opposition to the government's policies had offered a striking presentation of its positions" and this "gave them some slim consolation." They could not imagine that their own certainties now meant so little in metropolitan decision making.[41]

Excluded from the ballot box, those angered by this denial of their citizenship loudly expressed their discontent: they first took to the streets, beginning with a strike that shut down the major cities of Algeria immediately following the announcement of the cease-fire and moving on to noisy demonstrations filled with tricolor flags and echoing with patriotic songs. In addition, the French of Algeria used every means at their disposal to summon

[38] Goguel, "Les circonstances du référendum du 8 avril 1962," 190.

[39] Direction centrale des RG, "Sommaire général" (Paris, 3 April 1962), 1, in CAC/AN 800280, article 216.

[40] Direction centrale des RG, "Sommaire général" (Paris, 5 April 1962), 1, in CAC/AN 800280, article 216; Direction centrale des RG, "Sommaire général" (Paris, 6 [sic, 7] April 1962), 2, in CAC/AN 800280, article 216.

[41] Lt.-Colonel Cousin, "Bulletin hebdomadaire de renseignements. Semaine du 24 au 30 mars 1962" (SP 87.000, 31 March 1962), 27, in SHAT 1H/1436/D(1).

metropolitans to recognize a situation that to them was clear. The song that rallied defenders of French Algeria opened with the verses "We are the Africans, / we return from afar / to save the Fatherland."[42] "The Africans" was the battle hymn of the Army of Africa (or First French Army), most memorably of the regiments raised and stationed in Algeria after the Allies had liberated these departments from the Vichy state in November 1942. These regiments, with a majority of "Muslim" Algerian soldiers, had landed in Provence at the end of World War II to participate in the liberation of metropolitan France.[43] For those who intoned "The Africans," as with the deputies who referred to these people until days before the cease-fire as "Algerians," the idea that they were not French was more than unthinkable: it meant that France itself was in danger. Confronted with the referendum of 8 April, a vote that excluded them, they were summoned, as an OAS flyer distributed in Oran announced, "to renew the war of subversion and above all psychological warfare on the metropole." To achieve this, the flyer suggested, "OAS tracts must no longer be thrown away, but must find their way to the Metropole." The arguments therein, the diehards believed, would convince their compatriots.[44]

In the days leading up to the referendum, those who spoke in the name of French Algeria used every available means of what the OAS tract termed "psychological warfare." Among the most active were the organizers of a manifesto titled "We Are French." By late March, hundreds of thousands of Algerians had signed this rallying call, and the sponsors of the manifesto remained convinced that its message would suffice to block Algerian independence. "France," one of their tracts told their fellow Algerians, "is going to vote on 8 April. France . . . but not us." Perhaps to disassociate themselves from OAS terrorism, perhaps to further a critique of the government's violation of the law and their rights that left them little room to maneuver, they emphasized that they were denied the vote and other legal means to express their resistance. In response, they implored all Algerians, "*We Must Tell the Truth!* . . . We will let the world know our will to remain French, to bear witness before History." Their summons to "cover Algeria with the Bleu Blanc Rouge," the national colors, over the weekend of the referendum was addressed to "*Union Members, Veterans, Reserve Officers, Students, Intellectuals, and Workers.*"[45]

---

[42] Army intelligence in Algeria repeatedly noted the role of this song, e.g., Commandant de la Gendarmerie en Algérie/Oran, "Fiche de renseignement n. 789" (Oran, 10 October 1961), in SHAT 1H/1735/1.

[43] See Anthony Clayton, *France, Soldiers, and Africa* (London, 1988).

[44] OAS ZONE III, T/600, "*Oranaises, Oranais . . .*" (26 March 1962), in AN 78 AJ/32.

[45] Comité de la patronage de la Campagne, "Je suis Français," "*Diffusez, Diffusez—La France va voter le 8 avril*" (March–April 1962), in AN 78 AJ/32l. For the number of signatures, see Ministre d'Etat chargé des Affaires algériennes, service de l'information, "Ephémerides n. 5" (1–15 March 1962), 5, in SHAT 1H/1128/5; Lt.-Colonel Cousin, "Bulletin hebdomadaire de renseignements. Semaine du 10 au 16 mars 1962" (SP 87.000, 17 March

Partisans of a "No" to Evian brought this campaign to the metropole. Relying on the post-1955 paradigm of "integration," which promised to reconcile the recognition of difference and republican equality, those who rejected Evian were able to present themselves as drawing from social groups and advancing arguments associated with the political Left: antiracism, the Rights of Man, and republicanism. *L'Esprit public*, a journal founded by right-wing anti-Gaullist intellectuals in 1960, published under the title "They Are French" the accounts of "two French citizens of Algeria" and "their will to live and die French: the one," deputy and mayor Ahcen Ioualalen, "is of Muslim origin, the other," René Moatti, "of Jewish origin." The article's preface noted that the same issue reproduced a speech given at the National Assembly by Deputy Pierre Portolano. "A 'Muslim,' a 'Jew,' a 'Pied Noir,' all three born on Algerian soil, proclaim that they are brothers, sons of the same Fatherland and that this patrie is France. The policy," incarnated in the Evian Accords, "the one that today tends to see them as different from each other and wants to exclude them from the national community, is a policy of racial segregation."[46] Their argument that "the guarantees granted to Europeans but denied to Muslims, *so many illusions, so many lies*" emphasized at once the racism and the hypocrisy of a government that violated laws and the constitution while it asked Algerians to put their trust in a legal arrangement.[47]

The argument that Algeria was French territory allowed opponents of Evian to synthesize their claims to represent both antiracism and republican legalism. The focus on territory was starkest in those warnings that depicted a geographically diminished France, for example, a broadside from the National Committee for the Defense of Territorial Integrity that urged a "*No! to Atomic Suicide!*" Noting that "de Gaulle wants atomic missiles," the tract explained that "in case of nuclear warfare, the farther away our missiles are, the safer you will be. While France plus Algeria and the Sahara makes 2,700,000 km2, France without . . . makes 500,000 km2." The point was clear: "*Lose Algeria and the Sahara and Bring the Atomic Menace Closer to Your Home,*" or keep them and "*Push Away This Threat.*"[48] More subtly, foregrounding the juridical truth that the boundaries of France included Algeria and the Sahara allowed a facile elision of the actual history of the exclusion of most of Algeria's population from legal equality until 1958.

1962), 25, in SHAT 1H/1436/D(1). The numbers are not verified, but all observers reported a mass phenomenon.

[46] Ahcen Ioualalen, deputy mayor of Aomar [Grande Kabylie], and René Moatti, "Ils sont français," *L'Esprit public* 28 (March–April 1962): 3.

[47] OAS, "*Algériens, Algériennes!*" (21 March 1962), in AN 78 AJ/32.

[48] Comité national de défense de l'intégrité du territoire, "*Non!* au suicide atomique!" (March–April 1962), in AN 78 AJ/32. This message also mobilized the large number of French people, politicians, and military men opposed to de Gaulle's plan for a nuclear strike force. De Gaulle explicitly put forward nuclear deterrence as a replacement for the security and grandeur provided by the empire.

Pro–French Algeria evocations of Algeria's place in French history made colonialist oppression disappear; they concurrently described a France open to religious and ethnic differences. The syncretism of republican arguments articulated by individuals or organizations associated with the Far Right was particularly revelatory in this regard. The rather frequent and certainly symptomatic use of the term "province"—with its echoes of the Kingdom of France and old traditions—to describe French Algeria in anti-Evian tracts was one of a number of syntactical signifiers rooted in the political language of the Far Right. (The invocation of conspiracy theories was another.) In this context, its deployment worked to rhetorically lengthen Algeria's historical attachment to France; it also suggested false depth to the French citizenship, since World War II, of Algerians with Koranic civil status. This idiom allowed even the royalists of Action Française to publish propaganda that failed to distinguish itself from the republican and antiracist line the OAS espoused. "Never has France victorious surrendered a French territory," one royalist mimeograph began, "and when the recourse to arms failed her, never has France ceased to fight for the return of a province momentarily lost. De Gaulle," it charged, "wants to drive out of the national community a province French for 132 years (French longer than the Savoy or the County of Nice)," and claimed that "to vote 'Yes' would be to *turn over to the Assassins of the FLN* the 90% of French Christians, Muslims, and Jews who, in 1958, again said yes to France." Republican legalism book-ended these patriotic lines, which were introduced with the phrase "[this referendum] *is in violation of our nation's laws,*" and which was followed by a paragraph explaining, "We say '*No*' because this referendum *plebiscite violates the constitution* (the Council of State said so)." Action Française offered as proof, not Salic law or eternal French values, but the Constitution of 1958's Articles 2 ("France is an *indivisible* Republic") and 5 ("The President of the Republic . . . is the guarantor . . . of *territorial integrity*"), while contesting de Gaulle's use of article 11.[49] This tract's admixture of classic far-right coding and tone with arguments alien to this tradition was typical of the propaganda that such groupings pumped out in this brief, intense moment of ideological upheaval.[50] The various elements backing the OAS, determined to keep Algeria French, insisted on what they presumed were the most compelling arguments: the laws and history of the Republic and the French identity of all Algerians. For ideologues and activists attached to the Far Right, repro-

[49] Action Française/la Restauration nationale, "Voici pourquoi nous disons *Non*" (March 1962), in AN 78 AJ/32. The deployment of constitutionalism, in and of itself, was not out of character for the post-Vichy French Far Right. As Richard Vinen discusses, the struggle to defend accused collaborators in French courts, which consumed many in this microcosm after Vichy's collapse, renewed the French Far Right's reliance on the laws of the Republic. See Richard Vinen, *Bourgeois Politics in France, 1945–1951* (Cambridge, 1995), 105.

[50] For assessments, see AN F/1cII/640, folder titled "Référendum du 8 avril 1962. Rapports de préfets sur les résultats," in which Action Française plays a notable role. For examples of tracts that were distributed, see AN 78 AJ/32.

ducing these arguments also posed obvious problems. Yet their attempts to grapple with such contradictions cannot be reduced to simple hypocrisy: this instance of far-right political confusion—the embrace of a rhetoric of "integration" in the (failed) defense of the province of Algeria—prepared the ground for new theoretical certainties. In the summer of 1962, far-right journals in France and Belgium began to publish harsh self-criticism of their movement. How could they ever have pretended that Algerian "Arabs" could be French? Among these journalists were those who would soon found the racialist "New Right" movement. (This as yet unexplored history is ill served, it must be noted, by Pierre-André Taguieff's efforts to rehabilitate one of those journalists, Alain de Benoist.)[51] In any case, the brutal violence of the OAS overshadowed all of these arguments for French Algeria. Radio journalist Claude Terrien told his listeners the week before the ballot that "there are two referendum campaigns, one of thought and one of blood." Referring to the Algiers' suburb where a recent brutal OAS attack had killed dozens of "Muslim" Algerians convalescing in hospital beds, he insisted that "many cannot help but think of Bouzareah," in listening to the arguments of three deputies from Algiers for the "No" vote.[52]

Rather than arguments, it was the register of sentiment (to which Louis Joxe appealed when he spoke of "good sense" and "trust") that permeated the isolated attempts to respond to the anguish of French Algerians. The Socialist Party leader, Guy Mollet, addressed French Algerians, arguing that "I have the right to ask them" to reflect on what they were doing. "I took several important decisions to guarantee their basic liberties," he recalled in a spring 1962 statement. "I am committed—insofar as I and my friends can exercise any influence—to do everything to prove that we are in solidarity with them."[53] On the verge of Algerian independence, scattered invocations of empathy began to give depth to what until then had been difficult to articulate: yes, Algerians were different from French people; perhaps, however, some people from Algeria could be French. Like arguments that French laws would guarantee their Frenchness, these calls to trust the intangible bonds between French people encountered little discernible echo among those in Algeria who wanted to remain French. Their unwillingness to believe in the weight of a sentimental understanding of French identity

[51] For examples of this self-criticism, see Jean Pleyber, "Les travaux et les jours: 'Soldats devoyés et aventuriers criminels'," *Ecrits de Paris* (March 1962): 10–20; Gilles Mermoz, "Connaissances de l'OAS: Illusions lyriques," *Ecrits de Paris* (October 1962): 50–57; and "Connaissances de l'OAS: Les hommes de la dernière chance," *Ecrits de Paris* (November 1962): 55–64; as well as *Europe-Action*, which began publishing from Belgium in the summer of 1962. This magazine was quickly joined by de Benoist and other disappointed far-right French supporters of the OAS, who later founded the Nouvelle droite. Taguieff ignores the specific historical context in which de Benoist and others began to develop their new vision of race and European identity. See *Sur la nouvelle droite* (Paris, 1994).

[52] Europe 1, 4 April 1962, 8:30 a.m. Cited in Michèle Cotta and Nicole Racine, "La Radiodiffusion," in *Le référendum du 8 avril 1962*, ed. Goguel.

[53] Etienne Maquin, *Le parti socialiste et la guerre d'Algérie* (Paris, 1990), 37.

largely explains why such people soon fled Algeria to remain in French territory.

A widely noted and reproduced editorial, "Beyond a Monosyllabic Yes," by former prime minister Edgar Faure intimated what he called "the perplexity, the disarray" of many who had defended French Algeria under republican auspices, yet were now ready to accept independence.[54] The Radical deputy implored his local electors and all metropolitans to understand the anguish of French Algerians and to reach out to them. This plea was conjoined with an injunction to French Algerians, "who must look to the future and must understand." His was a delicate negotiation between sympathy and condemnation of their support for the OAS, what he summed up as French Algerians' "collective aberration." Searching for balance, he presented France as a harmonious combination of territory and people. The text begins with soil, what the French term *terroir,* invoking "this France, which is theirs," a land composed of "our hamlets, our cantons, our villages, rural France," a double of which French Algerians had sought "obsessively to recreate." It was a grafting, he implied, that could not take "on that African land." Yet while his pastoral imagery drew from a republican mythology of the French *province,* Faure did not reduce the Republic or France to local color:

> In the National Assembly, an orator who does not share my views, said to his adversaries, "You have lost faith." I would say, to those who agree with him, "It is you who have lost faith, for you have placed your faith in a past that will never return; we still have faith, and because we hold on to this faith all can be saved, we can be saved together." This faith is never opposed to destiny, it is with it.[55]

Faure relied on "faith" to reach beyond law and history. His summons was linked both to the land and to what he called "destiny." Yes, he argued to those who doubted, those people from Algeria were truly French, although—the caveat is crucial if tacit—from a land that only pretended to be France. French people must express their knowledge that these Algerians are French, they must "cry out to them . . . let us group together so they will be touched—for it is this that can save them—by our warmth, which they so need." An editorial in *Paris-Match* entitled "The Unique Guarantee," called on metropolitans to offer "the only guarantee that is valid, pacifying, and decisive: the friendship of French people for French people." *Paris-*

---

[54] For the SFIO, see "Déclaration televisée de Guy Mollet au nom du Parti socialiste, le 2 avril 1962."

[55] Sent by the Préfet du Doubs, "Article paru dans la presse régionale JA/SB cab" (7 April 1962), 1 and 14, in AN F/1cII/640; Edgar Faure, "Au-delà du oui monosyllabique," *Le Comtois* (6 April 1962). See also Léo Hamon, "Après le cessez-le-feu," *Le Comtois* (29 March 1962), 1 and 12.

"Il faut dire à nos compatriotes, les Français d'Algérie, ce qu'on ne leur a pas jusqu'ici assez dit."
Edgar Faure.

...MERDE !

Cartoonist Siné's response to Edgar Faure's plea, "We must say to our compatriots, the French of Algeria, that which we have not, as yet, told them enough." In *La Voie Communiste*, March–April 1962. Reprinted by permission of the artist.

Match left unstated how the French would know which people from Algeria were French.[56]

These pleas for friendship (which avoided using the word "fraternity") were not simply echoed, they also brought responses. One explicit rebuttal appeared on the front page of *La Voie Communiste*, the monthly publication of an oppositional group within the PCF. Above an outtake from Faure's editorial, the phrase "We must say to our compatriots, the French of Algeria, that which we have not, as yet, told them enough," the far left periodical's cartoonist Siné appended a drawing of a happy fellow shouting: "Merde!"[57] A poll reported that "sixty-two percent of French people believe that France had no obligations to assist potential repatriates from Algeria."[58] As Siné's drawing suggests, the far and new left accused those on the traditional left, who in the heat of the campaign expressed understanding for the "colonists," of sympathy with the enemy.

In March and April 1962, despite some concerns about Gaullist manipulation of the referendum results, virtually all of the French media and political class came out in support of a resounding "Yes." Desperate not to quell the voters' eagerness to see the war over, to be done with Algeria, all but the most ardent opponents veiled their criticisms of the accords and the referendum. French political scientist Jean Touchard, writing soon after the referendum about what he characterized as "the brief and dull campaign" for the "Yes" vote, argued that "most political formations acted as if it was really more of an 'observation round' before the decisive confrontation." Certain that de Gaulle would call early elections, no one wanted to leave the political peace dividend to the Gaullist Union for the New Republic (UNR). Touchard remarks that "before 8 April it seems that few politicians, including [prime

[56] Editorial, "La seule garantie," *Paris-Match* 673 (3 March 1962), 27.
[57] *La Voie Communiste* n.s., 27 (March–April 1962).
[58] Cited in Michel Abitbol, "La Cinquième République et l'accueil des Juifs d'Afrique du Nord," in *Les Juifs de France,* ed. J.-J. Becker and A. Wieviorka (Paris, 1998), 302.

minister Michel Debré] had predicted" de Gaulle's decision not to immediately call elections.[59]

When the results were in, the various experts grouped in the Ministry of the Interior, whether electoral analysts or police intelligence, agreed that the referendum's primary message was clear: "The referendum confirms that the majority of the French are attached to the style and the orientation that the head of state has given to the ensemble of French politics," the RG estimated, "and consecrates the failure of the activists and their supporters."[60] In the following months, public pronouncements as well as more private discussions by de Gaulle's government and allies continued to connect these two elements: a popular mandate for presidential primacy, opposed only by "the activists and their supporters."

What those who voted "No" meant proved somewhat confusing. Most analysts identified "No" votes as emanating from the "nationalist opposition," or the Far Right, most recently incarnated by Pierre Poujade and his allies. From this perspective, the far-right vote had plummeted by some seven hundred thousand voters. Certain internal government assessments of what one identified as "less weak percentages of the 'No' centered in the departments of the Garonne Valley and the Mediterranean region," pondered a different explanation: "Can we tie this to the presence in these regions of numerous repatriates from North Africa?"[61] Political analysts struggled to explain votes not easily assigned to the "Far Right" or to "repatriates." Two political scientists, interpreting the relatively elevated "No" vote in the south of France, counted traditional far-right clienteles with the add-on of recent repatriates from North Africa, but this addition did not account for all the votes. They could only "point out the ambiguous attitude of a number of local notables from the traditional Left for whom sympathy for the ultras strangely joined with concerns for republican 'legality'." The thematic constancy of the "No" campaign, which, as I have shown, fixated on republican catchphrases and invocation to raise concerns about government abuse of the law and the republic, did not matter. It did not make sense, it was only strange. To vote "No" revealed sympathy for the OAS and nothing else.[62]

The Emotional End of the "Long Fourth Republic"

After the 8 April 1962 referendum in the ninety departments north of the Mediterranean affirmed metropolitan acceptance of Algerian independence,

[59] Jean Touchard, preface to Goguel, Le référendum du 8 avril 1962, x.

[60] Direction centrale des RG, "Sommaire général" (Paris, 9 April 1962), 1, in CAC/AN 800280, article 216.

[61] Ministère de l'Intérieur, "Physionomie du scrutin de référendum" (n.d.), 3, in AN F/1cIV/634.

[62] Alain Lacelot and Jean Ranger, "Analyse des résultats," in Goguel, ed., Le référendum du 8 avril 1962, 135.

a second referendum, on 1 July in France's fifteen Maghrebin departments, confirmed the enthusiasm in Algeria for this evolution. Large turnouts and overwhelming support promised, finally, the end of the Algerian War, the end of French colonization, the end of French Algeria. On 3 July, in Paris, the Fifth Republic acknowledged the "Algerian populations'" vote for independence; two days later, in Algiers, the leader of the Provisional Government of the Algerian Republic, Benyoucef Ben Khedda, proclaimed the liberation of the Algerian nation, exactly one hundred and thirty two years after the capitulation of Algiers to the French invaders.

Yet during the same period that direct French governance and the eight-year war with Algerian nationalists was ending, another battle, born from the first, occupied the forefront of French public discussions: defenders of French Algeria fought on. Spearheaded by the "activists" of the OAS, they rejected the peace the French government and the FLN had agreed on. On both sides of the announced Mediterranean frontier conflict was engaged with plastic bombs and assassination attempts, and it was overwhelmingly supported in the heavily "European" areas of Algeria. Although almost all Muslim French citizens from Algeria vigorously rebuffed or simply ignored the claims of these combatants, the activists professed to light the way toward a different future, where the promise of French Algeria finally would be realized. However, most people in metropolitan France perceived them as wanting to prolong the nightmare in France and Algeria—in order, government officials and intellectuals on the left suggested, to restore the dark days of Vichy, or worse.[63]

These fears provided the justification for government action, just as the referendums of 8 April and 1 July 1962 offered the government new tools. In the name of repressing the OAS, the government made impressive and durable changes to French law. To do so, the government instrumentalized popular eagerness to make real and irreversible the assertion that Algeria and Algerians were not French. By consistently adopting "the broadest possible conception" of the powers the 8 April referendum authorized, the president introduced a number of previously "exceptional" practices—which left-wing and other critics heroically had contested when used to fight the FLN—into permanent elements of the criminal code. These ensured executive oversight of judicial decisions and expanded police powers. A number of studies explore how the repression of actual or suspected nationalist activity affected French law and justice. Yet the ways that policies and politics premised on the novel certainty that Algeria was not French altered French law and ideas of justice have received little attention.[64] These developments, however, di-

[63] In addition to metropolitan departments, voters in the four DOM (*départements d'outre-mer*) and seven TOM (*territoires d'outre-mer*) also voted on 8 April. For the most detailed analysis of the limits of OAS control over terrorist activity in Algeria, see Jean Monneret, *La phase finale de la guerre d'Algérie* (Paris, 2001).

[64] See the pathbreaking special issue of *Genre humain,* Juger en Algérie (To Judge in Algeria) (September 1997), esp. the preface by Nadine Fresco, 7–9. See also Karine Vartanian, "Le

rectly extended—indeed, accentuated—forms of legal repression first tried out against nationalists; French jurist Arlette Heymann suggests that "the same writer employed the same formulas."[65] Two factors (both structured by racism) made the latter less efficacious than the former: first, the much smaller scale of state-sanctioned violence employed. While the legal edifice erected to fight pro–French Algeria terrorism was similar to that used to combat nationalist efforts, the incidence of extralegal use of torture and, in particular, on-the-spot executions was not comparable (although examples of both did occur, most notably as a result of the Gaullist *barbouzes,* the nickname given to members of a violent anti-OAS group that the French secret service set up in late 1961).[66] Second, the complicity, explicit or otherwise, that significant numbers of the military and judicial personnel offered to individual activists or their cause. Yet, unlike the antinationalist struggle, the fight against the OAS was a government victory, won, on the one hand, by direct and constant executive intervention in military and judicial decisions and, on the other hand, by silencing all political and ideological support for French Algeria.[67]

No assessment of the Republic's "life or death" struggle against the activists pretends that measures made possible by the referendum altered the scope, nature, or effectiveness of government anti-OAS practice. Heymann's study of judicial repression against the FLN reinforces the argument the Council of State had made in rejecting the second clause of the 8 April referendum: disturbances linked to Algerian independence could be fully countered through existing French institutions. What these measures did do was ensure the longevity of legal practices implemented in response to the nationalist uprising in Algeria, "to permanently modify French law."[68] Whereas FLN "outlaws" were charged with crimes whose definition denied their political nature, a series of ordinances identified OAS associates as criminal "activists." Nationalists had been indicted for participating in activity related to a certain place, the departments of Algeria and Sahara, at a specific time, after 1 November 1954; in 1962, to agree with the OAS and support its agenda became crimes. All this was done with little political opposition. Faced with the choice of protesting the obvious excesses of the gov-

droit de la guerre d'Algérie: Réflexions sur l'exceptionalité," PhD diss., Université de Paris–X, 1995.

[65] See the articles in *Genre humain* (September 1997).

[66] On the use of torture against suspected OAS activists and supporters, see Pierre Vidal-Naquet, "Documents: L'OAS et la torture," *L'Esprit* n.s., 5 (May 1962): 825–39; and Raphaëlle Branche, "La torture pendant la guerre d'Algérie," in *La guerre d'Algérie, 1954–2004: La fin de l'amnésie,* ed. Mohammed Harbi and Benjamin Stora (Paris, 2004), 381–401, 400–401. On the "irregular" assassins that the government installed in Algiers to kill suspected OAS activists and sympathizers, see Jean Monneret, "Les 'barbouzes' contre l'OAS: Nouveau regard," *Guerres mondiales et conflits contemporains* 191 (1998): 89–116.

[67] Arlette Heymann, *Les libertés publiques et la guerre d'Algérie* (Paris, 1972), 188. For the juridico-military combat against the FLN, see Sylvie Thénault, "Assignation à residence et justice en Algerie (1954–1962)," *Genre humain* (September 1997): 108.

[68] Heymann, *Les libertés publiques et la guerre,* 43. On measures taken, see p. 44.

ernment's efforts to crush the OAS, most public figures decided that complicity with the pro–French Algeria terrorists, with what Edgar Faure identified as their "cynical exploitation of republican scruples," constituted the greater risk to liberty.[69]

The president of the Republic presented various executive measures as necessary to speed punishment of OAS activists. The authority the 8 April vote extended made this possible. Why were such wide-reaching reforms necessary when ministerial intervention and exceptional measures had proven so effective? It is clear that they were not implemented primarily to combat the OAS. In fact, a top secret overview of anti-OAS judicial methods prepared for Prime Minister Debré, while not opposed to the planned reforms, insisted that the two top priorities, the choice of magistrates and close government control of their decisions, did not require expanded executive jurisdiction. The second clause of the 8 April referendum advanced not the fight against the OAS but de Gaulle's desire to establish presidential primacy for the long term.[70]

The new powers the referendum authorized acted most efficiently to make permanent the marginalization of parliament that de Gaulle had "exceptionally" established in 1958, and to rewire the French legal system. At the war's close, de Gaulle consistently and without opposition authorized arbitrary justice and condoned a general disregard for traditional juridical procedure in cases concerning accused activists. He exercised control through the Select Council for Algerian Affairs, a body constituted in 1959, which allowed him to decide French policy in Algeria in consultation with a limited number of ministers and military advisers. In the months preceding Algerian independence, preparatory memos and summary accounts detail that juridical matters and the redeployment and withdrawal of French armed forces from Algeria were the only subjects the Select Council considered.[71] Briefs that advisers prepared for a council meeting on 3 April 1962 show how de Gaulle brooked no "legalistic" rigmarole in suppressing OAS resistance. The agenda was wholly concerned with questions of military justice and prisoners.[72] The overall focus of "juridical" concerns was what one note termed

---

[69] Faure cited in Goguel, "Les circonstances du référendum du 8 avril 1962," 184.

[70] For a list and description of these ordinances and decrees, see Heymann, *Les libertés publiques et la guerre*, 43–48; Ministère d'Etat chargé des Affaires algériennes, "Note pour le Premier Ministre en vue du Conseil restreint du Mardi 3 Avril 1962 à 17h" (Paris, 2 April 1962), 3 and 7, in MAE 117.

[71] See MAE 117.

[72] The official agenda was typical: "(1) Operations of the Military Tribunal; (2) State of primary judicial investigations in progress; (3) Measures taken for the installation of the Tribunal for Public Order in Algeria; (4) Problems linked to the application of the Evian Accords concerning the liberation of prisoners." See Secrétaire Général de la Présidence de la République, "Ordre du jour: Conseil restreint du mardi 3 avril 1962 à 17h, 1 avril 1962," in MAE 117. On the procedures used against suspected "activists," see the preparatory note for Conseil restreint, 3 April 1962: Ministère d'Etat chargé d'Affaires algériennes, "Fonctionnement du Tribunal militaire" (3 April 1962), in MAE 117.

"the acceleration of judicial repression," which was currently subjected, the author complained, "to inadmissible delays." The minister of justice was instructed to make the judgment of certain "exemplary crimes a priority." De Gaulle's instructions—one note spoke of "what the President would like to see"—guided his ministers' constant and emphatic intervention in the legal process. Government intervention accelerated significantly after the referendum. Invoking Article 2 of the Law of 13 April, the government sought to inscribe into law "exceptional" practices (that limited the rights of the accused) the military had used against the FLN.[73]

It was civil servants who most energetically opposed efforts to abandon legal protections for the accused and traditional legal norms. French courts as well as government administrators, whose modus operandi was steeped in legal procedure, acted quickly to stymie what was perceived as executive overreaching. The Paris Court of Appeals restricted one ordinance (Ordinance of 1 September 1962) that "modified the procedure to follow for 'certain crimes of a nature to threaten public peace'"; the decision limited its application to "criminal infractions related to the events in Algeria." By insisting that the government provide proof that such a relationship existed, the ruling narrowed the ordinance's claim that an ambient OAS threat to public peace authorized any police action the government deemed necessary.[74]

Still, the authority the executive had gained to reverse republican precedent was impressive. The author of a 1962 legal commentary, while approving the letter of the Paris Court of Appeals' decision, despaired that, in spirit, "this ordinance changes the character and the nature of justice, promoting summary and exceptional justice over standard justice [droit commun]."[75] The jurist admitted that the executive had the right to do this, emphasizing how law and judicial practice (not to mention the absence of judicial review of laws in France) limited the scope of opposition available to the courts. But a number of very public judicial decisions did directly challenge executive efforts. The most important legal rebuffs were the Military High Tribunal's verdict in the Salan trial and the Council of State's ruling in the Canal case, in which jurists acted to curb urgent efforts by government officials to deliver exemplary verdicts against OAS leaders. Scholars have recognized both cases as revelatory of the government's efforts to ignore and override the rule of law. Jurist Christian Guery cites the two to argue that "at each unwelcome judicial decision, the law was changed."[76]

[73] Gerard Wolff, "Note à l'attention de M. de Leusse" (8 May 1962), 2, in MAE 117.

[74] Paris Court of Appeals decision of 11 October 1962; commentary by Pierre Chambon in JCP 1962 bis, note Chambon.

[75] Ibid., 43.

[76] Christian Guery, "La justice pénale pendant la guerre d'Algérie," Genre humain (September 1997): 97. Although all his examples concern the repression of the OAS, Guery's argument focuses on French justice faced with the FLN during the war. See also Anne-Marie Duranton-Crabol, Le temps de l'OAS (Brussels, 1995), 234–36; and Jean-Louis Queyremonne, "Les décisions et les avis du Conseil d'Etat et du Conseil constitutionnel: Enjeu politique," Con-

What has gone unnoticed by commentators is that both of these court decisions that restricted government efforts were argued in historical terms. "Historical" questions (Are the "events in Algeria" over? How are ongoing developments in the metropole related to them?) could and did perturb executive efforts, because they undermined the political assumptions that legitimated such actions. Each ruling undermined one of the anti-OAS registers on which the government relied to make institutional changes that had little to do with Algeria. "The law was changed" after each decision not only to obtain the desired condemnation of the accused: executive intervention acted to end such instability, to reaffirm that terrorism and fascism still threatened, and thus that aggressive government action was legitimate. Whereas against the FLN the French government had sought to deny the possibility of nationalist claims competing with republican order, against the OAS the government worked to present new laws and decisions as necessary to exclude the activists from the body politic. Furthermore, government intervention reinforced public suspicion that the jurists had been corrupted by Algérie française sympathies, that their decisions were not based in the law, which they claimed to defend against government tampering, but served the OAS terrorists. The government could then present its insistence on arbitrary judgments and disregard for legal procedure as, in fact, reinforcing the judicial system as well as fighting fascistic terrorism.

These two "historical" rulings sowed trouble by placing the events presented in narratives different from those the government and most commentators embraced. They were all the more striking because of the legal limits meant to prevent any such deviation. Salan was tried by the Military High Tribunal, which the government established—in order to judge the captured putschist generals of April 1961—using the emergency powers of the constitution's Article 16 (Decree of 27 April 1961). This tribunal had already condemned Generals Challe and Zeller, who had surrendered; in absentia, Jouhaud and Salan were found guilty as well. It presented, Guery comments, "all the characteristics of an exceptional jurisdiction." Sharp restrictions on the rights of defendants—"the decision that the prosecutor had made in the preparatory phase could not be appealed, the accused had only two days to choose his defense counsel"—were exacerbated by the arbitrary basis (by executive order) on which an individual was sent before the tribunal. The 4 June 1962 ordinance establishing the Military Court of Justice, which the Canal decision later overturned, went even further in eliminating the rights of the accused: it allowed the Military Court of Justice to deny the defense the right to make any statements.[77] As with most of the legal mea-

---

seil constitutionnel et Conseil d'Etat (Paris, 1988): 405; J. B. King, "France: The Canal Affair and the OAS Case," in Politics and Civil Liberties in Europe: Four Case Studies, ed. R. F. Bunn and W. G. Andrews (London, 1967); Y.-F. Jaffré, Les tribunaux d'exception, 1940–1962 (Paris, 1962).

[77] See Guery, "La justice pénale pendant la guerre", 95.

sures pursued in the name of combating the OAS, changing the law reproduced a tactic already seen in earlier repression of pro-independence militants. After the Jeanson trial, in which defense depositions had proposed a
political context to explain the actions of the "suitcase carriers," the Ordinance of 6 October 1960 restricted depositions to "facts for which the
accused are reproached," as well as those addressing the accused's "personality" and "morality."[78] Like the trial of the suitcase carriers, the trial of
OAS chief Raoul Salan brought all of these contradictions into focus.

The capture of the ex-army general, who was picked up at a military roadblock on the outskirts of Algiers (despite his fake moustache and dyed hair)
on 20 April 1962, was a major blow to defenders of French Algeria. Following the late March arrest of ex-General Edmond Jouhaud, OAS second
in command and chief of operations in Oran, the incarceration of the OAS
chief removed the activists' top military leadership. Salan's trial began on 21
May, under intense press scrutiny in a tightly guarded Hall of Justice on the
Ile de la Cité, Paris. It was expected that the judges, hand picked by the government, would return the same verdict as they had given Jouhaud just weeks
before: the tabloid daily *France-Soir* headlined its 13 May edition "Already
Condemned to Die!" Nicknamed "the Mandarin," Salan had been hailed in
pro–French Algeria propaganda as the true "homme providentiel" even as
he was vilified in the French press as an opium-addicted colonialist and racist
killer.

Salan's defense team chose a very different courtroom strategy from that
of Jouhaud. The "number two man" of the OAS had responded at length to
questions about his actions in the failed putsch and with the activists. His
lawyers had emphasized the deep attachment of the "pied noir general" to
his Algerian birthplace. In contrast, in the trial of the last of what de Gaulle,
when rallying resistance to the putsch, had famously called "an insignificant
foursome of retired generals," Salan's defense chose political history over
emotion or personal biography. The accused traitor offered a short prepared
statement that began with his recognition that "I am the head of the OAS.
My responsibility is thus total." He then continued with his version of
France's history and achievements outside the metropole and what he
claimed was his role in that project, first as an officer, then with the OAS. He
refused to answer any questions.[79]

Jean-Louis Tixier-Vignancour, a long-time defender of far-right clients
and a future far-right candidate for president, led Salan's legal team. They
confronted the prosecution's damning evidence of the ex-general's activities
since the April 1961 putsch, what the newspaper of reference *Le Monde*
termed "One Year of Crime," with a strategy the same headline summarized

---

[78] Article 331, *CPP.* See Heymann, *Les libertés publiques et la guerre,* 269.

[79] See *Le procés d'Edmond Jouhaud: Compte rendu sténographique* (Paris, 1962) and Fab-
rice Laroche, *Salan devant l'opinion* (Paris, 1963), 209–10. Laroche later published under the
name Alain de Benoist and became a leading figure in the ultraracist Nouvelle droite.

as "For the Defense: Ten Years of History."[80] There was an initial challenge—at once almost ritual, yet fully coherent with OAS propaganda
claims—to the High Military Tribunal's competence to judge activities occurring after the state of emergency expired on 30 September 1961.[81] From
then on, through the testimony of witnesses ranging from serving officers to
former prime minister Debré, Salan's lawyers offered a courtroom narration
of the defense of French Algeria, punctuated with the testimony of actual actors in that drama.

The defense's announced goal was to show that Salan's indicted actions
were coherent with both his previous engagements as the commander of
French forces in Algeria and those of de Gaulle and his government in Algeria. They did so with some success. Writing in *L'Express,* Françoise Giroud
commented that "the invisible defendant is the head of state. . . . As for the
jury that is summoned to render a verdict, it is History!" A week later, she
marveled that because Salan was not taking the fall, "all the dirty laundry of
the extended family of 13 May [1958] already is snapping in the winds of
history." Still, much of the media, while recognizing the rhetorical éclat
of the defense team and its tactical victories in the courtroom, insisted, as
France-Observateur's André Delcroix (pen name of François Furet) wrote,
"There is only one trial, that of the OAS." They refused to let context obscure Salan's responsibility for OAS terror.[82]

When the verdict was returned on 23 May 1962, the majority of the
judges found Salan guilty of all charges. However, a majority also found that
there were "extenuating circumstances": instead of death, he was to be confined in perpetuity and stripped of the Légion d'honneur. Among Salan's partisans and critics this conviction was greeted as a victory for the defense. The
PCF daily *L'Humanité* reported, "Tixier-Vignancour yelled. At this signal, in
a room filled with fascists, the reaction was delirium." Those who objected
to the verdict presented it as yet another example of judicial "reaction"; a
number of periodicals attempted to identify the lenient judges by tracing
their links to pro–French Algeria acquaintances.[83]

Immediately, press commentators examined the decision's possible effects

---

[80] 15 May 1962.

[81] The charges against Salan included two sections: one concerned the April 1961 putsch,
for which he, like Jouhaud, had already been condemned to death in absentia; the second concerned his subsequent leadership of the OAS. The April 1961 application of Article 16 of the
Constitution of 1958 was the authority by which the Military High Tribunal's jurisdiction had
been established; crimes committed after its expiration, the government had announced, would
be added to the tribunal's authority by a law, a law that had not yet been passed when Salan's
trial began.

[82] "Le procès: La dernière lessive," *L'Express* 570 (17 May 1962), 12; *L'Express* 571 (24
May 1962), 12; A. Delcroix, "Le vrai procès Salan," *France-Observateur,* 629 (24 May 1962):
5–7.

[83] See for example, A. Delcroix, "Les contacts avec l'OAS", *France*-Observateur 630 (31
May 1962): 7. Unlike common law procedures in the United States and Britain, French judges
do not sign opinions.

on the continuing convulsions over Algeria. Excepting known OAS sympathizers, the critics far outweighed the few who chose to see the verdict as part
of bringing necessary closure to the war's torments. Both those who condemned the judgment as too precipitous and those who welcomed it as wise
saw it as anticipating a future reconciliation between metropolitans and
pieds noirs. "History," pronounced *Paris-Match*, "has never moved so
quickly, and Justice, which decides today in anticipation of the eventual rec-
onciliations of tomorrow, helps it turn the page."[84] This interpretation was
made possible by the escalating exodus, which had taken on dramatic pro-
portions since the ex-general's arrest. In Algeria, one intelligence officer
twinned verdict and exodus as the "epilogue to French Algeria." A *France-
Observateur* commentator suggested that the pieds noirs "also want to benefit from extenuating circumstances"; a reader wrote to the same magazine
in response to the judges' moderation to condemn "a part of the press that
is trying to make us more indulgent vis-à-vis the OAS, by presenting us with
the distress and the moral drama of the repatriates."[85]

Most accounts, however, expressed concern that the verdict would revive
the war. De Gaulle reportedly was enraged. The RG described French opinion as "surprised" by it, "believing that the High Tribunal's indulgence may
encourage the OAS."[86] A military commander in Algeria reported that "Europeans" greeted the verdict as a "divine surprise," not doubting that "the
judges were afraid of the OAS."[87] A reader's letter to *France-Observateur*
made clear that the concern was not really that now the OAS would win:
"What is tragic," he contended, "is that from now on we can no longer qualify them as mad [*fou*], but instead, au contraire, as logical criminals." Given
that just one week before, in *L'Express*, Giroud had identified pro-Salan witnesses as "logical madmen" [*fous logiques*], the change the verdict worked
seemed palpable.[88]

The jurist Robert Badinter responded to the decision by noting that if
"each trial is a battle," that of Salan was de Gaulle's "Sedan."[89] For Badinter and others, the defeat broke de Gaulle's authority. Yet what was imper-
iled was not, as Badinter presumed, the legal scaffolding of the regime, rather,
the legal defeat jeopardized the historical master narrative on which de

[84] Editorial, "La paix anticipée," *Paris-Match* 686 (2 June 1962), 7.

[85] Lt.-Colonel Rivière, "Bilan hebdomadaire de renseignements intéressant la Sécurité militaire en Algérie, n. 20. Semaine du 18 au 24 mai 1962" (SP 87.265, 26 May 1962), 1, in SHAT
1H/1456/2; A. Delcroix, "Les contacts avec l'OAS," *France-Observateur* 630 (31 May 1962),
7; M. Didier Saint-Maxen, de Saint-Die, "Nos lecteurs écrivent: Réfuser l'amalgame," *France-
Observateur* 630 (31 May 1962).

[86] Direction centrale des RG, "Sommaire général" (Paris, 24 May 1962), 1, in CAC/AN
800280, article 217.

[87] Rivière "Bilan hebdomadaire de renseignemnts intéressant la Sécurité militaire en Algérie", 5.

[88] M. J. Dufresne, Bar-le-Duc, "Nos lecteurs écrivent: Ces circonstance attenuantes," *France-
Observateur* 630 (31 May 1962), 2; "La dernière lessive," *L'Express* 571 (24 May 1962), 11.

[89] *L'Express* 572 (31 May 1962), 11.

Gaulle's extension of his authority depended. The tribunal's acknowledgment of the defense team's *petite histoire de l'Algérie française* (abridged history of French Algeria) upended the interpretation of events in Algeria that de Gaulle, with the accord of most French politicians and opinion makers, had crafted. After taking into account recent events in Algeria, the Military High Tribunal recognized that the tide of History—during his testimony Debré argued that "everything to do with decolonization has become . . . a force"—was *not* the only logical conclusion to draw from the situation. Whereas most politicians in France had refused to respond to the arguments of French Algeria partisans, de Gaulle's exceptional tribunal acknowledged that these claims were not simply irrational, all the while condemning the blood crimes committed in their defense. De Gaulle acted quickly to eliminate the institutional site that had broken, briefly, the tide of History narrative. On 24 May, the Minister of Information announced that the Military High Tribunal would be abolished, a maneuver one journalist saw as "somewhat incoherent." Yet, the pundit explained, having chosen the Military High Tribunal, de Gaulle "juridically had no way out." Eliminating the jurisdiction, the president of the Republic acted to reassert his authority.[90] Badinter had invoked the wrong "realm of memory." The end of the French overseas empire would have more in common with 1851 and the emergence of a plebiscitary regime than with 1870 and its collapse.

Legal authorities continued to interfere with de Gaulle's plans by offering historical interpretations to narrow de Gaulle's exercise of new powers. In the Canal decision (19 October 1962), the Council of State exercised what one jurist has termed "its maximum possible control" over the legality of government actions. The council rejected the presidential insistence that all ordinances taken under the authority of the Law of 13 April 1962 had the force of law;[91] this nullified the ordinance that had established the Military Court of Justice (announced as replacing the Military High Tribunal) specifically in order to judge accused OAS activists. The council rejected the opinion of government experts that the authority that the second article of Law 62–421 of 13 April 1962 gave to the executive was valid until such a time as an Algerian "National Assembly" approved by vote an Algerian government. Given, as the government insisted, that Algeria was not France, the context that determined the French government's actions should not be Algeria but events in France.[92] "The Algerian War was over," legal scholar Arlette Heymann concluded. "The Council of State asked itself if the prejudice the ordinance inflicted on general principles, in this case the rights of the de-

---

[90] A. Delcroix, "Les contacts avec l'OAS," *France-Observateur* 630 (31 May 1962). Decrees on 25 May and 1 June 1962 removed the tribunal's jurisdiction and established the Military Court of Justice to replace it.

[91] See Queyremonne, "Les décisions et les avis du Conseil d'Etat," 405.

[92] VS/SR, "Note. Objet: Durée des pouvoirs conférés par la loi du 13 avril 1962" (24 September 1962), in CAC 19960393, article 1.

fendant," she summarizes, "was justified by the circumstances of the moment." While admitting that such an assessment was possible, the councillors decided that, after Algerian independence, the actual context did not justify such an exception.[93]

In relying on their own historical interpretation, the councillors unveiled the abyss between what de Gaulle and his government were doing with the powers the April referendum offered them—altering the republican legal tradition—and the reasons they claimed the extension of executive authority was needed: the defense of the Republic. In their decision, the councillors, unlike Salan's judges, did not in any measure accede to the merit of pro-OAS arguments.[94] Yet the Council of State's seemingly uncontroversial historical judgment—that the events in Algeria were over—threatened de Gaulle and his allies. The government wanted to continue to use "what made sense to the French," the end of the Algerian War and the defeat of defenders of French Algeria, to make permanent post-1958 institutional and legal arrangements that had emerged exceptionally (and, most French politicians and scholars thought at the time, temporarily) to fight Algerian nationalists.

Once again the government reacted quickly and firmly to upend the legal roadblock, abandoning yet another "special jurisdiction" in order to force a quick trial that would produce the judgment they wanted. Eventually Law 63–23 of 15 January 1963, Article 50, affirmed that all ordinances taken under the authority of Article 2 of Law 62–421 of 13 April 1962 had "the force of law."[95] Despite his angry threat following the Canal decision, de Gaulle did not try to dissolve the Council of State. As with the corps' criticisms of the April referendum project, however, he in large measure succeeded in imposing his interpretation of why the council had rejected his project. For him, it was a pro-OAS institution that was riddled with right-wing anti-Gaullists.[96]

Only after the autumn referendum and elections, which assured the executive's new powers as well as presidential primacy, would this final offensive against "historical" challenges slacken. Two months later, a presidential pardon commuted Canal's death sentence, as well as that of ex-General

[93] See Heymann, Les libertés publiques et la guerre, 46.

[94] Beyond ruling on the principle, the judgment overturned the new Military Court of Justice's condemnation of André Canal, an Algerian businessmen and OAS member who had been sent to the metropole to run "Mission France III," the organization's continental propaganda wing. On Canal's activities on behalf of the OAS in the metropole, see Direction centrale des RG, "Sommaire général" (Paris, 17 April 1962), 1, in CAC 800280, article 216. On the organization of the OAS, see Rémi Kauffer, OAS: Histoire d'une guerre franco-française (Paris, 2002).

[95] VS/SR, "Objet: Validation des ordonnances prises en application de la loi n. 62–421 du 13 avril 1962 (Algérie)" (Paris, 17 January 1963), in CAC 19960393, article 1.

[96] For de Gaulle's reaction then and in his Memoirs, see Queyremonne, "Les décisions et les avis du Conseil d'Etat," 406. On the ways that the Canal decision and the Council of State's actions in the October referendum dispute reshaped the council's role, see Le Conseil d'Etat: Son histoire à travers les documents d'époque, 1799–1974 (Paris, 1974), 896–914.

Jouhaud, to life imprisonment. *Paris-Match* described how "the Left interpreted these pardons . . . as an 'opening toward the Right,' and the Right as a promise of reconciliation. In fact," the photo weekly posited, "it is the electoral rout of activist tendencies that made the pardons possible, by eliminating the risk that they would have any political significance."[97] Although the election results made possible de Gaulle's mercy, it was not the OAS threat that had disappeared; rather, the voters' affirmation and authorization of presidential primacy reduced the regime's need to rely on such a menace in order to obtain the powers it pursued. In this book's final chapter I explore this development.

The chapters of the next part return to the period when Algerian independence had come to seem inevitable to most French people and look at the ways that officials and public opinion defined people from Algeria and sought to keep them in Algeria.

---

[97] Editorial, "La peine capitale," *Paris-Match* 713 (8 December 1962), 5. There were two elections: a referendum to approve the direct election by universal suffrage of the president of the Republic on 28 October; and an election of deputies to replace the outgoing National Assembly (in two rounds of elections held 18 and 25 November). Following the parliament's refusal to accept the legitimacy of the second referendum of 1962—a resistance that inspired the first (and only) successful vote of no confidence in the Fifth Republic—on 6 October President de Gaulle dissolved this body (see chapter 10).

PART II

BETWEEN FRANCE AND ALGERIA

But, you will say, but, we live in the mother country and we
disapprove of her excesses. It is true, you are not settlers, but you
are no better. For the pioneers belonged to you; you sent them overseas,
and it was you they enriched. You warned them that if they shed
too much blood you would disown them, or say you did.
JEAN-PAUL SARTRE

The settler makes history and is conscious of making it. And
because he constantly refers to the history of his mother country, he
clearly indicates that he himself is the extension of that mother country.
Thus the history which he writes is not the history of the country
which he plunders but the history of his own nation in regards
to all that she skims off, all that she violates and starves.
FRANTZ FANON

Chapter 5

Making Algerians

The period during which Algerian independence appeared to most in France to be a fait accompli but was not yet a fact was a short one. President de Gaulle's 5 September 1961 press conference remarks, which abandoned French pretensions that the Sahara must be treated as an entity separate from Algeria, effectively marked the beginning of this phase. Numerous journalists had reported that "secret" negotiations with GPRA representatives, in Melun in May and June, then at Evian in July, had failed both times when the nationalists walked out over French insistence that the Sahara was not part of Algeria. Yet, responding to a question concerning "sovereignty over the Sahara," the general shocked even his closest advisers. The president of the Republic placed his response in the context of "finishing with the Algerian question by the year's end," adding that "in the Franco-Algerian debate . . . the question of sovereignty over the Sahara is not a consideration, or at least it is not for France."[1] Journalists reported (incorrectly) that this shift had led Prime Minister Debré to tender his resignation. De Gaulle's public acceptance of the claims of Algerian nationalists about the boundaries of the territory in question ("Algeria") radically simplified negotiations with the men French officials always publicly called "representatives of the rebellion," that is, the GPRA and, through them, the FLN. It also crystallized a new certainty in government circles about the inevitability of independence.[2]

---

[1] "Conférence de presse tenue au Palais de l'Elysée (5 septembre 1961)," in Charles de Gaulle, *Discours et messages, t. iii: Avec le renouveau, mai 1958-juillet 1962* (Paris, 1970), 357–58. On French claims to have "created" the Sahara and its "non-Algerian" status, see Michèle Cointet, *De Gaulle et l'Algérie française* (Paris, 1995), 209–12 and esp. 217–22.

[2] In defending the accords, French government officials admitted that they were negotiating with the FLN but not the Provisional Government of the Algerian Republic (GPRA). Important

Yet even when, with seeming ease, France abandoned its claim to the land and resources of Algeria (including the Sahara), what to do about the people living there remained a troubling question. On 5 September 1961 de Gaulle had initialed, rhetorically speaking, an agreement with the FLN on territory: now, the status—in all senses of the term—of the people living in the land under negotiation emerged as the central conflict between FLN and French government negotiators. A 1 November 1961 "top secret" assessment of ongoing talks noted that two disagreements remained between French "views and those of the FLN." One concerned "self-determination for the Sahara." Hand-written editing clarified that while this was "a problem," there remained only one "fundamental opposition," which was "how to deal with nationality." With the Sahara problem out of the way, it was the nationality question—who could be Algerian, when and how—that was at the heart of subsequent French government discussions with the FLN. It also grabbed the attention of French legislators, the French executive, and the metropolitan public. Other questions about nationality—who could be French, when and how—remained unspoken.[3]

"The Category of 'People' Is Juridically and Politically Imprecise"

In the months leading up to the Evian Accords (and a few months beyond), when outlining multiple definitions of people from Algeria, the French government officially maintained the primacy of categories that existed in French law. In doing this they downplayed more abstract, yet seemingly more rooted, categories such as ethnicity, race, religion, "Frenchness," or "Algerian-ness." These French plans ignored Algerian nationalist claims. They did not integrate popular presuppositions. They did not consider the arguments of early metropolitan supporters of independence, such as Sartre and Aron, who had offered relatively clear definitions of how to distinguish French from Algerian. An early 1961 preparatory memo for negotiators involved in an aborted set of negotiations with "representatives of the rebellion" at Evian warned that "the category of 'people' is juridically and politically imprecise. No one of the possible elements used to determine this notion is sufficient or decisive." Using different examples (all—from Pakistan to Togo—drawn from the annals of European decolonization), the Foreign Ministry expert elaborated, "Neither geography; nor ethnography; not religion; not language . . . is a suitable base on which to define the notion of a people." Referring to

---

in terms of French attention to the law, and to French insistence that they alone possessed sovereignty in Algeria until the 1 July 1962 referendum they organized, this was only a pretense. The GPRA named and authorized the nationalist negotiators with the French government.

[3] See "Projet de proposition en vue de la reprise des négociations" (21 November 1961), 1, in MAE 93.

"the English colonies in the Americas," he argued that "not even the accumulation of all of these criteria" was enough. Instead, shifting subtly from a definition of "people" to that of "nation," he cited Ernest Renan's maxim that "it is a spiritual principle," which allowed him to insist that "what constitutes a people is the consciousness of the individuals that make it up . . . their will to constitute a national unit." While invoking a still ongoing "elaboration of the Algerian personality," the policy paper studiously avoided any reference to "a daily plebiscite" à la Renan.[4]

The "tide of History" explained the imminent secession of Algerian *territory*. Rather than offering additional abstract considerations, this official of de Gaulle's Fifth Republic pinpointed a "juridically and politically" precise procedure that would constitute a national unit: "the Algerian *people* will be born, eventually, via a popular vote."[5] French officials in the early 1960s, now certain that Algeria was a foreign territory, retained a description of the Algerian "people"—however hesitant—that was very French. For the planned referendum to work, the author cautioned, "all the significant groupings of those who will have the right to vote for self-determination need to join together in a shared sentiment of making up a people."[6] In its rejection of "preexisting" or "organic" criteria and its embrace of a political process, this early memorandum suggests how French elected officials and functionaries would continue to privilege the connection between membership in the nation and territory. This tack held even after the process of self-determination announced by the 8 January 1961 referendum shifted decisively, with de Gaulle's statements in September 1961, toward independence.

Until Algerian independence—and its precursor, the crisis of the exodus— almost all commentators, official and not, in the Hexagon presumed that when independence happened most people from Algeria and living in Algeria would become Algerian. As late as early March 1962, Minister of the Armed Forces Pierre Messmer explained to the heads of the different military branches that "a large-scale return of Algerians to the metropole would have the effect of emptying Algeria of the qualified personnel it needs to survive and to develop, as well as confronting France with enormously complicated human and financial problems." For this reason, French negotiators were continuing to proceed under the assumption that "it is highly desirable that the great majority of Algerians decide to continue to live in their country of birth."[7] To allow most French citizens in Algeria the best chance to become members of the Algerian people-to-be, the French had to offer "guar-

---

[4] Ministre d'Etat chargé des Affaires algériennes, untitled note: "Sans qu'il soit nécessaire . . ." (1961), 1, in MAE 103.

[5] Ibid. Emphasis added, 2.

[6] Ibid.

[7] Pierre Messmer, ministre des Armées, "Le Ministre des Armées à Messieurs les Chefs de Corps des Armées de Terre, de Mer et de l'Air" (Paris, 8 March 1962), 2, in SHAT 1H/1784/1.

antees."[8] Already, in February 1961, weeks after French voters approved "self-determination" for Algeria (but not the Sahara), Foreign Ministry functionaries were certain that twin guarantees were necessary to husband the birth of the Algerian nation. The French government would need (1) to elaborate a status for "repatriates," applicable in the metropole, while (2) agreeing with their nationalist negotiators on some form of minority status that would operate in the future self-ruled Algerian state. They believed these guarantees would help produce an Algerian people out of almost all the inhabitants of Algeria.

This official vision was premised in the certainty that government experts knew what Algerians, in particular "European" Algerians, wanted. In an April 1961 confidential report on the "Europeans of Algeria," an Algiers-based political affairs specialist explicated the complexity of "Europeans'" current attitude of "lassitude born from despair." The writer reported that "the European asserts that Algerian independence is ineluctable and will mean departure [*l'exode*] for himself and his family. And yet," the analysis nuances, "he does not foresee leaving voluntarily"; the European "grabs onto the smallest hope" of staying. Moving even further from the paraphrased words of the "European," the author diagnoses that "in their hearts, many Europeans hope to stay here while also holding on to their French nationality, which in their eyes constitutes the primary guarantee." Absolutely certain that Algerian independence would occur, French planners struggled to realize the "primary guarantee." Whether doggedly arguing for a special minority status in Algeria with negotiators sent by the FLN, or pushing to create the status of "repatriate" in the French Parliament, officials of the Debré government sought to work with what seemed a productive paradox: "Europeans" said they wanted Algeria to stay French, but what they really wanted, metropolitan experts agreed, was to stay French in Algeria. The government wanted them to become Algerians, but in order for that to occur the "Europeans" had to stay in Algeria. Everyone, then, wanted this population to stay in Algeria: this provided the seemingly solid premise from which French experts made their predictions. Yet the reference to "Algeria" hid incommensurable meanings. French officials relied wholly on their idea of Algeria-about-to-be-decolonized, while French Algerians were sure of their Algeria-integral-part-of-France.

The idea that "Europeans'" attachment to the land of Algeria and to their homes was a greater value to them than remaining French persisted despite massive evidence to the contrary. In one of a series of sociological studies that the General Delegation of Algeria commissioned during the final months of French Algeria, Suzanne Frère, an employee of the Division of Political Affairs and Information, analyzed "The Youth of Algiers."[9] Her summary

---

[8] Ibid.
[9] Suzanne Frère, "Enquête sociologique: La jeunesse européenne d'Alger" (Algiers, Spring 1962), 1, in MAE 92.

of the responses of fifteen-year-old "European" boys when asked "What does the idea of fatherland [*la patrie*] mean to you?" begins with the assertion that "the idea of *la patrie* is represented in many cases by the place of birth:—'To live and die where my ancestors have lived and died.'" Yet her analysis immediately suggested that the concept was

> caught up in their dearest wish:
> —"My uncles and brothers fell on the field of battle so that *la patrie* would survive; they sacrificed themselves to remain French."
> —"to remain French until death."
> —"to live and die as a good Frenchman."
> —"to remain an honest and loyal Frenchman all of my life."[10]

Young men of seventeen years and older, she claimed, "let it be known that besides their work they participate in a secret activity 'to serve *la patrie*.'— 'To serve the cause of French Algeria, so that any children I might have would be French.'"[11] Yet, as in the 21 April 1961 report, officials transformed a barely discernible "small hope" that "Europeans of Algeria" would accept independence into the baseline of their previsions. In doing this they utterly failed to probe what it meant for French citizens, in this case "Europeans," "to stay here," as the report said, "while also holding on to their French nationality." Metropolitan commentators did not think historically or politically about the impossibility of this equation, when "here" meant a place that was no longer a part of France—exactly what Algeria promised to become. It was not until the exodus that the apparently productive paradox was revealed as simply an irreconcilable contradiction.[12]

In preparation for Algeria's independence, officials acted to preserve the fundamentals of a "French" understanding of national identity: they took as a given the foreign nature of Algerian territory and acted to encourage the elaboration of an "Algerian nation" founded on *jus soli*. Rather than acceding to nationalist demands or recognizing FLN claims, they acted *as if* their plans would determine the shape of the future state and create an Algerian nation. They insisted that it was the process of self-determination they had come up with—not the history of Algeria, Algerians, or Algerian nationalism—that would produce the Algerian nation. Such a republican Arab Kingdom would be a sign of the universality of French conceptions, rather than of a crisis in France's capacity to make people on French territory French. Government officials treated the exceptions to traditional republican *jus soli* approaches that they proposed—the elaboration of "repatriate status" in French law and "minority status" in the accords—as stopgaps,

---

[10] Ibid., 12.
[11] Ibid., 21.
[12] Affaires politiques, Délégation générale du gouvernement en Algérie, "Les Européens d'Algérie III. Considérations d'ordre politique" (8 April 1961), 6, in MAE 103.

meant to allow all people living in Algeria to become citizens of Algeria. The system the French government put in place was premised on the same logic as that of French Algeria's defenders: living on national territory and rule by a national government would produce people who would share a national identity. Nothing else would.

Repatriate Status

The French government first used the term "repatriate" to name people who were *not* from Algeria. Throughout the 1950s, in Egypt, Pondichéry, Indochina, and later in other colonies and protectorates where indigenous nationalist agitation ended or diminished direct French domination, French government decisions obligated most "overseas French" to leave their homes. In Paris, these officially incited and desired repatriations were the object of concern and, occasionally, action.

When, in fall 1961, the government acted to establish a legal definition of "repatriate," it did so in the name of helping these people who were not from Algeria. The evidence clearly shows that the government and most legislators passed the so-called Boulin Law of 26 December 1961 on Repatriate Status in order to help French people from Algeria, yet they did so while seeking to avoid any reference to Algeria and in order to encourage people from Algeria not to repatriate to the metropole.[13]

Government officials had first discussed the repatriaton of French people from Algeria as part of the policy of "integration," rather than as preparation for "decolonization." With the range of policies designed to make real the French nationality of all Algerians, "the problem of the repatriation to the metropole of a certain number of French people from Algeria is posed, *Europeans or Muslims,*" as a March 1961 memo from G. de Wailly of the Algerian Affairs Ministry warned.[14] In planning for "even the most favorable circumstances" some repatriation to the metropole was certain to take place. The note foregrounded "the necessity to transfer to Muslims public- and private-sector jobs, the perspective of agricultural reform, the diminution of the armed forces, and the subsequent reduction of commerce." Given the significant proportion of FSE who worked as low-level civil servants in Algeria, it was widely if quietly acknowledged that official efforts to promote the hiring of FMAs would displace many "Europeans" from posts in Alge-

---

[13] J.-J. Jordi and Emile Temime, eds., *Marseille et le choc des décolonisations* (Aix-en-Provence, 1996).

[14] G. de Wailly, mission d'etudes, Ministère d'Etat chargé des Affaires algériennes, "Note sur le rapatriement éventuel des Français—européens et musulmans—d'Algérie" (Paris, 28 March 1961), 1, in MAE 100. Emphasis added.

ria and back to the metropole.[15] Yet, only one year before the Evian Accords were announced, this "note on the eventual repatriation of French people— Europeans and Muslims—from Algeria" had to admit that Algeria's connection to France would probably diminish, rather than increase. It was necessary to act, whatever the future might hold. "Already," the note signaled, "the first repatriates—victims of the Oran incidents of December—have appeared" in Paris.[16] By early 1961, functionaries adjusted plans for how to accommodate "Europeans," particularly in light of self-determination.

The government encouraged repatriations from other decolonizing French overseas possessions as necessary elements of French efforts to manage decolonization. De Wailly's note captures how officials' attempts to make plans for potential repatriates from Algeria, on the contrary, sought to dramatically reduce, and hopefully avoid, any departures from Algeria. Repatriate status was announced as helping people from former colonies as they returned to their French homeland; it was meant to prevent French citizens in Algeria from coming back to the metropole.

The government wanted to guarantee that the vast majority of so-called European Algerians would remain in Algeria after independence. Government planners saw the establishment of repatriate status as a way to reassure them that, because they would be welcome to the metropole, they did not have to come. Algerian repatriation was "difficult for the government to address because of the counterproductive repercussions" effective measures might have "on French and Algerian opinion." Yet government planners were confident they knew what needed to be done to avoid mass departures. Still, they recognized their bind, what the same 28 March 1961 note called the "political aspects of the problem." They wanted to avoid publicly raising the possibility that mass repatriation might occur, but to prevent such repatriation they believed that publicizing their plans was necessary. "The certainty given to French people who feel threatened in Algeria that they will find an efficient welcome, available housing, and, above all, the possibility of [jobs], would work to calm the distress of most of them." (For those unconcerned about pied noir spleen, he emphasized that these guarantees would "eliminate the reasons for political agitation.") Unfortunately, "these two considerations are clearly contradictory."[17] Repeatedly officials sought to draw lessons from recent events in Tunisia and Morocco. They did so explicitly to preclude French Algerians from embracing more pessimistic interpretations, because they were well aware that much remarked reports about "the discontent of repatriates" from Morocco and Tunisia risked "in-

[15] Ibid.
[16] Ibid.
[17] Ibid.

citing" French Algerians "to have doubts about the nation's solidarity with them."[18]

Government planners, then, in considering eventual repatriates from Algeria, were consistent with official thinking about Algeria since the 1830s: Algeria was unique. They envisioned possible measures for the meridional departments under a very different lens from the still-ongoing repatriation of French people from recently independent colonial holdings. Rather than addressing what they understood as a unique problem with potentially dramatic implications for the French Republic, they tried to deal with Algeria as typical, another colonial territory. Whether or not independence came, some measure of repatriation from Algeria was inevitable. Yet, unlike for "French" inhabitants in other "decolonized" overseas possessions, reinstallation in the metropole could be avoided for most French Algerians. This approach dominated official thinking until the exodus began.

In elaborating repatriate status, the government relied on a pragmatic falsehood: they camouflaged decisions concerning Algeria within a larger process. This prefigured the "tide of History" argument that would dominate French explanations of Algerian independence in the months following 5 September 1961. To deal with the evident contradictions government experts discerned in planning this aspect of Algeria's future, they decided "to prepare discreetly and immediately for the return of French Algerians under the guise of operations already under way for other territories."[19] The office of Minister of State Louis Joxe prepared a special repatriate status so as to "intervene at the governmental level in order to ameliorate" the spotty assistance afforded repatriates from Tunisia and Morocco. Joxe's note continued that by doing so "the apprehensions of our compatriots from Algeria over their future situation" will be "calmed." Unfortunately for "repatriates" from Tunisia, Morocco, and elsewhere, calming Algerians was not just a side effect. While presented as meeting their needs, this initial summary suggested that, because of legal complications, none of the "improvements" should apply to "repatriates" from Tunisia and Morocco already in the metropole.[20] A summer 1961 report by the left-wing republican Club Jean-Moulin that urged the government to enact a "repatriate status" made explicit that doing so would allow France to "complete the process of decolonization better than it had begun it." The report also made explicit what the government did not want to state: the repatriates in question would be from Algeria.[21]

---

[18] Signed G. de Wailly, "Rapatriement éventuel de Français d'Algérie. Sommaire des principaux problèmes à approfondir dans le courant des prochaines semaines" (Paris, 8 February 1961), 2, in MAE 103/b1; G. de Wailly (Paris, 28 March 1961), 2, in MAE 100.

[19] G. de Wailly (Paris, 28 March 1961), 2, in MAE 100.

[20] Like "FMA" before 1956, "repatriate" was not yet legally defined, although the phenomenon was officially recognized. Secrétaire général, Ministère d'Etat chargé des Affaires algériennes, "Note à l'attention du M. le Ministre concernant un éventuel retour en metropole des Français rapatriés d'Algérie" (14 April 1961), 1, in MAE 100.

[21] Club Jean Moulin, "Les perspectives d'emploi des européens en Algérie" (s.d.), 43, in CAC 80 AJ/254 [930275/94].

The Boulin Law of 26 December 1961 did establish "repatriate status," but it continued to evade making the connection to Algeria.

Legislating Repatriate Status

Throughout fall 1961, the government pressured the parliament to pass a law that seemed to prepare for the coming conclusion of French colonialism by defining a new legal category: the repatriate. Yet Prime Minister Debré insisted to the committees studying the proposal that the measure in no way concerned Algeria. There were, after all, already 304,000 French citizens who had fled to France from former French possessions, now decolonized.[22] It was too early to discuss measures dealing with Algerian independence. Through careful phrasing, most senators and deputies publicly discussed the statute as if it were limited to the French inhabitants of already decolonized territories, although they proceeded to amend it, as committee records reveal, with soon-to-be independent Algeria in mind. From their place on the far right of the parliamentary hemicycles, through catcalls and speeches, ardent defenders of French Algeria once again sought to force a debate on Algeria's future and on what they termed the government's plan to divide French territory and to abandon French citizens—Algerians "French in descent or French of heart." Critics of government policy in Algeria struggled to prove that the law was not an opportunity to give benefits to those who had already fled former colonies. It was, they claimed, a tacit admission of the impending disaster government policy in Algeria would produce. This policy, they asserted, would in short order lead to multitudes of abused French Algerian compatriots, forced to flee a foreign dictatorship—ruled, variously, by Communists, religious fanatics, or racists—seeking refuge in the metropole. These "traitors" met with no direct response. For if almost everyone acted as if Algerian independence was about to happen, almost no one in the first government of the Fifth Republic was willing to talk about it—yet.[23] Others insisted that the legal guarantees were part of a strategy of convincing "European" holdouts of the wisdom of an independent Algeria: with the guarantee they would be welcomed in the metropole, more "Europeans" would be likely to stay in their homeland. While this argument reproduced the reasoning that had led the government to propose the text, it is significant that the government's point man on these issues, Secretary of State for Repatriates Robert Boulin, did not enunciate such an explanation in public. The government sought to give as few arguments and as little publicity to its support for the law as possible.

The project's connection to the Algerian situation was so unclear that one

---

[22] For details of the development of administrative responses to the arrival of "repatriates," see M. Tomasini, "*Avis* . . ." (16 November 1961), 3–4, in CAC 780058/206 [F/60/01980].

[23] For transcripts of the committee meeting and parliamentary debates, see CAC 780058/206 [F/60/01980].

amendment, eventually adopted into the law, was approved because, as a
senate committee summarized, "the term 'repatriate' is incorrect where
refugees from Algeria are concerned." The National Assembly committee
that proposed the change sketched a distinction between those French people who were "constrained to return to the metropole and departing a territory that has obtained or regained sovereignty" and those coming from "a
territory still under French sovereignty." Although using "the word 'repatriate'" for all, the report cautioned that "it is clear that in the second case,
this word is incorrect and should not appear in the text of a law." The
amendment extended eligibility to "French people forced or who judged it
necessary to leave a territory not included in the first article." Yet the amendment the National Assembly approved made no mention of Algeria. Only
the Senate committee's summary of what was said in the National Assembly
committee made clear that this meant Algeria. In any case, it was not until
a decree of 2 April 1962 that French people from Algeria arriving in the
metropole could automatically benefit from the law's provisions.[24]

The press offered extensive coverage of parliamentary discussion of the
proposed repatriate status. Commentators focused both on the procedure
and the content. Exceptionally, for the Fifth Republic, the government's initial proposal was much amended as it "shuttled" between Senate and National Assembly. The Constitution of 1958 gave the government multiple
"exceptional" means to impose laws without having to compromise with
members of either legislative chamber. So the ongoing consideration and in-
corporation of legislators' amendments into the proposed law led to much
press speculation about whether this discussion augured the renewal of parliamentary prerogatives, as if the parenthesis the Algerian crisis had opened
was now closing.[25] In terms of what was at stake, French media concentrated
on the intense parliamentary conflict over what the state's obligations were
to its citizens who would have repatriate status. At the heart of this dispute
was the question of whether the French state should offer compensation to
those so classified. Parliamentary discussion of the proposal revolved around
whether the bill should establish a principle of "solidarity" or one of "compensation." In support of the former, Chairman René Tomasini of the National Assembly's Commission on Cultural, Familial, and Social Affairs
characterized the goal as "making existing mechanisms of aid or assistance
work in favor of the repatriates as well as eventually putting in place some
new ones." This must be done "without allowing their status as repatriates
in and of itself to confer them rights vis-à-vis the state or the nation."[26] The

[24] See the conclusion. Sénateur André Fosset, "Rapport . . . (Annexe au procès-verbal de la
séance du 6 décembre 1961)," 4, in CAC 780058/206 [F/60/01980]; M. Bernard Le Douarec,
Deputy, "Rapport . . . (Annexe au procès-verbal de la séance du 17 novembre 1961)," 2 n. 1,
in CAC 780058/206 [F/60/01980].
[25] Jean Vacher-Desvernais analyzes press coverage of parliamentary discussion of repatriate
status in L'avenir des Français d'outre-mer (Paris, 1962), 110.
[26] M. René Tomasini, "Avis . . . (Annexe au procès-verbal de la séance du 16 novembre
1961)," 5, in CAC 780058/206 [F/60/01980].

deputy's reasoning was consistent with the proposal the government had forwarded to the National Assembly in September and that the second chamber, expeditiously, but with significant amendments, had approved.

In amending the project, the Senate "had introduced the novel principle of compensation for lost property," as Deputy Bernard Le Douarec summarized. This, he continued, "recalled" the idea of "the state's 'responsibility,' which does not necessarily imply that it assumes 'fault.'" Unlike private parties, public acceptance of responsibility was not "linked to the existence of a real or presumed fault." Despite eluding discussion of the republic's moral responsibility toward potential repatriates, the amendment broke with the government-supported logic of "solidarity." A project of solidarity allowed a new category to be created to which the French government *could* extend assistance: if, when, and to whom among those designated it deemed necessary. This was very different from the obligation(s) that the creation of rights for repatriates would entail. The preeminent French scholar of pied noir repatriates, Jean-Jacques Jordi, terms the government's conception, as written into the Boulin Law, the "moral right to integration," as opposed to "actual rights."[27] Deputy Robert Szigeti, writing in the name of the assembly's Commission on Foreign Affairs, cast the project as one of "social justice." By this he meant to privilege "the guarantee of housing, work, school, and fraternity" for all repatriates above "the compensation of property," which would benefit only a few. The report noted, however, that while "this commission accepted the principle of national solidarity," this did not mean "in consequence that we definitively reject the other [principle] of compensation of lost goods."[28]

The question of compensation touched on what senior civil servant and author Jean Vacher-Desvernais identifies as "a classic theory of French public law, that of 'government deeds.'" According to this theory, "the government's exercise of its prerogatives can necessitate certain decisions that, although inevitable, result in damage to the individual." This theory posited that the state was not responsible for damages incurred from its actions and so had no obligation to give compensation. Repatriates, like other French citizens in comparable situations, had no legal grounds to ask the government or the courts to assist them. In turn, without a law the government and the courts had no preexisting legal authority to offer that assistance. The project proposed a means to negotiate the government's attachment to the "theory of government deeds" with the perceived need to address the problem of repatriates from overseas. The means was the project's assertion of a "fundamental right" to solidarity, an underlying principle that would authorize all future laws on the subject. The Law of 26 December 1961 explicitly recognized this right "by virtue of the national solidarity that the preamble of

[27] Jean-Jacques Jordi, *De l'exode à l'exil: Rapatriés et pieds-noirs en France; L'exemple marseillais* (Paris, 1993), 77 n. 27.
[28] M. Robert Szigeti, deputy, "*Avis* . . . (Annexe au procès-verbal de la séance du 17 novembre 1961)," 2–3, in CAC 780058/206 [F/60/01980].

the Constitution of 1946 affirmed." The government now could act and should be expected to act to extend national solidarity to those defined as "repatriates."[29]

Despite wide-ranging debate over the law's content, the government succeeded in avoiding any affirmation of the state's responsibility for compensation. This success came despite the push by key legislators, who believed that more should be done, to admit the principle of compensation. Was it the government's success in avoiding any explicit discussion of the Algerian situation that prevented any variant of compensation from becoming law? Whatever the reason, the government's legislative victory did not include the most novel element of its initial project. Here, content and form were tightly linked. The original bill's second article, in effect, would have "authorized the government to act by ordinances and, during a period of one year following the law's publication, to take all measures to apply it." This article would have given the executive the right to exercise powers that, constitutionally, were wholly the purview of parliament. Vacher-Desvernais argues that the National Assembly's opposition to the proposed wording of Article 2 of bill was hardened and "embittered" by the government's constant effort "to avoid giving any details" about what the bill would do or why. In a resolutely technocratic book, he describes the assembly's struggle to amend the bill as "a constant effort to push back the line between light and shadow."[30] In a surprising vote on 24 November, the National Assembly reaffirmed the senate's rejection of this aspect of the bill. It was an unprecedented defeat for a Fifth Republic government.[31]

At the time, this setback received considerable media attention. Journalists took the vote as another clear indication that the parliament was ready to take back its prerogatives after three years of de Gaulle-induced somnolence. It seemed like a reassertion of Fourth Republic governmental practice, where the role of the legislature was preeminent. The Algerian crisis—the reason the president of the Republic had been allowed to exercise powers that went far beyond what the 1958 Constitution gave him—was nearing its conclusion. The true institutional nature of the Fifth Republic, one not so different from the Third and Fourth Republics, would start to emerge. Instead, the legislators' success in taking back some of their prerogatives proved a pyrrhic victory.

Retrospectively, the vote sheds light on what became the government's strategy vis-à-vis the parliament in the months ahead. The 8 April referen-

---

[29] Vacher-Desvernais, *L'avenir des Français*, 117. It is important to understand the role of legislative powers versus executive powers of regulation in the Fifth Republic. Article 34 of the Constitution of 1958 defines the roles of laws as establishing general principles and defining essential rules. Beyond these domains—and while respecting the laws and the constitution—the government had the power to regulate through ordinances and decrees.

[30] Ibid.

[31] Vacher-Desvernais, *L'avenir des Français*, 118.

dum gave the president the exercise of legislative powers that the article would have authorized (after 8 April, however, repatriate status was only one element among the vast and ambiguously defined "measures necessary to implement the accords signed at Evian"). Compared to their success with the referendum of 8 April 1962, it is clear that the government's reticence to give details in fall 1961, its failure to evoke Algeria, led to legislative defeat. No one in fall and winter 1961 argued that granting the executive extraordinary powers was necessary to bring an end not only to the situation of repatriates but to the Algerian crisis itself. In seeking to avoid any mention of Algeria, the supposed urgency of giving the executive the means to act decisively—and without further consultation—remained unconvincing. The government learned this lesson well. In hard-fought campaigns in spring and fall 1962, de Gaulle successfully extended executive control over legislative prerogatives by linking each of his plans directly to getting out of Algeria. With the Evian Accords, the legislature overwhelmingly accepted his demands. Concerning the direct election of the president of the Republic, most legislators were unsuccessful in their attempt to deny that there was a connection with the Algerian situation (see chapter 10). In both campaigns, the urgency most French citizens gave to severing France's relationship with Algeria overcame all other legal or historical concerns.[32] This was not, however, the only sign of things to come that the elaboration of this law revealed.

Debates over repatriate status also allowed legislators a rare chance to detail how they conceived of repatriation. Those who preferred to evoke national solidarity bolstered their explanations with proposals to assimilate the repatriates completely into the nation. One senator observed that "no rights are extended to repatriated French people, but solidarity will work fully for them, to make them full participants [les faire participer] in the economic development of the nation."[33] These lawmakers insisted that national solidarity in and of itself would make repatriates indistinguishable from their fellow citizens. A repatriation policy premised on national solidarity could overcome the sense of group identity that shared ties to the land repatriates had left and the potentially difficult conditions of repatriation might accentuate. Remarking on the "misfortune of our compatriots," one assembly committee emphasized that "it would be dangerous for the unity of the nation to let a class of distrusted and desperate people emerge." This was why public monies needed to be spent. To counter a suspicion that none of the deputies publicly raised, the document pointed out that repatriates would not be "rich colonists," but "people of modest means."[34]

Mass exodus needed to be avoided. Concern over what repatriation of

[32] Ibid.

[33] Sénateur André Fosset, "Rapport . . . (Annexe au procès-verbal de la séance du 10 octobre 1961)," 3, in CAC 780058/206 [F/60/01980].

[34] M. René Tomasini, "Avis . . . (Annexe au procès-verbal de la séance du 16 novembre 1961)," 5, in CAC 780058/206 [F/60/01980].

French people from Algeria would mean was a constant in these debates, as it was in bureaucratic consideration of the "Europeans" and how to end the war. A "first attempt at a historical discussion of the Algerian problem" commissioned by the Algerian Affairs Ministry gave a rather long title to its analysis of this possibility: *"The Return of a Significant Proportion of the French of Algeria Will Provoke a Political Crisis Fatal to the Political Regime of the Parliamentary and Liberal Republic."* This "often expressed fear," it suggested, "is without doubt well founded."[35] Debates over the proposed law grappled with these fears. Legislators again attempted to maneuver between contradictory impulses: on one hand, they sought to dampen metropolitan fears about the potential negative effects of repatriation; on the other, they acted to impose mechanisms designed to combat any menace to the Republic that repatriates from Algeria might pose. To calm metropolitan qualms, one senator suggested that it was "on the psychological level that we should focus most of our attention." The government must first make the repatriates familiar to metropolitans. He argued that "a vast information campaign" would prevent metropolitans "from embracing an unacceptable Malthusianism regarding our compatriots from overseas." Without putting into place any specific measures, deputies and senators alike called for structural constraints on the choices and decisions that eventual repatriates would be able to make in regards, for example, to where they would live. So that they could be quickly assimilated into the metropolitan population, it was urged that no concentrations of repatriates be allowed to form.[36]

Fundamental policy disagreement within the Debré government fomented this inarticulate uncertainty about the future of French Algerians. Boulin, named on 24 July 1961 to the newly created post of secretary of state for repatriates, worked to prepare for eventual departures from Algeria. His fellow ministers, in turn, opposed all such efforts. Even in the relatively discreet confines of parliamentary committee rooms, Boulin was the only government representative who would state what many deputies strongly believed, that repatriate status was linked directly to the future of Algeria. "Starting now," he told them, "without prejudging any definitive solution, we need to consider how to extend these texts to Algerians forced to leave their territory."[37] Boulin's isolation went beyond parliamentary discussions, or even official actions. Other ministers sought to impede any discussion of eventual departures, particularly of any endeavors that encouraged such departures. While deputies and senators debated the fate of repatriate status, the ministers of foreign affairs and the interior acted forcefully to avoid any sign of official approbation for group departures from Algeria. They had work to

---

[35] J. S., mission d'etudes, Ministère d'Etat chargé des Affaires algériennes, "Essai d'une discussion historique sur le problème algérien" (28 September 1960), 5, in MAE 5.

[36] M. René Tomasini, "*Avis* . . . (Annexe au procès-verbal de la séance du 16 novembre 1961)," 14, in CAC 780058/206 [F/60/01980].

[37] *J.O. Débats* (24 October 1961), 1243.

do: on the one hand, Boulin's office was attempting to sponsor a covert operation to facilitate the emigration of French Algerians to South America; on the other, the mayor of Angoulême invited a group of so-called harkis (FMAs who had worked with the French armed forces against the "rebellion") and their families who were under threat in Algeria to settle in his commune. Among a number of private initiatives to prepare future settlements for French Algerians in various South American countries only one, the RG detailed, was "on the verge of realizing" its objectives. The Technical Office for Economic Studies and Migration (OTEM) planned to install three hundred farming families from North Africa in Argentina. The RG analyzed that this "necessarily nonprofit" organization was seeking "to make preparatory studies and to facilitate the reinstallation of families and groups of North African emigrants in other foreign countries." Headed by former agriculture minister and current head of the Peasant Party for Social Union, Alphonse "Paul" Antier, the OTEM made the Argentine settlement its initial effort.[38]

The romance of a new French Antarctica (the name of the sixteenth-century French colony in what became Brazil) did not seduce most government officials. While Robert Boulin offered his "complete backing" to Antier's organization, the secretary of state's letters to the ministers of foreign affairs, finance, and industry garnered no positive response. The Ministry of Foreign Affairs (often referred to as the Quai d'Orsay) refused any contact with OTEM representatives, the RG explaining that diplomats did not want OTEM "to be able to evoke such exchanges, which might easily be qualified as 'official' nor to offer grounds" to French or foreign observers "for extensive interpretation." In his unsuccessful effort to garner Foreign Minister Maurice Couve de Murville's support for the Argentine scheme Boulin presented it as a self-contained project. In letters to Valéry Giscard d'Estaing, minister of finance, and to the minister of industry, he announced that this was a "first step" that might prepare the way for other settlements.[39]

In offering assurances that the scheme involved only a small number of French families, Boulin failed to understand why the Quai d'Orsay would not support Antier's project. At first, the Quai did not actively oppose the efforts of Antier and others to establish a South American connection. While they rejected official support at any level, Foreign Ministry officers made no attempt to prevent emigration. As with the government's introduction of repatriate status, official willingness to accept that people would leave Algeria was combined with a commitment not to admit publicly that this might happen.[40] Whereas Boulin worked to prepare the flight of at least some

[38] See Directeur des RG, "Objet: a/s de l'installation en Amérique latine des familles françaises de colons émigrés d'Afrique du Nord . . ." (8 January 1962), 4, in AN F/7/16108.

[39] Ibid., 8, Robert Boulin, secrétaire d'Etat aux rapatriés, "Lettre à M. Antier Paul, ancien ministre" (Paris, 13 November 1961), in AN F/7/16108.

[40] Direction des RG, "Objet a/s de l'OTEM," joined to "SN/RG/ENQ.-n 7388" from Commisaire Divisionnaire au Préfet Directeur des RG (4 January 1962; 29 December 1961), 3, in AN F/7/16108: ref. CAC 880502/3.

French Algerians, the Quai d'Orsay sought to quash suggestions that the peace it was negotiating with Algerian nationalists would require any French departures. Boulin's efforts—under the table as well as in front of parliamentary committees—contradicted government claims about what would happen in Algeria. Reporting in January 1962 on the South American scheme, the RG remarked that "until now the official thesis is based in the claim that the negotiated settlement of the Algerian question will permit the immense majority of French people to remain in place." To maintain this position it was crucial, the report continued, "to deny the necessity of massive emigration." In giving meaning to repatriate status and in preparing possibilities for potential emigrants, Boulin's maneuvers suggested that France should prepare for "emigration," massive or otherwise. Made aware of his covert actions, the Foreign Ministry used backdoor pressure on the Argentine and Brazilian governments to stymie the plan they previously had left untouched.[41]

While the Quai d'Orsay sought to keep French officials from involving themselves in plans to establish colonies of French Algerians in South America, the Ministry of the Interior acted to block initiatives to bring to the metropole Muslim French citizens from Algeria who had publicly opposed the FLN. When the mayor of Angoulême offered housing and assistance to a group of forty harkis and family members in mid-1961, officials at all levels, from the cabinet to the local prefect, sought to undo his efforts. The project, the head of the Service for Muslim Affairs (SAM) warned, "raises serious problems of principle as well as on a material level." It risked "being politically exploited without helping those concerned." The prefect of the Charente worried about "serious disturbances" among different groups in the metropole (particularly pro-FLN Algerians) as well as what effect "at a psychological level" this might have on "Europeans" considering repatriation.[42]

These attempts to prevent any appearance of government encouragement for leaving Algeria show what might seem obvious: the government perceived clear differences between "Europeans" and "Muslims" from Algeria. By avoiding public discussion of what the end of French Algeria might mean, however, the government kept such considerations of difference outside of legislative or public debate. Discussion of repatriate status, for example—whether in bureaucratic or parliamentary consideration—rarely attended to distinctions between potential repatriates. Algeria entered almost not at all into public debate over repatriate status. The primary impulse behind the establishment of the category was to overcome the high

---

[41] Directeur des RG (8 January 1962), 3–4.

[42] Lamassoure, Préfet, chef du Service des Affaires Musulmanes et de l'Action sociale, "Note . . ." (29 September 1961), 1, in CAC 770346/10; Balut, conseiller technique, Préfecture de la Gironde, "Pour Lamassoure" (Bordeaux, 27 September 1961), 1, in CAC 770346/10.

costs and the inefficiencies of an individualized system—and to avoid mass repatriation from Algeria.[43] Legislators expressed great concern that people who did not need public assistance not receive it, but this problem was addressed in the debate over compensation; even those who argued that compensation should be only for those "forced" to come to the metropole (thus excluding those who "chose") who were not rich "colonists" did not demand that the unworthy be excluded from "repatriate status." Legislators trusted bureaucratic and political scrutiny of "merit and need" to make distinctions between repatriates.

Official policy made no distinction among potential repatriates based on national origin, ethnicity, race, or religion, hewing to republican "color blindness." Indeed, officials proved willing to apply repatriate status at times to people with non-European ancestry who did not have French citizenship.[44] Repatriate status was first and foremost a "primary guarantee," meant to placate people in Algeria, and not the important category of political and social identity it, in and after the exodus, would become. As in their thinking about repatriate status, French officials considered the second "primary guarantee"—setting up of a minority status for independent Algeria—critical to their goal of keeping most "French Algerians" in Algeria. While discussions to put in place repatriate status presented this goal in terms of avoiding turmoil in the metropole, officials defined the benefits of minority status in terms of more abstract goals. "European" Algerians becoming simply Algerians would serve French interests.

Negotiating Minority Status

The French constantly used their negotiations with FLN representatives to try to establish institutions that would limit the leeway available to the coming Algerian state; they constantly were tempted to believe that it would necessarily and rationally follow the French model. What I call the always-imaginary "Arab Kingdom" deeply influenced the French approach to the negotiations. For the studies and analyses that French diplomats relied on evinced a confidence similar to that of Napoleon III in their capacity to shape the "Arab" state to come. The facts necessitated their success. An expert in the Justice Ministry, for example, suggested that guaranteeing a certain number of "minority" judges "would probably result more from factual conditions than legal condition," given that, in this expert's opinion, "judges in the new Algerian state should have equivalent professional qualifications as

---

[43] Commissariat à l'aide et à l'orientation des Français rapatriés, Ministère de l'Interieur, "Dossier analytique: Crédits d'intervention" (March 2 or early March 1961), 1, in MAE 100.

[44] See Colette Dubois, "Les retour de rapatriés d'Egypte 1956–1957: Repli ou rapatriement?" in Jordi and Temime, *Marseille et le choc des décolonisations*, 39–53.

French judges." Since France had provided the necessary education to very few Algerian "Muslims," ipso facto Algeria would have to employ "European" judges.[45]

French negotiators sought to impose the accords that French experts had imagined and blueprinted, an architecture with markedly hexagonal features. But negotiations with FLN representatives, of course, did have an enormous effect on French propositions, first and foremost because their struggle made such proposals necessary. Even with the principle of territorial separation won, however, FLN negotiators never obtained French acceptance of their definitions of people in Algeria. Rather, their success in forcing changes in French projects resulted, first, from their rejection of successive French plans and, eventually and most effectively, when they succeeded in demonstrating that French projects for Algeria were inconsistent with French law and republican principles.

The confrontation with the nationalists' arguments, exigencies, and rebuttals most affected how officials formulated minority status and its corollary, minority rights, at two levels: ideological consistency and reciprocity. Reciprocity represented a desire to present each French demand for minority rights as either reflecting or announcing a right that Algerian citizens would have in France. This shaped all attempts to formulate exceptional categories of individuals. Early in the negotiations, a senior Algerian Affairs official proposed in the form of a top secret "general remark, a remark that concerns above all the presentation, rather than the fundamentals," that in the dealings that would shape the future Algeria "the guarantees we are asking for must appear to be the normal application of general rights and liberties and only if necessary as the consequence of minority status."[46] This meant, for example, that France offered "to maintain the French nationality" of "Muslims living on metropolitan territory," this to buttress their insistence that Algerian nationality be offered to all "Europeans" living on Algerian territory. Distinct from minority status per se, this point became one of the most charged issues that was negotiated. Officials explained parallelism as not a "systematic application of reciprocity" but as part of an effort to "keep our arguments coherent while remaining true to our general approach." The example given concerning nationality emphasized that "the French thesis is its acquisition by all inhabitants of Algeria . . . without the necessity of asking for it." The corollary was that "we cannot, without weakening our position," ask that Algerian "Muslims" not have a parallel right to French nationality.[47]

---

[45] Touren, Service législatif, 1ère section, "Organisation judiciare en Algérie" (15 May 1961), 1, in CAC 950395/76.

[46] R. Cadet, Ministère d'Etat chargé des Affaires algériennes, "Remarques suggérées par le dossier des négociations [3ème phase]" (25 October 1961), 8–14, in MAE 93.

[47] [Ministère d'Etat chargé des Affaires algériennes], "Note de principe: Musulmans" (12 December 1961), 1, in MAE 97.

Because of parallelism, Quai d'Orsay goals of copying the French Republic in Algeria implied changing elements of the original republic in France. When the juridical constructions Foreign Affairs experts proposed for the Algerian republic-to-be were transposed onto the metropole, official doubts increased. Early in the negotiations, to support their goal of installing special electoral regimes for the municipalities of Algiers and Oran, French negotiators considered explicit reciprocity. To guarantee "European" representation in these heavily "European" cities of Algeria, "in communes where the importance of the Muslim community justifies it" in the metropole, the government should be ready to "grant them specific rights to be represented."[48] This was consistent with the principles that had led to the post-1958 extension to the metropole of integrationist policies, such as hiring quotas for public-sector jobs. Still, a handwritten note beside the last suggestion—"Huh? And the Basques of Paris?"—gave a telling indication of widespread resistance to the structural implications reciprocity demanded.[49]

An early reflection on the "future Algerian state" pinpointed the ideological confusion in which French negotiators ensnared themselves. Writing in September 1960, a senior Quai d'Orsay official argued that the "ultimate error" would be to consider "maintaining the European minority in Algeria" in conjunction with "the survival of a certain number of democratic institutions." "Order," he argued, "is more important for the [minority] than democracy. It is not always democracies that have given the most protection to minority rights." Indeed, "democracy in its French variation is, au contraire, voluntarily centralizing and unifying." This model "transposed into the Algerian situation raises fears of a Muslim centralism that would be very dangerous for the minority."[50]

Quite simply, republican ideology and French post-1789 practice made accepting minority rights difficult. A jurist's note that laid out responses to "the political argument that Krim Belkacem" had put forth in negotiations at Evian in late May 1961 struggled to make a case for minority rights. Although the note insisted that French positions were straightforward, in reality French officials had trouble agreeing among themselves what their positions meant. Belkacem, the head of the GPRA's delegation at "First Evian," had argued that "the application of the right to popular self-determination meant that in Algeria the minority would have to accept the verdict of the majority."[51] The French position foregrounded the need to "reconcile collective rights with the rights of individuals." That was why they wanted to nuance majority rule when it came to the "process of self-determination"

---

[48] Ministère d'Etat chargé des Affaires algériennes, "Instructions" (2 May 1961), 8, in MAE 93.

[49] Ibid.

[50] J. S., "Essai d'une discussion historique sur le problème Algérien" (28 September 1960), 10, in MAE 5.

[51] Citation of Belkacem in [Professor Gros], "Note" (late May 1961), 2, in MAE 92.

that could produce an Algerian state. "In effect," the jurist argued, "democracy considers first man and not the groups he forms. Even a summary examination of the texts of the Declarations of Rights proves this." After quoting the *Declaration of the Rights of Man and Citizen* (1789) and the *Universal Declaration of Human Rights* (1948), he sought to demonstrate "democracy's" capacities to guarantee the rights of members of a minority. This was made possible, first by "recognizing the fundamental rights of man" and guaranteeing their "respect," second by "the actual operation of democracy by which the minority has the possibility of becoming a majority," and, finally, by political representation that allows "a minority at the national level to be a majority at the local level."[52]

Having relied on French examples to prove the important protection democracy offers minorities (in order to refute Belkacem's rejection of minority status), the Algerian Affairs jurist had to shift the discussion away from the case of a "political" minority—since the *absence* of political consciousness was exactly how the government chose to think about the "Europeans" of Algeria. Referring to the Treaty of Versailles (1919), he explained that "effectively, in the Algerian case, the minority defines itself not by mere political orientation but by objective elements, which are its ethnic origin, its civil status, its religions, its language, and its way of life." Leaving the uncertainty of political orientation behind, he argued that the "contours" of the minority "are clear: they result from certain specificities."[53] Exactly what those specificities were remained unclear, at least to those trying to establish a juridical definition. The laws of the Fifth Republic did not distinguish between people from Algeria: "All Algerians," one high-level assessment recalled, in reference to nationality, "are French people who become Algerian." This legal reality encouraged the invocation of nonlegal categories to define the minority that any agreement with the nationalists was supposed to protect. The same note from de Gaulle's chief of staff instructed that references to "French origin [*origine*]" be replaced by "European origin [*origine*]," before slipping more comfortably to "replace French origin and Europeans with 'minorities'."[54]

Studies made by the Foreign Affairs Ministry concluded that France had no usable history of minority rights. Whereas diplomats addressed all other issues negotiated with the GPRA's representatives through references to French examples, French treaties, French colonies, or episodes in French history, they justified and presented double nationality and other concepts related to minority rights through evocations of developments more peripheral to France, such as the Treaty of Versailles, the constitutions of (former French League of Nations mandates) Lebanon and Syria, or the recent "suc-

---

[52] Ibid., 3 and 5.
[53] Ibid., 7.
[54] J. J. de Bresson, Secrétariat général, présidence de la République, "Note d'observation sur le dossier" (11 November 1961), 2, in MAE 93.

cessful" compromise on the island of Cyprus. "The term minority," one preparatory memo noted, "has never been the object of a definition that the League of Nations or the United Nations has accepted, and no general principle for the protection of minorities has been formulated." Still, examples from "between the two world wars" as well as "the work of the Commission on the Rights of Man of the UN" suggested "a certain number of factors permitting a definition of the minority in Algeria."[55]

In an April 1961 proposal, in which government experts struggled to come up with a definition of the minority they wanted independent Algeria to recognize, they set out the terms and assumptions about difference that would emerge forcefully in the exodus. "In the independent Algerian state that the self-determination referendum will bring forth, the Europeans of Algeria will constitute a national, open, and organized minority." Each of the three qualifiers was important. "National" meant conjoined with Algerian nationality: "the Europeans will not be foreigners in Algeria." Their status, "covering the totality of rights and guarantees granted to these Europeans by a Franco-Algerian convention," would be recognized by international law, "analogous to those that [the Treaty of] Versailles conferred upon diverse European minorities." This meant that "their juridical situation will be radically different from that of the French in Morocco or Tunisia."[56] The reliance on "the systems of minority protection put in place by the League of Nations in the interwar period" had been advanced as "desirable" by Algerian Affairs experts because, "originating in international treaties and law," they would "impress" the FLN, which itself "had made great use of such arguments." If nationalist negotiators were impressed, it is not revealed in the sources I have seen, or in the results of the negotiations. Rather, many French officials as well as the FLN rejected these systems founded in international law.[57]

"Organized," in the April 1961 proposal, meant joined "in a legally recognized corporation that groups all the members of the minority and is dedicated to playing the role of something like a union for the defense of minority rights." The role of this "community" could range from "making up for an insufficient or inefficacious participation of members of the minority in political institutions (in particular at the state level)" to intervening "in the management of certain public services (like teaching, etc.)." Determining how these roles might operate proved difficult for French experts. They were foreign to French experience and to republican ideology.

---

[55] Ministère d'Etat chargé des Affaires algériennes, "Définition de la minorité" (24 March 1961), 1, in MAE 99. See also M. De Wailly, "Hypothèses de travail retenues par la mission d'études en ce qui concerne les garanties de la minorité européenne d'Algérie" (7 April 1961/sent 13 April 1961), 1–2; and J. S. [Salusse], "Essai d'une discussion historique sur le problème Algérien" (28 September 1960), both in MAE 5.

[56] M. De Wailly, "Hypothèses de travail" (7 April 1961/sent 13 April 1961), 1–2, in CAC 950395/76.

[57] D. L., Ministère d'Etat chargé des Affaires algériennes, "Plaidoyer pour l'association communautaire" (3 November 1961), 1, in MAE 96.

It was de Wailly's middle term, "open," that made clear how resistant minority status was to consistent, sensible, and legal prescription. Minority status usually was considered as a category in which some "Muslims" would be included. In this expectation, the French explicitly deflected Algerian nationalist claims about the definition of Algerians. While it was necessary to give "Muslims" the possibility of abandoning or "declining" their French citizenship, it was also, as one Algerian Affairs senior official framed it, "a very serious matter" for France that its "citizens with Muslim status can be part of the community at their request."[58]

"Named 'European' for reasons of convenience, the minority nevertheless should include some non-European Algerian citizens," de Wailly wrote. If "all French citizens whose personal status is governed by the Civil Code (which is to say all the Europeans, all the Israelites, and a small number of Muslims who have renounced Koranic Law personal status) should be presumed members of the minority," still this postulate could not be definitive. Minority status, "premised on each individual's free choice," should be open to "other Algerians who request inclusion." It would also exclude those "Europeans who reject Algerian citizenship," as well as those who "although having Algerian nationality, declined to join the minority community."[59]

Algerian Affairs experts had isolated "two sets of criteria," each of which could "determine membership in a minority." The first they termed "objective criteria": this would encompass "every person possessing the group's characteristics: race, language, religion, etc." The second they termed "subjective": this would include "each person who in their estimation believes that s/he possesses the group's characteristics." The choice under this second approach would be "strictly individual" and not open to reversal by "either an administrative authority or a tribunal."[60] The assessment of the "two sets of criteria" that follows in this October 1961 report is particularly telling, for it reveals both official thinking about the groups of people involved and suggests how difficult it was for French officials to accept the logic of minority rights. The writer regretted that "it does not seem possible to use objective criteria to define the minority in Algeria." The term "race would exclude Frenchified Muslims"; the term "religion" would leave out "Israelites"; the term "language is very imprecise." Not only is the distinction between "Muslims," who have "race," and Jews, who have religion, significant, but the desire to fix membership criteria, the unwillingness to embrace

[58] R. Cadet, Ministère d'Etat chargé des Affaires algériennes, "Remarques suggérées par le dossier des négociations [3ème phase]" (25 October 1961), in MAE 93.

[59] M. De Wailly, "Hypothèse de travail" (7 April 1961), 2, in CAC 950395/76; Ministère d'Etat chargé des Affaires algériennes, "Garanties de la minorité européenne en Algérie" (31 March 1961), 2, in MAE 96.

[60] Ministère d'Etat chargé des Affaires algériennes, "Définition de la minorité" (24 March 1961), 1, in MAE 99.

a "strictly individual" choice resonates with the confused French history of "assimilation," "coexistence," and "integration." This note urged caution in using the legally precise criteria that historic tension between "assimilation" and "coexistence" had produced: "civil status or membership in the First College," it warned, "would 'freeze' the minority at a moment far in the past." This effort to include the recent possibilities of post-1955 "integration" policies (and even post-1944 policies) soon disappeared. Negotiators finally abandoned their efforts to include "minority status" in the Evian Accords in the final days before both sides initialed them.[61]

Instead, the French opted to affirm the outlines of identity that the older policy of assimilation had established. They abandoned complicated distinctions in favor of a reassuring binary. The Evian Accords offered a series of guarantees to a subset of people living in Algeria, to those who were "Citizens with General Law Civil Status." French negotiators abandoned their pretensions to articulate guarantees for any other "citizens," which is to say French citizens: "objective" and limited criteria based in the law were preferred. In 1947 participation in the "First College" had been offered to some 65,000 "elites," and the 1958 Constitution had asserted equal citizenship for all, regardless of "civil status." Both reforms were put aside. The ironic importance of negotiations over minority status, then, was that, never applied in Algeria, they revealed the contradictory representations by which French officials understood people from Algeria. These myopic understandings also prefigured, in the way that they defined groups and the relationship to "French" identity they assigned each group, a newly racialized logic that crystallized in the exodus and shaped post-Algeria France.

During the conflict over Algeria, all sides struggled to define the people living there, in a conflict that took place as much on the ground as in discussions of principle, public debate, and in diplomatic negotiations. At the war's end, having abandoned legally factual claims that all Algerians were French, the government tried to assert that all people living in Algeria would be both French and Algerian. Algerian nationalists rejected this position—arguing that "Europeans" would have to prove they were fit for Algerian nationality—as did many metropolitans, who claimed that the pieds noirs were not really French. The exodus would resolve these questions, when the government and many others recognized "Europeans" as French and "Muslims" as Algerians: two mutually exclusive categories. During the course of the war, French officials had denied that there were any definitive differences between "French" and "Algerian," and integrationist policies aggressively sought to overcome existing distinctions by taking them into account. Still, longstanding popular and official understandings of insurmountable racial and ethnic difference had continued to develop. The war's end saw a hardening of such popular understandings of who was different from whom;

[61] Ibid.

these popular understandings eventually—in response to the exodus—shaped official definitions.

"Movements of Populations and of Segregation between the Two Communities"

Written between January and March 1962, which is to say more than seven years after the beginning of the Algerian Revolution, sociologist Suzanne Frère's study, conducted for the government and entitled "The Two Communities of Algeria," observed with concern that "for several months the relationships between . . . Europeans and Muslims have become strained." Identifying "attitudes that run from basic prudence to hostility," Suzanne Frère cautioned that "what seems to be a widening divide is more complicated and perhaps shallower than visible signs might lead one to believe." Drawn from her general research, this study was more personal than others she submitted to the General Delegation in Algiers. Its claims are frequently dubious, lacking any analysis of the colonial situation, of the long-term segregation that divided Algeria's towns, or of the anti-"Muslim" racism that shaped French Algeria and, often, informed her analyses. Yet Frère's work is representative of a broad current of observations in early 1962 that stressed the novelty of near-complete segregation in French Algeria and that remained certain that this development would be ephemeral.[62]

What she and numerous other commentators most remarked, what she termed the most "spectacular" proof of segregation, were "movements of populations and of segregation on the part of the two communities," a division Frère characterized as "more or less complete in the large cities such as Algiers, Oran, Constantine, and Bône." Her study highlighted the numerous and distinct shifts—different from city to city, from neighborhood to neighborhood, different in what started the local movement, or in what ambiance, from hostility to complicity, the separation took place—that together produced this general phenomenon. Frère extended her analysis of "segregation" to other and, she argued, equally recent developments: "In the last several months, Europeans no longer wander through Muslim neighborhoods, or even near them," while, in European areas, particularly downtown, "Muslims still come but less and less as [OAS] attacks" continue. On certain days, "Muslims disappear completely from European neighborhoods." Taxi drivers from each community were now "refusing to transport clients not from their community"; "Anyone who takes public transportation now notes . . . that Muslims and Europeans avoid looking at each other."[63]

---

[62] Suzanne Frère, "Les deux communautés d'Algérie" (Algiers, January–March 1962), 1, in MAE 92.

[63] Ibid., 11–12.

In January 1962, as if confirming Frère's point, the Algiers Army Corps' "Weekly Psychological Intelligence Report" introduced a new heading: "Movements of Racial Segregation." They indicated that, while "a few" such movements had been noted in previous months, now "they tend to be more important and more widespread." In "sensitive" areas, such as Bab-el Oued ["European"] and Climat de France ["Muslim"], they "tend increasingly toward the elimination of one or the other of the two communities." In the Montplaisant neighborhood of Bouzareah, a suburb of Algiers, "780 of 832 FSE left between 14 December 1961 and 1 January 1962." These departures started, the report claimed, when "Muslims had come through forcing the FSE to leave, or face reprisals." Other European departures were attributed to "an OAS tract demanding their retreat to Bab-el Oued."[64]

Analyzing the same phenomena that Frère considered, army observers described a shift in the attitude of "Muslim" Algerians. In late January 1962, one army report noticed "the antagonism between the two communities tends to lose its purely political nature, becoming instead more and more racial." By December 1961, reports spoke of "Muslim" hostility toward all "Europeans"; with OAS terror reaching new levels, most "Muslims" now "tend to consider the European population" as wholly complicit with "violent attacks against Muslims." What was new, as the January report made clear, was not "Muslim" anger at "Europeans'" stubborn refusal of the inevitable—independence—but the "racial" character of this resentment.[65]

Official French sources in Algeria and the metropole described the emerging physical and racialized segregation between the two communities, but they could identify no particular actor or organization that wanted this to happen. An early January military analysis of developments in Constantine reported that the FLN "affirms that, when it is free and independent, democratic Algeria will be the shared fatherland of Muslims and Europeans." The author, Colonel Guerin, paralleled this promise with "OAS tracts that began in October to appeal to the Muslims." He noted ten documents, some "summoning them to choose between Communism and Europe," others "proposing to build a French and fraternal Algeria" or "asking Muslim youth to join in lifting up Algeria." Despite the novelty of the two movements' shared appeal across communitarian divides for Algerian unity, he noted that the two "terrorisms continue unabated." The colonel concluded with twinned questions: "Is such propaganda sincere and, if it is sincere, have the two movements lost control of their supporters?" Guerin's queries suggested that tension existed between, on the one hand, the leaders of the OAS

---

[64] Colonel Cavard, "Bulletin hebdomadaire de renseignement psychologique. Semaine du 10–16/1/62" (Algiers, 18 January 1962), 11, in SHAT 1H/2549/2.

[65] Lt.-Colonel Cousin, "Bulletin hebdomadaire de renseignements. Semaine du 20 au 26 janvier 1962" (SP 87.000, 27 January 1962), 11, in SHAT 1H/1436/D(1); 3ème Bureau EMI/Commandement Supérieur des Forces en Algérie, "Bulletin mensuel des activités des forces en Algérie: Décembre 1961" (December 1961), 15, in SHAT 1H/1855/12.

and the FLN and, on the other hand, their respective "European" and "Muslim" popular base. The former were each hoping to use unity to triumph, while the masses were eager for confrontation.[66]

Other official observers, however, argued that the "two populations" also wanted to keep some semblance of unity among all the people of Algeria. "Despite the movement of segregation," the officer in Algiers claimed, "both communities are attempting to live with a minimum of confrontation and exist side by side without acrimony."[67] Officer Cousin's report insisted that "moderate nationalists" were worried about the racialization of the conflict, estimating that "the separation of the communities would begin a process of compartmentalization, of a partitioning they see as undesirable." Concerning segregation, an army observer in Algiers reported that one "opinion that is widely shared among FSE and FSNA is that if this continues, it will no longer be in Berlin, but here that they will need to build a 'wall of shame'."[68] Indeed, Cousin pinpointed January 10 as the "high tide in Algiers," an argument, like his description of the ongoing "decrease in [OAS] terrorism," that subsequent reports and other evidence did not confirm.[69]

Like official sources, early 1962 press reports emphasized the novelty of segregation. A France-Observateur report claimed that the first week of January saw "tension between the two communities reach a critical point." Official assessments presented OAS and FLN leaders as well as the people of Algeria as surprised by these developments. The media, however, presented racialized segregation and conflict as normal. For them, this movement was not ephemeral but a defining and definitive shift in the conflict. Unlike official sources, metropolitan journalists drew direct connections between moves toward segregation and FLN and, above all, OAS tactical decisions. Each organization was presented as representative of both their "community's" leadership and the militant minority within each "population."[70] For the French media, the leaderships of the FLN and the OAS were co-opting "popular" segregation. The "isolated" and "spontaneous" movements of recent weeks had been, journalists André Delcroix and Hector de Galard asserted, "organized and taken control of" by the OAS and the FLN: "In the

[66] Colonel Guerin, "Bulletin hebdomadaire de renseignements. Semaine du 31 decembre 1961 au 7 janvier 1962. n. 64 CAC/2–A-S" Secret (Constantine, 10 January 1962), 2, in SHAT 1H/2836/3. The history of the FLN is beyond the limits of this study, which is researched in French sources and attentive above all to the dramatic changes that Algerian nationalism brought to France.

[67] Ibid.

[68] Colonel Cavard, "Bulletin hebdomadaire de renseignement psychologique. Semaine 10–16/1/62" (Algiers, 18 January 1962), 17, in SHAT 1H/2549/2.

[69] Lt.-Colonel Cousin, "Bulletin hebdomadaire de renseignements. Semaine du 20 au 26 janvier 1962" (SP 87.000, 27 January 1962), 11, in SHAT 1H/1436/D(1); 3ème Bureau EMI/Commandement Supérieur des Forces en Algérie, "Bulletin mensuel des activités des forces en Algérie: Decembre 1961" (December 1961), 19, in SHAT 1H/1855/12.

[70] A. Delcroix, H. de Galard, "Les négociations franco-FLN et le tournant de l'OAS," France-Observateur 610 (11 January 1962), 7.

neighborhoods most damaged by hate and violence precisely because they were mixed and 'little people' lived there . . . each organization is regrouping its community." Relying on a comparison of demographic distribution with territory, they described the creation of a "partition on the ground."[71] Also in *France-Observateur,* Philippe Hernandez argued that "there is a new development: the countryside [*le bled*] has jumped on the bandwagon." Previously observers had praised the countryside's "'wisdom' when faced with urban unrest"; now, even there, the OAS had gained Europeans' support.[72] On the eve of the cease-fire, a *Paris-Match* editorial lamented that "two communities that had blended together over a century are now, hastily and chaotically, splitting apart in a dispirited exodus *intra muros.*" For the media, the self-segregation of Algeria's people had created "two pained cities that still reject peace: Algiers, capital of anguish, Oran, prefecture of terror." Yet media accounts also implied that the "exodus *intra muros*" fomented peace, as it put an end to "blending together" (*brassage*). Neither Frère nor the army officers agreed.

Press presumption that growing segregation between "Muslims" and "Europeans" was normal echoed the general desire among most metropolitans for a total separation between "Algerians" and "French." In the same weeks that physical segregation dramatically increased in Algeria, the relationship between "Muslims" and non-Muslims was changing in the Hexagon as well. In 1958, as part of the policy of "integration," the government had established the SAM to address the near total segregation of FMAs in the metropole. The earliest reports of Muslim Affairs' technical consultants claimed that the "events in Algeria" had produced new suspicion among "metropolitans" toward Muslim French citizens from Algeria. By the summer of 1961, a quarterly summary described how the recent accentuation of the conflict had "deepened the reservations of most metropolitan milieus toward all things Algerian." The summary, in turn, evoked how "Muslims, for their part, have turned inward and have few contacts with those around them."[73] In the final months of 1961, consultants continued to describe "people's unease" in dealing with "Muslims"; this was true even, they remarked, "among groups that proclaim their solidarity and their sympathy for Muslim workers."[74] The reports need to be read within the context of integration, for they reveal both the novelties and the strict limits of this approach. On the one hand, they presumed that there were important differences between FMAs and "French people" but that these differences were neither essential nor in-

[71] Ibid.

[72] Philippe Hernandez, "En Algérie, j'ai vu la France assiegée par l'OAS," *France-Observateur* 610 (11 January 1962), 9.

[73] SAM, "Synthèse des rapports trimestriels établis par les conseillers techniques pour les affaires musulmanes—3ème trimestre (1/7–30/9/1961)," 35, in AN F/1a/5014.

[74] SAM, "Synthèse des rapports trimestriels établis par les conseillers techniques pour les affaires musulmanes—4ème trimestre (1/10–31/12/1961)," 32–33, in AN F/1a/5014.

evitably the cause of separation and suspicion. Integration, unlike assimilationist policies, was designed to accept certain Algerian "Muslim" particularities without describing them as necessarily divisive. But, on the other
hand, the need to accommodate actual difference did not lead to any radical
critique of French society: SAM and integration policy assessments presumed
that racism and colonialism were things of the past. Further, they viewed integrationist policies that took account of the historically produced differences between the group FMAs and other French citizens as a more effective
way to achieve, eventually, the assimilationist goal of turning FMAs into individual French citizens.

For SAM officials, therefore, it was not underlying racism or colonialist
presumptions but the ongoing "events in Algeria" that produced metropolitan "unease" or "suspicion" of FMAs. In the fall 1961 report they claimed,
for example, that there was no "systematic hostility" among neighbors of
Algerian "Muslims," as long as "the latter did nothing that could bring un-
favorable notice." This attempt to identify a rationale for metropolitan refusal (both by individuals and municipalities) to have "Muslims" as
neighbors was novel. Earlier reports simply noted such acts. Even in early
1961, however, official understandings still did not even consider linking
metropolitans' suspicions to metropolitan racism, although the evidence presented certainly offered grounds for such a conception.[75]

The reasons SAM officials did give for metropolitan suspicions of FMAs
changed over time. Early 1961 reports had highlighted overly lax parenting
as "the principal complaint" among neighbors. At the beginning of 1961,
the quarterly report remarked that "relations between European and Muslim families are generally correct although only rarely developed." In public
housing, it was claimed, "Muslim" families "are fairly well accepted after a
short adaptation period as long as"—and here a crucial premise of SAM efforts emerged—"they do not make up too large a percentage" of the inhabitants. It was not until late 1961, as war seemed to be arriving in the
metropole, that SAM reports identified fear of terrorism as potential neighbors' great concern about "Muslim" Algerians.[76]

Impending independence also sharpened other fears. The March 1961 report expressed "concern that certain businesses that have made an effort to
employ French Muslims rather than foreigners will no longer feel bound by
the same moral obligation when Algeria becomes independent," and it reported worries among employers that independence would inspire "massive
and unannounced departures" of Algerian workers. The December report
further emphasized this anxiety, insisting that employers "are worried that,
if Algerian independence occurs, there will be massive departures, voluntary

---

[75] Ibid.
[76] SAM, "Synthèse des rapports trimestriels établis par les conseillers techniques pour les affaires musulmanes—1ère trimestre (1/1–31/3/61)" Confidentiel, 35, in AN F/1a/5014.

or not, which will completely disorganize their businesses." It was for this reason—wholly rational to any reader of Adam Smith—that in the Moselle, it was claimed, "metalwork factories are no longer hiring new Algerian workers."[77]

The Evian Accords effected a slight but noticeable shift in the attitudes of "metropolitans" and "employers" toward FMA: among the former, "some hope, tacitly, that Algerian workers, now become foreigners, will go back to their homeland"; employers expressed greater reservations concerning "the Algerian workforce, either for emotional reasons, or because they worry that the evolving Algerian situation will lead to massive and unannounced departures." The SAM technicians' identification of the emotional and irrational nature of both hopes and concerns reflected the depth of the certainty mixed with desire that France soon would be rid of Algerians.[78]

In early 1962 popular anticipation that "Muslim" Algerians would leave joined official certainty that what they termed "French Algerians" would not come to the metropole. Before empirical information either had confirmed or invalidated them, these joined expectations—that some nine million French citizens all living on French territory (FMAs in the metropole and everyone in Algeria) would prefer overwhelmingly to live in an independent Algeria—give one measure of the profound crisis that the end of empire produced in France. The belief that "Algerians" would prefer to live in a territory that was to become not French, in order to become themselves no longer French, signaled a rupture in French confidence in the power and attractiveness of their national identity. This was new. More than most other European nation-states, modern French people had shown enormous confidence in the nation's capacities to refound and form as French all individuals within the boundaries of the state. Rogers Brubaker argues that this was critical to the establishment of nonethnic definitions of French nationality and citizenship. If the end of empire had produced this unprecedented lack of confidence in the power of French institutions to create French people, the sentiment itself had yet to take institutional or discursive form: the institutionalization of "confidence," which is how Brubaker explains modern French attribution of citizenship and nationality via *jus soli*, remained in place.[79]

The French Republic soon regained this confidence by embracing an ethnicized vision of the nation: although still explicitly "universal" in pretension, to be French became more closely wedded to being "European." The

<hr>

[77] Ibid., 34–35; SAM, "Synthèse des rapports trimestriels établis par les conseilleirs techniques pour les affaires musulmanes—4ème trimestere (1/10–31/12/61)," 32–33, in AN F/1a/5014.

[78] SAM, "Synthèse des rapports trimestriels établis par les conseillers techniques pour les affaires musulmanes—1ère trimestre (1/1–31/3/62)," 34–35, in AN F/1a/5014.

[79] Rogers Brubaker, *Citizenship and Nationhood in France and Germany* (Cambridge, Mass., 1992).

collapse of integrationist measures in the months leading up to the Evian Accords set the stage for the institutionalization of this understanding of French identity, which took place during the exodus. In their secret negotiations with Algerian nationalists, French officials had worked to craft terms that maintained the continuity of republican definitions and practices that determined who was French, as well as to reproduce them in Algeria. Popular understandings in France provided the basis for what would emerge, without discussion, in the exodus: a rupture.

One key factor that allowed this rupture to disappear was that, in the months leading up to the "exodus," a more long-standing tension in French conceptions of national membership reemerged. The "Jewish Question" once again played a key role in shaping French discussion of who was French. In the next chapter I explore debates among French officials and among defenders of French Algeria about Jewish Algerians. These worked to eliminate the uncertainties about identity that "integrationism" had embraced, which attempts to formulate "minority status" had brought to the fore. Concurrently, taking Jews into consideration reinforced claims that republican assimilation had worked in Algeria, at least for some people.

Chapter 6

Repatriation Rather Than Aliyah

The Jews of France and the End of French Algeria

The collapse of thirteen decades of assertions that Algeria was part of France confronted republicanism with the limits of its post-1789 claims about universalism and French identity. Concurrently, the Algerian crisis once again confronted the French with the "Jewish Question" that had so troubled the Republic since the 1789 Revolution. Jews, as a growing scholarly literature emphasizes, were the French citizens whose supposed "group" differences had obsessed and shaped French culturalist xenophobia, itself the force that both had refounded the Far Right after the Dreyfus Affair and molded much of modern French politics and history. In the last months of the Algerian War, French politicians, bureaucrats, and political movements engaged a number of discussions about whether the Jews of Algeria were the same as or different from the "Europeans of Algeria." Their answers suggested that the French Republic might finally have found a way out of this obsession.

The close of the Algerian conflict capped a period that began on 21 October 1943, when the Provisional Government of the French Republic in Algiers reinstated (after much hesitation) the Crémieux Decree.[1] The Vichy government's Law of 7 October 1940 had overturned the Decree of 24 October 1870, the landmark text that had "declared all Indigenous Israelites of Algeria French citizens." The 1940 law reassigned anyone who had citizenship as a result of the Crémieux Decree—that is to say, not only any person who had been "naturalized" in 1870 but their descendents as well—to "Indigenous Israelite" status, a group whose political rights were the same as

---

[1] See Patrick Weil, *Qu'est-ce qu'un Français? Histoire de la nationalité française depuis la Révolution* (2002), 139.

"Indigenous Muslim Algerians."[2] Following World War II and the collapse of the Vichy state, the Republic and most French Jews emphatically reaffirmed the assimilation of Jews—metropolitan and Algerian—into the nation. Events during the Algerian War consolidated this development. In turn, the urgency with which the French government and other French people insisted that Algerian Jews were wholly French helped fix a new boundary for the nation, which now excluded Algerian "Muslims."

"Individuals," Not an "Ethnic Community"

Leaders of Jewish organizations in Algeria and the metropole made great efforts to avoid getting drawn into the post-1954 struggles and debates over Algerian independence.[3] Yet a spring 1961 article by SFIO leader and former prime minister Guy Mollet forced them to enter the public fray. He described a recent conversation with Charles de Gaulle in which the president of the Republic evoked "the rights of the Arab, Chaouia, Mozabite, Jewish, and French communities." This comment—distinguishing the "Jews" from the "French" in Algeria—shocked Algerian Jewish leaders, despite Mollet's admission that he was not certain he had quoted de Gaulle correctly.[4] The specter of 1940, and the Vichy regime's revocation of the Crémieux Decree, had risen again. To counter what they saw as the clear implications of this "'communities' policy," Algerian Jewish leaders denied any political importance to their history as a group. They turned instead to a history in which French laws had made them all, as individuals, French citizens, emphatically reasserting the assimilationist rhetoric central to what the historian Pierre Birnbaum describes as "Franco-Judaism." Like all "French people," as one of the preeminent community organizations, the Alliance Israélite Universelle (AIU), laid out in a position paper on minority status, they should be considered as "individuals," and not as "belonging to an 'ethnic community.'"[5]

---

[2] See *J.O.* of 8 October 1940. For the political rights of "Indigenous Israelites," see Article 2. "Indigenous Israelites" as individuals had the same legal rights as "Muslims" to apply for "naturalization." See M. Camboulives, directeur des Affaires civiles et de Santé, "à M. le Chef du Gouvernement, Ministre Secrétaire à l'Intérieur, Sous-Direction de l'Algérie" (Vichy, 17 July 1942), which states, "Given the very terms used in the Law of 18 February 1942 . . . we must admit that 'indigenous Jews' have the possibility of obtaining citizenship" through the terms of the Senatus-Consulte of 14 July 1865. Dossier "Statut des Juifs en Algérie," MJ/FA S54 113. This last point contradicts the claims of Jacques Cantier, *Algérie sous le régime de Vichy* (Paris, 2002), 73; see also Michel Abitbol, *Les Juifs d'Afrique du Nord sous Vichy* (Paris, 1983).

[3] See Sarah Sussman, "Changing Lands, Changing Identities: The Migration of Algerian Jewry to France, 1954–1967" (PhD diss., Stanford University, 2002), 92–142.

[4] See Mylène Sultan, "La synthèse impossible, 1954–62," in *Les Juifs d'Algérie: Textes et images*, ed. Jean Laloun and Jean-Luc Allouche (Paris, 1987), 46.

[5] Alliance Israélite Universelle, "Note concernant les modalités de conservation de la nationalité Française et l'acquisition de la nationalité Algérienne dans l'Algérie future" (Paris, 17 April 1961), 5, in MAE 99. Pierre Birnbaum, *The Jews of the Republic: A Political History of*

Beginning in late 1954, Algerian Jewish organizations began to repeatedly affirm the French citizenship of Jews, while also trying to avoid appearing as if they were taking a political position in the name of "the community." Now, faced with de Gaulle's assertion of their existence as a group distinct from other French citizens, they wanted, as one General Delegation in Algeria memo summarized, explicit official recognition that their French citizenship was "acquired by paternity and no longer by virtue of the Crémieux Decree."[6] What made each Jew French was being born of parents with French citizenship and/or on French soil. Anti-Semites and then the Pétainist state had argued that their citizenship, even generations after 1870, was not a birthright, but a reversible "naturalization," which would end if the 1870 decree was revoked.

In the metropole, the AIU among others also actively sought to counter "the so-called communities policy." In a note to Minister of State Louis Joxe, Alliance president René Cassin, a jurist who also served as vice president of the Council of State (and who in 1968 received the Nobel Peace Prize for his work on human rights, especially the drafting of the UN Declaration of Human Rights), argued that officially only "Muslims" and French people should be identified in Algeria. He recognized the historic distinctions between different "Muslim" groups—Arabs, Kabyles, Chaouris, Mozabites—yet argued that history and events since 1954 effectively had effaced them. As for non-"Muslims," he pointedly remarked, "French law does not allow the identification of French people by their origins." History here explicitly made all Algerian "Muslims" one people, just as, here implicitly, decolonization should make them—although currently French citizens—not French. Note the critical role the law played in this definition of French identity.[7]

Rejecting references to the Crémieux Decree, metropolitans and leaders of Algerian Jewish organizations recalled the shame of Vichy. They also spurned the position of the GPRA, announced at the Congress of Soummam in 1956, which argued that the 1870 decree's mass assimilation of the Jews of Algeria was not a generous reform but a colonial act that arbitrarily divided one group of Algerians from the rest. From this historical interpretation, the 1956 GPRA Congress had insisted that "Jewish Algerians" were fully part of the Algerian nation. In 1961 such claims, which had made little headway except among certain Jewish members of the Communist Party (PCA), were further discredited by the FLN's assassination of several well-

---

State Jews in France from Gambetta to Vichy, trans. Jane Marie Todd (Stanford, 1996); Michael Laskier, *North African Jewry in the Twentieth Century* (New York, 1994).

[6] Direction générale des Affaires politiques et de l'information, Délégation Générale en Algérie, "Note sur la réaction de la communauté Israélite d'Algérie face à l'évolution du problème algérien" (Rocher Noir, 24 January 1962), 1–2, in MAE 121 bis.

[7] Direction générale des Affaires politiques et de l'information, Délégation Générale en Algérie, "Note sur la réaction de la communauté Israélite d'Algérie," 1–2.

known members of the Jewish community. On 22 June, for example, frontists in Constantine murdered Cheikh Raymond Leyris, the widely popular Jewish star of Malouf (a form of classical Arabo-Andalusian music). By invoking French law and the recent Vichy episode of French history, Jewish leaders and their allies successfully made sure the government adopted a position that wholly rejected Algerian nationalist claims. These efforts made quick headway within the government. The point men were Bernard Tricot, a diplomat on the staff of the president of the Republic, and Louis Joxe, Algerian Affairs minister. Both served as negotiators at the two Evian conferences, the latter as the head of the French delegation.[8]

Their rejection of any invocation of Jewish specificity weighed heavily in resolving official uncertainty over how to define the "European minority." Tricot repeatedly intervened to point out the implications for Jewish Algerians of proposed French position papers. He edited out all formulations that appeared to admit the existence of a Jewish community in Algeria. In one note, with respect to the "Definition of the Minority" section, he warned against "talk of extending access to the European community to the Israelite minority." The French position "up to now," he chided, "considers them as belonging without question [de plein droit] to the European community."[9] Tricot's emphasis on the nonexistence of the group "Israelites" in French law inadvertently emphasized how in defining "the minority" Algerian Affairs officials had begun by isolating group identities not anchored in French law. Early proposals made few if any references to civil status: the minority was to be "European." Thus, one study identified the people concerned as "Europeans," "Israelites," and "Arabs loyal to France." Among the first group, the document proposed only one distinction: between those who lived in Algeria and those "passing through." Civil status was not the primary criteria, although it constantly was taken into consideration. In the above proposal, while arguing that both of the other groups should also be offered minority status, the "Israelites" were included because they "have the right," whereas self-selecting "Muslims" "could" enjoy the benefits minority status would offer.[10]

Tricot's attention to protecting the inclusion of Algerian Jews in any definition of "European" clarified this definitional confusion. In his response to the 17 May 1961 study, he criticized the attempt to "parallel" Israelites and

---

[8] Minister for Veterans Affairs and War Victims Raymond Triboulet also lent his offices to the assimilationist agenda, while Chief Engineer Louis Kahn worked to present AIU concerns to a number of ministers. Cf. René Cassin, président, Alliance Israélite Universelle, "Pneumatique à M. le Ministre Louis Joxe" (17 May 1961), 1, in MAE 100; [Joxe] Ministère d'Etat chargé des Affaires algériennes, "Personnelle à Raymond Triboulet, Ministre des Anciens combattants et Victimes de la Guerre" (March 1961), 1, in MAE 100.

[9] Bernard Tricot, présidence de la République, "Note au sujet du dossier relatif à la minorité" (8 May 1961), 1, in MAE 99 folder.

[10] Ministère d'Etat chargé des Affaires algériennes, "Contenu du dossier des pourparlers d'Evian" (17 May 1961), 5, in MAE 103.

"loyal Muslims." After repeated interventions by Tricot and other high-ranking government officials, "Israelites" disappeared from French proposals, except in affirmations that they were part of the group to be included in the "European minority." The effect on French demands was immediate: it attenuated the claim that certain "Muslims loyal to France" necessarily should be offered minority status. Efforts to solidify the definition of a "European minority" in order to eliminate any reference to Jews as a group worked to exclude "Muslims" altogether. Tricot made clear his strong agreement with the reticence one study expressed about including any "Muslims," an inclusion described as "barely compatible" with the "European character" of the proposed minority.[11] It was Tricot's articulation of a distinction between "Muslims" and "others" that had the most impact on the revised proposal. While affirming the full "assimilation" of "Algerian Jews," Tricot's reticence to include any "Muslims" in the proposed definition—he noted that "for Muslims it certainly [would be] an extension"—undermined French efforts to have the accords with the GPRA take integrationist policies into account.[12]

Rather than try to negotiate using existing religious and ethnic differences, as integrationism had begun to attempt, Tricot's position reaffirmed pre-1944 assimilationist efforts. Civil status, rather than French citizenship or desire to retain French citizenship, eventually emerged as the primary determinant of "European" identity. Indeed, no "Muslim French citizens from Algeria," even those who had "French civil status" or who legally had "assimilated," should be included automatically in the "European minority."[13] The new position did admit that "Muslims who expressed the desire" could be included "for political reasons," but not as a right and with an impressive condition: "as long as they merit benefiting from the same protection as French people." Further, documents increasingly referred to the "Muslim"-free category not as "Europeans" but as "French."[14]

Countering the Jewish "Exodus"

While Jewish community leaders and well-placed insiders pressured Paris-based Algerian Affairs officials to include Jews in the category of "Europeans," other French bureaucracies worked strenuously in late 1960, 1961, and into 1962 to prevent the separation of Algerian Jews from "European"

[11] Ministère d'Etat chargé des Affaires algériennes, "Définition de la minorité" (24 March 1961 with revision 18 April), 1, in MAE 96; Bernard Tricot, présidence de la République, "Note au sujet du dossier relatif à la minorité" (8 May 1961), 1–2, in MAE 99.

[12] Ibid.

[13] Ministère d'Etat chargé des Affaires algériennes, "Garanties de la minorité européenne en Algérie" (31 March 1961), 2, in MAE 96.

[14] See particularly Ministère d'Etat chargé des Affaires algériennes, "Définition de la minorité" (24 March 1961 with revision 18 April), 1, in MAE 96.

Algerians. In the midst of the government's brutal fight to crush Algerian nationalists, Interior and Foreign Affairs officials engaged in a tug-of-war with Jewish nationalism, Zionism, over Algerian Jews. Although there was a general effort by the French government to keep Algerians with French civil status from leaving, the involvement of the government of Israel and the Jewish Agency gave a particular valence to their efforts concerning Algerian Jews. Just as the challenge of Algerian nationalism had led to an "integrationist" ferment of new republican policies, so the challenge of Zionism reshaped republican certainties and provoked new possibilities.

The biblical term "exodus" was used, not surprisingly, precociously and repeatedly to characterize Jewish departures from Algeria. As early as 1960, first in the region around the eastern city of Constantine and then elsewhere, police and army intelligence noticed that a good number of Jews were leaving with no intention of returning.[15] Official attention to such activity began in early 1961, when civil servants attributed this growing phenomenon to foreign intervention. These bureaucrats made considerable effort to see that the "approximately" 128,380 Algerian Jews one list claimed were living in Algeria at the beginning of 1961 remained in Algeria. Their aim was to allow most Jews, like most other non-"Muslims," eventually to become citizens of Algeria.[16]

French sources detailed two types of foreign contacts with Algerian Jewish leaders and organizations: the first involved rumors that members of the Israeli right-wing extremist organization Irgun were in Algeria to train OAS commandos. In January 1962, *Paris-Match* claimed that there was a violent Jewish underground in Algeria.[17] That the far-right Zionist terrorist organization, known for its brutal killing of Arab civilians and British soldiers in pre-1947 Palestine (and a precursor of Israel's Likud Party), would be linked to the OAS was little surprise. French officials, however, never took these unproven claims seriously.[18] (The idea of a "plot," however, remained plausible to many long after independence.[19]) The Jewish Agency, also based in Israel, was the second contact. French functionaries had verifiable intelli-

---

[15] See Secrétaire d'Etat aux Affaires algériennes, "La communauté Israélite d'Algérie" (19 October 1962), 1, in MAE 121 bis, which offers an overview of developments up to that point.

[16] For reports on Jewish departures, see CAC 920172/08. For early 1961, see "Liste approximative des Juifs en Algérie par localité au début de 1961," in CAC 920172/08. For choice of France versus Israel and other countries, see Secrétaire d'Etat aux Affaires algériennes, "La communaute Israélite d'Algérie" (19 October 1962), 2, in MAE 121 bis.

[17] Jean Maquet, "A Oran comme Alger un passant invisible: La peur," *Paris-Match* 667 (20 January 1962), 26–31.

[18] See, for example, Jean Sicurani, "Note sur les 'commandos juifs' d'Oran" (16 January 1962), 2, in MAE 121. Karim Rouina affirms that there was an "organization established by the Israeli secret services, called Hagana Magen." See the roundtable discussion transcribed in Jean-Louis Planche, "Français d'Algérie, Français en Algérie? Jacques Chevallier ou les impossibles compromis," in *Intelligentsias françisées au Maghreb colonial*, ed. G. Meynier and J.-L. Planche (Paris, 1990), 92.

[19] See, for example, H. Argod, ambassadeur, haut représentant de la République Française en Algérie, "a/s Les Juifs d'Algérie" (Algiers, 9 August 1963), 1, in MAE 121 bis.

gence that delegates of the paragovernmental organization were encouraging French Jews in Algeria to leave and go to Israel, "to make aliyah" in Zionist parlance. In January 1961, the French government's highest civilian official in Algeria, Delegate General Jean Morin, alerted the Ministry of the Interior to the request for entry permits by "ten delegates of the Jewish Agency," who wanted, they stated, "to calm the apprehensions of the Israelite population of Algeria." Morin argued that they had a different agenda, noting that the "most important activity of the Jewish Agency always has been to encourage emigration to Israel." He asked whether the French government "would facilitate such an enterprise." He stressed "above all" that emigration to a foreign country was being urged on "a population that was the first autochthonous population to acquire French nationality."[20]

In response, not only did the minister of state for Algerian affairs deny entry to the delegates but a July letter made clear that France "refused to accept applications for entry on Algerian territory from representatives of *any* Jewish organization." This "rigorous position," the letter announced, "is impossible to maintain for much longer."[21] The Israeli government was aware that France had blocked the agency's access to Algeria. On 9 March 1961, the French ambassador in Tel Aviv told the Quai d'Orsay that Foreign Minister Golda Meir had summoned him to inquire about a visa problem for Jewish Agency officials wanting to go to Algeria. He pleaded ignorance.[22] Morin, however, appeared unaware of this decision. In mid-March, complaining that, since his first warning, the government had taken no action, Morin now reported that Jewish Agency representatives had shifted from "facilitating the emigration of Israelites who wanted to leave" to "exhortations to leave for Israel."[23] In July 1961, Morin's earlier concerns about the Jewish Agency's encouragement of departures to Israel now were twinned with a warning about how Agency envoys "laid out new reasons for the general malaise of the non-Muslim population." This argument was typical of all efforts to prevent groups of French citizens from definitively leaving Algeria. "It is not so much the results" that were worrisome, for there was, he asserted, "no question of anything like an exodus of Algerian Jews"; it was rather "because of the psychoses it encourages that this activity by the Zionist movement is troublesome."[24] Morin again touched on the issue of Algerian Jews' unique history of successful assimilation. Jew-

---

[20] C. Viellescazes, dir. du Cabinet, Délégation Générale en Algérie, "A l'attention personnelle de M. Aubert n. 699 CC" (24 January 1961), 1, in CAC 920172/08.

[21] Délégation Générale en Algérie, "à M. le Préfet . . . n. 7059 CC" (18 July 1961), 2, in CAC 920172/08. Emphasis added.

[22] Bourdeillette, ambassador to Israel, "Télégramme no. 175/76/80" (Tel Aviv, 9 March 1961), 1, in MAE 121 bis.

[23] Jean Morin, "Objet: Activité des mission israéliennes en Algérie" (Algiers, 24 March 1961), 1, in MAE 121 bis; see also Délégation Générale en Algérie, Affaires politiques, "Télégramme n. 2784" (22 March 1961), 1, in MAE 121 bis.

[24] Ibid.

ish Agency speakers claimed, Morin reported, that "Algerian independence is inevitable in the short term" and that Israel "merited their trust more than France."[25]

The Jewish Agency's denigration of the Republic, following Morin, was the heart of the matter. Israel's first prime minister, David Ben-Gurion, had stated in 1958 that the French should trust no Algerian Arabs "no matter how assimilated." In 1961, internal documents repeatedly invoked Ben-Gurion's remark. His assertion of inassimilable difference—and necessary enmity—revealed the ethnic nationalist crux of the Zionist project the Jewish Agency advanced. French republicans found the idea anathema. Most French politicians supported Algerian independence while avoiding any consideration of what it meant for republican ideology that France had been unable, via assimilationist policies pursued (or announced) since 1830, to make most Algerians French. Proving that French citizens who were at once Jewish and Algerian could "trust" the Republic more than Israel (and that, in turn, the Republic could trust them) allowed republicanism to emerge reinforced.[26]

Official efforts to prevent Jewish departures at first seemed futile. Throughout fall 1961 and into 1962, all government observers emphasized Jewish departures. The RG estimated that barely half of Constantine's 1954 Jewish population remained in Algeria.[27] As part of his tabulation of French nationals "definitively leaving" Algeria, the secretary of state for Algerian affairs made special note of those bound for Israel: 302 of 1,913 in September; 173 out of 2,086 in October; 21 of 2,530 in December. The report warned that "the real destination generally is no longer given by voyagers of the Jewish faith." The Jewish Agency had given instructions to this effect.[28] By early 1962, whatever their destination, the abandonment of Constantine by its Jewish population had become a source of continuing interest to the metropolitan press.[29] Yet in official reports a counterrevolution seemed to be occurring. At the end of 1961 and, more markedly, the beginning of 1962, in what proved the last months of French Algeria, military and civilian officials noted a slowdown in Jewish departures. Concurrently, they evoked a new

[25] Ibid., 1 and 2.

[26] For Ben-Gurion, see *Le Figaro* (10 April 1958). For invocations of this comment see Sicurani "Note sur les 'commandos juifs' d'Oran," 2, in MAE 121 bis. See also Morin, "Activité des mission israéliennes en Algérie," 2, in MAE 121 bis.

[27] RG d'Alger, Bône, Constantine, Orléansville, "Etat d'esprit de la communauté israélite" (27 and 30 November 1961), 45, in MAE 121 bis.

[28] "Statistiques des départs définitifs d'Européens d'Algérie" (7 November 1961 and 6 December 1961), in MAE 121 bis. Note that these statistics do not correspond to those given elsewhere, for example, "Débat budgetaire Fiche ii/p. 6, 'Départs définitifs d'Algérie'" (1 April to 31 October 1961), in MAE 121 bis.

[29] Christian Mouly, "L'exode des familles israélites d'Algérie . . . ," *Le Monde* (17 February 1962); for official concern, see MAE 121 bis and SHAT 1H/1436/D(1). For an example of discussions of "repatriation" to Spain, see Lt.-Colonel Cousin, "Bulletin hebdomadaire de renseignements. Semaine du 10 au 16 fevrier 1962" (SP 87.000, 17 February 1962), 2, in SHAT 1H/1436/D(1). Such reports also began to identify "Europeans" who were leaving as "of Spanish origin" and "of Maltese origin."

and increasing solidarity between Jewish and non-Jewish Algerians with French civil status. Across the divide that anti-Semitism had enforced, as with the other divides—"ethnic," partisan, and, most important, class—the joining together of Algerian non-"Muslims" occurred through the OAS.[30]

The "Rapprochement between Israelites and Europeans *d'origine*"

Until January 1962, intelligence sources had emphasized Jewish suspicion of the OAS. One RG report spoke of Jewish notables' doubts about "a clandestine movement in which some leaders are said to want to establish totalitarianism in France, with all its sinister historical ancestry."[31] A National Security report on "one particular ethnic group . . . the Jewish communities" of Algeria, examined their "obstinacy before FLN propaganda as well as that of the OAS." Overwhelmingly opposed to FLN claims about belonging to the Algerian nation, nevertheless, "Jews in general avoid association with the diverse French Algeria movements. Nazism remains too alive in their memories for them to accept any connection with local leaders of the far-right movement." Jews in Oran and "to a lesser degree, Algiers" were picked out as atypical in their sympathy for the activists.[32] Yet, outside of Algiers, Oran, and, to a lesser extent, Bône, most "Europeans" shared a similar reticence— and occasional enthusiasm—for activist engagement. Where active support for the OAS now dominated among "Europeans," it did so among "Jews," and vice versa. While official reports and the press clung to indications of Jewish difference, the evidence they reported pointed increasingly to a coming together of all Algerian non-"Muslims" around shared political goals and analyses.

The press quickly remarked on signs of Jewish activism. Most prescient was *El Moudjahid,* the voice of the FLN, which warned Algerian Jews away from such a course.[33] In January 1962, when *Paris-Match* made its accusation of Irgun involvement in Algeria, the journalist wrote first of the "Jewish" victims of an FLN attack: "the schoolboy, grandson of the greengrocer

---

[30] Although all subgroups shared the same legal status, the infamously intense engagement with anti-Semitism of non-Jewish "Europeans," which began a few years after the Crémieux Decree, had anchored a distinction between Jews and gentiles far more important than the other "ethnic" fissures that divided "Spanish" from "Italian," or "Maltese" from Algerians "of [French] origin" with French civil status.

[31] RG de Constantine, "Malaise au sein de la communauté israélite de Constantine" (27 December 1961), 46, in MAE 121 bis. On Cagayous, see David Prochaska, "History as Literature, Literature as History: Cagayous of Algiers," *American Historical Review* 101 (June 1996): 671–711.

[32] Direction de la Sûreté nationale en Algérie, Jean Fachot, "La communauté Israélite face au problème algérien" (January 1962), 2, in SHAT 1H/1255/2.

[33] "Les ratonnades et l'avenir de l'Algérie," in *El Moudjahid* (Arabic edition: 30 September 1961; French edition: 1 October 1961), in SHAT 1H/1152/1.

... his throat cut"; "four bullets in her stomach" that killed "a young
woman seven months pregnant"; and a "seventy-five-year-old man struck
down." The article then describes the "lynching" that followed. "They were
horrible, the Israelites," according to a witness who linked "Jewish" violence
to the fact that "during seven years they watched and waited, even flirting
with the FLN." After invoking the Irgun's arrival, the article concludes,
"Ready to defend themselves against the Muslims or the Christians, they
have chosen sides: the OAS."[34] Military reports of anti-"Muslim" vigilan-
tism also increasingly noted Jewish participation. Unlike years past, when on
rare occasions Jewish Algerians had been accused of spontaneous "lynch-
ings" in response to FLN violence, these actions suggested a new communi-
tywide response. On 8 March, in Mascara, Army Intelligence reported that
four explosions attributed to the FLN were followed by "a European demonstration, principally led by Israelites." The result: "eight Muslims injured,
one of whom died at the hospital."[35]

After October 1961, the OAS aggressively reached out to Jewish Algerians, as well as to "Muslim" Algerians, emphasizing that their definition of
French people included Jews as well as "Muslims." The OAS celebration of
Jewish Algerian Frenchness included explicit recognition of the twentieth-
century history of anti-Semitism. This differed from pro–French Algeria
claims that Algerian "Muslims" were fully French. The OAS only acknowledged colonialist racism—by the government and among Algeria's "Europeans"—when it argued that the "fraternization of the May Days" of 1958
had offered a clean slate. Unlike their silence about past racism, references
to Nazi persecutions, pogroms, and even Vichyite collaboration peppered
OAS propaganda. All revealed how Gaullist policy and metropolitan support for Algerian independence were anti-Semitic as well as racist. They repeatedly attacked the Gaullist state as "Nazi" and "SS", and accompanied
these condemnations with specific reference to the exterminationist anti-
Semitism inherent in this link. Again and again, pro-OAS propaganda described the martyrdom of young Noah. On 19 January 1962, a French
soldier shot at a group of high school students who, in the words of one
handbill, were "sticking patriotic posters on a wall." As the soldier walked
on, "the blood of a young boy, who looked Israelite, drained away on the
sidewalk." The author of "My Dear Friend" explained that "this scene did
not take place in Warsaw, 1942, but in Bône, in the European Quarter. No,
the man in the uniform is not an SS, but an officer with the Military Court
at Bône."[36] Jacques Soustelle, former governor general of Algeria and the
architect of "integrationism," wrote a syndicated column entitled "Gan-

---

[34] Maquet, "A Oran comme Alger un passant invisible," 26–31, 27. The article suggests
that all the violent undergrounds in Algeria "are trying to copy the methods" of the Jews.
[35] Lt.-Colonel Cousin, "Bulletin hebdomadaire de renseignements. Semaine du 3 au 9 mars
1962" (SP 87.000, 10 March 1962), 27, in SHAT 1H/1436/D(1).
[36] OAS, "Mon cher ami . . ." (1962), AN 78 AJ/32.

grène" (the title appropriated from one of the first French books to detail the state's habitual use of torture against accused nationalists).[37] He compared the French Army's "roundup of all boys between sixteen and twenty-five whose physique gives away their ethnic origin" to the Gestapo "when it organized dragnets to capture Jews in occupied France." The goal of this "physiognomic roundup of young Europeans," he argued, was "to strike out against the French of Algeria as a people, as French people, Christians or Jews."[38] References to pogroms also were common in Algerian OAS propaganda. OAS handbills directed at soldiers serving in Algeria reminded them that if they left, as the open letter addressed to "My Dear Friend" stated, "the harkis you served with will have their throats slit," while "the Israelites will fall victim to pogroms."[39]

Some on the far right, in an evolution forced by their overwhelming desire to keep Algeria French and their support of the OAS, sought to hold on to the premises of Maurrassian xenophobia, yet to assert that Jewish Algerians were fully French. This move broke with the history of the new Far Right that emerged in late nineteenth-century France, where suspicion and demonization of "the Jew" played such a foundational role.[40] These Jewish Algerians were French not because of Crémieux, nor assimilation, nor the rules of the *pays légal* (the legally defined country) but because of their actions in the *réel* (the actual). The anonymously authored paperback *The Activist* rehearsed the old Action Française chestnut about "not calling French someone who acts like a member of a foreign community," yet denied that this was a sign of "racism or anti-Semitism." The "Algerian Jew fighting against the secession of this province" was just as French as "the German or Hungarian or Russian" who had "served under our flag in the Foreign Legion."[41] "OAS-Métropole," an operation particularly infested by militants from far-right groups, went further. In defense of Israel, they claimed the mantle of anti–anti-Semitism, identifying anti-Semitism (or, in Pierre-André Taguieff's terms, Judeophobia[42]) as a key element motivating de Gaulle's desire to abandon French Algeria. OAS-Métropole argued that de Gaulle wanted France to "take its place in the anti-Semitic concert of nations" alongside the Soviet bloc and the Arab states. Algerian independence was part of an international conspiracy "to strangle the State of Israel." It would turn the nation that in 1956 had fought at Suez beside the Israelis against Arab na-

---

[37] *La gangrène* (1959).

[38] Jacques Soustelle, "La gangrène," *Indépendante du Sud-Ouest* (Agen, 15 June 1962), 1.

[39] Ibid.

[40] See, e.g., Raoul Girardet, *Le nationalisme français: Anthologie, 1871–1914*, parts 3 and 4 (Paris, 1983); and Zeev Sternhell, *Maurice Barrès et le nationalisme français* (Paris, 1972).

[41] Anonymous, *L'Activiste* (1962), 28, in AN 78 AJ/31. Although Jews here are named only to celebrate their patriotism, the phrases used to denigrate those who "act foreign" depend on anti-Semitic stereotypes for their resonance, invoking high-placed conspiracies in the banks and government.

[42] *La nouvelle judéophobie* (Paris, 2002).

tionalism into two states that accepted Arab nationalism. The end of French Algeria would deform France in order to destroy Israel.[43]

Commentators on the left noticed the lull in far-right anti-Semitism, which they attributed to hypocrisy. In late spring 1962, the editor of *L'Esprit* Jean-Marie Domenach remarked that "they have muted their anti-Semitism." Even the 14 April 1962 nomination of Georges Pompidou, an "employee of Rothschild's," to head the government had brought only "a serial in *La Nation Française*" (a neo-Maurrassian weekly), and not the apparently expected onslaught of anti-Semitic outbursts from far-right journalists about Jewish money and hidden cabals. "A single racism is enough for the moment," Domenach argued—"against the Muslims." In this schema, anti-Semitism was not downgraded in favor of anti-"Muslim" racism. Rather, Domenach identified pro–French Algeria muting of anti-Semitism as part of a larger cynical denial of their essential racism. As he reminded his readers, "The OAS's antiracist alibi is the support it has among a portion of Algerian Israelites."[44]

From Jewish Algerians to Europeans

It is reasonable to qualify as hypocritical the embrace by the OAS and supporters of French Algeria of a strategy that emphasized its antiracism and its opposition to anti-Semitism. Yet such an interpretation risks ignoring the actual effects of these tactics. Not only did this propaganda propose a nonracialist vision of the French nation that explicitly embraced "Jews" and "Muslims," as with the Plan Salan, the rhetoric paralleled as well as contributed to on-the-ground developments. The definitive departures of Jews from Algeria, so remarkable and of such concern to French bureaucrats, slowed. More significant, as an army summary in October 1962 described it, "In the spring and early summer of 1962, the emigration tendency for both communities [Jewish and non-Jewish "Europeans"] followed a parallel curve." The curve, in fact, fluctuated wildly, swinging in tandem with pied noir confidence in the OAS-led struggle to prevent independence as well as with pied noir discipline in following OAS orders. What is undeniable is that, in these months, departures—like confidence and discipline—became pied noir, and no longer "Israelite," "Spanish," or "of French origin." Army intelligence in late 1961 and early 1962 reported that Algerian "Israelite" opinion shifted definitely from *attentisme* (waiting to see what happens) to pro-OAS activism.[45]

---

[43] See OAS Presse Action, "Information semaine du 21 au 28 octobre 1962," 2, in AN 78 AJ/30; OAS Délégation en Métropole, "OAS/Métro/APP Presse Service" (Paris, 17 April 1962), in AN 78 AJ/30. The same OAS-Métropole bulletin ended, however, with a characterization of newly named Prime Minister Georges Pompidou as "Rothschild banker."

[44] Jean-Marie Domenach, "Journal à plusieurs voix: La droite nihiliste," *L'Esprit*, n.s., 6 (June 1962): 972–76, 974.

[45] Ibid.

At the war's end, the Far Right presented Algerian Jews as first and foremost French, as were all Algerians. For most people in the metropole, however, they were above all "French of Algeria": they were, that is, not really French, but in the same way as all pieds noirs were not really French. This conception underlay the government's establishment of repatriate status as well as French diplomats' efforts to insert "minority status" into the Evian Accords. In the next chapter I describe metropolitans' definitions of pieds noirs in the months before the 1962 exodus and the emergence of a strongly anti–pied noir public discourse, which included "Jews" as well as "Europeans." Yet the successful efforts of Tricot and others to distinguish the relationship of Algerian Jews to French identity from that of any "Muslim" Algerian was a precursor: their shared exodus demonstrated that Europeans, and Jews in particular, were French in ways that were greater than the citizenship they shared with Algerian "Muslims."

Between March 1960 and March 1962 French officials stopped referring to Jewish Algerians as a group apart, first in presidential rhetoric and then in policymaking. A concerted lobbying effort from inside and outside the executive branch joined with a reflexive but intense bureaucratic resistance against Israeli efforts in Algeria to silence considerations of Jewish difference. This process changed official thinking about how to define all people from Algeria. While these tactics failed in their explicit goal of preventing mass departures from Algeria, the results were striking: in overwhelming numbers, Jews left Algeria and "repatriated" to France. Since the State of Israel's establishment in 1948 in Palestine this remains the only example of the flight of a group of Jews where most did not go to the self-proclaimed homeland of all Jews.[46]

The shift in government assertions, from distinguishing between Algerian Jews and Algerian "Europeans" to collapsing all references to Jews into the category "European," offers grounds for two, somewhat contradictory, points of assessment. The most important implication (and that which has dominated scholarly consideration of this question) is that in 1960 it was still possible to consider Jews as a group apart from other French citizens. In this optic, the developments this chapter has charted reinforce a narrative of republican progress. What such a perspective obscures, however, is the early history of the Fifth Republic: presenting a narrative of republican progress effaces how France had used integration to recognize the existence of certain (cultural, religious, and ethnic) differences as fully compatible with the Republic. The second perspective from which these debates must be viewed places them within the history of efforts to make Algeria French. In the assimilationist approach, which dominated official thinking (if often not official actions) in Algeria before 1944, any bureaucratic or political recognition of distinctions between Jewish and non-Jewish Algerians with French civil status can and should only be seen as evidence of anti-Semitism. Recent

[46] See Sussman, "Changing Lands, Changing Identities," 162–68.

work—on popular anti-Semitism among Algerian "Europeans" and campaigns to reverse "Crémieux" as well as on bureaucratic efforts to distinguish between Jewish and non-Jewish "citizens with French civil status"—proves the important effects and disastrous consequences of such official "recognition." Yet post-1955 integration proposed new means to officially consider and discuss religious and ethnic differences within the Republic. Legal definition of FMAs was one sign of this. With civil status no longer a marker of citizenship, it became possible politically or bureaucratically to "recognize" group differences without necessarily implying that such people were not as fully French as others from Algeria. In 1961 and 1962, the disappearance of official references to Jews as a distinct Algerian group prefigured the political collapse of French integrationist policies and pretensions. Alongside discussions of repatriate status, this process marked the return of classic assimilationist strategies; now, it was an assimilationism where the inassimilable was starkly indicated: "Muslims." The 1962 exodus would make clear that it was the emergence of this boundary that allowed republican ideologies of national belonging to be reasserted without reference to the limits and incoherencies that integrationism had worked to address.

Beyond 1962, the victory of those who had struggled for Jewish assimilation, the long-delayed acceptance by French elites of the tenets of "Franco-Judaism," ironically created the context in which Jewish critics of assimilation à la française garnered new influence and importance in the Hexagon. The post-1962 context offered newly solid grounds for the arguments of those self-identified Jews in France who called for affirmations of Jewish specificity. French Jews could and did begin to speak about their political identity as Jews. This was the new context from which, five years later, French people stunned by de Gaulle's antagonism toward Israel for its aggression in the Six-Day War and his infamous characterization of Jews as "an elite people, sure of themselves and domineering" began to speak politically as Jews.[47] Many of these Jews had come from Algeria as part of, not a Jewish exodus, but the pied noir exodus.

---

[47] See Birnbaum, *Jews of the Republic,* and *Jewish Destinies: Citizenship, State, and Community in Modern France,* trans. Arthur Goldhammer (New York, 2000).

Chapter 7

Veiled "Muslim" Women, Violent Pied Noir Men, and the Family of France

Gender, Sexuality, and Ethnic Difference

On 7 February 1962 OAS commandos set off a bomb in Minister of Culture André Malraux's apartment building. The explosion's only victim was his four-year-old neighbor "little Delphine," left permanently blind in one eye. A widely reprinted black-and-white close-up showed the young brown-haired girl covered with blood; the snap-shot that usually accompanied it showed the white-skinned child amid a field of flowers, her eyes smiling. This could have been yet another incident in the terrorist campaign that OAS activists had begun in spring 1961, which through late April 1962 killed some 1,660 people and injured an estimated 5,148, the vast majority "Muslims." Yet this time was different: "Delphine Renard," as the historian Rémi Kauffer remarks, "immediately became the symbol of the almost universal rejection of the OAS." During the winter of 1961–62, popular revulsion at these lost lives and the shattered bodies—Delphine's in particular—seemed to offer proof that the newly pressing French desire to leave Algeria revealed something more than ennui. OAS violence, in this interpretation, had done what nationalists and their metropolitan supporters had been unable to do, catalyzing a political reaction among French people against racism and colonial oppression and for the right of the Algerian people to self-determination. Before December 1961, of course, such a public reaction to events in Algeria had not been evident.[1]

---

[1] See Rémi Kauffer, "OAS: La guerre franco-française d'Algérie," in *La guerre d'Algérie, 1954–2004: La fin de l'amnésie,* ed. Mohammed Harbi and Benjamin Stora (Paris, 2004), 451–76, 51. For the casualty figures until 20 April 1962, see Guy Pervillé, *Pour une histoire de la guerre d'Algérie* (Paris, 2002), 242–43. Between 19 March and 19 May, the OAS killed 1,658 and injured 2,450. Besides the chronological overlap between these two sets of statistics, reliable numbers for the last weeks of French Algeria are unavailable, so that an overall number is not available.

A collage of titles from the international press about the OAS threat against Brigitte Bardot, published by *L'Express* in December 1961. Reprinted by permission of *L'Express*.

To understand what was going on among metropolitans in this period, it helps to focus on the public uproar over another victim of OAS criminality, Brigitte Bardot. The victim was not an otherwise anonymous young French child, but a young French woman, surely the most famous young French woman of her generation. In a letter to the weekly magazine *L'Express* in early December 1961, the French starlet announced that "I do not want to live in a Nazi state" and made known her rejection of an OAS demand that she give them 50,000 NF (new francs). The OAS, which in Algeria relied on bank robberies as well as a form of "revolutionary taxation" to obtain cash, was now extending its fund-raising efforts to the metropole. OAS operatives targeted prominent, rich individuals for "contributions" and threatened violence if they refused. If everyone from whom they sought to extort cash would "resist and go public" with their response, Bardot declared, the OAS "threat quickly will be disabled." A *France-Soir* headline announced "Brigitte Is Going to War against the OAS."[2] The press jumped at the chance to do battle alongside the actress against the nefarious OAS. The "new left" press, *L'Express* and *France-Observateur,* and even the Communist daily, *L'Humanité,* joined the media pack along with pro-Gaullist journals like *Paris-Match* and *France-Soir* in defense of the woman "God created" and of the France that B. B. so flamboyantly represented. Of course, neither the ink spilled on the OAS attempt to blackmail Bardot nor the more horrific images of the maiming of Delphine surprised readers of *Paris-Match* or *France-Soir.*

The ways that the metropolitan media reacted to these attacks, actual or threatened, helped redefine what was at stake in the crisis in Algeria, cathecting the shift from a fight against Algerian nationalists to one between people claiming to be French. A pro-OAS comic book, published and immediately banned one year after the event, exaggerated (perhaps) the role Bardot's defiance played in mobilizing metropolitan rejection of those who still supported French Algeria. The comic book, "The Journal of a Prisoner of the Bastille under the Fifth Republic," made no mention of Delphine Renard's suffering. Trading in the same macho jocularity that dripped from most Bardot coverage, the cartoonist spiced up his own faux–fairy tale narrative to recount how "the most beautiful derrière in the kingdom decided to join forces with the king against us. This was what shifted the balance to the 'other cheek.'"[3] The caption's sexist bitterness points to something that the heroic Joans of Arc and Mariannes who fill the comic book's pages only magnify—and that the author seems to have realized only after the fact: the battle that defenders of French Algeria lost was gendered.

"French Algerians" became identified as violent males who attacked help-

---

[2] "Brigitte Bardot: Je ne veux pas vivre dans un pays nazi," *L'Humanité* (1 December 1961), 4; *France-Soir* (1 December 1961), 7E.

[3] Coral, *Journal d'un embastillé sous la Vème République* (1962 [censored 20 December 1962]), preface and 65.

less women and children, and this made their claims to (and on) French identity almost untenable. Rather than a defense of stirring ideals—or oppressed
Algerians—what instead mobilized so many French people was their rejection of a group of people who, although they kept insisting on their Frenchness, now appeared to be clearly different from the French and, because of
that difference, committed to violating human rights and republican values.
Affirmations about normal and abnormal relationships between men and
women, men and men, and men and children anchored press representations
of French ("European") Algerians as different from the French, and as dangerous to both France and Algeria. More specifically, pieds noirs stood accused of embodying abnormal masculinity in ways that recalled charges that
orientalist writers and apologists of colonialism in North Africa long had
leveled at "Arabs" and "Muslims." Such accusations also worked to buttress the normalcy of relations between French men and women, which "the
family" embodied. In this way, too, decolonization redeployed tactics that
had often legitimated the pursuit of colonialism.[4]

During the Algerian War, the implicit reliance on the sexualized and gendered understandings that had so underwritten colonialism's role in building modernity became manifest. Wars and crises, as numerous historians of
gender and sexuality have shown, often force such revelations. What is noteworthy in this instance was how a new context, the invention of decolonization, allowed Algerian anticolonialists to draw much attention to the
French use of such tactics and to offer convincing rebuttals.[5] Indeed, nationalists' successful challenges on the international stage to French re-
hearsals of long-potent sexualized stereotypes about colonized men and
women helped force independence. Yet, as war's end discussions of the pieds
noirs emphasized, this failure in no way exhausted the potency of intersect-
ing ideologies of sexuality, gender, race, and imperialism.

The Battle of the Veil: Liberating "Muslim" Women from "Muslim" Men

In July 1958, a *New York Times Magazine* article identified a new front in
the French government's struggle with the FLN, one that the events of May
1958 had forced into view: "The Battle of the Veil."[6] This battle and the ter-
rain on which it was fought, the minds and bodies of Algeria's "Muslim"

---

[4] See Antoinette Burton, "Introduction: The Unfinished Business of Colonial Modernities,"
in *Gender, Sexuality, and Colonial Modernities,* ed. Antoinette Burton (New York, 1999), Edward Said, *Orientalism* (New York, 1977), and Ann Laura Stoler, *Race and the Education of
Desire: Foucault's History of Sexuality and the Colonial Order of Things* (Durham, N.C.,
1995).
[5] See the essays in *Behind the Lines: Gender and the Two World Wars,* ed. Margaret R.
Higonnet et al. (New Haven, 1987).
[6] Hal Lehrman, "Battle of the Veil," *New York Times Magazine,* 13 July 1958, 14–18.

women, quickly became central to French efforts to win the larger war of international opinion. As proof of the generous aims they were pursuing in Algeria, the French government even produced an English-language documentary for American audiences entitled *The Falling Veil.*[7]

By showing that women and their liberation were the targets of French efforts in Algeria, the government could avoid responding to the FLN or engaging a debate on the question of colonialism. Their real enemy was those who rejected the modernization that France and the West promised, or, as *The Falling Veil*'s narrator stated, the "many Muslims . . . who insist on total control and total obedience, whose wives are treated little better than chattel." The film joins these words with images of "European" women who show their "Muslim" counterparts shops, the post office, what the historian Matthew Connelly describes as various "practices of modernity for their protégés to mimic." This "battle" relied above all on propaganda aimed at an international audience, but it did include on-the-ground efforts. *The Falling Veil* informed audiences that General de Gaulle had appealed directly to "Muslim women" during his famous tour of Algeria in June 1958. Perhaps seeking to replace images of the increasingly well-known French Army practice of using portable generators to torture "Muslim" suspects (*la gégène*), the film assured Americans that de Gaulle's "confidence in the women acted almost as an electrical current to many of them, a kind of psychological shock which jolted them out of their old attitude of apathy into a new awareness of themselves."[8]

The key event that brought the battle of the veil before international audiences was the oft-cited "unveiling" of Muslim women on 16 May 1958. In the midst of the uprising that threatened to overthrow France's government, and that quickly led to the return to power of General Charles de Gaulle, thousands of "Muslim" Algerians were brought in from villages around Algiers to show their support for French "fraternity" and for "Algérie française." Among them, a small number of women became the center of media attention as, with the help of well-dressed "European" women in a highly choreographed ceremony, they took off their veils to reveal smiling faces. Their chant made clear that they looked to French women to lead them from backward-thinking patriarchy to modernity: "*Kif kif les françaises*" ("Let's be like French women").[9]

Algerian nationalists also engaged the battle of the veil. The FLN leadership denounced the "Muslim" women who had participated as "all-around maids of the General Government as well as boarders of whorehouses." Revolutionary thinker and FLN cadre Frantz Fanon, in his article "Algeria Un-

[7] Robert W. Schofield, director, *The Falling Veil*, Tangent Films, circa 1960, discussed in Matthew Connelly, *A Diplomatic Revolution: Algeria's Fight for Independence and the Origins of the Post–Cold War Era* (New York, 2002), 216.

[8] All quotes cited in Connelly, *A Diplomatic Revolution*, 216.

[9] David C. Gordon, *Women of Algeria: An Essay on Change* (Cambridge, Mass., 1968), 56.

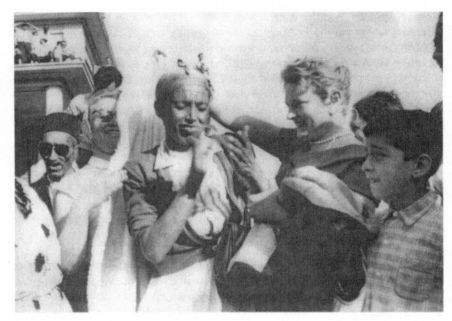

"European" women unveiling a "Muslim" woman in the Forum of Algiers on May 16, 1958.
Reprinted by permission of AFP/Getty Images.

veiled," referred to the women of 16 May 1958 as "servants under the threat
of being fired, poor women dragged from their homes, prostitutes."[10] The
women who participated in the choreographed "unveiling" were, in fact,
members of the Women's Solidarity Movement, a charity group whose proclaimed goal was bettering the lives of Muslim Algerian women. Mme.
Raoul Salan had launched the group; she was the wife of the man who com-
manded French armed forces in Algeria in 1958 and who later became the
leader of the terrorist OAS. Mme. Salan, along with the wives of some of the
other generals and top officers, personally helped her Muslim protégés take
off their veils in the Algiers Forum.[11]

As Fanon's article pointed out, the *haïk,* or "Islamic veil," had long been
an obsession of French observers of Algeria. In the 1860s one of the most
prolific early students of "native society" in Algeria, Gen. Eugène Daumas,
a key figure in organizing the Second Empire's Bureaux arabes, or Arab Offices—which collected information on the indigenous people and carried out
administrative functions—put together and commented on a large number

---

[10] FLN quote in Marnia Lazreg, *The Eloquence of Silence: Algerian Women in Question*
(New York, 1994), 135; Frantz Fanon, "L'Algérie se dévoile," in *L'an V de la révolution algérienne* (Paris, 2001), 46.
[11] Gordon, *Women of Algeria,* 56.

of primary documents. Not published until 1912, the aim of his "The Arab Woman," he announced, was "to tear off the veil that still covers the morals, customs, and beliefs" of Algeria's Arabs. In 1912, when the *Revue africaine* unearthed and published this work, the editors, too, regretted that the "indigenous family is still for us a closed sanctuary," a complaint that characterized both academic and official unhappiness with this situation.[12] Their frustration resonated with the orientalist fantasies that Algeria inspired in France. During the late nineteenth and early twentieth centuries, to give one mass-culture example, erotic postcards that evoked at once the heavily fetishized veil and the voluptuous and voracious nature of Muslim women that the veil and the harem supposedly locked up were wildly popular in France.[13]

A number of French feminists also discussed the veil. All of them criticized wearing it as a form of misogyny and as a means to oppress women. However, some of the most well-known militants also relied on feminist analyses to place their criticisms in the context of colonial domination. Hubertine Auclert, who founded France's first suffragist newspaper, *La citoyenne*, in the 1870s, later spent four years living in Algeria. She wrote of her shock at both the suffering of Muslim Algerian women and of the abuses of French rule. While condemning the veil, what she saw as the forced submission of Muslim women, and what she termed "the Arab marriage," she saved her most pointed criticisms for the French administration. She argued that French occupation had made the conditions of Muslim women worse. Auclert accused French officials of colluding with "Muslim notables" to maintain Algeria's women as "defenseless victims of Muslim hedonism" in order to guarantee the support of these elite men. She pointed to colonial officials' public arguments against establishing schools for Muslim girls: officials argued that cost was not the primary issue; rather, they wanted to avoid creating a group of educated Muslim women whom neither "European" nor "Muslim" societies would accept.[14]

The Algerian Revolution brought into focus and onto the world stage the long history of French fixation on the veil; once again, the veil worked as a sign both of all that was alien, premodern, and regressive in Muslim and Arab cultures, and of the difficulties the French faced in their efforts to fully conquer, not just the land of Algeria but the hearts and minds of the vast majority of its inhabitants. In the late 1950s, the symbol of the "falling veil" anchored official French efforts to present their fight against the FLN as a crusade for modernity. Fanon responded by celebrating both female FLN

---

[12] See Eugène Daumas, "La femme arabe," in *Revue africaine* 56, no. 284 (1912), discussed in Julia Clancy-Smith, "Islam, Gender, and Identities in the Making of French Algeria, 1830–1962," in *Domesticating the Empire: Race, Gender, and Family Life in French and Dutch Colonialism*, ed. Julia Clancy-Smith and Frances Gouda (Charlottesville, Va., 1998), 163–66.

[13] Malek Alloula, *The Colonial Harem* (Minneapolis, 1986).

[14] Clancy-Smith, "Islam, Gender, and Identities," 167–70.

militants who put on the veil to take part in revolutionary activity and Algerian women whose veils signaled to the French their opposition to colonial rule. He argued that women "who had long since dropped the veil once again donned the *haïk,* thus affirming that it was not true that woman liberated herself at the invitation of France and of General de Gaulle."[15]

The veil was not only the subject of political polemic—the fixation on it had concrete effects. In some instances, Muslim women felt increased pressure to take on the veil to show their rejection of French rule. At the same time, numerous reports detailed how certain French soldiers used forced unveiling as a tool to humiliate women, particularly in the countryside. Soldiers unveiled women as one way to punish those suspected of belonging to the nationalist movement, such as Zahia Arif Hamdad, who reported that, after she was arrested with her husband, a soldier tore off her veil, while another announced that "Enough is enough: the play-acting is over." The soldiers then tortured her with *la gégène* and beatings; during this treatment, she was nude, except for her stockings; her face was wrapped, not in a veil but in a blinding hood. Even the signing of the Evian Accords between FLN and French government representatives did not end the symbolic role of the veil: on 6 May 1962 the OAS abandoned its policy of not directly targeting women by shooting five veiled women on the streets of Algiers. Three died of their wounds.[16]

In the context of the Algerian Revolution, the battle of the veil led to specific positive effects for women, as government action gave force to official invocations of the French liberation of "Muslim" women from a backward culture into modernity. The orientalist discourse of Muslim difference and inferiority that historically had served only to explain and exacerbate French domination now guided reforms. Education of "Muslim" children finally became a priority, and girls benefited from this effort. Although the Ferry Laws (1879–86) had made primary education mandatory for both sexes, most Algerian "Muslims," despite their French nationality, had been denied schooling. By 1898 there were only 1,984 "Muslim" girls in school. By 1954 this number reached 76,610 in primary school (compared to 218,000 "Muslim" boys). In 1958, the number of "Muslim" girls attending primary school almost doubled, to 118,000, and the government announced plans to push toward universal primary education for "Muslim" children.[17] This was joined by other efforts to provide some education to unschooled adolescents, through the Youth Training Service of Algeria, and to adults in the Centres sociaux.[18] These programs presented their efforts as elements of French out-

[15] Fanon, "L'Algérie se dévoile," 46.

[16] Gordon, *Women of Algeria,* 55.

[17] Ibid. 45. On education in French Algeria more generally, see Fanny Colonna, *Instituteurs algériens, 1883–1938* (1975); and Barbara Harshav, trans., "Educating Conformity in French Colonial Algeria," in *Tensions of Empire: Colonial Cultures in a Bourgeois World,* ed. Frederick Cooper and Ann Laura Stoler (Berkeley, 1997), 346–70.

[18] On the Centres sociaux, see James LeSueur, *Uncivil War: Intellectuals and Identity Politics during the Decolonization of Algeria* (Philadelphia, 2001), chap. 3.

reach to "Muslim" women. Yet despite claiming to combat "Muslim" sexism, their own vision of women was far from egalitarian. As one internal brochure for the Youth Training Service of Algeria detailed, "While the evolution of the boy is absolutely necessary, that of the girl is equally necessary; the parallel evolution of both future parents makes domestic harmony possible." Thanks to French education "Muslim" adolescents would benefit from "preparatory professional training (insofar as possible for the boys, while the girls will receive preparatory training to be housewives)." Across the board, the education of girls and women was to focus on the "domestic arts" and hygiene.[19] This attention to "Muslim" Algerian women as the catalyst for transforming "Muslim" families into Frenchmen and women was particularly clear in the metropole. As Amelia Lyons argues in her study of Algerian families and the French welfare state, "Administrators considered influencing Algerian women one of the most effective ways to convert the Algerian family to French ways of life. . . . If women could internalize proper French homemaking skills, they would influence their husbands and the next generation." As Lyons shows, integrationist programs in the metropole privileged women and "family-building" in their unprecedented extension of benefits and protections to Algerian "Muslims."[20]

In terms of formal political rights, "Muslim" women in Algeria finally obtained equality with "Muslim" men, as well as with other French citizens, in 1958. Although in 1944 Charles de Gaulle had announced from Algiers the opening of suffrage to French women, "Muslim" women in Algeria had been excluded from even the restricted suffrage all "Muslim" men obtained in 1947. The 1957 Programmatic Law for Algeria extended suffrage to all adult women in Algeria, a reform guaranteed in the Constitution of 1958. A final element of French reforms explicitly aimed to improve the lives of "Muslim" women: in 1957 French legislators at last sought to reform the Koranic law code, which had been stultified since the conquest, to bring it in line with French family law. The government presented the Law of 11 June 1957, the Ordinance of 4 February 1959, and the Decree of 17 September 1959 as increasing the rights of women seeking a divorce, establishing the right of women to become legal guardians of their children, and protecting young girls by banning the practice of early marriage. As welcome as they were, Marnia Lazreg points out that French failure to extend these reforms to people governed by Mozabite customary law made the political motivation behind them clear: Mozabite notables strongly supported the French authorities.[21]

This same desire to guarantee the support of local notables had made the Debré government reticent to pursue these reforms, as indicated by documents

[19] "Le Service de formation des jeunes en Algerie (brochure)" (n.d.), 3, in CAC/AN 19830229, article 2.
[20] Amelia Lyons, "Algerian Families and the French Welfare State in the Era of Decolonization, 1947–1974," PhD diss., University of California—Irvine (2004), 6.
[21] Lazreg, *Eloquence of Silence*, 90–91.

from the office of Nafissa Sid-Cara, the first "Muslim" Algerian woman to serve in a French government (as secretary of state for social questions in Algeria, under Prime Minister Debré, 8 January 1959–14 April 1962). Sid-Cara twice had to threaten to resign in order for any reforms of Koranic civil law to be implemented; she finally decided to accept a reform that was much less far-reaching and much less focused on equality for women than the ones she had proposed.[22]

The battle of the veil reinvested preexisting understandings of "Muslim" Algerian misogyny and backwardness, which had long stabilized the moralizing and civilizing premises of French domination. Because of the Algerian Revolution, the veil and the condition of "Muslim women" now became a field of discursive combat: French and FLN spokesmen agreed that women wearing or not wearing the veil proved something about the relationship between France and Algerians. Each side presented their own concerns and the methods they used to advance them as a defense of women against "barbaric Muslim" or "colonialist French" men. This discourse provided the grounds both for the FLN's celebration of the role women played in the revolution, and French efforts to open up new possibilities in education, political participation, and civil rights for "Muslim" women and girls. Much has been written about how another gendered vision, one based on the masculine nation, shaped Algeria's revolution and FLN behavior once it took power. The veiled woman, it is now clear, was a symbolic site on which the FLN interwove its announced ideological project—modernizing, pan-Arabist, and socialist—with invocations of the Islamic past, references dear to the heart of the most conservative elements of Algerian society. Scholars have paid less attention to how French leaders, as well, relied on understandings of masculinity to help them claim victory, and (as the three chapters of the next section explore) reinscribed understandings of gender to help redefine the post-Algerian French nation.[23]

Pieds Noirs, Bêtes Noires

At the war's end, the question of gendered relationships once again re-emerged in French discussions of Algeria. It was in defense of women, children, and normal (nuclear and heterosexual) families that metropolitans mobilized to resist, and reject, those who defended French Algeria. They mo-

---

[22] See CAC 19770007/210, 211, 212.

[23] For a summary of such critiques, see Madhu Dubey, "The 'True Lie' of the Nation: Fanon and Feminism," *Differences: A Journal of Feminist Cultural Studies* 10 (June 1998); see also C. Kaplan, N. Alarcon, and M. Moallem, eds., *Between Woman and Nation: Nationalisms, Transnational Feminisms, and the State* (Durham, N.C., 1999); A. Parker, M. Russo, D. Sommer, and P. Yaeger, eds., *Nationalisms and Sexualities* (New York, 1992); Anne McClintock, *Imperial Leather: Race, Gender, and Sexuality in the Colonial Contest* (New York, 1995).

bilized, more particularly, to reject the pieds noirs as perverted men, men without women, who because of their perversions were not wholly French. For metropolitans at the end of the Algerian War, the OAS "lost soldiers" of 1961 came into focus as violent pieds noirs. Metropolitan media and politicians presented the activists as the emanation of a subtropical subculture that racist and colonial structures of domination had perverted. This new understanding recast previous images of French combatants who, disillusioned and dehumanized by their futile and misguided fight to defend the empire, had joined the OAS.[24] The decadence of the pieds noirs revealed itself through their abnormal masculinity, and the metropole—that is, France— had to protect itself (read: herself) as well as Algerian "Muslims" from the violent death throes of the pied noir old regime.

It was the so-called new left (see chapter 2) that was most aggressive in the gendering of the Algerian conflict in the months before the Evian Accords. This presentation was key to the new left's emphatic recasting of the conflict as a Franco-French civil war. In late 1961 and early 1962, they saw growing popular mobilization against defenders of French Algeria as revealing a nascent revolutionary solidarity catalyzed by the Algerian struggle. The February 1962 Charonne métro station demonstration and the subsequent mass protest inspired by the death of eight PCF militants convinced the new left that history was on the move. In acts and writings, militants and, in particular, new left journalists thus chose to privilege attacks on the OAS and "European" Algerians over their critique of the French state and society. It was the deviant characteristics of the pieds noirs that had nourished a new fascism during the Algerian War—the shocking violence, racism, the rejection of rationality—not anything French.[25] Writers of the new left recentered their antifascism—which previously had focused on de Gaulle, French society itself, or Western imperialism—on the OAS and, in an easy elision, on the "Europeans of Algeria." This buttressed a growing assumption that pieds noirs—like all people from Algeria—were not French and that it was their irrationality and violence that had produced "French" wartime abuses such as torture. France needed to stop the pieds noirs by getting out of Algeria, for neither the people nor the land was French. The editorial of one far-left monthly described the enemy as "Salan and the other fascist officers, the fanatics of Bab-el Oued, the legionnaire assassins, the [forcènes] paratroopers, the Nazis of Jeune Nation and other Poujadists." The editorial's title, "Yes to Algerian Independence, No to the Gaullist Re-

---

[24] See Claude d'Absac-Epezy, "La société militaire, de l'ingérence à l'ignorance," in *La guerre d'Algérie et les Français*, ed. Jean-Pierre Rioux (Paris, 1990), 245–56; Jennifer Yee, "Malaria and the Femme Fatale: Sex and Death in French Colonial Africa," *Literature and Medicine* 21, no. 2 (2002): 201–15.

[25] On this shift, see Direction générale de la Sûreté nationale, "Bibliographie de la guerre d'Algérie," in *Bulletin de documentation de la direction des Renseignements Généraux* 84 (Paris, March 1963), 2, in AN F/7/15581.

gime," put forward the need to fight on two fronts. The new left Unified Socialist Party also called for voters to say, "Yes to Peace, No to the Regime." Still, the article's focus on the Far Right's ravages in Algeria denoted how the movement increasingly downplayed the critique of France that previously had been primary. Most far-left propaganda and analysis gave even more attention to what Jean-Paul Sartre identified in early 1962 as "the relationship that unites [elements of the armed force] with fascism, with the pieds noirs." While Sartre insisted that this fight was primarily taking place in Algeria, most in the French Far Left, like the editors of *La Voie Communiste,* concentrated on what they could do to combat the menace in the metropole, an attitude the philosopher qualified as "absurd."[26]

Only Sartre seems immediately to have grasped that the new and radical left were failing to describe what was happening, or to analyze what was at stake. He complained, in an editorial entitled "The Sleepwalkers," that after the announcement of Evian, "All anyone wanted to hold on to was this: It's over, with Algeria, it's over. In corner restaurants, the nightly ritual altered little: people arrived, apologized for their tardiness, shook hands; they were informed, 'There's a cease-fire.' They sat down saying, 'Yes, yes, I know.' Then they spoke of other things." Sartre's simple, powerful, and ultimately unheeded demand was that the French recognize that they had lost. He asserted, "This cease-fire that everyone proclaims 'without winners or losers,' in reality, the Algerian people have imposed. Alone." Far from sharing this victory, the French had responded to the struggle as "witnesses, then as uncertain, then abandoning responsibility." If for Sartre the Algerian Revolution represented the exemplary challenge of the colonized to the oppressor, French acceptance of the Fifth Republic demonstrated their unwillingness to grapple with the new situation. Faced with the FLN's forcing of History, he remarked, "We gave all power to a dictator so that he could decide, without asking us, the best means to end the affair: genocide, resettlement and territorial partition, integration, independence, we have washed our hands, it is his deal."[27] Choosing to focus on an anti-OAS and anti–pied noir agenda offered the new left a valuable possibility to resituate the fight against the Reaction, the ongoing battle between defenders of the French Revolution and those who rejected it. Valuable because de Gaulle's reversal on the question of Algerian independence had so unsettled their initial redefinition. If opposition to French conduct in the Algerian War was central to the gestation of the new left, resistance to what many saw as the antirepublican developments of 1958 had given its nebulous forces institutionalized forms. As the historian of French republicanism Maurice Agulhon reminds

---

[26] Gérard Spitzer, *La Voie Communiste* n.s., 27 (March–April 1962): 1; Ministre de l'Intérieur, "Note à l'attention de M. Bonis-Charancle" (2 May 1962), 3–5, in AN F/1cII/634:II; "Les somnambules," *Les Temps Modernes* 191 (April 1962): 1397–1401, 1397, 1399, 1400–1401.

[27] "Les somnambules," 1397, 1399, 1400.

us, 1958 saw an attempt to raise a republican defense against the newest manifestation of Caesarist authoritarianism: Charles de Gaulle and Gaullism. In 1962, resistance to the OAS displaced this anti-Caesarism to focus on OAS leader Raoul Salan. To save the republic from another Napoleon, Patrice MacMahon, Georges Boulanger, or Pétain it was more important to prevent the man nicknamed "the Mandarin" from leading his storm troopers to power in Algeria or France than to struggle against the actual president of the Republic, the nation's "leader and guide." What authorized this temporary shift was an insistence that the "French of Algeria" embodied the reaction.[28]

In a deforming but reassuring recasting of Frantz Fanon's identification of the colonized as the equivalent of the proletariat and the colonizers as the bourgeoisie, new left writers in these months decided that only the colonists, the pieds noirs, dominated and exploited. While often invoking Fanon's wording, the new left's formulations broke with the revolutionary's careful knitting together of colonist and colonial excess with the metropole and, indeed, Western culture. Sartre, in his preface to *The Wretched of the Earth*, had warned against exactly such a misreading of Fanon. In *France-Observateur,* and in other new left journals (*L'Esprit, Témoignage Chrétien*), writers—both journalists and, in *France-Observateur,* readers—enthusiastically joined in fighting the enemy of the people. As Agulhon remarks, if in this moment political sentiment was understood as "no longer premised in class," it still "could be discerned by belonging to a group of people: colonists." This group was not defined purely by a position in the relationship of production, but geographically—they were from Algeria—and "ethnically": the pieds noirs. Formerly, Agulhon continues, enemies of the republic could be identified "by the *particule* [the aristocratic *de*], now names with other consonances, not French, would suffice."[29]

The template for new left representations of the pieds noirs at the war's end was the 1961 book *The French of Algeria* by the historian Pierre Nora. Usually cited as a scholarly study, prefaced by the prominent historian of Algeria Charles-André Julien (one of the first in France to break with the "colonialist school" of imperial history), the book synthesized a self-righteous anti–pied noir discourse that many French intellectuals shared. Nora foregrounded a defense of the rights of colonized "Arabs." Yet, like those who would take up his anti–"French of Algeria" jeremiads, the radical possibilities of such a project in fact served to put forward a definition of France

---

[28] On the "republican defense" against what she terms OAS "liberticide," see Sylvie Thénault, *Histoire de la guerre d'indépendance algérienne* (Paris, 2005), 233, 239. On how this shaped new left responses to the referendum campaign, see Jean Charlot, "La campagne des formations politiques," in *Le référendum du 8 avril 1962,* ed. François Goguel (Paris, 1963), 35.

[29] Maurice Agulhon in *De Gaulle et son siècle,* vol. 1, *Dans la mémoire des hommes et des peuples* (Paris, 1991), 190, 177; cf. Marc Heurgon, *Histoire du PSU,* vol. 1, *La fondation et la guerre d'Algérie, 1958–62* (Paris, 1994).

from which two groups of "Algerians" should be excluded: "Arabs," as different from the French and equally deserving of a state, and the "French of Algeria" as, despite their name, different from the French and dangerous to the Republic.

Nora had come to public attention as a journalist for *France-Observateur*, but he presented *The French of Algeria* as the work of a university-trained historian. The book, however, as American historian of French Algeria David Prochaska notes, "is not so much a work of history (it is not based on original research and is devoid of the usual scholarly apparatus) as a personal account written in a passionate, powerful style." Absent research, the book is grounded in the "tide of History" presumption so prevalent among those who, after 1959, merely accepted Algerian independence.[30] This consensus had accepted with muted resignation the necessity of "decolonization" that resulted from the "tide of History," while failing to discuss the question of Algerian difference that anchored articulations of this concept in the 1950s.

Nora embraced the cause of Algerian independence while positing the "French of Algeria" as wholly different from the French. That is, rather than the 1950s pro-independence dialectics of French colonizer/Algerian colonized à la Fanon and Sartre, or an Aronian affirmation of obvious noncongruence between French people and "Muslims," the categorical difference he sought to explain was between the French of the metropole and the so-called French of Algeria. He presented this difference in starkly hierarchical terms. Informed by his two years as a high school teacher in Algiers, Nora was able to explain that the "French of Algeria" were not individuals, nor were they composed of sociologically diverse groupings: all of them formed a group, and a group characterized by dangerous irrationality. He suggested that "from the capitalist 'big colonist' to the little Jewish tailor, from the descendants of old French families to the Maltese worker, from the big merchant to the small-time colonist of the interior, the nationalist fever is the same." But this was not, he cautioned, a temporary condition of cross-class solidarity: "That which psychologically unites all these categories is greater than that which sociologically divides them." Nora, in this passage and in his book, denied that a class analysis applied to these people, and he rejected claims that certain groupings of "non-Muslims"—most pointedly, Jews—were more "rational" or "liberal" than others.[31]

In Nora's diagnosis, it was irrationality that psychologically united them.

---

[30] David Prochaska, *Making Algeria French: Colonialism in Bône, 1870–1920* (Cambridge, 1990), 6, quotes from Pierre Nora, *Les Français d'Algérie*, preface by Charles-Andre Julien (Paris, 1961), 87, 98.

[31] Nora, *Les Français d'Algérie*, 252, 47. A number of prominent Jewish Algerian leaders and journalists repeatedly had affirmed that their "community" was more liberal than other non-Muslims in Algeria. See Sarah Sussman, "Changing Lands, Changing Identities: The Migration of Algerian Jewry to France, 1954–1967" (PhD diss., Stanford University, 2002), 136.

He had "never heard one of them respond with an argument." "If you have doubts about the marvelous climate, they act as if you've said that their mistress was cross-eyed; if you question their tendency to run down pedestrians as they try to zip past other automobiles, it's as if you've questioned their virility." Fixing on a Jungian-style archetype, he explained that "all the French of Algeria are like Cagayous," referring to a popular local fictional character, "humiliated and distrustful." Their "collective and constant temper tantrum, screams, tears, the bluff and the sudden collapse, the extreme sensibility, all this psychological distress" led Nora to begin his fourth chapter with a quote from Freud's "New Reflections on War and Death," which evoked "their lack of intelligence, their refusal of the most convincing arguments, the infantile credulity with which they greet the most debatable affirmations."[32] All the same, the "French of Algeria" were the antithesis of the French, despite their constant moanings to the contrary. "In the street, at the first incident, the argument appears: 'I am French' pronounced," Nora specified, "with an accent: 'I am Franch.' 'I am Franch, sir, I am just as Franch as you.'" Further, having asked a number of newspaper vendors what they read, he could report that none read *Le Monde* or any "national" newspaper: "Not even the elites, unlike any normal provincial town." The French of Algeria, Nora posited, should be considered as a powerful elite, but an elite that should be disdained not simply, or even primarily, because they exploited, but because they were without culture or education.[33]

Moving from these telling signs, Nora attacked the terms used to characterize Algeria's inhabitants as abusively inappropriate. He condemned the usual distinction between "European" and "Muslim" Algerians for "it gives too much credit to the minority while, under the guise of a pejorative designation, it limits the possibilities of the majority." Supposedly geographical, "European," he argued, should connote a "technological civilization, energetic and Nordic"; the reality of what the term referred to in Algeria was "some Andalusian or Calebresian worker closer to an Egyptian *fellah* [peasant] than the worker of [18]48 [exiled from the metropole by Napoleon III] or the Alsatian [fleeing German control in 1871]." The term "European," he lamented, "groups together in a community and ennobles" this mishmash of degraded humanity. He rejected its use. Nora was equally opposed to the idea that "all the non-Jewish natives would be classed as Muslims." The term, he explained, was a "religious criteria that evokes, as well, a theocratic religion emblematic of a sclerotic civilization [i.e., Islam] that has not advanced since the end of the Middle Ages." After an effort to delegitimize the term "French" to define people in Algeria, Nora resigned himself to its use.[34]

The folly of integrationist policies aimed at "Muslims," in Nora's critique,

[32] Ibid., 46, 50. On Cagayous, see David Prochaska, "History as Literature, Literature as History: Cagayous of Algiers," *American Historical Review* 101 (June 1996): 671–711.
[33] Nora, *Les Français d'Algérie,* 52.
[34] Ibid., 252, 161.

was the fallacious pretense that the "French of Algeria" were truly, or could be made, French.[35] The French Republic's great mistake, he explained, was the Law of 1889, which "automatically naturalized children born in Algeria of foreigners." It was this law that "created what we call the French of Algeria, who had lost their European anchorage, yet knew nothing about France."[36] Insisting on how un-French they were, Nora pointed out (incorrectly) that currently the most fervent partisans of French Algeria inhabited *le bled,* the Algerian countryside, where "they have suffered the influence of their Arab milieu." Sharing the "same climate and the same lives, they have finished by adopting the same habits." This explained their embrace of "integration" that "permits them to imagine that they will resuscitate their link with Europe and to recover that precious Western essence that they largely have lost."[37]

Nora conjoined disdain for the immigrant with his embrace of orientalist stereotypes to explain why the French of Algeria were worse than the indigenous people. In French Algeria, "the only common link between all the immigrants from France and from Europe," he argued, was "a psychology of backwardness vis-à-vis their own nations." This he deduced had come about because "for one reason or another," obviously, "all those who came to settle in Algeria had already failed at making a life for themselves." Rootless *apatrides,* what defined the "French of Algeria," and what produced their sickness, was their relationship with Algeria, a relationship based on the exploitation of the land and of its people. For the historian, this second connection also condemned the French of Algeria to a nonindustrial future: like Marx's peasants, their rejection of industry was first and foremost a reticence to engage in human relations, to the gathering together of workers: "men scare them." Their double exploitation of Algerians and Algeria paradoxically produced a sick society and allowed it to soldier on: it was only their certainty that they "all were better than the Arabs that allows them to survive," for all "would be little or nothing in the metropole."[38]

Nora's analysis of the pieds noirs resonated with and informed a widespread rejection of this group among the influential, if small in number, new left milieu. It offered a foundation for the new left's shift in focus away from French conduct in Algeria, such as torture, to support for independence. Nora recast the "tide of History," a philosophical framing concept that had become an ambient explanatory trope, filling in the absent term—Algerian difference—with a xenophobia directed at the "French of Algeria." This development also allowed metropolitans to think of themselves ("the French") as a society distinct from the pieds noirs (the so-called French of Algeria). In so doing, they could affirm what made people from Algeria different from

[35] Ibid., 51.
[36] Ibid., 81, 83. (On the Law of 1889, see chapter 1.)
[37] Ibid., 51.
[38] Cf. *The 18th Brumaire of Louis Napoleon;* Nora, *Les Français d'Algérie,* 252, 175.

other people with French citizenship—without taking nationalist claims into account, or offering their own definition of what made the majority of Algerians (the "Muslims") different from other French nationals.

Crucial to this move, his text also articulated an ongoing post-Vichy French political obsession with male same-sex sexual "perversion." Throughout the Algerian Revolution, French intellectuals and politicians had grappled with the challenge Algerian nationalism posed to French understandings of their identity by resorting to an idiom of male sexual perversity to address and assess who was truly French. During key public debates, all sides sought to tar those they criticized with the names and the signs of male same-sex perversion.[39] They did so to identify their opponents as abnormally French. If one could show that homosexual lusts motivated political adversaries, they would be understood as unworthy to speak as rational subjects, as citizens. As one early-1950s French critic explained, perverts are "high strung, their actions and reactions guided only by their attractions, in a word, eminently 'subjective.'"[40] At the war's close, as in earlier debates, for example, over the French Army's widespread use of torture against accused Algerian nationalists, left-wing writers identified their opponents as perverted males. However, while earlier criticism, such as in the banned exposé *The Gangrene* (1959), had highlighted how colonial domination of Algeria transformed French officials and soldiers into homosexual sadists, excited by the suffering they inflicted on "Muslim Algerian men," now the accusations exclusively targeted pieds noirs. They presented pieds noirs men as Janus-headed, divided between those obsessed with proving their masculinity and *tapettes*, faggots.[41]

In 1961, Nora proposed that those among the French of Algeria who supported OAS terrorism recognized a single value: "one's self-presentation as supervirile." In his argument, those few pieds noirs men (he "had been introduced to two") who as self-proclaimed "liberals" refused the OAS were not different in kind: rather their obsession with masculinity was explicitly focused on other men.

One quickly understands that they are famous for their folly. "Sows" [*femelles*], people say. Of the two to whom I was introduced, one wrote bucolic poems and found himself thanks to Roger Vaillant. "I, my dear," he repeated in a café, while turning around in his seat, "I am like Don César: *Je me désinteresse.*" The other loitered on the boulevard with several fellow bachelors and,

---

[39] The historian Florence Tamagne argues that in Third Republic France, unlike Weimar Germany or Great Britain during the same period, public fixation on same-sex sexuality remained out of domestic political debates, manifesting itself in medical, literary, and artistic discussions, instead, and included women as equally "perverted" as men. See Florence Tamagne, *History of Homosexuality in Europe: Berlin, London, Paris, 1919–1939* (New York, 2003), 47.

[40] Frédéric Hoffet, *Psychanalyse de Paris* (Paris, 1953), 104–5.

[41] *La gangrène* (Paris, 1959).

with all the graciousness in the world, distributed his favors to his friends, as well as spending his fortune on them.[42]

A new-left journalist, Philippe Hernandez, in a series of articles, further elucidated the idea that hypervirility and effeminacy were twinned sides of the pieds noirs' subtropical and homosocial subculture. For the "Europeans" the OAS plays "the role that Nazism played for the Germans: it is the proof of their virility." In pied noir society, "the essential thing is not to be a 'faggot.'" Hernandez explained that "the faggot is the one who, in the coming together of a couple, plays the role of the woman, even though he was destined by nature to play that of the man." To explain how this pseudo-ethnology joined with anti-imperialist and antiracist politics, he continued: "The pied noir is convinced that he is, by nature, the Arab's male." The pro–French Algeria struggle, therefore, should be understood as an attempt to maintain dominance in this homosexual economy. The article quotes a police officer who insisted that "when the OAS first seized control, Arabs would run to us to inform on the FLN." With talk of Algerian independence, "that is finished. We have our legs spread like faggots. We are dropping our pants, spreading our legs."[43] The report offered no engagement with what the OAS or their supporters argued, merely assertions of deviant masculinity. In the subsequent "Letter from One Pied Noir to Another Pied Noir" Hernandez concluded that it was time for pieds noirs to prove their manhood: "'We're no faggots,' you tell me? OK, comrades, this is the moment to prove it. The faggot is someone to whom things happen and things right now are happening to you." They needed to embrace independence. If they would not come to their senses, become true men, the French people must mobilize.[44]

New left writers, of course, did not invent this idiom; they were participating in a struggle to place opponents outside the ring of heterosexual—French—masculinity. (French historians of the period, including Jean-Pierre Rioux and Jean-François Sirinelli, note how widespread homophobic comments were in political debate in the 1950s and early 1960s, in order to insist that this was unremarkable.[45]) In another article of January 1962, Hernandez explained that the reason most pieds noirs hated de Gaulle was that he had transformed them "into his faggot." Weeks before, and in the same way, the most important publication of the OAS insisted that de Gaulle had "given up Algeria" to the FLN "in obedience to his inversion neuroses, which obliges him to give himself to the male." The editorial made sure to

[42] Nora, Les Français d'Algérie, 60.

[43] Philippe Hernandez, "En Algérie, j'ai vu la France assiégée par l'OAS," France-Observateur 610 (11 January 1962), 8–10.

[44] Philippe Hernandez, "Lettre d'un Pied-Noir à un Pied-Noir," France-Observateur 619 (15 March 1962), 10.

[45] Jean-François Sirinelli refers to such attacks as "banal" in Deux intellectuals dans le siècle: Sartre et Aron (Paris, 1995), 328; see also Jean-Pierre Rioux, The Fourth Republic, 1944–1958 (Cambridge, 1989), 349.

specify that Algerian nationalists "have only the sexual attributes, but lack the psychology [of] the male."[46]

Still, in early 1962, at the very moment when attacks on defenders of French Algeria were most widely echoed in the mainstream media, new left warnings about the pied noir menace depended on accusations of male deviancy. Indeed, male perversion rather than far-right political attachment often was identified as the primary signifier of what needed to be fought. A January editorial in *France-Observateur* that sought to rally the Left against the OAS evoked "a minority of dedicated men, fanatics . . . totally cut off from the masses." Claude Bourdet warned his readers that "they are counting on the nonintervention of the people and," more menacingly, "on the numerous contacts they have among the perverts" in the metropole. Reaffirming their concerns about male deviance among the pieds noirs, new left journalists presented an Algeria where women were never seen, heard, or even interviewed. (It is worth noting that it was harsh criticisms from the left in response to his 1957 affirmation that he "would place my mother ahead of Justice" that led the pied noir author Albert Camus to renounce speaking about violence in Algeria.) Nora's "historical" description of the "French of Algeria" grounds this absence in the early years of settlement when all the colonists, he claims incorrectly, were male. Nora fantasizes that the French(men) of Algeria "with the purest masculine intuition" recognized the competition the Arab posed was as "a man more than as a social or religious being," which drove them to assault Arab women, who used the veil and the harem to protect themselves and their families. The eventual arrival of Frenchwomen in Algeria changed little, for "the French woman, parasite of this colonial relationship to which she contributes nothing even if she works, is generally more racist than the man." She does have some agency, however, "strongly contributing to preventing any contact between the two cultures." Nora here rehearses what scholars describe as the "memsahib myth": the shared certainty among many male imperialists and subsequent historians of imperialism that white women played a uniquely destructive role in colonial practice. (As the historian of British imperialism Karen T. Hansen writes: "A crude version of this argument holds that when white women arrived in larger numbers, race relations deteriorated; white colonial society closed in upon itself, did not pay sufficient attention to indigenous political stirrings, and hid difficulties reckoning with the imminent end of the Empire.") Nora's primary focus, however, was that pied noir society had transformed its women, rather than becoming civilized by them. For Nora, it was not femininity in women that was the problem, but its absence: French Algerians' erasure of what made women different demonstrated how dangerous the

---

[46] Hernandez, "En Algérie, j'ai vu la France assiégée par l'OAS"; Georges Aubert, Editorial: "Le Mâle et l'Effort," *OAS Information* 4 (Bône, 20 December 1961), 1–3, in SHAT 1H/1735/ 1; Claude Bourdet, "Le temps du choix," *France-Observateur* 610 (11 January 1962), 24.

French of Algeria were. In this male society in constant struggle with Arab culture and its natural, healthy rapport between the sexes, the only "feminine" characteristic Nora identifies—besides the effeminate homosexuals—lies in the relationship between the French of Algeria and the metropole. In this rapport, they are like "those ugly women who have been lucky enough to find a man [the metropole] to support them and then resent him for the rest of their lives because, for the love of him, they abandoned a promising career."[47]

In descriptions such as Nora's, deviant masculinity defined pied noir society, a society that alternated between "hypermasculine" aggression and twisted effeminacy. This understanding appeared in representations of OAS-led actions to defend French Algeria, violent and otherwise. Following the heavy attention metropolitan media gave to the OAS attacks on young Delphine and on Brigitte Bardot, women and children continued to be presented as the primary victims of OAS terror, while the OAS seemed more and more the emanation of a pied noir society where both women and normal families were absent. Criticisms of the OAS presented violent Algerian ("European") men killing innocent Algerian ("Muslim") women and children. Socialist Deputy René Schmitt referred to the OAS as "a band of cowards who go after a cleaning woman returning from work, a Muslim child who sells flowers on the sidewalks." Gaullist Deputy Pierre Carous raised and elided the distinction between the OAS and Algérie française deputies, insisting, "It is acceptable to use democratic processes to defend any position, but it is inadmissible to shoot down women in the streets like pheasants." On 19 March, on the metropolitan radio station Europe 1, the "Twelve Noon Europe" announcer detailed the stark difference between the calm that reigned in the "Muslim neighborhoods" the day following the announcement of the Evian Accords versus in "European" Bab el-Oued, "one thousand men, but only men, in the streets, who look at everything, inspect everything," streets littered with "light barricades made of broken bottles and crates."[48] Evoking the departures of some Europeans to the metropole, Minister for Repatriation Robert Boulin spoke of "the atmosphere of insecurity, the attacks, the street fighting, the closing of schools—often by bombing—which brings mothers of families to send their children to the metropole, the economic difficulties, without mentioning the fear many of [these women] experience." The government continued to insist that most

---

[47] Nora, *Les Français d'Algérie*, 174–78, 151; Karen T. Hansen, "Review," *Signs* 14, no. 4 (Summer 1989): 930–34; on the memsahib myth, see also Nupur Chaudhuri and Margaret Strobel, introduction to *Western Women and Imperialism: Complicity and Resistance*, ed. Nupur Chaudhuri and Margaret Strobel (Bloomington, Ind., 1992). On post-1945 French intellectuals' celebration of the key civilizing role played by female difference and heterosexual exchange, see Joan Wallach Scott, "French Universalism in the Nineties," *differences: A Journal of Feminist Cultural Studies* 15, no. 2 (2004): 32–53.

[48] *J.O.* (1962), 1408, 1440, 1403. "Extraits du journal parlé 'Europe Midi' CSFA B2/EXT" (19 March 1962), in SHAT 1H/1784/2.

French citizens of Algeria would choose to stay in the soon-to-be-independent Algeria. Secretary of State Louis Joxe noted that those who were arriving in the metropole were "almost all women and children, coming to France, mostly still for summer vacations."[49]

French horror at the actions of the OAS and of the perverted pied noir society that produced them accompanied a growing sympathy for the Algerian people, the oppressed Arabs and Berbers. It seemed clear that the same pieds noirs who were now killing French young men, soldiers seeking merely to oversee the peace accords, had been responsible for the brutalization of the Algerian people. It was they, not French soldiers or politicians, who were to blame for the ongoing involvement and the activities that had sullied France's reputation. In the face of OAS terror, the French saw an army protecting "women and children" from other violent and questionably French men. The armed forces' new vulnerability tempered the abnormal hypermasculinity with which previous charges of torture had tainted the army. Conscripts, according to *France-Soir,* now chanted "Long Live Brigitte Bardot, the Anti-OAS Queen!"[50] OAS brutalities allowed the French Army to appear as defenders of the weak and of universal (French) values. Depictions of the OAS as made up of unnaturally violent men offered an explanation that could elucidate earlier French use of torture. It was not, as discussions of military torture had suggested, a crisis of French masculinity that provoked abhorrent behavior: it was the colonial society of Algeria.[51]

This was the ultimate certainty conveyed by the outpouring of new left, anti–pied noir sentiment. Again, Nora's book set the tone. The preface by Charles-André Julien presented France's history in Algeria as marked by the metropole making good-hearted efforts to improve and civilize life for all Algerians, a mission the "French of Algeria" had always deformed. (Nora went so far as to claim that torture and "excesses" on the part of French Army soldiers during the early 1830s resulted from "French of Algeria" refusal to condemn such acts. The horrors were real, but no "French" or "European" settlers had yet arrived.) Civil servants in Algeria were portrayed as "traitors" to the metropole. They had been "mostly recruited there or quickly converted by the milieu." What "gave the French of Algeria strength," he explained, was "their refusal of the liberal tendencies of the metropole."[52]

The only way to save France and Algeria was to end their unnatural bond. Reaffirming widely held understandings of gender, French intellectuals articulated a commonsensical definition of how "(European) Algerians" were different from French. It was an explanation that offered the reassuring certainty that what had gone wrong in French-ruled Algeria resulted from an

---

[49] *J.O.* (1962), 1398.

[50] "B. B. Boycotté à Alger," *France-Soir* (3–4 December 1961), 4CA.

[51] On torture in Algeria as a crisis of masculinity, see Kristin Ross, *Fast Cars, Clean Bodies: Decolonization and the Reordering of French Culture* (Cambridge, Mass., 1995).

[52] Charles-André Julien, preface to Nora, *Les Français d'Algérie,* 252, 26, 88.

absence of French civilization, rather than the inherent contradictions of France's civilizing mission. (The conviction that France has a unique history of male-female entente regularly reemerges in French intellectuals' attempts to distinguish and defend "French" ideals against foreign models. Three decades after Nora, the historian Mona Ozouf wrote—in a semischolarly essay attacking American feminists—that in France "the art of women civilizes men."[53]) Although it was new left writers who did the most to advance the presentation of pied noir difference, their efforts buttressed government activity, detailed in previous chapters, that worked to keep the Europeans of Algeria in Algeria and out of France. The exodus confronted both popular representations and government efforts with the insistent demands of hundreds of thousands of people to remain in "France." In the next section I explore the exodus and how the crisis it produced reshaped both French state institutions and understandings of who was French.

[53] Mona Ozouf, *Les mots des femmes: Essai sur la singularité française* (1995), 326. On the mid-1990s vogue among French academics for such arguments, see Eric Fassin, "The Purloined Gender: American Feminism in a French Mirror," *French Historical Studies* 22, no. 1 (Winter 1999): 113–38.

PART III

THE EXODUS AND AFTER

The truth is, there is a wave of panic sweeping over Algeria. . . .
Why deny it? Everyone wants to leave.
SOCIALIST DEPUTY RENÉ SCHMITT, IN THE NATIONAL ASSEMBLY,
30 MAY 1962

Forgetting—I would even go so far as to say historical error—is a
crucial factor in the creation of a nation.
ERNEST RENAN

Chapter 8

Repatriating the Europeans

With everyone certain that Algeria and Algerians were not French, nothing had been done to exclude them from France or from citizenship. People in Algeria would become Algerians; Algerians in France would leave. The exodus confounded these presumptions and wishes. Between mid-April and September 1962, a chaotic rush to escape Algeria—a migration that commentators immediately named the "exodus"—brought close to one million people to the Hexagon. The institutional reshaping of de Gaulle's "post-Algeria" republic would have to wait until fall to be finalized. It was in the unexpected exodus, however, that a post-Algerian definition of French national identity crystallized, as emergency policies, laws, and bureaucratic responses met popular and press understandings.

No one in France predicted the exodus of almost all of the so-called pieds noirs. Many people and organizations forecast what they considered large numbers of departures, yet even the most perceptive assumed that the majority would end up living in Algeria. An article on plans for "Operation Dunkirk" that *France-Observateur* published in summer 1961, for example, spoke of plans for a massive air- and sealift to bring back almost all French Algerians, but made clear that they meant only the minority of "Europeans" who had "French" ancestry, rather than those with Spanish, Jewish, Italian, Maltese, or other ancestors. The subtitle of a magazine article in the summer of 1962, "From Predictions (400,000 Repatriates in Four Years in Ninety Departments) to Reality (400,000 Repatriates in Four Weeks in Four Departments)," gives a sense of the distance between what was planned for and what happened.[1]

---

[1] René Delisle, "L'opération 'Dunkerque' est-elle possible?" *France-Observateur* 585 (20

Evidence was available for a prescient prediction of mass departures. Experts from the Algerian Affairs Ministry claimed that their analyses included a worst-case hypothesis, in which "300,000 families, that is, 1 million people," would return. They offered no suggestions as to how to prepare for this eventuality.[2] In late November 1961, an RG report on the state of Jews in certain cities in Algeria suggested that "we can speak, in effect, of a veritable exodus."[3] Insistently, however, this and similar indications were explained away with retrospectively remarkable ease. The RG report, for instance, laid out a series of reasons why the departures of Jews were slowing.

As with segregation in early 1962, no one wanted Algeria's "Europeans" to leave en masse and definitively, not the OAS, not the French government nor prominent nationalists. To get them to stay in Algeria, the French government had established repatriate status, and sought to negotiate other guarantees with representatives of the GPRA. A journalist reported that at a May meeting between the head of the provisional executive, Abderrahmane Farès, and de Gaulle, "the two men envisioned the future of the European community." Discussing a possible exodus Farès "insisted on the necessity of going all out to keep them" in Algeria. De Gaulle, the journalist wrote, "was in agreement: 'Above all, keep them,' were his exact words."[4] On the ground, the OAS had been instrumental in preventing mass flight in the first months of 1962, a success due in part to their orders forbidding departures and promising retribution to those who disobeyed. The first OAS order appeared in December 1961, when a tract forbade "university students, pupils, high schoolers" from leaving Algerian territory during the holiday season.[5] By late January, an order from ex-General Salan extended the ban on "unjustifiable departures" to all "Europeans," excepting those whom

July 1961), 6; Philippe Hernandez, "Les pieds noirs de Montpellier," France-Observateur 639 (2 August 1962), 9.

[2] G. de Wailly, "Notes sur le rapatriement éventuel des Français—européens et musulmans—d'Algérie" (Paris, 28 March 1961), 1, in MAE 100; see also President M. Chevry, "Transcript réunion du 16 mai 1961," 1, in CAC 80 AJ/254 [930275/94]; see also Commission de la Main-d'Oeuvre—Groupe de travail, Commissariat général du Plan, "Procès-verbal réunion du 16 mai 1961" (16 May 1961), 1, in CAC 80 AJ/236 [930275/76]; "Elements de réponses pour l'Assemblée nationale et Sénat/Lettre rectificatif du IVe plan" (14 February 1962), 1, in CAC 80 AJ/172 [930275/12]; M. Ripert, "Influence de la réduction du service militaire et du retour des Français d'Afrique du Nord sur le marché du travail" (March 1962), 1, in CAC 80 AJ/172 [930275/12]. For a different analysis of predictions of the size of the exodus, see Jacques Frémeux, "Le reflux des Français d'Afrique du Nord," in Marseille et le choc des décolonisations, ed. Jean-Jacques Jordi et Emile Temime (Aix-en-Provence, 1996), 21.

[3] RG d'Alger, Bône, Constantine, Orléansville, "Etat d'esprit de la communauté Israélite" (27 and 30 November 1961), 45, in MAE 121 bis.

[4] Paul Marie de la Gorce, "Alger: L'histoire de la trêve," France-Observateur 631 (7 June 1962), 7. On the FLN and the ALN, see Gilbert Meynier, Histoire intérieure du FLN, 1954–1962 (Paris, 2002).

[5] Lt.-Colonel Barthelemy, "Bulletin hebdomadaire de renseignement psychologique. Semaine 27/12/61–2/1/62" (Algiers, 4 January 1962), 5, in SHAT 1H/2549/2.

the OAS authorized to leave. It was an order that the local population took very seriously.[6] The OAS proclaimed such measures in the name of the "levée en masse" [general mobilization] of all to defend French Algeria; those who disobeyed, instructions from late January on made clear, would be "considered as traitors and dealt with as such."[7]

Many observers interpreted the fact that group departures largely stopped between January and mid-April 1962 as primarily a reflection of widespread belief in the eventual success of the OAS and not simply because of fear of OAS reprisals. Popular support for the OAS as well as fear of punishment also contributed to the notable cooperation that various companies and agencies gave to the activist ban on departures. Following an OAS order, moving companies rejected customers who could not prove they had OAS authorization. When Air France and Air Algérie decided not to sell tickets to "Europeans" who did not have an OAS laissez-passer, French authorities responded swiftly and aggressively to counter the activists' propaganda victory. After army officers sought to force the companies to abandon this policy, the personnel went on strike—whether in support of the OAS or in fear of it is unclear. The air force eventually took over all civilian air transport between 22 March 1962 and mid-June. The success of the OAS's ban on departures seemed to prove that its announced tactics were working: to take control of numerous institutions in the midst of a general mobilization.[8]

Segregation had increased pied noir unity dramatically. In turn, far more than the activists' rare tactical successes, this nurtured "European" confidence that, despite the government's betrayal, French Algeria—via the OAS—would triumph. Large cities offered the greatest support to the OAS, Algiers consistently and Oran—after the local Jewish population threw in their lot in with the activists—with growing fervor. Backing for the OAS was less widespread in other cities, as Bône, Tlemcen, and Mascara offered significant support, and Constantine relatively little. There was spotty and restrained support for the activists in le bled.[9] The growing "exodus intra muros" drained le bled and small towns, however, gathering most FSE into FSE-majority cities, while preventing these people from cohabiting with

[6] Lt.-Colonel Cousin, "Bulletin hebdomadaire de renseignements. Semaine du 24 février au 2 mars 1962" (SP 87.000, 3 March 1962), 24, in SHAT 1H/1436/D(1).

[7] Colonel Degas, "Bulletin hebdomadaire de renseignements. Semaine du 13 au 19 janvier 1962" (SP 87.000, 20 January 1962), 28, in SHAT 1H/1436/D(1); Lt.-Colonel Cousin, "Bulletin hebdomadaire de renseignements. Semaine du 20 au 26 janvier 1962" (SP 87.000, 27 January 1962), 27, in SHAT 1H/1436/D(1).

[8] Captain Landel, "Télégram official n. 345/CSFA/EMI/3/S. OPS-S" (Reghaia, 15 March 1962), in SHAT 1H/1870/1; Général Fouquet, "Compte rendu mensuel d'activité. Mois de mars 1962" (SP. 87.065.AFN, 23 April 1962); Général Gauthier, "Compte rendu mensuel. Mois de mai 1962" (SP. 87.065.AFN, 20 June 1962); and "Compte rendu mensuel. Mois de juin 1962" (SP. 87.065.AFN, 20 July 1962), all three in Service historique de l'Armée de l'Air (SHAA) I/E 274.

[9] 2ème bureau, signed by Col. de l'Espinay, "Bulletin de renseignements mensuel. Mois de mars" (SP 87.000, 11 April 1962), 10, in SHAT 1H/1428 /1.

"Muslims." The Accords had accelerated this process, precipitating a "regrouping in villages or large cities" of "the near totality" of "European" *bled* dwellers; then came the "abandonment of towns where the ALN will be stationed, in order to take refuge in large cities."[10]

In these "European" enclaves OAS propaganda dominated the available Algerian-based media, while encouraging widespread disdain for metropolitan reporting. OAS pirate transmissions interrupted regular radio and television broadcasts on a daily basis (until mid-June), while numerous local newspapers published (under duress, their editors claimed) front page decrees by the OAS.[11] As always, threats and intimidation were central to OAS efforts. The assassination of numerous "Europeans" in Algeria who persisted in publicly supporting de Gaulle or the French Left, or who publicly disagreed with the OAS, allowed the appearance of pied noir coherence and solidarity to be maintained. On 15 March 1962, for example, OAS activists murdered six educators associated with the Centres sociaux éducatifs (Centers for Social Education)—an adult education program for FMAs begun under integrationist auspices—on the basis of rumors that they were in contact with Algerian nationalists. Among those killed were the novelist Mouloud Ferraoun and the historian Max Marchand.[12]

The French-Algeria cause suffered setback after setback. Yet OAS action and propaganda succeeded in creating a widely shared certainty among most pieds noirs that Algeria would remain French so that they would be able to stay in French Algeria. One intelligence report on the "European" milieu graphed the ambiance in Oran on a "temperature curve of emotions." It found a "highly exaggerated bell curve: great anger is followed by immediate depression as well as vice versa." (To emphasize the importance of emotion, the report stated that Oran was "much less bourgeois than Algiers, as the 'petits blancs' who are mostly of Spanish blood compose three-fourths of the population.") Even after clear OAS defeats, such as the arrest of ex-General Jouhaud, "the man in the street believes that 'the fight's not over'."[13] From the viewpoint of the "Europeans," there were dramatic developments, such as the army's blockade of Bab el-Oued or when French soldiers shot between forty-six and eighty civilians during a peaceful protest against independence on the rue d'Issly in Algiers on 26 March. But like developments directly linked to the possibility of departures, these did not dramatically shift sentiments. Intelligence reports detailed growing waves of departures,

---

[10] Capt. Koch, "Annexe à joindre au rapport n. 555/4 du juin 1962" (5 June 1962), 2, in SHAT: 1H/3086/1; Col. Cavard, "Bulletin Hebdomadaire de renseignement psychologique (semaine 16-22/5/62)" (Algiers, 24 May 1962), 4, in SHAT: 1H/2549/2.

[11] See, e.g., 2ème bureau weekly intelligence reports in SHAT 1H/1436/1.

[12] See James LeSueur's introduction to Mouloud Feraoun, *Journal, 1955–1962: Reflections on the French-Algerian War*, trans. Mary Ellen Wolfe and Claude Fouillade (Lincoln, Neb., 2000).

[13] Direction de la Sûreté nationale, "Milieux Europeens" (Rocher Noir, 29 March 1962), 3, in SHAT 1H/1784/2.

yet still cautioned that decisions to leave remained under consideration and that conditions could and did change weekly.[14] Between January and April 1962, reports concerning the "Europeans of Algeria" varied wildly. They were staying, getting ready to go, only pretending to get ready to go. The OAS was universally supported, was widely mistrusted, was feared, had lost all popular confidence. "Europeans" were waiting to see what would happen, were prepared to fight to prevent any form of cease-fire, wanted to see what the FLN would do, had no confidence in the FLN.[15] "The *état d'esprit* of the Europeans," in the words of Officer Cousin, "varies from day to day, even hour by hour, driven by events, by measures taken by the authorities, and by the most unlikely rumors."[16] Popular sentiment was not coherent but, more important, it differed enormously both over time and according to location. This encouraged observers to privilege well-rehearsed presumptions over even acute insights. One of the earliest French critics to predict total repatriation immediately withdrew his prediction. In mid-May, writing in *France-Observateur,* Pierre Nora rehearsed his version of the "tide of History" thesis, evoking French Algerian "irrationality" counterposed with "the logic of their history cutting like a razor." Yet he was unable to follow through the logic of his analysis. Logically, he argued, "they should be forced to leave, every single one of them." Unfortunately, "such a plan is too beautiful, if I dare say so, to be true. This country, happily, is not serious. Something is happening that disproves even the logic of their irrationality." He was wrong on all counts. Throughout their shifts in mood and in plans, one thing held true: the attachment of "French Algerians" to remaining French and—reinforced directly by OAS propaganda—the linked conviction that this was possible only on French territory. Official efforts to convince FSE of the opposite failed utterly.[17]

As pieds noirs became certain that Algeria would be independent, the rush of departures that emptied Algeria of "Europeans"—"leaving by air or sea" —began. Departures had not occurred earlier only because this certainty was slow in coming. In Constantine, where concerns about Jewish departures had introduced the term "exodus" in 1961, it was in late April that military intelligence first announced that "definitive exodus to the metropole" was what "many Europeans" now planned. The reasons suggested were, first, a growing realization of "the uselessness of all the [pro–French Algeria] demonstrations"; second, the "persistent fear of future retribution by the Muslim masses or administration"; and finally, the pressure of "'taxes' that the

---

[14] Ibid., 1–6. On the blockade and the rue d'Issly tragedy, see Jean Monneret, *La phase finale de la guerre d'Algérie* (Paris, 2000), 91–105.

[15] See SHAT 1H/1437; 1H/1784; 1H/1428/1; 1H/2549/2.

[16] Lt.-Colonel Cousin, "Bulletin hebdomadaire de renseignements. Semaine du 12 au 18 mai 1962" (SP 87.000, 19 May 1962), 27, in SHAT 1H/1437/1.

[17] Pierre Nora, "Sept fois en un jour en Algérie," *France-Observateur* 628 (17 May 1962), 10.

FLN has been collecting since the cease-fire."[18] The previous weekly summary, like those before it, had made no mention of such plans, analyzing instead the "stupor" of the "European" population confronted with developments, "the referendum in France and the installation of the provisional executive," which "will determine their future but in which they play no role."[19]

Recognizing the Exodus

The arrest of ex-General Raoul Salan marks, empirically and symbolically, the beginning of what would be recognized as more than a variety of discrete phenomena, as an event: the exodus. Empirically because, from 20 April on, what would prove to be definitive departures to the metropole went up markedly and "continued with no slowdowns" until the exodus ended.[20] As a year-end chronicle asked: "Coincidence or consequence? On 21 April 1962, and for the first time ever, the constabulary had to refuse entrance to the Maison-Blanche airport, where numerous Algérois [inhabitants of Algiers] sought to board. Two thousand people were able to leave. The rest, pushed back, camped in their cars."[21] Symbolically, because Salan's arrest removed the individual who had embodied popular hopes for the victory of the forces supporting French Algeria, and it also precipitated the collapse of any semblance of OAS unity and, with it, of the organization's embrace of a republican project for France.

The Law of 13 April 1962, which inserted the Evian Accords into French law, had already sapped republican and juridical arguments within the organization, claims that the French government was acting outside the law in dealing with the FLN. The OAS, as the historian Rémi Kauffer argues, could no longer pretend to be defending the letter of republican law, which led many activist leaders, particularly those who had left the armed forces, to withdraw. Without Salan, this movement accelerated. In turn, once the exodus began, the influence of the OAS collapsed; its brutish methods, widely accepted in the early crucible of French Algerian resistance to Algerian independence, now inspired anguish among pieds noirs who did not want to

---

[18] Captain Koch, "Annexe à joindre au rapport n. 555/4 du juin 1962" (5 June 1962), 2, in SHAT 1H/3086/1; Colonel Cavard, "Bulletin hebdomadaire de renseignement psychologique. Semaine 16–22/5/62" (Algiers, 24 May 1962), 4, in SHAT 1H/2549/2; Lt.-Colonel Genestout, "Bulletin hebdomadaire de renseignements. Semaine du 15 au 22 avril 1962" (Constantine, 25 April 1962), 2, in SHAT 1H/2836/1. This report covers the week in which former general Raoul Salan was captured.

[19] Colonel Serafino, "Bulletin hebdomadaire de renseignements. Semaine du 1 au 8 avril 1962" (Constantine, 11 April 1962), in SHAT 1H/2836/3.

[20] General Cherasse, commandant de la Gendarmerie en Algérie, "Bulletin quotidien des informations et renseignements . . . Periode du 28 au 29" (Algiers, 29 June 1962), 7, in SHAT 1H/1784/4.

[21] Année Politique 1962, 282.

leave Algeria but who were desperate to remain French. Official reports remained vague as to the causes of this pied noir anguish. In early April, officers noted a growing feeling among "Europeans" that they were being "rejected by the nation [as] 'Pieds Noirs,'" which inspired "their stupor, their shock, their desperation, or their anger." In mid-May, other military observers noted for the first time "a certain queasiness among the general population." "The masses," wrote Cousin, "particularly in Algiers, have a sinking, sickened feeling as they face accusations made against the whole European community." The claims concerned their responsibility for terrorism, torture, colonial racism, and ongoing violence in general. Besides moral qualms provoked by metropolitan judgments, however, the same report also pointed to "fear of Muslim reprisals" inspired by the "machine-gun attack of 14 May" 1962 (by FLN commander Azzedine in Algiers) to explain a "timid" movement "to separate themselves from the OAS."[22]

After Salan's capture, the exodus began, did not stop, and was definitive. Numerous stages in the weeks between mid-April and early July can be traced: shifts in OAS strategy, or GPRA strategy; the repeatedly remodulated explanations and policies of Algeria's Provisional Authority; the so-called Susini-Mostefaï cease-fire, negotiated in early June between a student farright leader associated with the OAS and a representative of the GPRA; the splitting apart of the OAS, as different regional commands and factions followed their own courses—for example, the Oran command of the OAS, which supported dividing Algeria in order to establish a "territorial platform" for Europeans.[23] None affected the exodus, except to alter slightly its rhythm. Even the French Army's failure to stop the 5 July killing of Europeans in Oran by "Muslim" rioters, which changed French military protocols and shocked many in the metropole as well as in Algeria, did not alter radically the nature of the exodus. Pied noir repatriates were ready to come back, yes; but only to an Algeria that was again French.[24] What did change was what army intelligence officer Colonel Mangin called "the psychosis of the exodus," which "intensified or calmed in direct relationship to the possibilities of leaving." In May, Cousin noted for Algiers that "nascent hyste-

[22] On the OAS and legal arguments, see Rémi Kauffer, "OAS: La guerre franco-française d'Algérie," in La guerre d'Algérie, 1954–2004: La fin de l'amnésie, ed. Mohammed Harbi and Benjamin Stora (Paris, 2004), 451–76, 472; on pied noir sentiments, see Cavard, "Bulletin de renseignements mensuel. Mois de mars 1962" (JCM/JD, 6 April 1962), 43, in SHAT 1H/2716/2; Cousin, "Bulletin hebdomadaire de renseignements. Semaine du 12 au 18 mai 1962" (SP 87.000, 19 May 1962), 27, in SHAT 1H/1437/1.

[23] For these developments, see Lt.-Colonel Cousin, "Bulletin hebdomadaire de renseignements. Semaine du 19 au 25 mai 1962" (SP 87.000, 26 May 1962), 26, in SHAT 1H/1437/1, and Colonel Mangin, "Bulletin hebdomadaire de renseignements. Semaine du 2 au 8 juin 1962" (SP 87.000, 9 June 1962), 24–30, in SHAT 1H/1437/1. The latest historian to emphasize and detail the significance of these developments is Monneret (2000).

[24] For an overview of June, see 2ème bureau, signed by Colonel Mangin, "Bulletin de renseignements mensuel. Mois de juin" (SP 87.000, 13 July 1962), 11, in SHAT 1H/1428/1. For a very different analysis than my own of the last months of French Algeria, see Monneret (2000).

ria was wiped away by an increase in the number of planes and boats"; in June, Mangin stressed that the "psychosis" in Oran was "attenuated by the decreased harassment from the OAS."[25]

The movement out of Algeria was different in kind than the exodus intra muros, which had accentuated segregation. Even in the midst of this exodus, however, the belief that the pieds noirs necessarily would remain in Algeria was tenacious. The gendarmerie's commander, Captain Koch, reported that while movement within Algeria involved "entire families," that toward the metropole, although affecting "all social classes," was "primarily women and children. The head of the family generally stays behind." He made clear that his attention to pied noir men was not a warning about continued OAS violence but a hopeful sign that those who had left would return.[26] The government continued to hope that repatriate status would encourage most who had fled Algeria in fear to return and, more important, that official presumptions about what "Europeans" wanted were correct. After their vacations, politicians and press secretaries repeated, "Algerians" would return to their now independent homeland.[27] Even internal government documents referred straight-forwardly to vacations, perhaps envisioning the summer as a cooling down period. In late May, the Oran prefecture, calling attention to the masses of people "descending on the port of Oran and waiting day and night on the docks," urged the minister of the interior "to organize the transportation to France of thousands of women and children for summer vacation."[28] Others, although asserting that Europeans were "pretending to go on summer vacation" in order "to save face," still drew attention to "their hope that they will be able to return." Just as experts in the Hexagon continued to plan on no more than three hundred thousand repatriates from Algeria staying for good in Europe, official reports from Algeria maintained that, as the head of gendarmes in Oran wrote in early June, "although many Europeans try to convince themselves that staying in an independent Algeria is impossible, it is certain that in their heart of hearts they hope to stay." Noting the "massive exodus of Europeans toward the metropole," he highlighted the "small number of them who declare that they are giving up and

[25] Cousin, "Bulletin hebdomadaire de renseignements. Semaine du 19 au 25 mai 1962" (SP 87.000, 26 May 1962), 26, in SHAT 1H/1437/1; Mangin, "Bulletin hebdomadaire de renseignements. Semaine du 2 au 8 juin 1962" (SP 87.000, 9 June 1962), 24, in SHAT 1H/1437/1.

[26] Captain Koch, "Annexe à joindre au rapport n. 55 5/4 du juin 1962" (5 June 1962), 2, in SHAT 1H/3086/1; Colonel Cavard, "Bulletin hebdomadaire de renseignement psychologique. Semaine 16–22/5/62" (Algiers, 24 May 1962), 4, in SHAT 1H/2549/2.

[27] "Special Report of the Government, without Debate, on the Algerian Situation," ("Rapport spécial du Gouvernement, sans débat, sur la situation algérienne") J.O. 1962. I reemphasize that the term "repatriate" was defined in reference to French people who were not from Algeria but from "colonies" that had been "decolonized." See chapter 5.

[28] Parat, for Biget, préfet de police d'Oran, "Note à l'attention de M. le Ministre" (21 May 1962), 1–2, in CAC/AN 770346/08.

leaving definitively."[29] In July 1962, the Coordinating Commission for the Reinstallation of Overseas French did insist that "it seems reasonable to expect that some 50 percent of civil servants . . . will reinstall themselves in the metropole." This "reasonable" estimate was made even though 80 percent had already requested a transfer to the metropole. Once the current "climate" had passed, the commission presaged, the conditions that would allow most civil servants to remain in Algeria would reassert themselves.[30]

Officials repeatedly took fairly accurate statistical evidence and then worked to make the data confirm wholly inaccurate predictions. This process illustrated the continued dominance of a republican *jus soli* conception of citizenship and nationality, as well as other continuities in bureaucratic and government practice.[31] In looking at the total "French" population of Algeria, "the commission has retained," the July 1962 report explained, "a so-called normal hypothesis" based on "the application of the Evian Accords under the announced juridical and financial conditions." This led them to predict "the return of 160,000 working individuals out of a total of 350,000." Their hypothesis, they noted, "is premised on the hope that a certain number of families who came to France in June will resume their life in Algeria come September." In this case, "the possible number of definitive returns from Algeria realized in 1962 is around 80,000 people who previously were employed in Algeria."[32] Two weeks before this report, the government's spokesperson had announced that "since the month of May, a little less than 270,000 repatriates have arrived in the metropole." Alain Peyrefitte did state that it was "only in October" that the number who would stay in the metropole could be known.[33] In late August 1962, a note from the secretary of state for repatriates sent to President de Gaulle stated that his office had registered 506,644 individuals between 1 January and 12 August 1962. Prefects, he reported, estimated that there were "at least 100,000 people who have not approached [our] services," but judging the resulting figure of 600,000 "excessive, the figure retained as most likely is that of 550,000." Planning in his office therefore was done under a "working hypothesis for reinsertion based on the fact that 300,000 of those will definitively settle on the national territory." In other words, they were predicting the same number or less than what had been predicted before the exodus began.[34]

---

[29] Captain Koch, "Rapport . . . sur les événements survenus pendant la periode du 16 juin au 31 juin [*sic,* should read May] 1962" (Oran, 2 June 1962), 7, in SHAT 1H/3086/1.

[30] Commission de coordination pour la réinstallation des Français d'Outre-Mer, Commissariat général du Plan, "Rapport de la Commission. Annexe 3: Note relative au problème des fonctionnaires" (Paris, 18 July 1962), 16, in CAC 80 AJ/254 [930275/94].

[31] Rogers Brubaker, *Citizenship and Nationhood in France and Germany* (Cambridge, Mass., 1992).

[32] Commission de coordination, "Rapport de la Commission. Annexe 3," 5–6.

[33] Agence France Presse, "Bulletin Conseil de Ministres" (Paris, 27 June 1962), in SHAT 1H/1126/1.

[34] Secrétariat d'Etat aux rapatriés, "Note pour Monsieur le Président de la Republique" (Paris, n.d. [August 1962]), 1, in MAE 117.

French officials who sought to stop the exodus simultaneously assigned blame for it. Most decided, and many subsequent scholars and commentators agree, that it was the fault of the OAS or the FLN, or both, rather than the French, or French history. Some, however, recognized that the cause, rather than contingent, was structural: "What plunged them [in May] into deep despair and provoked an exodus verging on panic was the collapse of hope among the European community in an OAS victory that would keep Algeria French."[35] Lt.-Colonel Cousin, who synthesized intelligence reports for the Armed Forces in Algeria High Command, put more emphasis than most on FLN terror. Cousin portrayed the continuation of Algerian nationalist violence as being caused by imminent independence, with no connection to (notably increased) OAS terrorism. Rather, he linked "French" fear of the FLN's actions (whether future or present) with concern that the OAS would fail. France-Observateur's Paul-Marie de la Gorce described the Algiers raid on 14 May ("the first Muslim response to OAS violence") as having unleashed "the massive exodus of the European community." De la Gorce rightly maintained that this development was not what FLN and nationalist leaders had wanted.[36] Cousin emphasized (relatively minimal) FLN terror and disregarded (objectively significant) OAS exactions, yet more than most observers he captured the developing "European" exodus and assessed its primary cause: a rejection of Algerian independence. "Europeans," that is, responded to the OAS not in terms of its tactical shifts but as a means to keep Algeria French.[37]

On 30 May, an SFIO deputy insisted in the National Assembly that what was occurring was an "exodus. . . . The truth is, there is a wave of panic sweeping over Algeria." Speaking to the secretary of state for repatriates, he said, "Why deny it? Everyone wants to leave."[38] Yet, as "The Governmental Declaration without Debate on the Algerian Problems" that the deputy interrupted made clear, the government and its Algérie française opponents still shared a hope that what was happening was temporary, and each acted as if their plans for the people of Algeria would be realized: the government, that all would stay (or at least end up) in Algeria, OAS sympathizers that Algeria would stay (or at least end up) French. When the secretary of state evoked "the rhythm of repatriation or of return to metropolitan France, as it is now happening," an Algerian deputy protested: "The term 'repatriated' makes us tremble. Say the 'retreated' and we can agree." The secretary of state for repatriates' response, "I am not looking to fight about words with you," avoided

[35] 2ème bureau, signed by Mangin, "Bulletin de renseignement mensuel. Mois de juin" (SP 87.000, 13 July 1962), 11, in SHAT 1H/1428/1.

[36] "Alger: L'histoire de la trêve," France-Observateur 631 (7 June 1962), 8; on Azzedine's raid, see Cousin, "Bulletin hebdomadaire de renseignements. Semaine du 19 au 25 mai 1962" (SP 87.000, 26 May 1962), 27, in SHAT 1H/1437/1.

[37] "Bulletin hebdomadaire de renseignements. Semaine du 19 au 25 mai 1962" (SP 87.000, 26 May 1962), 1 and 26, in SHAT 1H/1437/1.

[38] René Schmitt, 30 May 1962, in J.O., 1409.

invoking the legal definition of "repatriate." Faced with another deputy's rejoinder, "This is more than a fight about words!" The secretary embraced the term "retreat."[39] By calling the French citizens coming from Algeria toward the metropole *replié,* or retreated, speakers defined them as pulling back, leaving in defeat from one part of their homeland—Algeria—to another—the metropole. They retained the possibility of returning to Algeria (French or independent, depending on the observer). *Rapatrié,* repatriated, meant to return to the fatherland. Its use in the debates was taken to indicate that Algeria was no longer part of the French *patrie,* that people were coming home to (metropolitan) France from (foreign) Algeria. "Retreated" resonated, for French Algeria diehards, with the history of the departments of Alsace and Lorraine (Moselle). The need to erase the shameful "retreat" of 1870–71 had been at the heart of the Third Republic's national mythology/history, and supporters of the OAS agenda imagined Algeria playing a similar role in the Fifth Republic. Rather than military or war-related terminology, the government invoked the need for vacations. The secretary of state explained to the deputies that the "rhythm of retreat to the metropole at present is around five thousand people a day." Whatever they might think, he cautioned, "what I would like to inform the Assembly is that this rate is exactly the same—for various reasons, of course—as at this time last year: 99,522 in May 1961, around 100,000 now." The government was not quite suggesting, as Ile de France Deputy André Laffin interjected, "So no one is leaving!" It asserted, simply, that nothing irreversible was happening. More important, nothing was occurring that needed explanation. Nor anything that required the precision of a term, such as repatriate, which French law defined.[40]

Elements of the OAS, too, disputed the reality of the "exodus" long after the movement had become a veritable groundswell. The OAS Zone III (Oran) refused to accept the early June Susini-Mostefaï agreements—which called for an end to fighting and the participation of "Europeans" in the independence process—and sought to establish a "territorial platform" governed by the OAS and independent from the French Republic as well as from Algeria. In mid-June, a communiqué explained that "we have asked that certain zones be evacuated, and the slightly more numerous departures of the last few days are the result of the evacuation of some families from the interior." Their definition of families, they specified, meant women and children: "*The men are staying put. They are ready to fight.*" An ever smaller group of diehards still argued that (part of) Algeria would remain French, and the French of Algeria would return.[41]

---

[39] Ibid., 1410–11.

[40] Indeed, OAS propaganda expressed shock at the large "Yes" vote on April 8 in Alsace-Lorraine. Direction centrale des RG, "Sommaire générale" (Paris, 24 April 1962), 1, in CAC/AN 800280, article 216.

[41] OAS Zone III, "Texte de l'émission réalisée sur les ondes de la TV le 16/6," in SHAT 1H/3167/1. Emphasis in original.

Even the metropolitan press, which seemingly had little interest in down-playing departures, was slow to challenge government claims that departures were merely the exaggeration of an annual phenomenon. After noting his hesitancy to contradict government experts whom he admired—thanks to their anti-OAS, pro-independence engagement—de la Gorce wrote in *France-Observateur,* "Still, it must be said that their explanations on the departures of Europeans are not convincing." Focusing on interpretation and not figures, he noted that "it is meaningless to compare the numbers of current departures to those of 'vacationers' each year." Instead, he pointed to the mass departures from Constantine, where "less than half" of the European community remained, or the Sersou Valley, where "nearly all the colonists" have left. Whatever their reasons, he maintained, "it is certainly not to take a vacation."[42]

"The Massive Effort Asked of the Nation"

At the 23 May committee meeting of the cabinet-level Committee for Algerian Affairs of the government of Prime Minister Georges Pompidou , the secretary of state for repatriates reported that "at this time the situation has changed profoundly." Now, and in the months to come, "circumstances lead us to predict massive arrivals at a rhythm that could easily be greater than 100,000 to 150,000 per month."[43] Despite earlier hopes that this movement was "seasonal" or simply irrational, in June military intelligence remarked that "departures to the metropole, in any case, have not ceased and their numbers are far beyond previous records for vacation-related voyages: 225,000 passengers recorded, versus 88,000 for June 1961."[44] This led top government officials in Algeria to predict, as the prefect of police in Oran wrote to Minister of the Interior Roger Frey, that "if the general tendency does not reverse itself between now and July 1, we are going to have a fairly important exodus of Europeans." It was time to face, he wrote, "the problem of organizing their departure, by sea and air, of transportation, of arrival in Marseilles and Port-Vendres."[45]

The Pompidou government decided that its most important task was shaping public understandings of what was going on, rather than committing resources or elaborating new measures. At the 23 May cabinet-level

[42] Paul-Marie de la Gorce, "Alger: L'histoire de la trêve," *France-Observateur* 631 (7 June 1962), 7.

[43] Secrétariat d'Etat aux rapatriés, "Comité des Affaires algériennes du mercredi 23 mai à 15h30. Objet: Personnes rentrant d'Algérie" (undated), 2, in MAE 39.

[44] 2ème bureau, signed by Mangin, "Bulletin de renseignements mensuel. Mois de juin" (SP 87.000, 13 July 1962), 11, in SHAT 1H/1428/1.

[45] Unsigned, "Pour M. le Ministre" (June 1962), 2, in CAC/AN 770346/08.

meeting, after enumerating the various measures that had been taken or needed to be taken (and paid for), Secretary for Repatriates Boulin emphasized that "for psychological and political reasons" it now was "essential to go before the parliament to detail the massive effort asked of the nation." What was most important, Boulin reiterated, was not what was going to be done: in addressing the National Assembly, the goal was to prevent the legislators from demanding that more be done—or more money spent—than the government recommended. As he said, "any other policy" except appealing to "the nation" in apocalyptic terms "might lead the Assembly to reject the budget we propose as ridiculously small."[46]

There was widespread and powerful resistance to taking any action to assist the repatriates. The archives of two interministerial committees chaired by President de Gaulle reveal the intense conflict among the Fifth Republic's leaders over the best way to respond. De Gaulle himself disdained the "pieds noirs." As Alain Peyrefitte reminds us, de Gaulle simply did not believe that people from Algeria, the Europeans included, could be made French.[47] The president privileged police responses to the exodus: the repatriates were a vector of OAS criminality and banditry and a potential locus for political upheaval. The attention to law enforcement met as well as inspired public concerns: during the summer of 1962 much of the popular press identified the repatriates as the source of a wave of banditry in the south and around Paris. Many on the left drew attention to potential political violence. If Socialist (SFIO) leaders were, according to the RG, "preoccupied" by "the problems posed by the repatriation of refugees from North Africa," the French Confederation of Christian Workers (Confédération Française des Travailleurs Chrétiens, or CFTC) warned its locals to be on guard against the threat of "infiltration by repatriates." A Communist deputy warned against letting "the retreated from Algeria become a reservoir of fascism." In *France-Observateur* the letters to the editor page was filled in early 1962 with criticisms of the pieds noirs, the repatriates, and what many readers thought was the weekly's too sympathetic coverage of their situation. Monsieur H. C. from Paris, "one of your earliest subscribers," questioned whether the "exodus" was necessary, given that "the French government has done everything to guarantee their safety and their property." He was opposed to assisting the repatriates, worrying that they would "reinforce metropolitan activism, which the press tells us is growing stronger and more violent." Against such

---

[46] Ibid. On the various agencies put in place, see Vincent Viet, *La France immigrée* (Paris, 1998), 163–302; Jean-Jacques Jordi, *1962: L'arrivée des pieds-noirs* (Paris, 1995) and *De l'exode à l'exil: Rapatriés et pieds-noirs en France; L'exemple marseillais* (Paris, 1993); and Jordi and Temime, eds. (1996). For an excellent study of how these agencies worked, see Sarah Sussman, "Changing Lands, Changing Identities: The Migration of Algerian Jewry to France, 1954–1967" (PhD diss., Stanford University, 2002), 143–251.

[47] See chapter 2.

concerns, Prime Minister Pompidou successfully played on de Gaulle's concerns about political upheaval to overcome scorn for the pieds noirs and to establish a more varied response to the exodus.[48]

The plans officials made under duress, however, worked most efficiently to eliminate the complicated set of definitions and structures that the Evian Accords and French law had established. In place of existing subtle subsets of French citizens—those with Koranic status, with double nationality, protected by European minority status, and so forth—the government embraced a simple division between "Algerians" and "French." The former were "Muslims"—a term that never appeared in official reports as a religion but always in reference to the majority "community" in Algeria—while the latter were not. These categories did not accurately capture some obvious realities, nor did they respect republican principles and French law. They were, however, easier to understand and easier to explain to a metropolitan population that had tired of trying to figure out what was happening with Algeria.

The abrupt transformation of the application of repatriate status captures this effort to clarify who was French. On 2 April 1962 the government had extended the status of "repatriate" to people who arrived in the metropole from Algeria.[49] Although the law had created the category of "repatriates" in the name of standardizing their treatment, it had individualized the process of obtaining benefits: potential repatriates would need to prove that they left under duress. Officials in the metropole were to assess each case and this judgment would determine the benefits available to each repatriate. The exodus destroyed this individualized system, creating a uniform class of "repatriates from Algeria." All repatriates now were eligible to receive specified benefits. As distinctions within repatriate status disappeared, the division that emerged instead was between repatriates and refugees. "Repatriates" came to refer almost exclusively to "Europeans," while "Muslims" became "refugees."[50]

In talks with the GPRA, French negotiators had already abandoned "integrationist" principles, which offered legal recognition to some forms of difference among French citizens. Now, the government responded to the exodus of "Europeans" with an ardent reaffirmation of the theory of assimilationism and of policies meant to assimilate the new arrivals. French authorities at all levels reiterated this principle and made clear their reasoning: the need to avoid the danger of any "pied noir community" emerging in the

---

[48] Direction centrale des RG, "Sommaire générale" (Paris, 18 April 1962), 1; Direction centrale des RG, "Sommaire générale" (Paris, 9 April 1962), 2, both in CAC/AN 800280, article 216; François Billoux, L'Humanité (5 June 1962); H. C., de Paris, "Nos lecteurs écrivent: Pourquoi cet exode?" France-Observateur 629 (24 May 1962), 2.

[49] See Maurice Faivre, Les combattants musulmans de la guerre d'Algérie: Des soldats sacrifiés (Paris, 1995), 195.

[50] Jean Vacher-Desvernais, L'avenir des Français d'outre-mer (Paris, 1962), 140. I will cover "Muslim refugees" in the next chapter.

metropole. Some articulated this imperative as necessary to overcome bitterness and homesickness (*le mal de pays*), while others feared the implantation of a far-right pro-OAS constituency in the nation. Both positions shared the same remedy: economic assimilation. In 1962 the General Commission for the Plan announced the outlines and directives of the Fourth Plan for Economic and Social Development. The ultimate expression of post-Vichy French technocracy and planned growth, the first economic and social plan (for 1947–53) had been drawn up by Jean Monnet during the heady days of Resistance-inspired reconstruction. A second plan covered 1954–57. With the birth of the Fifth Republic, the priorities and axes of development the third plan (for 1958–61) proposed had taken on a new importance. With a constitutionally defined role, "the Plan" was meant to embody de Gaulle's vision of the state-inspired technocratic reconstruction of a powerful yet fair France. In its details and as a much-cited abstraction, the Fourth Plan served as point of reference for most official responses to the exodus. In 1962 the General Commission for the Plan—which was responsible for creating a "Gaullist" technocratic model of economic and social development—published a series of revisions to its encyclopedia for future development in which high-level officials formulated an economistic panacea to the refugee problem.

The Fourth Plan's vision of assimilation was premised on the economic reinsertion of the repatriates, the purpose of which was to overcome cultural and political differences. Published proposals and popular discussions about the repatriates regularly raised cultural problems that might hinder the assimilation of a "Mediterranean" and "colonial" population. To address this threat, policies were established to avoid pied noir ghettos and to guide families from Algeria to jobs and housing throughout France, particularly to regions where the Plan prioritized development. Officials worked, as one late August 1962 memo to de Gaulle explained, "to encourage the repatriates to settle themselves throughout the metropole."[51] Cultural and political particularities, the planners presumed, would melt away in the rising tide of 1960s French economic growth. Certain voices within government agencies warned about the potential blind spots in official predictions based on assimilationist ideology. On 20 June, a business leader invited to address the General Commission for the Plan noted that "by his count the figure of forty-seven thousand [new] lodgings is valid only if the exodus stops," while the same meeting of the Coordinating Commission for the Reinstallation of French from Overseas heard Senator Armengaud and a public health official insist that efforts "should not seem too *dirigiste*." Instead, France should just "let integration happen." Not surprisingly, this advice was not taken.[52]

---

[51] Secrétaire d'Etat aux rapatriés, "Note pour Monsieur le Président de la République" (Paris, August 1962), 2, in MAE 117.
[52] Commission de coordination pour la réinstallation des Français d'Outre-Mer, Commis-

Numerous journalists and commentators insisted that the government needed to act aggressively to assimilate the new arrivals. In April 1962 Philippe Hernandez, a self-identified pied noir and a journalist with *France-Observateur,* explicitly linked a call for assimilation and anticorporatist language. Presenting a group interview with recently repatriated pieds noirs, he called on "Frenchmen" to "lend an ear," saying that "tomorrow, the thousands of pieds noirs who are going to arrive will group together and organize themselves because no one will help them." "I don't like that one bit," he added. He urged that the nation should take action to address their problems because "I would rather that any future associations made up of French of Algeria have nothing better to do than to organize an annual cocktail party."[53]

As had been the case with SAM and similar agencies in their approach to FMAs, observers attributed responsibility for metropolitan resentment, dislike, or suspicion of the pieds noirs to the pieds noirs. Accusations varied; what one witness referred to as "the black legend of the 'pied noir,' vain and exploitative" grounded certain accusations. A call for understanding Hernandez published in *France-Observateur* inspired one reader to write that bad feelings between metropolitans and new arrivals could be avoided, "but on one condition: once he sails for France, the pied noir must throw overboard his superiority complex, that of the colonist," offering as an example "that driver with the 9A [Algiers] license-plate who, when I signaled for room to pass him, told me 'I'm in the right!' while hogging the middle of the road." This complaint was joined by references to their use of the racial epithet *bougnoule* and similar belittling references to Arabs. It ended with the correspondent's bitter memory of being "refused bottles of water by pieds noirs . . . during the long marches of our military service."[54] Even the most serious and thoughtful observers held signs of pied noir *particularisme,* or difference, responsible for metropolitan reactions. One volunteer charged with organizing efforts to respond to the exodus argued that while "the misery and the disarray of most of those arriving today" largely had undermined the credibility of the "black legend," ending it would require "making 'pied noir' particularities disappear, on the one hand by breaking up all concentrations of refugees, on the other hand, by reregistering as soon as they arrive all automobiles brought over from Algeria." Separate them one from another and separate them from all signs that they were from Algeria: that way, French drivers, for example, would see rude drivers as just bad eggs and not as embryos of a coming fascist plague identifiable by their license plates.[55]

---

sariat général du Plan, "Procès-verbal du groupe 'Logement' réunion du 20 Juin 1962" (20 June 1962), 4, in CAC/AN 80 AJ/254 [930275/94].

[53] Philippe Hernandez, "Quatre pieds-noirs en métropole," *France-Observateur* 623 (12 April 1962), 10.

[54] M. J. Rosny, "Nos lecteurs écrivent: Ça pouvait s'éviter aussi!" *France-Observateur* 619 (15 March 1962), 18.

[55] Philippe Hernandez, "Les pieds-noirs de Montpellier," *France-Observateur* 639 (2 August 1962), 10.

Previously certain that Europeans would not leave and faced with a total failure in convincing them that they could remain French in Algeria, French officials encountered enormous difficulties in mobilizing transportation and accommodations to counter the "psychosis of the exodus." Over the summer, the government put in place aggressive social and political responses to the exodus. The extensive powers the Law of 13 April 1962 offered to the French executive made much of this possible in material as well as regulatory terms. The government, supported by a broad range of media sources, private agencies, and politicians, addressed metropolitan opinion to insist on the importance and the necessity of massive mobilization to help "French people in distress."

The connections were explicit between policies for assimilating the pieds noirs and the policies previously applied to a group now considered inassimilable. A number of existing or new government agencies were authorized to respond to the exodus. Most began as part of the Interior Ministry, although many moved into the new Ministry of Repatriation over the course of 1962. Among the first government agencies to respond to the exodus were several, such as the SAM and the Technical Assistance Section, designed and funded to facilitate the integration of Muslim French citizens from Algeria in the metropole. Faced with the dramatic change of this group's relation to the French state—most "Muslims," it was presumed, would move from citizenship to (privileged) foreigner status in France—these agencies were temporarily enlisted to deal with Algerian refugees and their employees reassigned to repatriate-specific duties. Their efforts were needed to ensure that the much-feared emergence of a pied noir colony in the metropole did not materialize. One government expert, called to advise on how repatriates should be settled, recommended following "the example of SONACONTRAL," a public housing agency, "that adopted the principle of never allowing more than 10 percent of its tenants to be Muslim families." If General de Gaulle compared French people and "Muslim" Algerians to "oil and water," according to this public housing official a more subtle comparison was in order: "We moved people around to arrive at this dose and, in terms of assimilation, the experiment proved satisfactory."[56]

What, in the eyes of planners and officials, were the conditions that would make this population assimilable? What made them seem enough like other French people that assimilation would work? The pieds noirs were, after all, deeply distrusted and resented. It is a question that occurs at the very moment that the Fifth Republic abandoned France's most ambitious attempt at assimilation—that directed at Algerian "Muslims." Their fundamental similarity was not their status as citizens, as this history of the exodus makes clear, but the "European" origins they shared with metropolitan French peo-

---

[56] Commission de coordination pour la réinstallation des Français d'Outre-Mer, Commissariat général du Plan "Procès-verbal du groupe 'Logement' réunion du 20 juin 1962" (20 June 1962), 3, in CAC/AN 80 AJ/254 [930275/94].

ple. Press discussions of the exodus, as well as government policy choices, presented the "Europeans" of Algeria as part of the same family as other French people. To make this argument, representations of the "Europeans" themselves as part of heterosexual families proved critical: this normalizing representation of gender relations countered the visions of male perversion that had shaped metropolitan rejection of the pieds noirs in the months leading up to the exodus.

Pied Noir Men Repatriating into French Families

Metropolitans and the French press were fixated on the exodus. The reactions varied enormously, although overall the press was much more welcoming than the people in general. The emerging official line, cobbled together once the collapse of all previous predictions became undeniable, urged metropolitans to welcome the pieds noirs. The mythic heterosexual family was the principal register that legitimated such appeals. Days after the "exodus" exploded, *Paris-Match* responded to "the announcement that some families from North Africa have begun to settle in the metropole." The editors dragged old-time natalism out of its retirement—which had been provoked by the post-1945 *bébé boum* (baby boom)—with an editorial titled "There Are Not Enough French People." The editors wrote that "today, economic progress depends on abundant manpower and the number of solvent consumers." The editorial's final line, "Have confidence in the future," became *Match's* mantra.[57] *Paris-Match* consistently urged its readers to embrace "the repatriates of Algeria," and its editorials, photos, captions, and, less singularly, its articles struggled to fabricate "the friendship of French people for French people."[58] Every element of the weekly's 2 June cover worked to evoke compassion: a blond baby holding a stuffed animal; a young, tall, dark (but not too dark) and handsome man; a young, petite woman with a Jean Seberg–style haircut and wearing a suede vest, both adults in profile, leaning on a railing, eyes fixed on land. The headline reads "France: Does She Still Love Us?" with the promise of a "major report" not *on* but "*with* the repatriates from Algeria." The front-page caption explains that "they met and were married in Algeria, he, a military man, she, a pied noir. They were teachers; today they return to the shores of the *mère patrie.*" Who could think they were in any way connected with France's enemies? In a white band at the top of the page, a bold-faced headline, "The Judges of Salan," reminded readers that the enemies were being dealt with, the article inside beginning with the observation that the judges had "looked to the future."[59]

---

[57] Editorial: "Il n'y a pas assez de Français," *Paris-Match* 681 (28 April 1962), 7.

[58] Editorial: "La seule garanté," *Paris-Match* 673 (3 March 1962), 27.

[59] Photo by Maurice Jarnoux, *Paris-Match* 686 (2 June 1962), 1; Editorial: "La paix anticipée," in ibid., 6.

"France: Does She Still Love Us?" A family of repatriates from Algeria arriving off the coast of the metropole, June 1962. Reprinted by permission of *Paris-Match*.

Images of "whole" families, men with women and children, were repeatedly produced to describe the people coming to France. Although not historically unprecedented, the use of familial descriptions to explain official responses to the exodus was particularly intense, working to extricate OAS from "pieds noirs" and to reinsert the latter in classic, comforting, and hierarchized gender relations. Men joined their women and children in metropolitan France. The separation between men, fighting for the OAS in Algeria, and women and children in France waiting to return to Algeria, had too successfully convinced metropolitans that the pieds noirs were un-French. Both pro-government and pro–Algérie française deputies worked to distinguish the innocent French refugees flooding into the metropole from recent and vivid descriptions of violent anti-French fanatics, who like the refugees were "Europeans" and from Algeria. Deputies from all sides, except the Far Left, called for French fraternity and solidarity. One Gaullist deputy urged, "It is necessary for those who returned with pain in their souls, with bitterness on their lips, who are somewhat maladroit because they suffer—they must be welcomed like distressed members of the same family." More than mere words, there was an institutional vector to this discursive deployment, as the state sought to cement depictions of the refugees as French families.[60]

The government announced that its repatriation program had opened "15,000 dossiers for heads of families. . . . we have had 19,000 families, about 50,000 people . . . each head of family receives 50,000 old francs, each person in their charge 20,000." One Algerian deputy questioned the functionality of such a system: "I would like the minister for repatriation to note that in order to receive these allocations, it is necessary that the head of the family be in the metropole. It would be just and it would be reasonable if these benefits were equally available to repatriated families where the head of the family has not come."[61] The genealogy of this dispute is compelling. Directing payments to the male head of the family was not the norm for French social spending. Only in the late 1930s, after the collapse of the Popular Front, did the Daladier government, under great pressure from the traditionalist Catholic and royalist Right, begin to utilize familial allocation. Earlier in the twentieth century, the French government had opted repeatedly to give money to needy mothers directly, whether married or not. Thus, while the deputy's complaints made sense in the context of the recent history of France, their political origins were novel. The pro–French Algeria Right, not the secular Left, was calling for a policy that ignored family status.[62]

Rather than a reflection of the traditional familial order or a choice made on the basis of efficiency, this criterion was forged in discursive necessity. Indeed, within weeks, certain payments to repatriates began to be distributed whether or not the male "head of the family" had arrived. Yet the government's initial policy, insofar as it broke with standard practice, political and bureaucratic, suggests how critical it was for responses to the unexpected

[60] J.O., 1440.

[61] J.O., 1404 and 1488.

[62] See Françoise Thébaud, Quand nos grand-mères donnaient la vie: La maternité en France dans l'entre-deux guerres (Lyon, 1986); Susan Pedersen, Family Policy and the Origins of the Welfare State: Britain and France, 1914–1945 (London, 1993); Ann Orloff, "Gender in the Welfare State," Annual Review of Sociology 22 (1996): 51–78.

"exodus" of "Europeans" to present them as grouped in heterosexual families. Representations of the pieds noirs as deviant men had been widely convincing, understandings that offered vivid proof that they were not French and were a threat to France. To be male and pied noir was enough to be associated with fascist terror. Although French Algerian men on their own were undeniably citizens, legally entitled to enter the metropole, only as "heads of family" could they be welcomed. If in late 1961 and January 1962 government reports on departures from Algeria had specified how many of those concerned were "Israelites," in June and July 1962 RG reports on "repatriates from Algeria arriving in France" distinguished the number of "men older than seventeen."[63]

Counterrepresentations that normalized these men as healthily heterosexual were at the heart of efforts to provoke metropolitan solidarity with people who, although from Algeria, were, it needed to be proven, French. This familial language worked to assert that the pieds noirs were directly linked to other French people, feeding into affirmations that they were "members of the same family." Familial images were readily articulated to disentangle the mass of pieds noirs from the actions of the OAS. As one Algerian deputy noted: "Already, in spite of official declarations and proclaimed optimism from the higher- ups, stories abound of facts that shame us. . . . In Marseilles, the [repatriates] have to sleep on the roadside in front of packed hotels or ones that refuse to accept refugees."[64] Through the multiple resonances of familial imagery, the repatriates were positioned as weak rather than violent, as themselves children, and as profoundly French, all exemplified in the words of one deputy urging his audience to look at the exodus and understand:

> Today, you can see the French who arrive on the docks of Marseilles, or the grounds of our major airports, poor and often miserable, their only baggage several sacks in which they were able to save the modest belongings that, over there, was all they owned. You need only to look at them to know that these are lower-middle-class Frenchmen, little people for whom life consists of work, of effort, and suffering. . . . Do not forget that these French people, our compatriots, our brothers, are the children of those who went before, pushed more by the need to give [to France] than greed.

The family—and above all the necessary place of males within it as fathers, brothers, and even children—was a privileged trope, mobilized to cleanse the pieds noirs, in particular the men, of the OAS stain and to guarantee their Frenchness.[65] Familial discourse offered tentative resolution to one of the

[63] Direction centrale des RG, "Sommaire générale" (Paris, 27 June 1962), 1, in CAC/AN 800280, article 218.
[64] J.O. (1962), 1427.
[65] J.O. (1962), 2353.

key questions the Algerian revolution forced France to address: Who could be French and why? In the next chapter I analyze how the government used powers the Law of 13 April 1962 offered to realize, at least partially, one pre-exodus metropolitan expectation: that Algerian "Muslims" would no longer be French.

Chapter 9

Rejecting the Muslims

There was, when the Evian Accords were announced, no official hesitation concerning what it meant for Muslim French citizens from Algeria. A telegram from National Defense headquarters in Paris to army headquarters in Algeria "conveys the prime minister's instructions" concerning their future:

> Question: Will they have the same possibilities as the "French of origin" to settle in the metropole with French citizenship and the benefits of the Law on Assistance to French repatriates? Response: *Yes.*
>
> Question: Will this possibility remain available to French Muslims? Response: Yes, by returning to the metropole at any moment after self-determination they can reclaim French nationality under French law and benefit from the Law.[1]

One month before, a six-page message from Minister of the Armies Pierre Messmer to all officers had assured "French Muslims serving in the armed forces and as auxiliaries that their legitimate interests as soldiers and citizens will be guaranteed."[2] Officials conveyed this message to officers in Algeria, who in turn announced it to French of North African Origin (FSNA) soldiers (there were 22,746 Muslim French citizens from Algeria serving in the French armed forces around the world[3]) as well as harkis, *moghazin,* and other auxiliaries. Radio France broadcast across the metropole the official

---

[1] DefNat Paris, "Télégramme au Bureau moral" (received 15 March 1962), in SHAT 1H/2467/6.

[2] Commandement Supérieur des Forces en Algérie, "Message n. 0560/CSFA/EMI/MOR" (22 February 1962), 3, in SHAT 1H/1260/1.

[3] Général du Corps Aérien Fourquet, "Militaires français musulmans d'Algérie présents sous les drapeaux a la date du 1èr avril 1962" (Algiers, 28 April 1962), in SHAT 1H/1319/2.

affirmation that continued French nationality and all measures of the Boulin Law were available to "every inhabitant of Algeria," whether "French Muslims or Europeans." In the metropole, supporters of the referendum of 8 April 1962 also specified that "French nationality would be maintained for all in Algeria who currently have it, Europeans or Muslims, and who do not explicitly renounce it."[4]

The exodus confronted republican bromides about the irrevocability of French citizenship—these legally binding facts—with their implications, and it was in this crisis that popular certainties about what made most Algerians different from French people took bureaucratic and juridical form. The suddenness of the unexpected confrontation certainly exaggerated its effects. Army sources, like other French officials, had believed that the transition between French sovereignty and independence would be one of stages. As the marginalia on one internal memo concerning "Muslim auxiliaries" presupposed: "It seems as though it will be progressive: cease-fire; provisional regime; consultations via elections; new institutions. We must prepare our activities for each phase, while planning for the next." The transition did not take years, as expected, but weeks. In that short period, the idea that those people French law defined as Muslim French citizens were part of an ethnoracial group different from that of other French citizens left the sphere of common sense to shape the legal categories established by the French government in July 1962. "Racialized ethnicity" explained why some people with French nationality ("Muslims") were Algerian, while other people from Algeria (pieds noirs) could remain French.[5]

From Muslim French Citizens from Algeria to Harkis

In late April and early May 1962, when it was publicly denying the existence of the exodus, the government acted to stop certain people from coming to the metropole: Muslim French citizens from Algeria. Or, as military orders and government decrees increasingly put it, "harkis," or simply "Muslims." Officials charged with assisting Algeria's "Muslim" population, a Top Secret note of 23 May from de Gaulle's office explained, must "cease all initiatives linked to the repatriation of harkis." To be "welcomed in the metropole, Muslims" must exit by permission of the Algerian high commissioner, and "their names must be on a list established to this end."[6] By late May, an officer directed that "Muslims" who were "too old, physically handicapped,

[4] Radiodiffusion Française, "Texte de l'émission diffusée au Bulletin de France II (13h) le 4 avril 1962: A qui s'appliquent les Accords d'Evian?" (4 April 1962), 2–3, in AN F/1a/5055.

[5] Colonel de l'Espinay, "Fiche: Problèmes posés par les harkis au moment du 'cessez-le-feu', RB/RC" (14 December 1961), 1 and 3, in SHAT 1H/1397/8.

[6] J. J. de Bresson, "Extrait du rélève des décision du Conseil des Affaires algériennes du 23 mai 1962: Rapatriés Musulmans" (28 May 1962), 1, in MAE 39.

or too young" as well as "single women" should not be transported. Such people, he remarked, "are destined effectively either to live off public charity or, with the young women, to turn to prostitution; all will become deadweights."[7] At the cabinet level, the shift in terms was more subtle—and easier to interpret. The secretary of state for repatriates' April report to the government referred to "Muslims" only as "auxiliaries"—harkis, whom the army would be in charge of dealing with. The May report referred to two distinct categories, "repatriates of European origin [souche]" and "repatriates of Muslim origin [origine]." With these categories, the government abandoned previous references that that tied identity to territory (Algeria), and instead identified people from Algeria on the basis of descent, or ethnicity.[8]

Still referred to in May 1962 as "Muslim repatriates," French citizens with Koranic civil status were increasingly referred to as "harkis" or "refugees," a shift that stripped them of the terms "repatriate" and "citizen." This was inextricably linked with another shift, in which "Muslim" was no longer an adjective for "French," or even for "civil status," but an "origin" [origine]. If the April report to the cabinet noted regarding "Muslim families whose head served in the French Army in Algeria" that their "lack of preparedness for metropolitan life poses special problems," the May report adopted a new tone and recommended a new approach: "As these Muslims are not prepared for European life, it would be inopportune to give them the aid reserved for repatriates as individuals."[9] De Gaulle pretended on 25 July that "the term 'repatriates' obviously does not apply to the Muslims. In their case, we are dealing only with refugees." His statement disregarded the Evian Accords and the definition of "repatriate," both of which had the force of (French) law. This disdain for legal definition was in marked contrast to the pointillist precision with which the president of the Republic, citing French and international law, asserted French sovereignty over Algeria up to and including 3 July, the date of the decree by which France recognized Algerian independence.[10] French officials already had affirmed that refugees were not repatriates. In the first weeks of mass departures for the metropole, government officials had embraced a distinction between repatriates and what de Gaulle's chief of staff characterized as "temporary refugees." This euphemism allowed officials to maintain that most French people fleeing to the

---

[7] Bureau du moral, Commandement Superieur des Forces en Algérie, "Recasement des supplétifs et civils FSNA menaces" (SP 87.000, 26 May 1962), 2, in SHAT 1H/1260/2.

[8] Secrétariat d'Etat aux rapatriés, "Comité des Affaires algériennes du 28 avril 1962: Accueil des rapatriés," 6, in MAE 39; Secrétariat d'Etat aux rapatriés, "Objet: Personnes rentrant d'Algérie," 5–6, in MAE 39.

[9] Secrétariat d'Etat aux rapatriés, "Comité des Affaires algériennes du 28 avril 1962," 6, in MAE 39; Secrétariat d'Etat aux rapatriés, "Objet: Personnes rentrant d'Algérie," 5–6, in MAE 39.

[10] Maurice Faivre, Les combattants musulmans de la guerre d'Algérie: Des soldats sacrifiés (Paris, 1995), 197.

metropole—"Europeans"—soon would return to Algeria. With the government now recognizing the exodus as a regrettable but durable fact, officials applied the term "refugees," with all its implications, almost exclusively to "Muslims."[11] At the beginning of 1963, the professor of medicine Robert de Vernejoul published *Study of the Problems Posed by the Repatriation of Refugees from Algeria.* The Economic and Social Council, one of the new representative institutions the 1958 Constitution had established, submitted it to the parliament and the government. Apart from "French repatriates who return to their fatherland," the official report stated, "there are Muslim 'refugees.'" The report clearly affirmed a distinction: "These non-French Muslims . . . are not repatriates in the true sense of the term." Instead, "they are refugees." De Vernejoul ignored their citizenship and pointed to their "choice in the last several years to side with France" to explain why they "have the right to the same benefits, to the same integrative measures," as repatriates. De Vernejoul followed de Gaulle, effacing law and history as well as the rights of harkis.[12]

Shifting Algerian "Muslims" out of the category of repatriates and into the category of refugees had serious effects. The most dramatic concerned the thousands of actual or suspected harkis who, abandoned by the French, were killed in Algeria during these months. Whether killed by armed units associated with the ALN or the FLN or as the result of local settlings of scores, Algerians claiming to punish traitors to the nation assassinated, using often inhumane measures, other Algerians accused of collaborating with the French. When, in September 1962, Prime Minister Pompidou gave instructions to the minister of the armies to "guarantee the transfer to France of former auxiliaries currently in Algeria who have sought protection from French forces," he made it clear that they were not French. They were "under threat of reprisal from their compatriots."[13] Pompidou's directive was grounded in humanitarian concern for human beings, not in fraternity or national solidarity for French nationals. A "personal note" in late October from the high commander of French armed forces in Algeria to all French generals in Algeria reinforced this point and made clear the limits this placed on humanitarian concern. Despite previous reminders, he observed, "the number of Muslims housed in our camps in Algeria grows steadily." It was thus necessary "as of now to suspend all new admission to our centers." In November 1962, official documents and the newspaper *Le Monde* estimated that over ten thousand Algerians had been killed for being harkis since the cease-fire. Although it remains difficult to ascertain verifiable numbers for

---

[11] J. J. de Bresson, "Extrait du rélève des decisions . . ." (28 May 1962), 1, in MAE 39.

[12] Robert de Vernejoul, *Etude des problèmes posés par le rapatriement des réfugiés d'Algérie: Rapport présenté au nom du Conseil economique et social* (Paris, 1963). The report repeated what legislators had noted about "repatriate status" excluding people from Algeria (see chapter 5). Here, though, the problem only concerned "Muslims."

[13] Prime Minister Georges Pompidou, "Note pour M. le Ministre des Armeés. Objet—Transfert en France d'anciens supplétifs menacés" (Paris, 19 September 1962), in SHAT 1H/1397/8.

these killings, estimates range from that figure to close to 100,000. Many who died, and others who did not, were subjected to various forms of torture.[14]

Those who made it to the metropole experienced other effects of being refugees in their own country. By early 1963, the head of the SAM could insist that "Muslim Algerian refugees in the metropole who have chosen French nationality cannot, ipso facto, be considered refugees." According to Circular 63–03 AGA.AS of 2 January 1963, they could benefit from refugee status only if they could "prove that they left their country of origin because in danger or for political reasons." While those whose "departure [*répli*] was arranged by the army automatically have this status," all others were required to establish a dossier, which would be examined by Technical Assistance Section counselors.[15] General Maurice Faivre (ret.), historian of the Algerian War and of the harkis, highlights how government leaders and officials stymied the efforts of numerous French officers to help harkis escape possible reprisals in Algeria. The most scandalous, and most well known, was Minister of State Louis Joxe's 12 May telegram to military authorities, marked "Top Secret Highest Priority," which laid out a new principle under which "all auxiliaries landing in the metropole outside of the official repatriation program will be sent back." Although the contents were quickly revealed by a number of press sources (*Combat, La Nation Française,* and *L'Esprit Public*) that were aghast at Joxe's proposal, the government persisted in its efforts to prevent "Muslim" Algerians from fleeing Algeria. Faivre pays little attention, however, to extensive documentary evidence of high-level military responsibility for these decisions. Military intelligence reports, for example, consistently downplayed the threats harkis confronted in Algeria and the military leadership shared basic assumptions about the dubious assimilability of "Muslims" with the government whose instructions they followed.[16]

It was officers and officials in the field who continued to take seriously French promises of equality to the "autochtones." This was particularly true of officers involved in "integrationist" programs or commanders of units made up of harkis in Algeria. Military officers repeatedly invoked the question of guarantees for their FSNA subordinates. In January, one report even argued that harkis "were more interested in how the new status recognizes that they are French than in the material improvements it promises them."[17]

---

[14] For estimates of the numbers of Algerians accused of being pro-French who were killed in the months following the cease-fire, see Guy Pervillé, *Pour une histoire de la guerre d'Algérie* (Paris, 2002), 243–44.

[15] G. Lamassoure, chef du Service des Affaires musulmanes, "à M. le Préfet de l'Isère. Objet: Anciens supplétifs et réfugiés musulmans" (26 February 1963), 1, in AN F/1a/5125.

[16] Louis Joxe, "à Haut Commisaire de la Republique en Algérie" (12 May 1962), in SHAT 1H/1260/2.

[17] Lt.-Colonel Barthelemy, "Bulletin hebdomadaire de renseignement psychologique. Semaine 27/12/61–2/1/62" (Algiers, 4 January 1962), 6, in SHAT 1H/2549/2.

These on-the-ground operatives struggled against the assumptions of higher-ups in Paris who ignored earlier French claims that all Algerians would remain French. Previously, in Algeria as elsewhere in the French overseas empire, it had usually been Paris-based officials that had held on to republican ideals despite local difficulties, whereas officers in the colonies had shown, at best, lip service to republican and universalist claims (often in the name of defending "indigenous" cultures and practices).[18]

When confronted with the exodus of "Muslims" to the metropole the government did not in fact treat them as French citizens with rights; the harkis were classed as outsiders whom the French Republic welcomed and assisted only out of charity and only in unavoidable circumstances. Defining them as a group rather than as individuals legitimated this shift. Summarizing the difference between their activities in 1958 and in 1963, SAM officials identified "320,000 legally French citizens" before Algerian independence; afterward, they were dealing with "a group of 480,000 foreigners."[19] The definition of the harkis as a group placed them outside the nation. Their fellow French citizens from Algeria, "repatriates of European origin [souche]," were able to avoid this fate. With "Muslims" moved into their own category, references to "Europeans" disappeared from official documents, replaced by references to a geographic origin (from North Africa) or, more usually, simply to the legally defined status "repatriates." The nation offered "repatriates from North Africa" its solidarity, as the discussions preparing the Boulin Law had announced. "Europeans," although part of a group (repatriates) that the government recognized in order to facilitate national solidarity, were above all French individuals. This was the type of solidarity that all French citizens could expect from the nation, rather than any form of special privileges given to a specified group. The model that "exceptional promotion" had offered was nowhere present. The post-1956 policy of integration had challenged that fundamental precept of republican thought, the rejection of "corporations," "subnational groupings," "particularism," or of any intermediate organization between the citizen and the nation. In the exodus, virtually all policies and practices linked to integration disappeared, swept away by executive fiat in the summer of 1962. Indeed, the government revised policies of exceptional promotion to include all French citizens from Algeria who were in the metropole. The new goal of reserving quotas for government hiring was to help French people in distress, rather than to redress the effects of discrimination. Later, government efforts to assist the pieds noirs were presented as having national implications, not as directed at any "subnational group." As Minister of Repatriates François Missoffe stated in May 1963, addressing himself to "pieds noirs": "The future of

---

[18] On this phenomenon, see, e.g., Alice Conklin, A "Mission to Civilize": The Republican Idea of Empire in France and West Africa, 1895–1930 (Stanford, 1997).

[19] Service des Affaires musulmanes, "Bilan des réalisations . . ." (28 November 1963), 1, in AN F/1a/5055.

other French people is in your hands. If you make good use of the grants, contracts, the exceptional institutions put in place especially for you, perhaps they will become permanent. Perhaps other people in need will be able to use them." His "wish" appeared in a newsletter that would be distributed to the "repatriates," in which each page was imprinted with images of black feet.[20]

In the midst of the exodus, contrary to the Evian Accords, the law, and government directives, only a few people insisted that France offer the harkis the same treatment as other repatriates. Harkis themselves did so with all the very limited means at their disposal. Numerous harkis signed individual copies of one form letter, with blanks for addresses and names of the signer, all addressed to M. le Colonel Commandant of the Bougie District, to "request my pullback and that of my family to the metropole." The appeal "to benefit from the advantages of repatriate assistance, in conformity with the applicable texts," was motivated "by the fact that I categorically refuse to stay in an Algerian Algeria. . . . I am French and want to remain French with my family."[21] Some state officials vigorously asserted that "Muslims" should be welcomed in the metropole. All affirmed that the potential repatriates in question were fully French. Military officers sent numerous messages seeking the reinstallation of individuals or groups of FSNA in the Hexagon. These letters exhaustively detailed the personal qualities of these "French Muslims" and the services they had rendered to the nation. The officers' letters stressed their assimilability to metropolitan life, most putting special emphasis on the applicant's fitness for work.[22] A battalion leader who sought the reinstallation in France of "a number of civilian families who are irremediably compromised with the armed forces in Algeria" asserted that the women and children "speak French and are physically and morally apt to settle in the metropole." Further, "their employment will cause no serious problems, as they will be immediately usable as maids. All [of the women]," he reiterated, "are highly moral."[23] Some officers tried to prove the true Frenchness of the individuals concerned. Battalion leader Roger wrote, in reference to "Mlle. Hamzaoui, Ratiba, social worker," that "through constant contact with Security Forces, she has acquired a life-style similar to a Frenchwoman *de souche* [of origin]."[24] Neither personal testimony nor "expert" certification guaranteed that either the harka in Ouadali or Ratiba

---

[20] Ministre des rapatriés François Missoffe, "Editorial: Votre exemple," *Bulletin special edité par la Ministre des rapatriés pour la campagne printemps 1963 "Priorité d'emploi aux rapatriés"* 4 (7 May 1963), 1, in SHAT 1H/1130/3.

[21] (Ouadali, 14 May 1962), in SHAT 1H/1260/3.

[22] See documents in SHAT 1H/1260/D3 folder "Récasement en France des FSNA menacées."

[23] Battalion Chief Troyes, "Objet: Récasement en France de militaires, de supplétifs, de civils FSNA et de leurs familles" (SP 86.292, 11 May 1962), in SHAT 1H/1260/3.

[24] Battalion Chief Roger, "Rapport sur les services rendus par Mlle. Hamzaoui, Ratiba, assistante sociale" (SP 86.900, 10 May 1962), in SHAT 1H/1260/3.

Hamzaoui, despite their French citizenship, would be given passage or authorized to go to the metropole. In both instances, as was generally the case, no investigation was made. No evidence in their folders remains that would indicate that they were being manipulated by an army officer. Yet the official presumption was that they were not French.

Charles de Gaulle left no doubt as to his own conception of what should be done, signing on 21 June 1962 a document concerning "the nationality problem." The note deployed terms without juridical value to assert that the people concerned were "Algerians of European origins" and "Muslim" Algerians. The document is striking because it employed terms so rarely used by French officials, terms that explicitly embraced group identities with no reference to territory or legal definitions in assigning national membership. It is noteworthy how he stripped both the military term "FSE" and the legally meaningful term "FMA" of their "French" anchor. While de Gaulle affirmed that the former should have their French nationality as before, for the latter, each individual should be required to file an application.[25] It was left to Christian Fouchet, high commissioner in Algeria, to remind the government that "the nationality question is strictly the domain of the law." Thus, he explained, "it does not seem possible, however desirable, to have a very general text that would give total liberty of interpretation to the administration."[26]

With the Ordinance of 21 July 1962, de Gaulle's government unilaterally altered one of the primary elements of the Evian Accord: the right of all people from Algeria to keep French citizenship. This "right" had been central to governmental explanations of the accords in the 8 April referendum campaign, which had wholly rejected opponents' criticisms of the "double nationality" measures. An 8 June 1962 draft of what would become the Ordinance of 21 July 1962 affirmed that

> French citizens with common law civil status living in Algeria on the date of the official announcement of the vote for self-determination will keep French nationality even if, at the close of the three-year period posited by the General Declaration of 19 March 1962 (Ch. II, art. II/2), they acquire Algerian nationality.

The opposite was done for French with local civil status, whose access to French citizenship was heavily restricted and dependent on the government's discretion. They could keep their French nationality only if they submitted "a declaration accepted by the judge responsible for the area where they live

[25] Signed: Charles de Gaulle, "Séance du jeudi 21 juin 1962. Rélève des décisions" (21 June 1962), 6, in MAE 40.
[26] Service des Affaires politiques, "Note pour le Ministre a/s Comité des Affaires algériennes du 21 juin" (21 June 1962), 2–3, in MAE 40. This note summarizes Christian Fouchet, haut commissaire de la République en Algérie, "Traduction du message chiffré n. 7859/51. Objet: Prochain Comité des Affaires algériennes–Questions de nationalité" (19 June 1962), 1–2, in MAE 117. Emphasis added.

in the territory of the French Republic." Not only did French citizens with local civil status have to claim a nationality they already possessed and do so while living outside of Algeria (and on French territory): (1) They would lose their nationality if this declaration was not accepted by a judge and then registered with the Ministry of Public Health and the Population by 1 January 1963; (2) the ministry had the right to refuse to register the declaration or, for a period of three years, to reject the declaration for "reasons of unworthiness." What these reasons might be remained vague, but they ranged from suspected or known nationalist activity to "moral" or personal character flaws.[27]

The government acted as if it was now clarifying uncertainties about "double nationality" that concerned all people from Algeria. In fact, the government moved to exclude Algerian "Muslims," not from the complicated situation of "double nationality" but quite simply from their right to hold on to their French nationality. On 19 June, High Commissioner for the Republic in Algeria Christian Fouchet expressed strong reservations about elements of this project, while at the same time confirming that "double nationality" for non-Europeans should be facultative and not a right. He urged that the ordinance be "brief and supple enough to respond to a situation in which numerous elements have not yet become clear."[28] According to the juridical counsel for the newly named French ambassador to Algeria, Article 2 of Ordinance 62–825 of 21 July 1962 meant that all "Algerians with local civil status . . . lost at the very least the use of this nationality as of the day Algeria became independent."[29]

Of course, the government wanted many "Muslims" who were in the metropole to stay, in order to provide needed labor, but only as Algerian citizens, not as French citizens. If not all could be sent back, the head of SAM urged that of "Algerian Muslims residing in France wishing to be recognized as French nationals," the government should exclude "the undeserving and all morally or physically retarded people who, later, will need to be gotten rid of." Immediate attention should be given, as "the prefects request, to sending back to Algeria any undesirables."[30] The late 1962 report empha-

---

[27] "Le President de la Republique sur le rapport . . . Ordonne" (Paris, 8 June 1962), 1–2, in MAE 117.

[28] Christian Fouchet (19 June 1962), 1–2, in MAE 117. The government excluded one group of Algerians with local civil status from the restrictions and the rigmarole to which it subjected all the others: civil servants. Like all functionaries from Algeria, the state dealt with "Muslim" civil servants not as repatriates (or refugees) but under a system specific to state employees. Despite this exception, functionary status was not perceived as transforming or fundamentally changing the racially charged identity of "Muslim Algerian." The government emphasized this by excluding retired functionaries from the exceptional system. See AN F/1cII/517, esp. Henri Le Corno, "Réponse à la lettre du Préfet de Seine-et-Marne" (2 April 1963), 1, in AN F/1cII/517.

[29] A. Bacquet, "A/S Acquisition de la nationalité française par un citoyen Algérien de statut civil local" (Rocher Noir, 29 September 1962), in SHAT 1H/1260/D3.

[30] Michel Lamassoure, chef du Service des Affaires musulmanes et de l'Action sociale, "Ob-

sized that the French "man in the street would welcome with relief the return of Algerians to their country, and he does not hide his surprise that new immigrants are arriving." Government moves to withhold from all "Muslims" their rights as French citizens—moves that left thousands to die often horrifying deaths in Algeria—were made not for legal or bureaucratic reasons, but in the name of common sense.[31]

Shifts in government terminology, which excluded all "Algerian Muslims" from French citizenship, aligned bureaucratic rules with the assumptions about people from Algeria that now dominated popular metropolitan discussions. This happened when the Hexagon finally began to confront the exodus: it saw not one flight from Algeria, but two. The media, to take one crucial vector of nongovernmental opinion, offered "Muslims" a welcome very different from other—that is, European—"families from North Africa." In *Paris-Match,* and this was true throughout the mainstream press, "Muslims" appeared, above all, as exotic additions to the exodus. One report describes "five families of harkis" arriving just as the boat is about to leave, "with haggard eyes, some twenty men, women and children" whom an "ex-officer had gone to find in their village in Kabylie, to get them away from reprisals."[32] Among many on the French left, there was concern that the harkis were the Trojan horse by which the OAS now threatened the metropole. An editorial, "Return of the Harkis," in *France-Observateur* primarily emphasized the role the "Muslim" arrivals might play in "reconstituting the OAS in certain regions." The article detailed what the government could do to restrict and monitor the arrivals of harkis and "reported" on numerous clandestine landings of harkis. While another editorial in the same issue, "Exodus to Marseilles," described "those who are leaving Algeria as acting 'despite the OAS' and 'in fear of the OAS,'" *France-Observateur*'s discussion of the harkis cautioned that "as normal as it is that France should shelter and protect the lives of the French Army's Muslim soldiers who consider themselves menaced by the FLN, it would be dangerous to allow the return to the metropole of veritable Muslim commandos of the OAS."[33] In late June, the Communist Party, the new left political party the Unified Socialist Party, and the Communist-aligned labor union, the Confédération Générale du Travail (CGT), protested against the favorable reception given to the harkis, comparing the conditions they encountered with what FLN

---

jet: Réunion des conseillers techniques pour les Affaires musulmanes" (20 November 1962), 4, in CAC/AN 770346/10.

[31] Service des Affaires musulmanes, "Synthèse des rapports trimestriels . . . —1ére trimestre (1/1–31/3/62)," 34–35, in AN F/1a/5014. According to SAM statistics, the months after the announcement of the Evian Accords witnessed a new tendency for more "French Muslims" to leave the metropole for Algeria than vice versa. By September, this had ended: once again more "Algerians" or Algerian "Muslims" were coming to the metropole than were leaving.

[32] Dominique Lapierre and Maurice Jarnoux, "Avec les passagers d'un nouvel exode," *Paris-Match* 686 (2 June 1962), 109.

[33] Editorial, "Points de repère. 'Retour des harkis' and 'Exode vers Marseille'," *France-Observateur* 629 (24 May 1962), 3.

prisoners were forced to endure. The PCF called as well for public vigilance against all the repatriates from Algeria, who risked becoming "a reservoir of fascism."[34] The government, unlike the press or left-wing politicians, was far more worried about activist infiltration among "French of European origin repatriates" than among harkis. But, despite significant concern about how to detect OAS operatives, at no point during the exodus did any official suggest that the government intervene to prevent non-"Muslims" from fleeing to the metropole. Agencies instead agreed on various intelligence-sharing and surveillance measures to stop such potential infiltrators. This concern eventually led to the reestablishment of the legal obligation of all French citizens to possess and carry a national identity card. Without debate, via the exceptional powers the Law of 13 April authorized, de Gaulle's government again made obligatory a responsibility that had been abandoned after the return of republican rule in 1944.[35]

If the government was most concerned about the infiltration of the OAS and its potential "European" supporters into the metropole, it chose to act aggressively to exclude "Muslim" Algerians, in particular the harkis. Rather than security concerns, or any kind of explicit embrace of the ideological terms of left-wing rejection of harkis as "collaborators" and OAS "storm troopers," de Gaulle's government affirmed a racialized exclusion. While government officials and the mass media struggled to convince the metropolitan public that the pieds noirs were really French and not Algerian, and that they were not all "fascists," they concurrently denied any right to French identity for Muslim French citizens from Algeria. The image of the isolated, unrooted, and violent harki man displaced descriptions of harki families seeking refuge. Policymakers, for example, began to focus on the former. Amelia Lyons shows that throughout the 1950s civil servants and academics in France grappled with the growing number of Algerian "Muslim" families that were settling in the metropole. She argues that 1962 saw a development that had lasting effects: "Algerian families became so invisible that [subsequently] social welfare administrators and the general public commonly denied their existence in France." This decision to focus on the harkis primarily as men was in stark contrast to the way the government addressed the "European" exodus. Such gendered definitions directly affected the process in which popular presumptions about the foreignness of all "Muslim" Algerians began to take legal form, in the shift in which harkis were no longer "repatriating citizens" but a group of refugees.[36]

If, in this context, most French people were willing to ignore the citizen-

[34] Direction centrale des RG, "Sommaire générale" (Paris, 27 June 1962), 1, in CAC/AN 800280, article 218.

[35] Direction de la Réglementation, Ministère de l'Intérieur, "Note pour M. le Ministre. Objet: Identification des Français de souche européenne rapatriés d'Algérie" (4 May 1962), 2, in CAC/AN 920172/09.

[36] Amelia Lyons, "Algerian Families and the French Welfare State in the Era of Decolonization, 1947–1974," PhD diss., University of California—Irvine, 2004, 286.

ship of the harkis and downplay French responsibility to them, significant
numbers of French officials—at the local level and in Paris, elected and not—
did express concern about the implications of the Decree of 21 July for what
one termed "Algerians having chosen to remain French." These concerns reinforce the reality of the French identity in question, reminding us of the importance of juridical definitions of citizenship; they also help graph the
contours of the denial of that identity that the end of French Algeria produced. The government spurned the rare bureaucratic efforts that proposed
to deal with arriving harkis as rights-bearing individuals. The Ministry for
Repatriates, for example, proposed establishing a workers hostel in Paris reserved for "Muslim repatriates." The letter spoke of "isolated Muslims arriving in Paris . . . civilians who have the right to the status of 'repatriate.'"
When an Interior Ministry official rejected the idea, he referred to "Muslims
who remained loyal to France" and compared them, not to other French people from Algeria, but to other (foreign) "migrants."[37] As the deadline for fil-
ing "declarations of nationality" approached and officials prepared to
exclude a group of some eight million people from French citizenship, the
secretary of state for Algerian affairs wrote to the minister of the interior. He
expressed his concern that "we risk taking the right to vote away from citizens who, according to the ordinance, were guaranteed that they could keep
the French nationality that they already possessed." Like the numerous prefects and mayors who wrote to Paris, he invoked not just French obligations
but the sensibilities of the harkis.[38] The secretary of state was more explicit
than most in pinpointing the racially charged character of the exclusion. He
warned the Ministry of the Interior that "no criteria exist that would allow
the authorities in charge of revising electoral lists to distinguish with certainty those Muslims with local status who were able to obtain French status from the others." The complication was purely juridical: "*A contrario,*
the only valid proof effectively results from the individual in question's incapacity to prove that he is governed by common law." The secretary of
state's approach was less subtle: he urged Interior "to not begin an automatic
exclusion [from the electoral lists] that would concern all electors who have
a name that sounds Algerian." Instead, he proposed an approach that at once
blatantly revealed the racial nature of the procedure and tried to bend it to
republican legality: "It would be better, it seems to me, to instruct those in
charge of voting stations to deny, when the case arises, access to the booth
to electors of Algerian origin [*souche*] who cannot prove that they have

[37] M. Peronu, "Lettre à M. le Ministre de l'Intérieur" (18 October 1962), 2, in AN F/1a/
5013; C. Ernst, "Lettre à M. le Ministre délégué . . . chargé des rapatriés . . ." (29 November
1962), in AN F/1a/5013. For the effects of Ordinance 62–825 on the Civil Service, see Marceau
Long, "FP/1 n. 003768. Objet: Application de l'ordonnance n. 62–611 du 30 mai 1962" (Paris,
23 August 1962), in CAC/AN 19770007, articles 210 and 212.
[38] Secrétaire d'Etat auprès du premier ministre, chargé des Affaires algériennes, "Inscription
et radiation" (12 January 1963), 1, in AN F/icII/517.

French nationality." In his system, that is, those who looked Algerian would only be dubiously—and not necessarily "un"—French.[39]

Concern about hurting the patriotic feelings or amour propre of harkis was not one of the primary elements shaping government policy. By 1964, government legal experts affirmed that it was the combination of submitting a declaration and official acceptance of that declaration that determined the French nationality and citizenship of harkis. It was a result of the government's generosity, not the fact that they previously held French nationality and citizenship. This decision broke with earlier interpretations, which presented the accepted declaration as confirmation of the "maintenance of French nationality."[40] After the exodus began no one accepted that having citizenship was sufficient grounds for "Muslims" from Algeria to keep it. De Vernejoul's report of January 1963 emphasized that it was "unthinkable to make things difficult for those who had fought under our colors," but the report presented this goal in tandem with excluding "people who took up arms against us or participated in terrorist activities." With Algerian "Muslims," excluding the "bad" was, at best, as important as admitting the "good," and often more so.[41] This bureaucratic gesture—the affirmation that the harkis or FMAs had French nationality, and thus citizenship, only as a result of official acceptance of their declaration—swept away not only integration but the entire history of French Algeria and the "failed" assimilation of "Muslims."[42] Government policy emerged as a series of experts and jurists interpreted texts and then interpreted their implications. Without any public debate, or even a single sweeping decision, the French citizenship of Algerian "Muslims" came to seem nonsensical. Distinct from the French, "not prepared for European life," they now appeared virtually inassimilable. Just months before, their membership in the nation still had seemed reasonable, at least to some.[43]

Government officials, in particular those in the SAM, had at first conceived the "regrouping" of harkis as a temporary measure, destined, as one note in the summer of 1962 described, "above all to offer them physical and moral comfort while their repatriate dossier is put together and their reclassification studied." Still working from the assumptions of "integration," SAM assessments of the harkis foregrounded the need to make the latter

[39] Ibid. On later interpretations that insisted that the declaration of nationality itself made the "Muslim" Algerians French, see, for example, CAC/AN 950236/09.

[40] See the September 28, 1962 letter from Marceau Long, secretary of state attached to the prime minister in charge of the Civil Service, "FP/1 n. 4330, à M. Messaoud Djeghloul, attaché de préfecture, Poitiers (Vienne)," in CAC/AN 19770007, article 210.

[41] de Vernejoul, *Etude des problèmes posés par le rapatriement des réfugiés*, 119.

[42] Henri Le Corno, "Application de l'ordonnance n. 62–825 du 21 juillet 1962 . . ." (4 February 1963), 2; and, in response, Bernard Lory, Ministère de la Santé publique, "Réponse à . . ." (18 February 1962), 1, both letters in AN F/1cII/517.

[43] Commission de coordination pour la réinstallation des Français d'Outre-Mer, Commissariat général du Plan, "Rapport général du 5 decembre 1962" (5 December 1962), 14, in CAC/AN 80 AJ/254 [[930275/94].

"feel like free men." This reflected a significant body of official opinion that maintained assimilationist or integrationist assumptions. A December 1962 report for the General Commission for the Plan posited, referring to "repatriated French Muslims," that for the "young" a "near total assimilation is possible."[44] Such reports presented possibilities for assimilation, first and foremost, as based on material conditions—housing and employment—and not "moral" conditions. Describing the harkis as "much more primitive than [Algerians] who normally settle in France," the SAM reports still made clear that their "integration into metropolitan life" could be achieved. The SAM and the Economic and Social Council persisted until early 1963 in asserting that, as the latter's official report stated, "the harkis and their sons, when they reestablish a normal life here, can integrate perfectly into the French national community."[45] On the copy stored at the Bibliothèque nationale in Paris, two vertical lines and a question mark score this passage. The frequency of such written interrogations next to similar assertions suggests more than one unfriendly reader: they indicate that "integration" no longer made sense for the harkis. Historians, harkis themselves, and their sons and daughters have only begun to recount the isolation, poverty, and misery to which their fellow citizens subjected them. The status of harkis as a group— and what would become their long-term exile in the supposedly temporary camps in abandoned corners of the provincial "French desert" where they were placed—came to seem normal, natural, as they were considered no longer citizens but refugees. By insisting during the exodus that all French citizens with Koranic civil status prove their suitability to have French citizenship, the Republic institutionalized what had been an uncodified, if widely held suspicion: "Muslims" were so different from the French that only exceptional individuals (and their families) could be assimilated into the nation.[46]

The Mozabite Jews

To grasp how being "Muslim" seemingly became incompatible with French nationality, it is useful to look at the ways that government officials claimed

[44] Commission de coordination pour la réinstallation des Français d'Outre-Mer, Commissariat général du Plan, "Projet d'avis sur le rapport général du 5 decembre 1962" (14 December 1962), 7, in CAC/AN 80 AJ/254.

[45] SAM, "Synthèse des rapports trimestriels établis par les conseillers techniques pour les Affaires musulmanes—4ème trimestre 1/10–31/12/62," 41, in AN F/1a/5014.

[46] SAM, "Synthèse des rapports trimestriels établis . . . —3ème trimestre 1/7–30/9/62," 25, in AN F/1a/5014. On the metropolitan welcome of the harkis, see Abderahmen Moumen, *Les Français musulmans en Vaucluse: Installation et difficultés d'intégration d'une communauté de rapatriés d'Algérie, 1962–1991* (Paris, 2003); Mohand Hammoumou, *Et ils sont devenus harkis* (Paris, 1994); and Mohand Hammoumou, with the collaboration of Abderahmen Moumen, "L'histoire des harkis et Français musulmans: La fin d'un tabou?" in *La guerre d'Algérie, 1954– 2004: La fin de l'amnésie*, ed. Mohammed Harbi and Benjamin Stora (Paris, 2004), 317–44.

another group from Algeria as French in these months. In 1961, by extending "French civil status" to the several thousand French Algerians "with Mosaic civil status" the government completed the assimilation of Algerian Jews last engaged by the Crémieux Decree (and its reestablishment, along with "republican legality," in 1943). This mass "naturalization" clearly revealed a key role played by the newly undeniable Frenchness of Algerian Jews: naturalizing the emerging boundary between French national identity and Algerian "Muslims."[47] At the war's close, while almost all Algerian "Muslims" were denied the right to make claims on France, the French Republic welcomed this long isolated group of Algerian Jews as fellow French people, even though their "way of life and morality"—which included polygamy— showed no sign of being easily assimilable. To be Jewish, to quote a pre-Evian secret document, was a "religion," compatible with French citizenship, while to be "Muslim" was "a nationality," thus necessarily foreign. It is worth recalling that this new alignment was in no way foreordained. From the late nineteenth century until World War II, anti-Semites regularly asserted that Algerian "Muslims" were more "truly French" than Jews.[48]

The indigenous (non-Sephardic) Jews of the M'zab, a territory the French conquered in 1852 but did not put under French law until 1882, had been the only French subjects to enjoy "Mosaic civil status" since 1870. In the process of replacing their "local civil status" with "French civil status," the Fifth Republic applied none of the restrictions—beyond the abandonment of their "privileges" in the metropole or governance by "Mosaic civil status" in Algeria—that post-revolutionary French authorities had placed on the assimilation of other Jews. Further, when these Algerians—who were ruled by *caïds* (traditional leaders), and dressed in "traditional costumes"—arrived in the metropole during the exodus with no proof that they benefited from "French civil status," extraordinary efforts were made to affirm that they were French.[49]

Several thousand inhabitants of the M'zab, most of them grouped in the communes of Ghardaïa, Laghouat, Ouargla, and Touggourt, had maintained what French officials called interchangeably either "Mosaic" or "Israelite" civil status. This resulted from the late date when French laws were extended to the area. When, in 1882, all Mozabites were placed under French law for

[47] See Patrick Weil, *Qu'est-ce qu'un Français? Histoire de la nationalité française depuis la Révolution* (Paris, 2002), 227–29.

[48] See Richard C. Vinen, "The End of an Ideology? Right-wing Antisemitism in France, 1944–70," *Historical Journal* 37, no. 2 (1994): 365–88, 380; and Daniel Leconte, *Les pieds noirs: Histoire et portrait d'une communauté* (Paris, 1978), 208. Judith R. Walkowitz has noted parallel claims that certain of Britain's South Asian colonial subjects were "more British" than European Jewish immigrants to the United Kingdom. See "The Indian Woman, the Flower Girl, and the Jew: Photojournalism in Edwardian London," *Victorian Studies* 42, no. 1 (Winter 1998–1999): 3–46, 6–7.

[49] Sarah Sussman, "Changing Lands, Changing Identities: The Migration of Algerian Jewry to France, 1954–1967" (PhD diss., Stanford University, 2002), 178–80.

criminal and public matters, Mosaic law for civil status questions reemerged in the administrative space that the Territories of the South made up alongside the Algerian departments. The 1870 Crémieux Decree had ended its role elsewhere in this area. French recognition of the jurisdiction of existing legal regimes over "civil status" allowed this development. No move to replicate the mass assimilation of the Crémieux Decree seems to have been considered, because of growing anti-Semitism in the metropole and, particularly, in Algeria.

After 1947, French authorities repeatedly considered whether to make the Mozabite Jews into French citizens with "common" civil status. In 1953, the first proposal was introduced in the Assembly of the French Union. The French National Assembly in April 1956 discussed a bill similar to the one eventually approved in 1961.[50] The Jewish communities of the M'zab were reluctant to abandon Mosaic civil status, French bureaucrats agreed, because of the "complete liberty," the absence of "any oversight or administrative or judicial sanctions" that local status offered. This was most important in matters concerning women. Not only did Mosaic civil law allow polygamy, it also authorized "repudiation," a man's right to end his marriage by putting his bride out of the home and returning her dowry. Mosaic civil law also excluded women and girls from any inheritance.[51]

In 1961, the "evolution of the situation in Algeria since 1960" was given as the reason that the Mozabite Jews themselves had requested their assimilation, overcoming the resistance of "traditionalist Jews." Law 61–805 of 28 July 1961 transformed these "French citizens of Algerian departments and the Departments of Oasis and of the Sahara [the former Southern Territories, which had become departments in 1958] who have kept their Israelite personal status" into French citizens with "common law civil status." The government's action was extraordinary in that it was the first group assimilation in North Africa since 1870 and the Crémieux Decree. The post-1958 "policy of integration" already had extended full French citizenship to these "Berber Jews." With integrationism's promise to reconcile all Algerians with France no longer tenable, this "naturalization" reproduced assimilationist precedents.

Like 1870, the 1961 entry of Mozabite Jews into common civil status af-

---

[50] Proposition n. 259 of Assemblée de l'Union française séance du 24 juin 1952; 6 April 1956, Legislation 713 6 A3. On the Jews of M'zab, see Régine Goutalier, "La 'nation juive' de Ghardaïa," in Communautés juives des marges sahariennes du Maghreb, ed. Michel Abitbol (Jerusalem, 1980), 115–36.

[51] Charles Kleinknecht, administrateur des Services civils, ancien sous-préfet de Ghardaïa, "Lettre à M. Cotte" (Barr, 17 May 1965), 1–2, in CAC 950236/9 [C/3614]. On polygamy, see Jean Moriaz (former Commissaire de l'état civil des Juifs du M'zab), "Situation des Israélites de M'Zab" (Lyon 29 March 1963); see also M. Meylan, "Précis de la législation coloniale: Les mariages mixtes en Afrique du Nord"; Senateur Abel-Durand, "Rapport . . . rélatif à la constitution de l'état civil des Français des départements algériens . . . qui ont conservé leur statut personnel israélite, et à leur accession au statut civil de droit commun: Annexe au proces-verbal de la séance du 19 juillet 1961," in CAC 950236/9 [C/3614].

firmed republican confidence in the powers of the French state to transform whole groups of people trapped by their particular differences into individual citizens of "universal" France. A Communist deputy in the National Assembly criticized this presumption when, referring to the "Algerian Israelites," he identified both the law under debate and Crémieux as "assimilationist," a policy that now, he argued, was "completely out of date." (This did not mean he supported integration.) Insisting that all Mozabites were Algerians, the deputy opposed the law both as a colonial holdover and as a tactic to bolster French pretensions that the Departments of the Oasis and Sahara were not part of Algeria.[52]

The Fifth Republic returned to assimilationism but ignored some of the key presumptions that underwrote it. The Mozabite population had had less contact with the French administration than their "Muslim" neighbors, the reason that, unlike most of their neighbors, they had not been required to take a family name. Like their neighbors, they were ruled by elders and practiced polygamy.[53] For these reasons alone their assimilation was contrary to the entire rhetoric and history of French assimilation. Like Muslim French citizens from Algeria, the Jews of the M'zab had benefited from the affirmative action–style "exceptional promotion" measures applied in Algeria after 1956. Above all, the Mozabite Jews were assimilated in 1961 because it clarified who was whom in Algeria: it consolidated the emerging divide between Algerians who were "Europeans" (a category that now encompassed Jewish Algerians) and those who were not (and who were thus wholly Algerian).[54]

In 1961, the law made these Mozabites French people without qualification. The hand-corrected drafts of the proposal make this crystal clear, rejecting standardized legal formulations in order to minimize the "Jewish" and "Algerian" aspects of their juridical status and emphasize their Frenchness. The first draft referred to "French Israelites of the departments of Sahara and Algeria who have conserved their personal status." It relied on a ready-made formula that paralleled legislative references to "French Muslims of the departments of Sahara and Algeria who have conserved their personal status." On the page, someone crossed out "Israelite" and moved the qualifier to the end of the phrase: *statut personnel israélite*. The second draft incorporated the suggestion by redoubling the invocation of Jewish identity,

---

[52] Maurice Niles, "Discussion d'un projet de loi: Etat civil des Français israélites . . . ," in *J.O.* (1961), 1564.

[53] Jean Moriaz, "Situation des Israélites de M'Zab" (Lyon 29 March 1963), 1, in CAC 950236/9 [C/3614]. Between 1925 and 1960, the administration extended into the Sahara the regularization of "legal identity" (*état civil*) that the Law of 23 March 1882 had applied to all Algerian "Muslims." These efforts required all "Muslims" in Algeria and the Territories of the South to take a surname, an act that made them eligible for identity cards. As people not governed by Koranic civil law, the Jewish inhabitants of M'zab remained unaffected, more by legislative ignorance and bureaucratic rigor, it seems, than for any particular reason having to do with the law.

[54] CAC 19980260, article 4.

reading "French *Israelites* of the departments of Sahara and Algeria who have conserved their *Mosaic* personal status." After another version, which read "French people . . . who have conserved their *Israelite Mosaic* personal status," the final terminology reaffirmed the importance of the first correction in removing any qualifier to the subject: Français. It placed "Israelite," at the tail end ("Français des départements du Saoura et de l'Algérie qui ont conservé leur statut personnel israélite"), distant from the subject, where conveniently the law could make the distinction between these French citizens and most others disappear.[55]

In May and June 1962, the Mozabite Jews of the southern communes left Algeria for France. In the course of their exodus and that of local French officials all the documents that registered their accession to French civil status were lost. These new arrivals in the metropole had no proof of their "French civil status"; most, to make matters worse, had forgotten their names! Exceptionally, the former French citizens with Mosaic civil status had been allowed to choose not only family names but new first names as well, this despite the protests of the local official charged with applying the law. In early 1963, as part of an administrative effort to assess what should be done, he recounted that many of those affected by the accession to common civil status had sought his assistance, not only to choose family names that sounded French but to rid themselves of first names that "sounded Arab— Youssef, Aïcha, Brahim, Guemra." A list of their new names appeared in the *Journal officiel 1961*. But after the exodus, there was great uncertainty about which names could be supposed to belong to whom. There was no documentary proof of the link between the names of French citizens with French civil status published in the *J.O.* and the individuals and families claiming repatriate status. After failing in their attempts to recover the lost records from local Algerian officials, the French government agreed to rely on the testimony of the former officials who had overseen the initial operation.[56]

In the 1930s, an explicitly anti-Semitic law had demanded that Algerian Jews provide documentary proof that their ancestors were living in the Ottoman territories that became the Algerian departments (an almost impossible task) or risk losing their citizenship. In 1962, France did all it could to recognize the status and rights of its Jewish citizens from the M'zab who came over in the exodus. Not only that: Mozabite Jews who had left Algeria, who sought refuge in Israel, and who now wanted to relocate to France (who like their fellows had no proof of their "French civil status") also benefited from this bureaucratic generosity.[57] The Law of 20 December 1966,

---

[55] Emphasis added. See CAC 950236/9 [C/3614].

[56] See Moriaz, "Situation des Israélites de M'Zab."

[57] Two years later, a similar generosity was extended to several Jewish North Africans who were not French citizens and who did not have French nationality. Writing on behalf of a group of Tunisian and Moroccan Jews, Guy de Rothschild, president of the Fonds social juif unifié, urged that France extend citizenship to people he described as "culturally French, francophone,

which set forth new regulations on the access of people from Algeria to French citizenship, again reaffirmed official insistence that Jewish Algerians were French, whether they had documentary evidence of their citizenship or not. Several mayors and deputies had expressed concern about how this law would affect a number of Jews, most from the M'zab, who had emigrated to Israel and now sought to have their French nationality recognized. Among its measures, the law excluded from French nationality people from Algeria who had obtained any other nationality but French. The 1 March 1967 circular, which detailed how the law was to be applied and directly responded to the elected officials' concerns, pointed to the law's preamble: the reference to "other nationality refers only to Algerian nationality." What was implicit was that Israeli nationality did not count.[58] This recalled other French efforts, in 1961 and 1962, to counter Zionist claims on Jewish French citizens from Algeria at the very moment that they were abandoning efforts to counter Algerian nationalist claims on Muslim French citizens from Algeria.

The Algerian War's reaffirmation that Jews from Algeria were fully French provided crucial support to the pretension that the French Republic shorn of Algeria was the same as that which had included Algeria. French actions guaranteed that all Algerian Jews were French citizens and, in doing so, insisted that assimilation—and, far more important, republican universalism—did not need to be rethought in light of Algeria, its French history, or its revolution. Assimilation still functioned, a belief that plans to assimilate all pieds noirs into the Hexagon reinforced. It no longer made sense for Algerian "Muslims," however. Republican ideology, too, emerged unscathed from France's failure to transform Algerians into French people. What immediately did change, as the next chapter assesses, was the Republic itself, and its relationship to people who remained French. In a series of elections in fall 1962, de Gaulle's allies mobilized understandings of who was French that had crystallized in the exodus: the thorough restructuring of state institutions achieved in the fall depended on popular anxieties about French identity that the events and debates of the spring and summer had pushed to the fore.

---

and profoundly tied to the European community." Accentuating the reliance on assimilationist rhetoric, de Rothschild described his organization's attention to "geographic decentralization" in settling them. Within days, this request was granted. See "Lettre à M. le Ministre de l'Interieur" (Paris, 15 July 1964), 1–2, in CAC 880502/44; and M. Cantan, "Réponse à Guy de Rothschild, President du Fonds social juif unifié" (15 July 1964 and 24 July 1964), in CAC 880502/44.

58 See MJ/FA S54 113 for letters of inquiry and circular.

Chapter 10

The Post-Algerian Republic

On 20 September 1962, President Charles de Gaulle summoned his fellow citizens to the year's second referendum. Confirming a decision taken at the Cabinet meeting of 12 September, the speech came a few weeks after members of the OAS made a spectacular but failed attempt to assassinate him on 22 August 1962. The assassination attempt made as he was passing by the village of Petit-Clamart in his Citroen DS20 left his car riddled with bullets but those on board untouched. In the 28 October 1962 referendum French voters would decide whether to choose by direct universal suffrage all subsequent presidents of the Republic. One somewhat unexpected result of the speech was that French voters returned again to the polls in November 1962, this time to elect a new National Assembly, after the deputies' rejection of his proposal for a referendum led de Gaulle to dissolve the lower house of parliament.

In *Paris-Match*, political gossip columnist Jack Chargelègue explained that according to inside sources de Gaulle "had always had the idea for this reform [direct election]." Delayed by Debré's caution, then by the 14 April 1962 appointment of Georges Pompidou as prime minister, "Petit-Clamart changed everything. The General reacted as a general: act quickly, take risks, assure himself the element of surprise. He figured that the resistance of the political parties [would] be less redoubtable than that of the pieds noirs or the army."[1] The war continued and, once again, the OAS thugs were only

---

[1] Jack Chargelègue, "Ils se sont tous confiés à *Match!*" *Paris-Match* 705 (13 October 1962), 54–57), 56. There are numerous opinions as to when and how de Gaulle came to embrace this reform. For two very different analyses, see Odile Rudelle, "Table ronde sur le thème 'La genèse des institutions'," in *"L'Austerlitz politique" de la Ve République*, ed. Hervé Maurey et al.

the visible tip of a submerged enemy conspiracy. Once exposed, however, that tip allowed de Gaulle to rally the nation, as he had done against the unruly armed forces in Algeria in 1960 and 1961 and against the pieds noirs earlier in 1962. With those threats sidelined, the pro-OAS forces' formerly unremarked "allies"—the "men of the Fourth Republic," the parties, intellectuals, and journalists who opposed de Gaulle's constitutional reform—swung into sight.

As with the campaign for the 8 April referendum that approved the Evian Accords, de Gaulle's allies used the fall campaigns to advance their own political fortunes. To do so, they presented their efforts, once again, as necessary to end the Algerian War and fight the threat of fascism. As in the spring, their anti-OAS message allowed the government to effect dramatic changes in the institutions of the Republic with little debate about what that would mean. Once again, their efforts had unexpected implications that reshaped France: the realignment of government institutions depended on and consolidated recodifications of French national identity that Algeria's decolonization had quickly precipitated.[2] Both fall campaigns, for the referendum and then for the legislature, began with hard-hitting Gaullist accusations that all who opposed the general should be considered objective allies of the OAS. Only by supporting de Gaulle could the still-dangerous activists be beaten. *Paris-Match* warned that the OAS, in Petit-Clamart as they had done before, sought to "eliminate the head of state," but not "because they hope to reverse the flow of decolonization." Rather the OAS activists believed that France would be "handed over to them" in the chaos that followed.[3] De Gaulle himself went first, presenting the reform as the only way to protect the Republic against violent terrorist attack. André Malraux, confidante of the president, opened the government's official media campaign for the legislative election by contrasting Gaullists with those "who did not agree with us on peace in Algeria." The brilliant wordsmith defended what de Gaulle's critics saw as the president's solitary and authoritarian exercise of power by opposing it to the cacophony of voices united only, he argued, by their complicity with the Republic's most ardent adversaries. While they pretended to defend Marianne, he warned, "they could not unite even in the face of the Algiers putsch [of April 1961]."[4]

(Paris, 1988), 67; and Jean-Paul Brunet, *Gaston Monnerville* (Paris, 1997), 217. See also François Goguel, "Les circonstances du referendum d'octobre 1962," in *Le réferendum d'octobre et les élections de novembre 1962*, ed. François Goguel (Paris, 1965), 10.

[2] On the relationship between "techniques of government" and the definition of "population," see Michel Foucault, "Governmentality," in *The Foucault Effect*, ed. G. Burchell et al. (London, 1991), 99–101.

[3] Editorial: "Ce n'est pas la France," *Paris-Match* 699 (1 September 1962), 11.

[4] Author, *Gaulliste historique*, minister of culture, and president of the newly formed Association for the Fifth Republic, which anointed pro-presidential candidates, he acted as the general's avatar, camouflaging "the guide's" abandonment of the role "above the partisan fray" the man of June 18th had always assigned himself. See "Discours radiotélévisé de M. A. Malraux,

Against what, in October and November, was named the "'No' Cartel," those who rallied around President de Gaulle upheld the necessary and evolutionary nature of direct election of the president by universal suffrage. More remarkably, their rhetoric equated those who opposed de Gaulle now and those who had said "No" to the Evian Accords in the spring. They accused their opponents of being in league with the OAS, of collaborating with "fascists" and "terrorists." Only intermittently did they criticize the parties and politicians they tagged the "men of the Fourth Republic" for seeking to return to a past system of governance, one resembling the parliamentary preeminence and weak president of the Third and the Fourth Republics. Although that is how most subsequent analysts describe the campaign, and that is how de Gaulle described them in private, this broad theme fogs the concerted focus of most public Gaullist criticisms. The president's allies portrayed their opponents as rejecting the "tide of History" by opposing the decolonization of Algeria. This message was relayed (in descending order of influence) by government-controlled television and radio, *Paris-Match*, the pro-Gaullist press, and the president's provincial allies.

Gaullists insisted that the Algerian War, in its anti-OAS variant, still threatened the Republic. Gaullists sought to extend the historical context that, since May 1958, had allowed them such success. They spent little time trying to convince people that de Gaulle's vision of how the nation should be governed was superior to previous republics. That was the tactic that de Gaulle had tried after the Liberation with the Rally of the French People political party (1947–53), which had failed. Their fall 1962 strategy did not rely therefore simply on public confidence in the president who had maneuvered France out of the Algerian morass, or on the citizenry's trust in the wisdom of his vision and his political choices.[5] War footing and the popular support it produced, to paraphrase Clausewitz, were necessary means for the Gaullists' political ends. As with the Evian Accords, their reform blatantly disregarded the constitution, French law, and republican precedent and principle. Unlike in the spring, however, the anti-OAS sacred union shattered. Linking autumn opposition to de Gaulle with the OAS allowed government allies to reproduce—with less efficacy—the spring's successful strategy of barely responding to the substance of opposition arguments. This time, how-

---

président de l'Association pour la Ve République au Palais Chaillot, le mardi 30 octobre 1962, à 20h40," in *La campagne électorale (octobre–novembre 1962) discours et débats*, vol. 1, ed. Monica Charlot et al. (Paris, 1963), 1.

[5] De Gaulle's decision to dissolve the National Assembly endangered the state's campaign against OAS criminality. Once the dissolution was published, an Interior Ministry senior official informed Interior Minister Roger Frey that "the obsolescence of the law of 3 April 1955 [Article 4] concerning the state of emergency, the regime under which we operate currently, will result ipso facto." A wide range of exceptional policing powers, then maintained by Ordinance 62–797 of 13 July 1962, would be forbidden by French law as of "zero-hour, 26 October 1962." See Bureau de la Sûreté de l'Etat, sous-direction de la réglementation intérieur, "Objet: Problèmes posés par le maintien de l'ordre public à la suite de la démission du gouvernement" (8 October 1962), 1–2, in CAC 940560/42.

ever, the marginalization of opponents was only relative, whereas that of French Algeria diehards was nearly total. Significantly, the one opponent de Gaulle and his allies most demonized was—following Algeria's independence—the only person of color to hold an important post in the French government, the president of the Senate, Gaston Monnerville.

Rejecting the Fall Referendum

For months before the 20 September announcement, French politicians and commentators, prodded by rumors of de Gaulle's intentions, had sought to circumscribe presidential tampering with the constitution, reciting constitutional text and verse and providing juridical exegesis. By repeatedly raising the hypothesis and asserting what options were (legally) available, they tried to delineate the realm of the (politically) possible. In late spring, *France-Observateur* published an article titled "De Gaulle, Can He Change the Constitution?" by the jurist Georges Vedel. Constitutional revision alone, according to Vedel, could alter, for example, "the mode of electing the president of the Republic." The simple and obvious answer to the title query was yes, but only, Vedel exhaustively demonstrated, with the approval of both National Assembly and Senate. Having proven the unconstitutionality of revising the constitution without legislative approval, he dismissed as juridically untenable "the argument by which the sovereign people, by ratifying the proposal submitted to it, would overcome the unconstitutionality of the procedure. The constitution determines the conditions under which national sovereignty can be exercised."[6] Enumerating a similar list of arguments in 1963, two French political scientists described them as the "clear and uncontested reading of the constitution" in its first four years. "The ambiguity appeared in spring 1962," according to Jean Touchard and Jean-Luc Parodi.[7]

---

[6] While the president of the Republic could submit by referendum ordinary laws and organic laws (those which organized the operation of constituted authorities) "over the heads of parliamentarians" for popular approval, this was not the case for "constitutional questions." The constitution proposed (Title XIV, Article 89) two forms of revision: (1) via a text to be submitted to popular arbitration by referendum; (2) the positive vote for a text of a majority of three-fifths of all deputies and senators summoned to sit, at Versailles, in parliament. To occur, both forms necessitated, first, that majorities in both chambers vote separately and favorably for an identical text. See Georges Vedel, "De Gaulle peut-il modifier la Constitution?" *France-Observateur* 630 (31 May 1962), 8–9.

[7] Ibid.; Jean Touchard et Jean-Luc Parodi, "L'enjeu du référendum du 28 octobre 1962" in *Le référendum d'octobre et les élections de novembre 1962*, ed. François Goguel (Paris, 1965), 39–42. See oral questions with debate by A. Courriere, J. Duclos, F. Mitterrand, G. Petit in the Senate, 17 July, and M. P. Brocas, on 20 July 1962, in the National Assembly. See also Brunet, *Gaston Monnerville*, 217–19. For jurists' interest, see, for example, Bernard Chenot, *Le Conseil constitutionnel, 1958–1985* (Paris, 1985); René Chapus, "Les fondements de l'organisation de l'Etat définis par la Déclaration de 1789 et leurs prolongements dans la jurisprudence du Conseil constitutionnel et du Conseil d'Etat," in *La Déclaration des Droits de l'Homme et du*

When de Gaulle summoned "Frenchmen and Frenchwomen" in September 1962 to approve the constitutional revision he proclaimed to be "the keystone of our new institutions," he invoked the authority granted to him in Article 11. The storm of controversy he raised was immediate, predictable, and energetic.[8] Faced with the government's refusal to consider submitting the referendum proposal to the legislature, the National Assembly, by an overwhelming majority, passed a vote of no confidence. As the constitution ordained, the government was dismissed (although it remained as a caretaker until a new government was named). De Gaulle responded by dissolving the National Assembly. Elections were scheduled for 18 and 25 November 1962.

The outlines of the campaign to approve the referendum already were in place: these included support for de Gaulle, who defined himself on 20 September as the nation's "guide and leader," and opposition to the OAS and its associates. How those who might resist the will of the president would respond was less certain. François Goguel suggests that, at least among parliamentarians, the widespread and vociferous rejection of the proposal "was not, a priori, obvious." The public precautionary debate about legal principles and constitutional theory had been ignored. Yet the same politicians had let pass the equally questionable constitutional maneuvers of the spring. Now, however, politicians invoked the same arguments that they had dismissed as without substance in reference to the 8 April referendum. This led Minister of Information Christian Fouchet to ask television viewers on 9 October, "Why such acceptance yesterday and such indignation today?" and then to insist, "It is because there is no real constitutional problem."[9] In fact, on opinion pages and in public forums the rejection of the presidential proposal was massive and swift. Among legal experts and authorities who publicly commented on the affair, only two law professors, Larue and René Capitant, argued for the legality of the procedure. In a much remarked violation of official secrecy, Le Monde revealed that all but one member of the Council of State had voted on 1 October to condemn the proposed referendum as illegal.[10] An Interior Ministry summary of press coverage preceding the referendum described strong editorial support for a "No" vote. Although the Parisian dailies were more evenly divided, the Office of Elections and Po-

Citoyen et la jurisprudence (Paris, 1989), 182–207; Philippe Ardant, "Le contentieux électoral devant le Conseil constitutionnel et le Conseil d'Etat," in Conseil constitutionnel et Conseil d'Etat: Colloque des 21 et 22 janvier 1988 au Senat (Paris, 1988).

[8] What needs to be explained is why so many subsequent historians have treated the controversy as an aberration. See Rudelle, "Table ronde sur le thème 'La genèse des institutions'"; Pierre Pactet, "Gaston Monnerville et le Conseil constitutionnel," in Le Président Gaston Monnerville, ed. Jacques Augarde et al. (Paris, 1995).

[9] François Goguel, "Les circonstances du référendum d'octobre 1962," in Goguel, Le référendum d'octobre et les élections de novembre 1962, 26. For Senate President Monnerville's argument to approve, see Brunet, Gaston Monnerville, 211. For the text of Fouchet's prime-time speech, see AN F/41/2234.

[10] See Jean-Luc Queyremonne, "Les decisions et les avis du Conseil d'Etat et du Conseil constitutionnel: Enjeu politique," in Conseil constitutionnel et Conseil d'Etat, 399.

litical Studies remarked that "by an overwhelming majority, the provincial press, abandoning its traditional restraint, actively campaigned in favor of the 'No.'"[11] Government-controlled radio and television, however, vigorously supported the "Yes."[12]

It was the partisan opposition that most forcefully fought the proposal. Faced with de Gaulle's defiance of constitutional arguments, opponents struggled to shape compelling arguments and explanations for a "No" vote. Politicians at all levels of the French government and from virtually every non-Gaullist political party came out against the executive's position. The National Assembly's vote of no confidence was joined by one in the Senate, which condemned in form and in principle the proposal by an overwhelming and enthusiastic majority. A Ministry of the Interior report counted motions condemning the referendum in thirty-one departmental general councils.[13] Among political parties, the so-called "No" Cartel—the SFIO, Christian Democrats, Radicals, and Independents—saw the PCF, the Unified Socialist Party, and former RNUR deputies align with them in opposition. In favor of the referendum, members of the Gaullist Union for a New Republic (UNR) and a number of independents—people that a new organization, the Friends of the Fifth Republic, soon anointed as "pro-Gaullist"—rallied behind the president of the Republic and against his "enemies." In a move that threatened (yet failed, in fact, to affect) the Gaullist description of the conflict, populist leader Pierre Poujade and his stridently anti-Gaullist and pro–Algérie française Union of French Forces actively campaigned for the "Yes."[14]

Partisan resistance to de Gaulle's reform quickly gained a spokesman. The government already had placed the Radical Party member and president of the Senate, Gaston Monnerville, under surveillance. Beyond his activities in Paris, the RG had kept the government informed about a series of speeches the senator made before provincial audiences in the aftermath of the Evian vote. Their content was constant, as one note summarized, "calling for the application of the constitution, coming out against the practice of repeated referendums, and declaring his opposition to an increase in presidential prerogatives."[15] It was, however, in the days following de Gaulle's September

[11] Bureau des Elections et des études politiques, Min. de l'Intérieur, "Objet: Attitude de la presse a l'occassion du référendum du 28 octobre" (7 November 1962), 1–3, in AN F/1cII/641.

[12] Already a trademark of the Gaullist regime (and one that would be repeated in subsequent political controversies), this bias provoked a strike of Office de Radiodiffusion-Télévision Française (ORTF) personnel.

[13] The General Council of the Meuse was alone in signaling its support. Bureau des Elections et des études politiques, Min. de l'Intérieur, "Objet: Motions politiques des assemblées locales. AP/ELEC. GZ 2131" (25 October 1962), 1–2, in AN F/1cII/641.

[14] An ardent supporter of French Algeria, the far-right populist preferred to abandon his allies in anti-Gaullism in order to advance a proposition—for a strong French presidency—that his movement long had supported. See unsigned, "Objet: Position du Mouvement UFF à l'égard du prochain référendum" (14 September 1962), 1, in AN F/1cII/641.

[15] Direction centrale des RG, "Sommaire général" (Paris, 20 April 1962), 2, in CAC 800280, article 216.

referendum summons that Monnerville seized center stage. In an unscheduled speech at the Radical Party Congress in Vichy, Senator Monnerville—the party's highest elected official—dared to utter an accusation heavy with implication: "Forfeiture." Narrating a history of republican resistance to the establishment of presidential primacy and assigning such a project to those from the Napoleons to the generals—MacMahon, Boulanger, and Pétain—who had sought to subvert this ideological tradition, the senator rejected de Gaulle's proposition. He then celebrated the institutional brakes to such an ambition embodied, by popular will, in the constitution and the constituted institutions: the National Assembly, repository of the "will of the people"; the Senate, representative of the nation's territorial units; and the Constitutional Council, the newly empowered adjudicator of constitutionality.[16] Monnerville accused the government of violating its members' oath of office, by trying to use Article 11 to ignore constitutional strictures. "Forfeiture," Article 166 of the Penal Code determined, was "any crime committed by a public servant in the exercise of his functions." Although Monnerville's words accused the government of Prime Minister Pompidou, Minister of Culture Malraux was far from alone in discerning a "clever ricochet" aimed at de Gaulle himself. French scholars Odile Rudelle and Geneviève Kieffer characterize Senator Monnerville's term as "a very 'big word,' immensely and completely insulting, which translates the political will to put [de Gaulle] to death." This assessment reflects that of most current scholars; it also reiterates Gaullist propaganda in the fall of 1962.[17]

The opposition Monnerville came to symbolize, although anchored in juridical reasoning, was forthrightly political in its message, its vision, and its actions. On the one hand, he argued that the Republic, its principles, its ideals, and its history—a history written into French laws and into its constitution—were incompatible with the proposed reform and its affirmation of presidential primacy. Above all, the "No" camp rejected what it claimed was the proposal's antirepublican content and unconstitutional form. In addition, they used every institutional and political tool the offices they controlled and the electoral legitimacy they claimed made available to them to defeat the referendum. Monnerville, who as president of the Senate was the second highest officer of the state (preceded, constitutionally, only by the president of the Republic), was thus uniquely qualified to head the effort. He not only mobilized senators and used their influence among local officials to work for the "No," he also later appealed the validity of the referendum

---

[16] "Points de repère: Emotions radicales," *France-Observateur* 648 (4 October 1962).

[17] Brunet, *Gaston Monnerville*, 224. For Malraux, see Charlot et al., eds., *La campagne éléctorale (octobre–novembre 1962)*, 1. For a description of the Vichy speech and its public echo, see Jean Charlot, "La tactique et la campagne des partis," in Goguel, ed., *Le réferendum d'octobre et les élections de novembre 1962*, 51–102; Jean-Thomas Nordmann, *Histoire des radicaux, 1820–1973* (Paris, 1974), 430; and Odile Rudelle and Genviève Keiffer, "Vers la révision de la Constitution," in *L'attentat du Petit-Clamart: Vers la révision de la Constitution*, ed. Jacques Delarue and Odile Rudelle (Paris, 1990), 59.

to the Constitutional Council. He was the sole non-Gaullist empowered to do so.

Attempting to place the law at the center of public debate, Monnerville, as he stated in a speech before the Senate, embraced republican ideology to reject accusations of petty legalism. "We do not fetishize the constitution," he insisted. Yet, "to violate the constitution is to threaten the very rights of citizens." Expounding on the role of the law in republican regimes (above all, France), he argued that "respect for the law concretizes the guarantees granted to men of the polis" and that "liberty consists in being dependent only on laws," not, he implied, on one man, however worthy his past actions. At Vichy he called for a vote of no confidence in the government from the National Assembly and summoned "a common front of republicans from all parties" to resist the project. In the following days, Monnerville was triumphantly reelected to his presidency (211 votes out of 244 possible and 215 cast), the National Assembly passed the no-confidence measure, and Monnerville's speech opening the senatorial session, which reiterated his message of Vichy (if omitting the word "forfeiture"), was met with wild applause. The Senate voted to reprint it under the heading "The Constitution Is Violated, the People Abused" and to post it in every French commune, but prefects prevented the application of this decision.[18]

The Radicals, the Socialists (SFIO), Christian Democrats (MRP), and Independents (CNI) worked hand in hand for the "No." The PCF and PSU were also fervently opposed. The broad-based opposition, which was tagged the "No" Cartel by the press, through its presence in public meetings, local militancy, and much of the printed press, made the government worried about the vote's eventual success. Stymied by the overwhelming rejection of the "Yes" by political and media elites and the legal profession, the minister of the interior urged prefects to "conduct polls among each social group of the population" in order to measure support for the referendum. "Do not," he warned, "be satisfied with the information habitually picked up from political notables."[19] Polling revealed neither overwhelming backing for the referendum nor a wave of support for the "No."[20]

Presidential allies acted in concert to assert that the contest engaged was one between Charles de Gaulle and those who wanted him to go. The prime minister himself wrote to each prefect noting that their obligation to ensure that all sides could express their positions equally was conjoined with their role as "the government's representative to foreground the reasons that led

---

[18] Speech before Senate, 9 October, quoted in Brunet, *Gaston Monnerville* , 12–13. Monnerville, along with the other leaders of the "No" Cartel, would always acknowledge the enormous debt France and the Republic owed to de Gaulle.

[19] Roger Frey, "à MM les Préfets. Circ. téléphonique n. 634" (16 October 1962), 1, in AN F/1cII/641.

[20] IFOP, "Le point de l'opinion à 15 jours du référendum du 28 octobre 1962" (15 October 1962), in AN F/1cII/641.

Gaston Monnerville leaving a meeting at the Elysée Palace in Paris on 1 May 1958. This photo appeared in *Time* magazine, which identified the President of the French Council of the Republic as the "President of [the former French colony of] Guinea." Reprinted by permission of Loomis Dean/Time & Life Pictures/Getty Images.

the chief of state to propose" the reform. "I am sure," he closed, "that I do not have to implore you to oppose vigorously allegations of 'forfeiture' and of 'violation of the constitution' that are occasionally formulated, aimed as much against the government as General de Gaulle." Ignoring the former, the head of the government insisted that the president's "past and the exceptional services offered to his country shelter him from such insulting accusations."[21] Opponents, Malraux reminded listeners when he opened the campaign for legislative elections, could act as if the will of the French nation was embodied by the National Assembly. "But if, in 1940, in 1958, France had only been there, and *not elsewhere*," not with de Gaulle in London or at Colombey-les-deux-Églises, "it would have gone pretty badly for her." Those who were with the general, and not those who opposed him, were the true republicans.[22]

Similar arguments blocked any intervention by the Constitutional Council in the referendum process. When the prime minister submitted the proposed text of the referendum to the Constitutional Council, a majority of its members (called "sages") raised all of the juridical and constitutional hesitations that legal commentators already had detailed before the French public. Sage Marcel Waline reminded his fellows that he "had always been a fervent supporter of referenda and direct democracy." He added that when he had participated in the elaboration of the present text,

> I tried in vain to give the president of the Republic the power to submit any kind of proposal to referendum. I was beaten. The constitution being what it is and not what I had hoped it would be, I am forced to admit that not utilizing Article 89 is not in conformity with the constitution.

The small minority of council members who defended the proposal's constitutionality did so, paradoxically, by denying that the actual text of the constitution was a possible measure of judgment. They offered the exigencies of the historical moment, the irreproachable biography and character of the president, and the "spirit of the constitution."[23]

De Gaulle's former justice minister, Bernard Chenot, argued that "the debate is serious enough that it goes beyond the reach of a juridical controversy. These are our institutions that are in question." In such an instance, "juridical notions must be situated in a political context. In 1945, if we had been limited by juridical consideration, we would have restored President Lebrun to his functions." He suggested, instead, that the "spirit of the consti-

[21] Georges Pompidou, "à MM les Préfets" (10 October 1962), 1–2, in AN F/1cII/641.
[22] See "Discours radiotélévisé de M. A. Malraux, président de l'Association pour la Ve République au Palais Chaillot, le mardi 30 octobre 1962, a 20h40," in *La campagne éléctorale (octobre–novembre 1962) discours et débats*, vol. 1, ed. Charlot et al., 2.
[23] Conseil constitutionnel, "Compte rendu, séance du 2 octobre 1962" (2 October 1962), in CAC 910411/12.

tution" should be their guide. This was embodied, he said, in Article 3—
"National sovereignty is an attribute of the people, who exercise it by their
representatives and by means of referenda"—and was revealed in the Constitution of 1958's three novel elements: "(1) the preponderant role of the
president of the Republic, made particularly evident by the powers offered
in Articles 16 [declaration of state of emergency] and 11 [convocation of a
referendum with legislative authorization]; (2) the direct intervention of the
people; (3) the possibility of direct contact between the head of state and the
people by means of referenda." It must be remarked that while these were
elements unknown in any previous *republican* regime, Chenot avoided any
mention of another innovation of the Fifth Republic: the possibility for judicial review of constitutionality. The institution of the Constitutional Council embodied this innovation, which was unknown under any previous
French government—imperial, royal, as well as republican.[24] Chenot's former colleague in the Debré cabinet, Edmond Michelet, argued that because
of the OAS their primary consideration in autumn 1962 must be that "every
single day the president of the Republic is faced with the threat of death. We
are not in a normal period." He challenged the reliance on "legality" and
asked, "Where was the legality of 18 June 1940?" The current historical context, according to Michelet, was similar to what France faced after the invasion by Nazi Germany. Listing a series of other arguments against ruling
on the question of constitutionality, he ended by saying, "I believe that constitutional law is circumstantial." Faced with Vichy and the Occupation,
France had needed de Gaulle and the Resistance; faced with the OAS, France
needed to establish direct election of the president, whether it was constitutional or not. Former president of the Republic René Coty harrumphed, "Ah,
non!"[25]

After Council President Léon Noël reminded the sages that they had sent
an "unofficial note" indicating to de Gaulle that the proposed second article of the 8 April referendum appeared unconstitutional, a large majority of
the members "observed that the procedure envisioned by the president of the
Republic could not be seen as constitutional." The same majority "believes
it necessary to make known to the president of the Republic that the use of
Article 11 is not in this case in conformity with the constitution."[26] While

[24] Ibid.
[25] Ibid.
[26] Ibid. The first vote was seven for, three against (Michelet, Chenot, Michard-Pellissier), the
second vote, seven for, two against (Michelet, Chenot), and one abstention (Michard-Pellissier).
In both, one member (M. Le Coq de Kerlan) did not participate in the vote. The note sent begins: "The Constitutional Council does not recognize its competence to give an opinion on the
text of a proposed bill to be submitted to referendum," then affirmed that the proposed vote is
not, constitutionally, a referendum and cautioned de Gaulle about "the serious consequences
that may result, on the level of the consultation's validity, from the use of the procedure envisioned." Conseil constitutionnel, "Note à M. le Président de la République suite à la séance de
2 octobre 1962" (2 October 1962), 1, in CAC 910411/12. For the names and votes during these
meetings, see Yves Beauvois, *Léon Noël: De Laval à de Gaulle via Pétain* (Paris, 2001).

two sages announced that they would not fulfill their oversight duties for an unconstitutional process, President Noël insisted that such acts, which implicitly would make public the nature of their confidential discussions, would be partisan. When the discussion continued in the following session, Michelet suggested that if the theses the two members defended were accurate, "we would have to convoke the president of the Republic before the High Court, as there is forfeiture."[27]

"If He Had Not Been Born in Guiana and If He Had Been White"

While his supporters vaunted General de Gaulle's biography as more important than legalistic quibbles, they cast personal aspersions on their opponents, most particularly Gaston Monnerville. His criticisms, a journalist wrote in the Parisian daily *Combat,* resulted from pure ambition. For if success for the "No" forced de Gaulle to resign, the president of the Senate would succeed him. Although a wholly accurate reading of the Constitution of 1958, this speculative interpretation of Monnerville's actions remains unconfirmed by any evidence, documentary or testimonial. Various other periodicals referred to rumors of what they termed "Operation Monnerville," in which de Gaulle's resignation would allow Monnerville to name former minister of the economy Antoine Pinay to head an interim government.[28] Yet neither Monnerville nor his allies ever called on de Gaulle to resign or even had the means to force him to do so; it was de Gaulle and his allies who repeatedly threatened that he would resign if the "Yes" did not prove overwhelming. Further, Jean-Paul Brunet, Monnerville's biographer, asserts that the senator for the department of Lot definitively had abandoned any hopes of becoming president of the Republic after his own party failed to consider his candidacy for the election of 1953. He believed, a friend and fellow Radical Party member recalled, that "if he had not been born in Guiana and if he had been white," his election would have been probable.[29]

That Monnerville, president of the upper chamber (Council of the Republic and later the Senate) of the French Parliament for twenty-two years, was of African descent played a role in the campaigns of autumn 1962. The evidence is uncertain, the contours of the silence around his "difference" less discernible than that which I have mapped around Algerian "difference" at

[27] Conseil Constitutionnel, "Compte rendu, séance du 2 octobre," 28, and Conseil Constitutionnel, "Compte rendu, séance du 11 octobre 1962" (11 October 1962), 5, in CAC 910411/12.

[28] See, e.g., Claude Estier, "Histoire d'une rupture," *France-Observateur* 648 (4 October 1962), 6; and "Le 'plan Monnerville'," *L'Express* 589 (27 September 1962), 6.

[29] Article by Maxime Blocq-Mascart, cited in Rudelle and Keiffer, "Vers la révision de la Constitution," in Delarue and Rudelle, ed., *L'attentat du Petit-Clamart,* 59; on 1953, see Brunet, *Gaston Monnerville,* 182; testimony of Roger Genebrier in Georgette Elgey, *Histoire de la IVe République,* vol. 2, *La République des contradictions, 1951–1954* (Paris, 1993), 219–20.

the war's close. Certainly, in the early 1960s, he was among the most brilliant examples of republican color blindness. He had been one of the first men who claimed African descent to be named to a French cabinet (1938), and his election to head the Council of the Republic in 1947 (renamed, after 1958, the Senate) propelled him to a leading role in republican institutions. Having supported de Gaulle's taking of power in 1958, Monnerville contributed to the significant increase of authority attributed to the second chamber and particularly to its president.

The events of 1962 brought his exemplarity center stage. First, Algeria's independence removed virtually all of the men and women "of color" from the French legislature. Until 3 July, when a much contested presidential decree ended the mandates of all officeholders elected in Algeria, the French Parliament numbered some fifty-five FMA members, among them National Assembly vice president Bachaga Boualem.[30] The collapse of the French Union closed the curtain on France's efforts from 1944 and 1962 to reconfigure citizenship and the Republic to somehow include its colonial subjects. Indeed, former prime minister Debré often referred to the newly "European" character of France's citizenry to clarify his own conversion to the direct election of the president of the Republic—thus explaining why the constitution he largely had elaborated did not include it. Back in 1958, he told *Paris-Match*, "the body of electors was the body of electors of the French Union, with all the African peoples and the Muslims of Algeria. This was stated explicitly." Under those conditions, he continued, "election by universal suffrage was impossible."[31] Second, Monnerville's concerted exercise of all of his political and institutional power to oppose de Gaulle's October referendum ended up leaving him completely marginalized by the government during and after the election. Unlike the slippery contours of race, this isolation was concrete and demonstrable. He was excluded, according to a memo sent to the Constitutional Council, from French television and radio coverage during the election campaign. Once the referendum was approved, de Gaulle instructed his staff to do everything possible to ignore the Senate and its president. (This shunning continued until Monnerville left office in 1968: Georges Pompidou did not appear in front of the full Senate for the six years that he was prime minister; when Monnerville took the podium to give his final speech as president of the Senate, the only member of the government present, the Gaullist secretary of state for agriculture, Jacques Chirac, stood up and ostentatiously left the chamber.[32])

---

[30] On 3 July 1962, Ordinance 62–737 excluded all Algerian representatives from the National Assembly and Senate.

[31] Guy Mollet, Edgar Faure, Michel Debré, "Trois anciens chefs du gouvernement s'expliquent sur le référendum," *Paris-Match* 704 (6 October 1962), 58.

[32] On radio and television coverage of Monnerville, see Constitutional Council, "Les inconstitutionalités de la Constitution" (5 November 1962), 3, in CAC 910411/12. On the shunning of Monnerville by members of the government, see Paul Smith, "Le Sénat de la Cinquième

Only Monnerville, among the leaders of the "No" Cartel, suffered a concerted effort to humiliate him. This led a high school teacher writing to *France-Observateur* to express his "surprise" that the Elysée "does not demonstrate such intransigence in regard to Guy Mollet, for example; is this maybe because the latter is a metropolitan?"[33] Such a cause and effect relationship is difficult to prove. But during the fall campaign, the idea that "because he was not white" he was not fit to lead France went from the informed suspicions of political insiders onto the printed page. The far-right press, which had supported the "No," offered this development as a partial explanation for defeat, remarking that "there are men of color . . . at the highest level of [the French] hierarchy . . . however, it is hard to imagine [Monnerville] as the head of the country, a post to which he could accede." Few French citizens, indications are, had ever thought about the possibility. The referendum campaign brought news of the senator to the front page of most newspapers, along with the inevitable photo. Monnerville himself never publicly considered the possibility that French racism affected him. He told *Paris-Match*:

> Remember, there is one phrase that leaves Americans stupefied; that is when they ask who stands in for de Gaulle and they are told, "Monnerville, from Guiana." It is because in France this is possible that I am so touchy when it comes to the Republic. France is the country of equality, equality for everyone.[34]

Any serious study of French Algeria, of France's other overseas possessions, or of the metropole itself casts doubts on this claim of color-blind egalitarian practice. Still, at the close of the Algerian crisis, as France chose to forget that Algeria was France and to stop pretending that ("Muslim") Algerians could be French, this promise seemed less and less a concrete possibility—for which Monnerville was a role model—and more and more an abstract principle with limits marked by ethnic or racial difference. At the same time, of course, Monnerville's continued political role, although dramatically diminished after the autumn 1962 campaigns, suggests the partial nature of this break. Although it became very difficult to imagine that "Algerians" could be French and, in response to the exodus, the government enacted laws and bureaucratic measures to impede non-Europeans from Algeria from maintaining their citizenship, most French would still claim that being French was not tied to race or ethnicity.

République: Evolution d'une chambre de contestation," in *Transgression et Contestation: Essais sur la littérature française et francophone: II*, ed. Russell King (Nottingham, 2000), 102.

[33] On postreferendum reprisals, see AN F/1cII/552; also, Brunet, *Gaston Monnerville*, 230–48; M. R. Dodin, "Nos lecteurs écrivent: Défense de Monnerville," *France-Observateur* 660 (27 December 1962).

[34] E. P., "Dictonnaire critique," *Ecrits de Paris* (July–August 1963): 97–101; Jack Chargelègue, "Ils se sont tous confiés a *Match!*" *Paris-Match* 705 (13 October 1962), 54–55.

"Women Voters" and "Repatriates from North Africa"

Beyond this biographical issue of race, the referendum campaign waged by
de Gaulle and his allies subsumed explanation and rational debate to sentiment and personality.[35] Government observers reported to Paris that the
Elysée's strategy was working. The appeal to direct democracy resonated
widely, first through the practice of referendums, now through the direct
election of the president, conjoined with the fear that de Gaulle would leave
power if he lost. Accusations of unconstitutionality and nonrepublicanism
left most voters perplexed. Prefectural reports to the Ministry of the Interior
assured that the electorate was not interested in what one dismissed as "doctrinal or juridical quarrels." To a point that "makes difficult, even useless,
the normally close examination of the reactions of different social classes"
most people in the department of Hérault, the prefect there observed, perceived the question as whether de Gaulle should continue to serve or should
abandon his presidency. Rather than analytic, he explained, their reaction
was sentimental.[36] The prefect of the Gironde related that "the voter—and
above all the woman voter—does not care about juridical policy stands. He
does not try to understand them. He does, however, link his notion of democracy with that of universal suffrage." Another prefect offered a more reasoned presentation of the public's "fear that the president's departure [if
defeated] would be followed by a period of serious hardship, which the OAS
would take advantage of to drag the nation back into civil war." The widely
reported call by the OAS to vote "No" reinforced this suspicion.[37]

In this referendum campaign, however, unlike in April 1962, opponents'
arguments did reach the public imagination. Prefects reported a sharp rise in
the registration of new voters. Shortly before election day, the prefect of the
Aveyron cautioned that "each day public opinion is becoming better informed. . . . The constitutional problem that, [previously] inspiring nary an
echo, the parliament had been trying to pose, now has become a topic of discussion." Voters were cognizant, his colleague from Tarn-et-Garonne advanced, "that on this vote depends the future political orientation of the
country." Yet the overwhelming factor weighing on these considerations remained concern that de Gaulle would leave office (and he made clear in his
four TV and radio addresses that if the "No" triumphed, he would). This
anxiety was sharp and short-term; it was directly linked, all sources confirm,
not to an uneasiness about a return of the Fourth Republic or of political

---

[35] Rudelle celebrates this approach, writing that "General de Gaulle proceeded by action
rather than speech, by 'practice' rather than a discussion of principles," in "La leçon des évène-
ments," in Delarue and Rudelle, eds., *L'attentat du Petit-Clamart*, 76.

[36] Préfet de l'Herault, "Référendum du 28 octobre 1962" (19 October 1962), in CAC
780654/09.

[37] Préfet de la Gironde, "Référendum du 28 octobre 1962" (18 October 1962); Préfet de la
Nièvre, "Référendum du 28 octobre 1962" (19 October 1962), 1, both in CAC 780654/09.

choices to come but to fear that the OAS would take control. It was de Gaulle as defender of "the Republic" and not as architect of the institutional arrangements of the Fifth Republic that voters supported. In the "eventuality" of de Gaulle's retreat from politics, the Aveyron prefect assured, "no one believes that the ["No" Cartel] will be strong enough to take over if the worst happens." The electorate was "disturbed" by the "artificial conjunction" of parties that were normally "opposed on every issue," another reported.[38]

Amid this general development, two groups of French voters obsessed the government in the lead-up to the referendum: women and repatriates from Algeria. "Women voters" were to be galvanized; it was believed that the female attachment to the general and anxiety about the OAS threat to France could guarantee victory. In the new Gaullist republic, (female) political irrationality was to be cultivated. "Repatriates" from North Africa, on the contrary, needed to be kept under close scrutiny. Presented as predictable and rational, their opposition to de Gaulle introduced a new element into the electoral process. The government could depend, provincial observers asserted, on public distrust of this group, which was perceived as violent, irrational, even fascist.

Over and over, prefects closed their observations with suggestions for targets for government propaganda; over and over, they counseled an emotion-based appeal to women voters. The prefect of the Gironde explained that "women voters are very sensitive to sentiments, and they are faithful to the man their feelings have given them confidence in." It was a description torn from the pages of anticlerical opposition to female suffrage in the 1920s and '30s, only now it purported to describe a presumed pro-Gaullist constituency. "If the president's final appeal included a sentence such as 'my dear old country,' the number [of Yes ballots] could grow larger," the senior official suggested. "The female voter in front of her radio or television is waiting more for a cordial summons than a rational explanation." The government's man in the Nièvre followed his discussion of the fear of OAS-inspired civil war with the suggestion that "the female electorate would be very sensitive to this argument."[39] These descriptions did not present the "woman voter" as aberrant. Rather, she was presumed to possess exactly the qualities the government's referendum campaign required. This portion of the electorate—which Gaullist orators never tired of pretending received the vote thanks to General de Gaulle—could be counted on to line up behind the nation's "guide and leader."[40] Neither abandoning traditional republi-

---

[38] Préfet de l'Aveyron, "Objet: Référendum" (24 October 1962), 2; Préfet de la Sarthe, "Référendum du 28 octobre 1962" (18 October 1962), 3, both in CAC 780654/09.

[39] Préfet de la Gironde, (18 October 1962), 2; Préfet de la Nièvre (19 October 1962), 1, both in CAC 780654/09.

[40] On the preeminent role of the Consultative Assembly in Algiers, 1944, in this reform, see Paul Smith, *Feminism and the Third Republic: Women's Political and Civil Rights in France, 1918–1945* (Oxford, 1996), 252.

can conceptions of female irrationality and political immaturity nor seeking to educate or "assimilate" French female voters into a polis premised on the citizen as rational individual, these Gaullist operatives put their trust in the whole French electorate behaving as the "woman voter" was supposed to. They more than made do with the "depoliticization" that concerned so many French commentators in this period.[41]

The mirror image of the "woman voter" was the "repatriate from North Africa." When compiling the requested analyses of voting intentions, virtually every prefect included a new "sociocultural group": "Algerian repatriates" appeared alongside "civil servants," "large and small businessmen," "farmers," as well as more culturally fraught categories such as "women voters," "clergymen," and "the elderly." Interior Minister Roger Frey's original request for such detailed analyses had not specified that repatriates be included. Yet, counting and qualifying the political behavior of this category was more than a recognition of its existence in French law: beginning in the campaign for the April vote, and accentuated as France confronted the exodus, the government interrogated prefects and local officials about the activities and political proclivities of this group. Bureaucratic interest mirrored public attention. The French press and political commentators now routinely discussed the voting and the political behavior of "Algerian repatriates," a term these nonbureaucrats used interchangeably with "pieds noirs."[42] In virtually every department, the number of repatriates who had taken advantage of the opportunity to register to vote in the fall elections was minimal.[43] Numerically insignificant, their opposition nonetheless both troubled and comforted the regime's electoral calculations. They were "hostile to the president's proposition"; their hostility, however, was seen as increasing the impact of pro-government warnings about the ongoing threat from the OAS. The anxiety of French voters—especially the "female voter"—could be counted on to keep General Charles de Gaulle as a bulwark against the return of fascism. Almost incidentally, the executive prerogatives that had emerged since 1958 would become the law of the French Republic.[44]

Having ignored parliamentary oversight, it was now necessary to overcome the possibility that the law could prevent the institutional affirmation of presidential primacy. Monnerville requested that the Constitutional Coun-

---

[41] On depoliticization, see Direction générale de la Sûreté nationale, "Les clubs," in *Bulletin de documentation de la direction des RG 96* (April 1964), 1, in AN F/7/15582.

[42] Henri Le Corno, "à MM les Préfets" (13 October 1962), 1, in AN F/1cII/641.

[43] The government decided to allow repatriates to register to vote in the commune where they were living, dropping the normal requirement for six-month residency. See Jacques Bonis-Charancle, "à MM les Préfets. Circ. téléphonique n. 602" (3 October 1962), 2, in AN F/1cII/641; and Roger Frey, "à MM les Préfets. Circ. telephonique n. 604" (4 October 1962), 1, in AN F/1cII/641. For the number of repatriates registered, see Ministre de l'Intérieur, "Repartition par département des rapatriés d'Algérie inscrits sur les listes éléctorales" (date unknown), 3, in AN F/1cII/641; see also CAC 780654/09.

[44] Préfet du Vaucluse, "Référendum du 28 octobre 1962" (18 October 1962), in CAC 780654/09.

cil examine whether the text submitted to the referendum on 28 October 1962 was in conformity with the constitution. (As president of the Senate, along with the president of the Republic and the president of the National Assembly, he had the authority to do so.) This semijuridical institution, if so called upon, was empowered to stop the promulgation of a law it judged, in part or in whole, to be unconstitutional (although its role was to make legal judgments, the Constitutional Council was distinct from the court system). Former president of the Republic Vincent Auriol, a Socialist, prepared a draft decision that concluded: "The request of the president of the Senate is valid in form and justified in content. The law voted by means of referendum the 28 October 1958 [*sic*] does not conform to the constitution and cannot therefore be promulgated." But, by a vote of six to four, the council declared itself incompetent to judge.[45]

In a postreferendum summary, the new category "repatriates" was identified as the only one that predominantly had voted "No."[46] Still, with a majority of 61.7 percent, the "Yes" vote was substantially smaller than in previous Fifth Republic referendums. For the first time, only a minority of enrolled voters (46.4%) had voted "Yes." (A number of observers, among them the German-born philosopher Hannah Arendt, expected that de Gaulle would be compelled to resign, since in previous referendums he had suggested that nonvoters should be presumed to be opposed.) The campaign based on fear of the OAS and confidence in de Gaulle to conquer that threat had worked, but far less effectively than previously. In the clearest indication of this, Communist support for the party's position ("No") returned to pre-1958 levels. Before Algerian independence, Communist voters had abandoned party discipline and turned to de Gaulle: many had not followed the PCF's call to reject the new constitution in 1958, and they had offered significant support to the referendum of 1961.[47]

The legislative campaign that followed began as a continuation of the October debates. The SFIO, Radicals, MRP, and Independents signed pledges to support the best-placed candidate for the second round of voting in districts where a supporter of the "Yes" vote remained in the running. What had been termed the "No" Cartel now called themselves the "Cartel of Democrats." The pro-government, pro–de Gaulle campaigners once again accused their opponents of being in league with the OAS and called on voters to support the president by giving him a working majority. In addition, they derided their opponents' capacity to offer a viable alternative government.

---

[45] Vincent Auriol, "Vu la requête du Président du Sénat . . ." (unpublished draft), 5, in CAC 910411/12.

[46] Bureau des Elections et des études politiques, Min. de l'Intérieur, "Objet: Prévisions sur les resultats . . ." (23 October 1962), 2–3, in AN F/1cII/641.

[47] See Carol Brightman, ed., *Between Friends: The Correspondence of Hannah Arendt and Mary McCarthy, 1949–1975* (San Diego, 1995), 142. Ministre de l'Intérieur, "Elections legislatives des 18 et 25 novembre. Conclusions" (6 December 1962), 1–4, in AN F/1cII/590.

The weeks leading up to the first round of voting revealed enormous tensions among the Cartel of Democrats: in district after district Socialists, and to a lesser extent Radicals and Christian Democrats, announced that they would not support candidates associated with the defense of French Algeria.[48] Two important factors further complicated the electoral alliance: the OAS and the repatriates. First, the Communists indicated that they would be willing to support Socialist and Radical candidates in the second round if that candidate firmly denounced the OAS and rejected the support of candidates who had collaborated with the activists.[49] This was a direct attack on the Cartel of Democrats' accord. Second, the press and prefectural reports focused on the mobilization of repatriates for certain candidates. The prefect of the Allier announced that the Socialist deputy Pierre Bourgeois was having trouble because his local party, citing his "statements in favor of French Algeria," had withdrawn its support. The prefect noted that in Vichy "a fairly significant concentration of repatriates" should assure reelection for an Independent (CNI) candidate. Most prefects, however, argued that repatriate mobilization and support would damage any candidate's popularity in the general population.[50]

Recognized publicly, politically, and bureaucratically, the repatriates from Algeria were presented as acting and voting in terms distinct from other French citizens. Like all people from Algeria, the pieds noirs were only dubiously French. Unlike most, they chose (and were able) to exercise fully their rights as citizens. This template for political action—a form of "identity politics"—played an important role in shaping post-Algeria France, as did the reemergence of a left-wing "Popular Front" alliance.

The night of 18 November 1962 in France might best be remembered for the ten-minute television show that introduced viewers to a young singer, Françoise Hardy, and her first single, "Tous les garçons et les filles de mon age." Yet on the same evening the results of the initial round of legislative elections also shaped French self-conceptions. These elections defined the institutions and the partisan alignments for the next twenty years—through May 1968 and (slightly) beyond 1981—of the society from which yé-yé youth culture and consumerism emerged. They rescued the PCF from decline, reestablished the Popular Front strategy as a possibility, and gave a coalition of Gaullists and economic liberals total control over the National Assembly.[51]

---

[48] Préfet de l'Herault, "Réponse au Ministre de l'Intérieur . . ." (3 November 1962), 3, in CAC 780654/13.

[49] Préfet de la Gironde, "Réponse au Ministre de l'Intérieur . . ." (3 November 1962), 3, in CAC 780654/13.

[50] Préfet de l''Allier, "Réponse à Ministre de l'Intérieur . . ." (3 November 1962), 1, in CAC 780654/13; Préfet de la Dordogne, "2ème réponse à Ministre de l'Intérieur . . ." (9 November 1962), 2, in CAC 780654/13 folder. See also Préfet des Bouches-du-Rhône, "2ème réponse à Ministre de l'Intérieur . . ." (11 November 1962), 2, in CAC 780654/13.

[51] For a description of Hardy's debut and an early assessment of yé-yé youth culture and consumerism, see the article "Riches à 18 ans," Paris-Match 717 (5 January 1963), 52–55.

Unable to convince party activists that countering de Gaulle's power grab should have priority over the settling of Algerian accounts, the party leaders who had assembled the Cartel of Democrats had even less luck with the electors. The first-round results promised a Gaullist landslide. In district after district, government experts highlighted popular rejection of anyone linked with the activists, explicitly or—through the "No" Cartel—implicitly. Among the vote's victims were many of the most prominent defenders of French Algeria. Yet, clearly marking the success of the Gaullist autumn campaigns, many of the leading figures in the September no-confidence vote also lost. The PSU, voice of the new left, was almost completely eliminated; Pierre Mendès-France, its most prominent figure, did not even make the second-round runoff.[52]

Prefectural reports reaffirmed that besides the obvious Gaullist success only the PCF, which had run the most stridently anti-OAS campaign, maintained and even improved its previous positions. Immediately, leaders of the SFIO and a number of local Radical sections abandoned the Cartel of Democrats strategy in favor of a Popular Front approach. Amiens was the showcase example, where the PCF pulled its candidate in favor of Socialist leader Guy Mollet, despite the fact that the Communist had more first-round votes. This approach, the very possibility of which had obsessed Interior Ministry experts for months, allowed a left opposition to emerge reinforced after the second round of voting. The PCF, able to profit from "republican discipline" for the first time since 1946, greatly bolstered its parliamentary troops. De Gaulle's designs to permanently marginalize the "Stalinists" had failed. After the fall elections, with the Algerian interlude over, the PCF was again the dominant force in opposition to de Gaulle. The key factor was a campaign against French Algeria far more ardent than the party ever pursued when French Algeria actually existed. The non-Gaullist Right, on the other hand, widely associated with the defense of French Algeria, was decimated: the Independents were left with 29 deputies, a loss of 92 seats, and were no longer numerous enough to form an official parliamentary group.[53]

Developments in the fall concretized the restructuring of state institutions that had begun in the spring. This occurred on the basis of understandings of who was French that crystallized in the exodus. In the spring, the text summoning the French to approve or not the Evian Accords simply excluded all

---

[52] See [Gaston Deferre], "Editorial," *Le Provencal* (26 November 1962). He cites Reynaud, Motte, Dorey, Simonnet, and Leenhardt as among the "No" leaders the vote eliminated.

[53] Marielle Bal, "Les indépendents," *Revue française de science politique* 15, no. 3 (June 1965): 537; see also *Année Politique 1962*, 130. No former members of the RNUR won reelection. Only nine of the eighty deputies who had voted for the "Salan amendment" were reelected, and only one deputy—Rémy Montagne of the Eure—who spoke out regularly in the National Assembly on behalf of Algérie française from late 1961 through 1962 was reelected. Deputies such as Jean-Marie Le Pen, Tremolet de Villiers, and Lefèvre d'Ormesson were heavily defeated. Interestingly, many outspoken opponents of Algérie française, who appeared in these same debates, were also defeated. The defeat of pro–Algérie française deputies was widely commented on; see *Année Politique 1962*, 103.

inhabitants of Algeria from the vote. This juridical fiction—that the departments of Algeria and the Sahara were already not France—offered definitional stability. By separating people living south of the Mediterranean from those in the metropole, it maintained the correlation between national territory and membership in the nation so crucial to post-revolutionary French identity. It also allowed the French to continue to avoid explaining why Algerians, all French citizens, were too different to be French. By autumn, things were more complicated. Almost all Algerian "Muslims" found themselves stripped of their French nationality. The campaigns that triumphed in the elections of October and November 1962 affirmed welcome certainties about who was French, while insisting that what was really at stake, even after Algerian independence, was support or opposition to keeping Algeria French. Questions of "race" and "ethnicity" worked to define the boundaries of the nation, while the reaffirmation of comforting presumptions about gender promised to guarantee the stability of the state.

The institutional architecture that coalesced in 1962 resembled that which de Gaulle had proposed after the Liberation in 1944, and which French citizens repeatedly rejected, through referendums and elections, between 1946 and 1953. De Gaulle's vision of the state had not become more republican: the nation had changed. De Gaulle had failed at the end of World War II, when he celebrated the unity of "the France that had resisted" but did not manage to end the regime of parties that he believed divided and weakened France. He succeeded when France became European, when he summoned the French to guarantee that Algeria was not part of France.

Conclusion

Forgetting Algerian France

Although untitled, the image is easy to recognize. Vaguely hexagonal, in black ink against a white background, it represents France. Inside the stark lines dots of varying sizes, each named, also make sense immediately. The biggest one indicates Paris; another is for Marseilles; marks for Lyon and Lille are there for those who know their Gallic geography. What makes this image remarkable is the names next to each dot: "Algiers," next to the point that should be Paris; "Constantine" instead of Marseilles; "Oran" instead of Lyon and "Bône" in place of Lille. Published on the front cover of the well-known surrealist journal *Les Lèvres Nues,* Marcel Mariën's work captures something that most analyses of "the Algerian War" avoid engaging. In it, Algeria is shaped like France, making visual the catch phrase of those who rejected Algerian independence, "L'Algérie, c'est la France." This does more than point out how ridiculous the concept is: it also suggests that what we know as France has Algeria written all over it. This would have seemed dubious, maybe troubling, to most of the journal's audience when "La dernière carte" was published in 1956. It would become difficult even to imagine after 1962, when Algeria gained independence and, as the historian Eugen Weber describes, the now obvious moniker "the Hexagon" began to be widely used to refer to France.[1]

The image encapsulates the central argument of my book: that the Algerian Revolution was the crucial conflict for French people over the shape and meaning of France in the post-1945 era. As the French philosopher Etienne

---

[1] Titled "La dernière carte" (Marcel Mariën), it appeared on the cover of *Les Lèvres Nues* 8 (May 1956). There are a number of possible translations for the title: "The Final Map," "The Last Card," "The Final Card," "The Last Map." On the Hexagon, see Eugen Weber, "L'Hexagone," in *Les lieux de mémoire,* vol. 2, *La nation,* ed. Pierre Nora (1986), 97–116.

Marcel Mariën, "La dernière carte," published on the front cover of the Belgian surrealist journal *Les Lèvres Nues* in 1956.

Balibar stresses, to insist that France and Algeria were one nation—as many
in France did for more than a century—worked to efface the reality of imperialism. Not only did popular and intellectual rejection of the claim—often violent and bloody—make possible the fact of Algerian independence,
the same struggle also exposed to international reprobation the profound injustices, the pervasive racism, and the fundamental inequalities camouflaged
by this pretension that Algeria was not a colony. Yet, Balibar argues, pretending *today* that France and Algeria are and were simply "two wholly distinct nations" impedes analysis of how formative colonialism was for France
and Algeria, its "impact on the so-called West as well as on colonized peoples." As he phrases it, "The France of today was made (and undoubtedly
still is being fabricated) in Algeria, with and against her."[2]

Throughout this book I have tried to show how the Algerian Revolution
brought to a head the long-term contradictions that had been at the heart of

[2] Etienne Balibar, "Algérie, France: Une ou deux nations?" *Lignes* 30, a special issue, "Al-
gérie-France: Regards croisés" (February 1997): 7.

the French republican project. By forgetting that Algeria was France, critics have ignored what the history of French Algeria and the Algerian Revolution reveals about French republicanism and liberal citizenship. This has made it easier to ignore that modern colonialism was a republican project. At the same time, it makes it easier to forget the Republic's capacity to imagine innovative policies to overcome discrimination and inequalities that affect groups of citizens because of their perceived differences. After World War II, to respond to the challenges anticolonial nationalists posed to French rule, the Republic dispensed with the post-1789 insistence that citizenship be one and indivisible, introducing for "Muslim French from Algeria" the possibility of both full political rights and the maintenance of local civil status. In 1958, following the return to power of General de Gaulle, this possibility was extended to all "Muslim French citizens from Algeria." "Exceptional promotion," along with the Constantine Plan for economic investment and development in the Algerian departments, worked to make what was called "integration" a reality. France abandoned all of these efforts once Algeria became independent. Moreover, it seemed as if all these attempts to make Algerians equal had to be exorcized. In the debates following the March 1962 announcement of a cease-fire, no one (except those whom mainstream opinion dismissed as French Algeria fanatics) bothered to ask what would become of the complicated system of statuses governing the French citizens of Algeria. It was not until after Algeria's independence that the government, with no consultation or discussion, announced that they all were to disappear.[3]

As I have demonstrated in this book, it was in struggling to master what they saw as a unique situation that French officials and people subsumed the events in Algeria into an instance of decolonization. This allowed Algerian independence, which had been unthinkable for most French intellectuals and politicians until the late 1950s, to become obvious to almost all in the early 1960s. Rather than representing an exceptional case, Algeria became the archetypal "postcolonial" case study. Decolonization was no longer only a descriptive explanation of what happened in Algeria by mid-1962: during the Algerian Revolution, the French embraced "decolonization" as prescriptive.[4] The war's end "invention of decolonization" saw the term itself became a historical category, which in turn defined a chronological period, and

---

[3] Jean Foyer, Ministre de la Justice, "Demande d'avis—Situation juridique en France des personnes de statut civil originaire d'Algérie/Législation 713–5F1d" (27 August 1964), in CAC 950236/09.

[4] My reference to "postcoloniality" is informed by arguments that the postcolonial is not merely what comes after decolonization but took shape as soon as imperialism took form or, as Stephen Slemon writes, "begins in the moment that the colonising power inscribes itself onto the body and space of its Others." Quoted in Patrick Williams and Laura Chrisman's introduction to *Colonial Discourse and Post-Colonial Theory: A Reader*, ed. Williams and Chrisman (New York, 1994), 12. Postcoloniality, in this sense, continues after the end of direct colonization in the former colonies and in the former metropoles, although differently.

both now seemed inextricable from the march of progress. Algeria had been a special and intractable case, complicated by laws and history; its independence was now the effect of an abstract force. In addition, the metaphor of the "tide of History" focused "decolonization" on independence for an Algerian state. In France as well as Algeria this foreclosed discussions of racism and other forms of domination and exclusion, which the Algerian Revolution had forced numerous critics and officials to recognize.

"Inventing decolonization" allowed the French to *avoid* facing the challenges that Algerian nationalism and the Algerian Revolution posed to classic conceptions of French values and history, at least temporarily. These conceptions depended on principles of universalism, the individual, progress, and the Rights of Man; what the French avoided discussing was the failure of the institutional forms that most embodied these principles—republican government, nationality, citizenship, and the constitution—to make Algeria French. Because France had made Algeria the preeminent example of how overseas conquest and a commitment to universal values coincided, the Algerian Revolution not only put paid to empire, it forced into view the inextricable links between universalism and imperialism. The ways the French institutionalized Algerian independence sundered them one from each other.

The "tide of History" consensus associated these choices with "republican values" (liberty, equality, fraternity, and the Rights of Man) while dissociating republican institutions from what France had done in Algeria. A France without Algeria signified a clean victory for republican values and not evidence that putting values premised in universalism into practice, institutionalizing them in the French republics, had depended on denying rights to certain people: in this case, "Muslims." It was under the guise of ending empire that the French government redefined the nation's boundaries to exclude Algerian "Muslims," sidelining republican "color-blindness" rather than confronting republican racism. In the name of fighting against "colonialist" OAS terrorism, presidential primacy trumped legislative authority and the exercise of new executive powers reduced individual liberties; "exceptional" methods used to crush Algerian nationalists, rather than be repudiated, reshaped metropolitan practices. In 1962, most French institutions and people chose to purge their past and present of signs that empire mattered, rather than either reinventing or repudiating the universal in defining themselves. The French invention of decolonization, that is, helped circumscribe what lessons could be drawn, in the West as in the former colonies, about the role of colonialism in state institutions and national pasts. This made it more difficult to address such tensions in the future. Understanding how this happened moves us beyond analyses of colonialism or the results of decolonization as simply positive or negative, to focus instead on how both still inform world history.

Bibliography of Primary Sources

Archives Nationales/Centre d'Accueil et de Recherche des Archives Nationales (AN)–Paris

65/AJ/1270
78 AJ/28
78 AJ/30–32
82/AJ/1–122
F/1A/5010 by Derogation
F/1A/5013–14 by Derogation
F/1A/5016–17 by Derogation
F/1A/5021 by Derogation
F/1A/5030–32 by Derogation
F/1A/5035 by Derogation
F/1A/5039–40 by Derogation
F/1A/5045
F/1A/5048
F/1A/5050
F/1A/5053
F/1A/5055
F/1A/5057
F/1A/5059
F/1A/5061–62
F/1A/5124–25 by Derogation
F/1A/5126–24
F/1CII/517
F/1CII/552–56
F/1CII/582–83
F/1CII/589–92
F/1CII/625
F/1CII/634
F/1CII/640 by Derogation
F/1CII/641–42
F1/CII/647 Partial Derogation
F1/CII/678

F/1CIV/164
F/1CIV/167–68
F/1CIV/634
F/1CIV/678
F/7/15581–82 by Derogation
F/7/16064
F/7/16108 by Derogation (See CAC 880502/37)
F/7/16124 by Derogation (See CAC 880502/44)
F/12/11809
F/17/16491
F/41/2013 by Derogation
F/41/2234–35 by Derogation
F/41/2239 by Derogation

Archives nationales/Centre d'archives contemporaines (CAC)–Fontainebleau

770097/30 and 35 by Derogation
770125/2
770346/3 and (by Derogation) 6–8 and 10
780058/187, 202, 204, 206 by Derogation
780654/7–8, 9–13
800273/287 by Derogation
800280/216–18 Partial Communication by Derogation
820599/83 (dossiers 77–79 and 80 by Derogation), 84 (dossiers 83–86), and 86 (dossier 105) by Derogation
880076/1 by Derogation
880502/37–44
910411/10–14 (12 by Derogation)
920172/5 (liasses 1), 8 (liasse 3), and 9–11 by Derogation
930275/6, 12, 76, and 94
930276/2
940560/1, 14 and 42 by Derogation
950236/7 and 9
950395/73, 76–77

Archives du ministère des affaires étrangères, Service des Affaires algériennes (MAE)–Paris

5
38–40
92–93
96–97
99–100
103–4
117
121 bis

Service historique de l'Armée de l'air (SHAA)–Vincennes

3916
H5/10278–80
H5/10300–303
H5/10314
I/E144
I/E 160
I/E 274

Service historique de l'Armée de terre (SHAT)–Vincennes

1H/1110
1H/1123
1H/1126
1H/1128
1H/1130
1H/1132/3
1H/1142–44
1H/1152–54
1H/1157
1H/1168–70
1H/1204
1H/1210
1H/1236/2 and 4
1H/1254–55 (1254/4 by Derogation)
1H/1260
1H/1263
1H/1265/7
1H/1269
1H/1269/3 by Derogation
1H/1319
1H/1385
1H/1392
1H/1397
1H/1428 (except dossier 2)
1H/1436–38 (1436/1, 1437/1 and 1438/1 by Derogation)
1H/1456
1H/1536
1H/1730
1H/1735–39
1H/1752
1H/1784/2–4 and 6
1H/1784/3 by Derogation
1H/1785–86
1H/1791
1H/1794 (dossier 3 by Derogation)
1H/1844–47

1H/1855–56
1H/1870
1H/1870/4 by Derogation
1H/1982
1H/2025
1H/2057
1H/2109
1H/2111
1H/2111/3–4
1H/2178
1H/2420/3
1H/2429/4–5
1H/2436/2
1H/2444/3
1H/2447/3
1H/2448/5
1H/2461/3
1H/2467
1H/2467 bis
1H/2515–16
1H/2549
1H/2552
1H/2649
1H/2703
1H/2709
1H/2716/2 by Derogation
1H/2725/1–3
1H/2726/1
1H/2743
1H/2745 (except dossier 1)
1H/2789
1H/2799/5
1H/2836 (dossier 3 by Derogation)
1H/2983–84
1H/3085/3 by Derogation
1H/3086 (dossier 1 by Derogation)
1H/3164
1H/3167–68
1H/3484/5
1H/4034
1H/4137/1–2 by Derogation
1H/4193/2
1H/4258/4–5 by Derogation
1H/4396/8–9
1H/4397 (dossier 2 by Derogation)
15R/95/1–2 by Derogation

Newspapers and magazines consulted

Ecrits de Paris, 1960–63
L'Esprit, 1960–63
L'Esprit nouveau, 1962
Europe-Action, 1962
France-Observateur, 1961–63
L'Humanité, 1954–62
Jeune Afrique, 11/1961–8/1962
Nation française, 1961–63
Paris-March, 1960–63
Observateur du moyen-orient et de l'Afrique du nord, 1/1962–9/1962
Rivarol, 1961–63
Témoignage chrétienne, 1961–63
Les Temps Modernes, 1961–62
La Voie Communiste, 1/1962–9/1962

Index

CPSIA information can be obtained
at www.ICGtesting.com
Printed in the USA
LVOW08s2300010317
525817LV00004B/298/P